HARY-O

'HARY-O'
FROM THE PASTEL BY JOHN RUSSELL, R.A.

HARY-O

The Letters of Lady Harriet Cavendish

1796–1809

Edited by
HER GRANDSON
SIR GEORGE LEVESON GOWER, K.B.E.,
AND HIS DAUGHTER
IRIS PALMER

LONDON
JOHN MURRAY, ALBEMARLE STREET, W.

First Edition . . . 1940

Made and Printed in Great Britain by Butler & Tanner Ltd., Frome and London

" E'en from the tomb the voice of Nature cries,
E'en in our ashes live their wonted fires."

GRAY.

CONTENTS

ILLUSTRATIONS

* *In the possession of Sir George Leveson Gower, K.B.E.*

ERRATA

p. 116, l. 25, *for* " whose daughter Lady Catherine Hamilton he subsequently married " *read*, " He married Lady Catherine Hamilton, daughter of the 1st Marquis of Abercorn "

p. 12, l. 18, *before* Strawberry Hill *add* Little

p. 48, l. 7, *after* Lawrence *add* [Sir Thomas L. the famous artist]

INTRODUCTION

By George Leveson Gower

IN 1894 my father, the late Honble. Frederick Leveson Gower, published two volumes of Letters of his Mother, the first Countess Granville, written chiefly to her sister, Lady Georgiana Morpeth, afterwards Countess of Carlisle. They were the daughters of the 5th Duke of Devonshire and were united by the tenderest affection. These letters began in 1810, the year after my grandparents' marriage.

Several years later my father had access to some further letters of his mother, written whilst she was Lady Harriet Cavendish. Most of them were addressed to her sister; others to her mother, the beautiful and talented Georgiana, Duchess of Devonshire; to her grandmother, the Countess Dowager Spencer; to her brother, the Marquis of Hartington, and to her governess, Miss Selina Trimmer. My father did not live to publish them, and for some years after his death in 1907 they disappeared, and have only recently come to light.

The reception of the first series by the press and the public was so favourable—I had almost said so enthusiastic—that I am encouraged to offer this second, although earlier, series to the public, which I am allowed to publish by the kind permission of my cousin, Earl Granville.

They display the same qualities of wit, humour, depth of feeling and delineation of character which were such marked features in the letters written after her marriage. It is true that the scene on which she moved was more restricted than that which she occupied later on as ambassadress and leader of society; but that does not hinder the free play of her talented pen.

My warmest thanks are due to my wife, who re-discovered the lost letters. I gratefully acknowledge the help of my daughter, Iris Palmer, who has co-edited the letters with me, and indeed without whose invaluable co-operation this book could not have been brought to a satisfactory conclusion. She has written introductory headings to the various chapters, in which she has incorporated some footnotes of my father's and of my own.

Nor must I omit mention of the valuable assistance which we received from our kinsfolk, the Howards of Castle Howard. It was there that Iris accidentally stumbled over a box in the Muniment Room containing further original letters of Harriet's which appear in this book.

Harriet Cavendish was certainly no beauty in the accepted sense of the term, as she herself frequently and readily admits, though this was largely compensated by her intelligence, vivacity and charm ; and, in spite of her admiration of Georgiana's looks, which must be attributed to her affectionate partiality, it cannot be said that in this respect her sister much surpassed her.

These letters begin in 1796 and continue till 1809, the last being an announcement of her engagement to my grandfather, one of the handsomest men of his day and already a distinguished diplomatist.

She was devoted to her mother and her position at Devonshire House, between the time of the Duchess's death in 1806 and 1809, the year of her marriage, was extremely delicate and disagreeable. She was the only unmarried daughter of the Duke ; Lady Elizabeth Foster, daughter of the 4th Earl of Bristol, Bishop of Derry and widow of Mr. John Thomas Foster, had resided for many years at Devonshire House and continued to do so after the Duchess's death. She assumed the general direction of the household, which should naturally have fallen to Lady Harriet. It is true that the late Duchess had had a certain liking for her and had never resented her living there ; this may possibly be attributed to her indifference as to the behaviour of her husband, who was, if the truth is to be told, a man who could command neither affection nor respect.

At the same time, in reading the correspondence, whilst feeling that Lady Elizabeth was a thorn in her side, one cannot help admiring the dignity and absence of loud complaint which mark Lady Harriet's letters.

Lady Elizabeth married the Duke in 1809. He died in 1811. She seems to have been a woman of considerable physical attractions, but deficient in judgment or indeed any mental qualities. After the Duke's death she went to Italy, where she made herself ridiculous by an affair with Cardinal Consalvi. She had two natural children by the Duke :

Caroline Rosalie Adelaide de St. Jules, born in 1786, who married George Lamb in 1809, and Augustus Clifford, born in 1788. He entered the Navy at the age of twelve, was knighted in 1830 and created a baronet in 1838. His half-brother, the 6th Duke of Devonshire, obtained for him, after some opposition from the King, the appointment of Black Rod, which he held from 1832 until his death in 1877.

Mention should now be made of Lord Granville Leveson Gower's two children by Lady Bessborough (Georgiana Duchess's sister), who were, according to my father, brought up by Harriet with the same care as her own. They were George and Harriette Stewart ; Stewart being the maiden name of Granville's mother, who was a daughter of the 6th Earl of Galloway.

The girl subsequently married the 8th Duke of Leeds, whilst the son became his father's private secretary. My father told me that one of his earliest recollections was being carried ashore by George Stewart, wrapped in a blanket, at a Dutch port, after a fearful storm in which the ship was nearly wrecked. This was when my grandfather had been made Minister to the Hague. Four valuable carriage horses had to be thrown overboard.

I remember George Stewart well, as I was twelve years old when he died. In appearance he was tall, upright and thin—indeed, he might have been called gaunt. He had a pale complexion, dark eyes deeply set in his head, an aquiline nose and a short pointed white beard ; not unlike the pictures of Don Quixote. He and my father were very fond of each other and travelled together for six months in Spain in 1847.

He was a wonderfully skilled turner ; indeed connoisseurs said that his work at the lathe, both for beauty and ingenuity of design and difficulty of execution, equalled, if it did not surpass, that of the best professional craftsmen. Luckily I possess several specimens of his art.

Chiswick House is often mentioned in the correspondence. This is a villa, built about the middle of the eighteenth century in the Palladian style, which Lord Hervey described as " being too small to live in, but too large to hang on your fob." On Lord Granville's death the Duke of Devonshire left it to his two sisters for their lives and, as my mother died a few days after my birth, my father and I lived there with my grandmother for four and a half years, until she died in 1862.

I think that I must be nearly the only person living who remembers her. She was an impressive old lady with her big black bonnet, dark clothes and downright manner, which, together with her mordant wit and caustic tongue, was apt to intimidate those who did not know her well. I cannot say that she alarmed me, which was perhaps the reason why she honoured me by saying that I was " one of the most agreeable of her acquaintance."

Chiswick was, in a way, a place of historic interest, as two great statesmen died there : Charles Fox in 1806 and Canning in 1827. It dwells in my memory as a pleasant place of wide lawns, with spreading cedars and masterpieces of ancient statuary, with long avenues and a lake on which swans floated, stately and serene.

The very fine gates were removed to Devonshire House and, on that mansion's demolition, were erected in Piccadilly by the Green Park.

I have dwelt at some length upon my description of Chiswick, as it was the scene of the close of my grandmother's life and of the early years of my own. Two lives which together comprise more than a century and a half.

I

A WHIG SCHOOLROOM

1796–1798

HARRIET CAVENDISH was born in August 1785 and was therefore 11 years old when these letters begin. Her elder sister, Georgiana, was 13, and their only brother, Hartington, was 6.

But the three Cavendish children were not the only inhabitants of the schoolroom at Devonshire House; their first cousin, Caroline Ponsonby, Lord and Lady Bessborough's daughter, was much with them. She too was born in 1785, and though delicate and often in the country, she and "Haryo" were the closest friends. There were also Caroline de St. Jules and Clifford, natural children of Lady Elizabeth Foster and the Duke of Devonshire. Their governess was Miss Selina Trimmer, who was the sister-in-law of the celebrated authoress, a writer of highly moral juvenile works. Miss Trimmer was devoted to the family, though they sorely tried her sense of the proprieties, and after her charges had left the schoolroom she remained as "watch-dog" to Haryo and as companion to the Dowager Countess Spencer, Georgiana Duchess's mother.

This little world moved between Devonshire House, Chatsworth and Chiswick. They also paid visits to their uncles and aunts at Roehampton, Althorp and Hardwick, and to their grandmother who lived at Holywell House, St. Albans.

The grown-up world was involved in war with France; Napoleon was carrying all before him, but such doings did not affect these little people.

The first two letters were written in 1796, and are much tidier than the later ones. "Lady Liz" is Lady Elizabeth Foster, "Sarah and Bob" the Spencers' children.

Just once the inexplicable point of view of the grown-ups appears; the whole party goes on an expedition and the presence of Lady Holland causes immense embarrassment. Why? We who are grown-up know that she had been divorced by her husband, Sir Godfrey Webster, after she had run away with Lord Holland, but it all seemed very funny to Harriet.

I have kept to Haryo's childish spelling on purpose and only wish that the faded ink, the gilt-edged note-paper and the childish hand could also be reproduced.

Neither Harriet nor her sister were good-looking and "Hart" afterwards told them, with a brother's frankness, that they had spoiled the looks of the two handsomest families in England. Harriet often talks of her "little eyes" and she was inclined to be fat and makes spasmodic efforts at slimming. But she is charmingly frank about her plainness and makes fun of it. There are only three portraits of her. One is a miniature by Cosway as a little girl with her sister; another a pastel, by Russell, also when she was a little girl. In this she has a dear, round, little face with very rosy cheeks, her "little eyes" are dark blue and very intelligent and her hair brown and straight. She is dressed in a low-necked muslin frock, white, with a pink satin sash and she wears a huge, gauzy mob-cap tied with beautiful pink satin ribbons. The third portrait is as an old lady; the mob-cap has changed into an immense black bonnet, but the little eyes are still full of wit and humour.

[The first letter is endorsed in the Dowager Lady Spencer's hand, "Harriet Cavendish." The end is missing, and there is no clue to whom it was written.]

As soon as you went we went into the green park. As we were walking round the pond we met Lady Pembroke, Mrs. Spencer, Little Lady Die and her governess. We walked a little with them and then they went home. As we passed Spencer house we saw Sarah and Bob playing on the steps. We spoke to them and they soon got leave to come with us. We met Lady Sephton [Sefton] and Miss Toley. After running a good deal with Caro and Hart, Sarah and Bob went home but when we got to S. house we went upstairs as my aunt was there. Lady Georgiana received us on the balcony and was very gracious. We found my aunt sitting in an inner room at work. When we got home I read and played till desert, after desert I wrote to you. I shall not be quite so exact in general but as I meant to shew it to G. [her sister] and fearful of being turned out of my office

I thought it best to be a little too exact for once. I am just going to bed so Adieu.

Saturday.

as soon as breakfast was over I read and played on the harp, after which Selina [Trimmer], G. and I walked in the park, we met the little Herberts, as we were speaking to them we saw the two Lady Howards, they spoke to us and then went. The eldest looked beautiful. we walked to Edwards and my new book comes tonight. Soon after we got home we had dinner. I am now writing to you. We are going to Chiswick and one of Selina's sisters comes to us there. I am so fond of the last new step in the Hornpipe that I go all over the House dancing it. mamma got Lady Lizes letter this morning and we're all very sorry for Lord H's accident. G. is very much interested in the " black penitent " and is now reading it in the window in mamma's little room. I am going to take my too new boxs to Chiswick and to lock them up with my books. I shall take everything out of my drawers this evening and put them in order on my shelves. I long to see how they will look. I did not tell you before you went my plan for the biggest of my drawers, I mean to keep in it all manner of Cloths of different sorts for the poor people and when I hear of any in distress I shall always have my drawer ready. give my love to dear Lady Liz. You are now at Salt Hill, pray write soon for I am very impatient to have a very minute journal from you. I shall expect one note (it is not much I am sure) every week and sometimes two in a week for a treat. Am I *too* exhorbitant?

To Lady Georgiana Cavendish

[This letter is directed in a grown-up hand to " Lady G. Cavendish, at the Countess Spencer's. St. Albans, Herts. From Devonshire. London, October the thirty first, 1796."

It is written in two parts and I believe the first part, which is evidently written by Caro Ponsonby, is supposed to be an imitation of Lady Hervey's style, as she has signed it in that lady's name.]

A thousand pardons, dearest Georgiana, for not writing sooner, for *'oo* know *dearest 'ove* that I *'ave* so *'ittle* time for *'ose* things *'at* it is impossible for me to *'ite*.

I have been studying to make meself Mad and uncommon and evrything thats dear and delightful but Have not been able to attain to the perfection of giving all the House a Headache. My dearest Love, believe me that all my professions of *amitié* I made you at Chiswick are sincere as Lasting. Ah, what pleasure I enjoyed whilst the children (pronounced with a contemptuous mean) amused themselves at the Bench ; what pleasure I say, we enjoyed pacing up and down the Lawn and expressing by words and actions our sincere Friendship.

Adieu my Love, your friend, ELIZ. HERVEY.

Now, G, *I* will write to you. Caro is journalist so I have no trouble. Roissere [one of their masters] is coming, so Adieu, dear G.

HENRIETTA CAVENDISH.

I forgot to say I was your sister but try and remember it.

To Lady Georgiana Cavendish

Saturday. 1797.

DEAR DEAR DEAREST G.,

I beg you a great many pardons for not having wrote so long but do write to me T. [Miss Trimmer ?] and I have been to Mrs. Shipley's today, there we beheld Mrs. Shipley looking very tol tol ; Kitty in a mob cap, an embroidered gown, a white cord, enquiring after you and Lady Spancer. Mr. Nailor and his sposa both *looking stark mad*, what they may be I do not know. Four, five boys quite *Italian* ; Mr. Sloper and Miss Sloper grown *plain*. Well sister Po, what may your productions have been ? Has any new specimen appeared ? I am going to publish my sweet pretty poem with the 8 *returns* in it. Oh, G. wherefore am I so stupid ? my dear sister when you are D——s of B——d, will you invite me to W——n ? We are just going to Roehampton to stay two or three days, the boys are coming from Harow. Oh G. excuse me any more and believe me your ever affectionate Henrietta Elizabeth Cavendish.

Selina Trimmer Adair sends her best love, her husband's bilious complaints are somewhat better.

[It was a schoolroom joke that Miss Trimmer should marry Bob Adair, one of the Devonshire House habitués. Georgiana had evidently decided to marry the Duke of Bedford and become châtelaine of Woburn.]

To Lady Georgiana Cavendish

HARDWICK.[1] *Saturday morning. November 1797.*

Indeed my dearest sister, I was very much in the wrong when I fancied I should not be happy here, it would indeed be impossible for me to be otherwise, my uncle and aunt [Lord and Lady Bessborough] are so very good to me . . . but I forgot, this is not remarkably *merry* and I fear my *poor letter* will have been already *doomed* to destruction. Heigho—'tis d. hard to be witty and I fear I must give it up for a time, so you must, shall and will excuse me. My dear, the wind blows bleak. At this present time uncle is a t'other side of the river taking a view on his little black poney, my aunt is at breakfast, my *hopeful* cousin yawning over a *column* of *spelling* and Hart, bless him, trotting all over the house with Mr. Fletcher and Pincher and your muz'd sister striving at wit, which poor soul, she cannot attain.

You can't imagine, G. how tourty [*sic*] we are of an afternoon, my aunt reads and tells us storys. The last thing she read us was Voltaire's "enfant prodige," it is beautiful. Only think how good my dear dear aunt was to me last night; I took some pills and she came and read me a very interesting story while I took them. I must hasten to subscribe myself your ever afectionate sister

HARYO CAVENDISH.

To Lady Georgiana Cavendish
SAVILLE ROW, LONDON

HARDWICKE CASTLE, *November, 1797.*

MY DEAREST G. AND CARO,

A thousand Thousand thanks for your kind Letter which I received last night. I was such a fool as to *cry* for joy when I got all the Letters, but I cannot help, I never knew how much I loved you till I was away from you. You will not envy me when I tell you Bowers [one of their masters] sticks here Tonight for my aunt wishes him to come as often as he can. Ohi, ohi, ohi. I have been riding with my

[1] Evidently lent to the Bessboroughs by the Duke of Devonshire.

uncle and aunt this morning. I must go to Bowers so when I am quite ashamed of this Letter I will write you each a long one soon.

yours ever afectionate, HARYO.

To Lady Georgiana Cavendish

MANSFIELD. *Nov. ye eighth, 1797.*

[The first part of this letter is in Haryo's handwriting, very sprawly and untidy; the second in Lord Bessborough's.]

DEAREST GEOARGIANNA, [*sic*]

I have only time just to thank you for your dear Letter which I received yesterday. My uncle will finish this for me.

We long to see you return here,—We have had but one bad Day since you went—we have been riding today. I have drawn this House from two different places—it looks beautiful from the other side of the Water in the Park.

All here are perfectly well & the Young Fry have been remarkably good. Hart sends his Love.

Believe me ever yours.

To Lady Georgiana Cavendish

Nov. 18th, 1797.

DEAR G.,

I have time only for a little scrap just to ask you not to write any more *aimiable* letters to Caro for my sake, for in consequence of the last, if her wishes had been accomplished, I should either have been quartered on a gibbet or at dispatch of *thousands of Devils.*

We are just going on a grand expedition to see Welbeck, the Duke of Portland's; Thoresby, Lord Newark's, and Clumber, the Duke of Newcastle's. It will take us seven hours and I believe we are to take a cold dinner in the coach.

Many thanks for your letter. I fancied you with your *hair down*, scratching your head, with the comb on the table before you, correcting Caro's letter with a bran new pen. I have had a conversation with Caro and she desires me to tell you that she *did not mean what she has said in her answer to you. There* I wish you would follow her example.

Yours ever afectionate HARYO.

[The 1798 letters are much better written, but Haryo and Caro indulge in their own private slang, mimicking their elders and they take a great interest in dress. After all, they were thirteen.]

To Lady Georgiana Cavendish

Thursday afternoon. D. HOUSE. *1798.*

MY DEAREST SISTER,

I cannot say that I have anything very interesting to communicate to you as yet nor have I seen hitherto your prediction fulfilled that we should be gayer than any little people ever were. However I will still hope for the best. My letters will not afford you much amusement as it is not very interesting to you to know which four masters smiled or frowned upon us etc. The dinner here consisted of Mr. Hare sitting all the evening with his taper legs crossed like a taylor's reading the *Gazette extraordinary* to the wondering [Lord] Coleraine all *dressed in green.* Foster [one of Lady Elizabeth's sons] exerted the pencil in characatures while John sat like what he is, a goodnatured f——l. mamma had got a book of prints from Mr. and Miss *Bull* so that entertained her and Lady Liz listened to the Battle. Adieu dear G. and that my next letter will be more entertaining is the sincere wish of

your ever affec^{t}, HARRIETT.

To Lady Georgiana Cavendish

Saturday evening. 1798.

Ten Thousand thanks my dearest G. for your dear letter. How very kind it was of you to write so soon. Caroline told you we went to Astleys [the Circus]. I will give you a *description* as you would not think it was me unless I describe *my dress* ; I must. *It was* a chip Hat with a wreath of grapes which looked very *small* and pretty, a white gown, gold chain and my Lilack cross. Lady Liz went with us of course and *mamma* staid with *pappa.* The first thing struck our eyes was Lady Holland, seated in the box. My aunt moved all her *ten fingers* at once. Mr. and Mrs. Peterson [the Bessboroughs' housekeeper and butler] who were there, made signs, Lady Liz twisted her *shawls* with a forbidding glance, Caroline held up her head a little higher than usual, John reddened and I who did not know who she was, thought it rather strange that a poor Lady looking so demure and quiet, should cause such evident confusion. I think her pretty. We came home rather crowded.

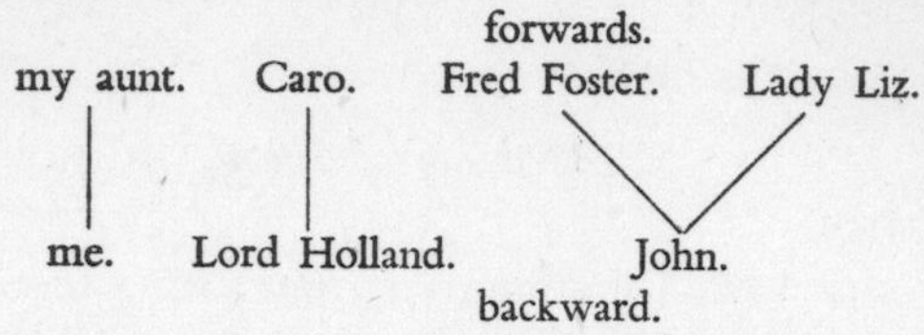

Capisce Miladi ! Lord Holland's tongue never ceased. He mimicked, talked, laughed etc. all in one breath. He said one drole thing, we were so crowded that he compared us to a *Coffel* where they stuff all the poor Indians in. My aunt said Lady Holland's coach would miss ours. Lord H. shook his head and said with emphasis, "ah no ! *she* will be sure to keep her *Coffel in sight.*" Ladamigella was here when we returned, cropped close to the head. I only saw him five minutes, he talked to aunt. I'll assure you I *looked as you bid me*, but in vain, I looked so good-humoured. He looked very handsome but seemed to *miss something* (I had a good mind to ask him *what*) and engaging and pleasing but alas, heeded nor approached me with his little finger. Adieu my own G., if I have entertained you my end is gained, if the contrary, forgive me. I must give you joy of your birthday and that you may live to enjoy many many more in happiness, peace and health is the most ardent prayer and wish of your ever affectionate

HARRIETTE.

To Lady Georgiana Cavendish

Tuesday morn^{g}.

I cannot thank you enough my *lov'd* G. for your letter, write often and long for never shall I be tired of hearing from you. I have been *nowhere* and seen *nobody* (I am sorry I have no better opening) excepting to Hopner's [*sic*]. He was out and Mrs. Ellis[1] and my aunt [i.e. their portraits] of course *locked up*, but poor Lady G. Gordon stood dancing in the middle of the room without respite. She is in a white gown which she tucks up behind with a fan, a thing like *that* round her waist, her hair en cheveux, her neck is very large and the

[1] Wife of Charles Rose Ellis, created Baron Seaford 1826.

GEORGIANA CAVENDISH, AFTERWARDS LADY MORPETH
FROM THE PASTEL BY JOHN RUSSELL, R.A.

whole of the figure seems larger than life. *I* do not think her pretty as I don't like her countenance or her eyes. Mamma is gone to Mrs. Grey's, she desires me to say she would have wrote but was too hurried. *Caro and I* and *Lady Liz* are going in the park. My dear sister how I love you, but I am in a stupid humour. My dear G., what will you say, Lady Liz is waiting. Adieu my beloved G.

your ever affectionate HARRIETT CAVENDISH.

To Lady Georgiana Cavendish

[The letter is endorsed: "Haryo. St. Albans. Feb. 24th, 1798."]

One *petit mot*, Dearest G., to tell you we are *safe* and *sound.* My aunt Bes [Bessborough] dines here today. I am so glad.

Your last charge to me was to write you a funny letter. Poor I. Knock at my pate and fancy wit will come, knock as I will there's nobody at home, *tho my dear so must make* shift without it.

We are to go to the play monday and to the Opera Tuesday. Write to me soon, my own G., a *long* letter. By the bye I am going to have my hair turned up. Caroline and I have composed a language with our *features*, for poor *little sings*, we were so moped in the coach for the rest of our party were so monstrous grumpy.

We should ask Papa for a frank for our two letters only Lady Liz will want it, and if we do, *my dear 'ady 'iz may chance* to give us a *spinkum spankum over her knee.* Lady Liz looks very well *considering* her illness.

Your own HARRYO.

I know you are as rich as Cresus or I would not send this without a frank, but necessity compels me.

To Lady Georgiana Cavendish

[This letter is endorsed: "Haryo. St. Albans. Feb. 25th, 1798."]

My own dear bonny girl. millions of thanks for your letter. Oh, what a *fuss*, oh what a *to do*, oh what a *bother* when we got it. Up stairs we scampered like two *march hairs*, read it with *such* eagerness and obeyed all your commands but that of burning; that was *un peu trop* fort, my G. My uncle and aunt Bes. dined here last night. Made me musicko girlico, *tous les Brebis* [the Lambs] *couvert d'or!* and Miss Lemb.

Car and I have looked over all our *old* letters last night. Oh, by the bye we have all been *stuffing* and *cramming* Lord H's *brick cake* and not content with it ourselves, we cram it down everybody's throat that comes here, just as Emy [their pet name for their Mother] and Haryo do *Mamselle's*. I think there must be a porter to stand at the gate (in case our visitors have *sickly stomachs*). *Gare au gâteau de Mylord*. Oh, how silly I am. By the bye we are to *gig it* with Derval. I hope he will not sneeze in his way, as I feel rather sick today.

Doody, Girl, yours HARRYO.

To Lady Georgiana Cavendish

[Endorsed: "Haryo. St. Albans. Feby. 25th, 1798."]

My own own funny G. Caro has just received your *Drola alina* enclosing Mademoiselle Mercier's, "you-a-a-a-a *a tomitala 'ittle-a monkey-a*." Hart has just received your letter but with all the *importance* of a MARQUIS keeps it to himself.

You see I mean to overpower you with letters as I have already sent you one today by Mr. Vigoureux. Mamma is gone to Town today and she means to go and see Lady Cha. Greville. If the post is not gone before she returns I will send you word how she does.

Have you heard that we go to the play twice, the first time to the "Castle Spectre" and some common farce, the second time to the same and "Blue Beard." Do you not remember I've seen them galloping etc? The opera is to be "Cinna," the one that has met with the most applause since "La Bonne Figluola" was first acted before Mama can remember. We have seen Mr. Vigoureux, he has, I see, got two *spectres* for you. We have not got *one*, however Mama has promised to bring us one.

HARRY.

Dinner calls, I must obey.

To Lady Georgiana Cavendish

[No address or date, but obviously written at the same time as the other letters from St. Albans.]

MY DEAREST G.,

We are going tonight to a *dance* and Monday to a *ball* at the same place. I shall like them both. Goodbye, Carro will finish.

HARYO.

DEAR G.

Haryo is *so so so* naughty not to write to *'oo* my love. Have I not imitated her well? [This is written in a very fair copy of Haryo's hand by Caro Ponsonby. She then writes in her own wild scrawl:]

Haryo forces me to write tho' I have no time, no interest, no anything and in a great passion, so goodbye.

To Lady Georgiana Cavendish

AT CHISWICK HOUSE, MIDDLESEX

MARGATE. *August 17th, 1798.*

DEAREST G.,—we arrived here yesterday, the road was beautifull, but the deuce a bit do you care about that, suffice it to say I sat *backwards* with cold meat and all manner of fruit. This morning I am so o'er whelmed with the buz of Margate beau's and Belle's in this, which is the *fashionable street* that I hardly know what I write. I had no peace before I got up with the noise my cousins made at my door, but Mrs. Peterson made a loud harangue, "for shame Mrs. P*onsonby*" which presently hushed it. Lady Anne [Hutton] was *ra*ther *strict* in the coach but *dove'd* and love'd me too. And does 'oo know that I'm very jappy, afectcha, a *coy* gal? "Be quiet little ape, an't she too bad Lady G.?"

Dalpini, we will if we can. I have not seen any of my cozs' yet, they are walking. Bless you, I will write an account tomorrow of today. Banister acts *here*, thats all I hardly *dare* hope . . . Will you excuse this letter but you know I have seen nobody. Give my love to all my friends and relations and tell them I long to throw myself at there feet. I will shew you the Margate dishabille for men. . . . [Here is a tiny drawing of a little man, with a cocked hat, high Empire trousers, a cane and a train.]

II

DEVONSHIRE DÉBUTANTE

1801

NO letters between 1798 and 1801 have come to light, and now we meet the débutante instead of the schoolgirl. Georgiana Cavendish married, in March 1801, Lord Morpeth, son and heir of the 5th Earl of Carlisle, and in the autumn of the year the Duke and Duchess, accompanied by Harriet, pay their first visit to their married daughter and son-in-law, who lived, as was the custom, with his parents at Castle Howard. The whole family had stayed at Castle Howard before the marriage, but this visit was invested in Harriet's eyes with much interest and glamour which centred in her beloved "G.," who was awaiting her first *petit paquet.*

The spring had been passed in gaieties. Harriet went to balls and did not lack partners ; Mr. Dillon, who dined so often at Devonshire House, Frederick Byng (whose name she spells with an "i,"), the Duke of Bedford, whom Georgiana had chosen as her future husband when she was still in the schoolroom, and her Ponsonby cousins.

The Misses Berry, whose friendship Georgiana Morpeth had cultivated, to Harriet's annoyance, were the friends of Horace Walpole, who left them Strawberry Hill. Their nicknames were Elderberry, Blackberry and Gooseberry.

Harriet's writing is now formed and clear, but Miss Trimmer had omitted to teach her punctuation. Omitted is the right word, for it is non-existent. I have therefore taken liberties in this respect for clarity's sake. Otherwise the letters are as Haryo wrote them, save for a few omissions ; protestations of affection, etc.

To Lady Georgiana Morpeth

DEVONSHIRE HOUSE, *Sunday evening, 1801.*

Thank you, Thank you, dearest G., for your second kind letter, but do not say you *take it very unkind* any more, and I promise to write.

Indeed you are the only person I write to without *absolute agony*, for as I cannot be with you it is even pleasure to me (that is not all very clear, however, non importa). By the bye, Nardini pines after you; I hope you correspond with him regularly to keep him alive.

We went the night before last to Lady Palmerston's, it was very pleasant indeed and not too full. The Berrys were there and (begging your pardon) quieter than usual. Mrs. William Locke was with them, looking beautiful. I danced with Mr. Dillon, Harry Temple, F. Ponsonby and Frederick Bing. Frederick Ponsonby has got a new friend, who does not do him credit, a branch of the W.W.W. [Watkins Williams Wynne] family, a Mr. Wynne. If you do not know him you cannot picture to yourself anything so goos-ish. I think Sir Watkin clever in comparison. This amiable youth and Fred are inseparable and of course we see nothing else.

We are going with a large party by water to dine at Richmond; it is Mr. Dillon's last day as he has had a summons to Ireland, therefore now or never.

Poor Lord Granville [Leveson Gower, her future husband] is ill and confined to his room. Mama and Lady Elizabeth went to see him today and saw there a very delightful letter from Lord Nelson.

Mr. Hare is dining here and more entertaining than ever. He has been quizzing poor Hart most unmercifully, who has been about an hour ordering his supper, and now Lady Elizabeth is endeavouring to prove that he ought to be humoured.

Goodnight my own dearest sister, how happy it would make me to come to you.

ever yours, HARYO.

To Lady Georgiana Morpeth

DEVONSHIRE HOUSE, *Monday morning, 1801.*

We go to Chiswick for good tomorrow, my dearest sister, to my great joy. Last night I sat up late but it was not worth it, for I was very, very dull, à l'ordinaire. Lord Cowper, Mr. Dillon, the Duke of Bedford, Mr. Crawfurd and Lord Granville were here, but Lord G. only for a minute or two as he is not at all well yet. Lord Cowper was all but asleep and the Duke of Bedford came very late. Mr. Crawfurd and Mr. Dillon kept up the conversation, so judge. They all dine here today and mamma and Corise [1] go to Vauxhall, alas! not us [Harriet and Caro St. Jules].

We went the other day to Mr. Townly's collections of Statues, they are most of them Beautiful.

When shall I see you, dearest G.? I do not hear papa say anything about Yorkshire which puts me in despair.

Adieu, dear own G., ever most affec^{ly} yours, HARYO.

Corise sends her love to you. If it was a possibility I would send you how Mr. Dillon goes on, but I defy anybody to discover. All I know is I have him in aversion, and the other night mama amused herself in making verses on him to [the tune of] The Dusty Miller beginning—

"Oh, the odious odious Mr. Harry Dillon."

Pray sing it, but do not leave this on the first landing place.

To Lady Georgiana Morpeth

CHISWICK HOUSE, *Tuesday morning, 1801.*

You would be very much flattered, my dearest G. if you could know how happy it makes me to hear from you. I received your kind letter yesterday and thank the two *Lords* [Carlisle and Morpeth] for not effectually hindering you from finishing it. A propos, you said to me in one of your letters, "it appears very strange to me, that you should not *like* Mr. Marsh." I am anxious to clear myself but I think find it rather more difficult to discover why you should fancy I had a prepossession against a man I never saw; for on the contrary, by all I have heard of him I am very much inclined to that *affection* which you so mournfully lament my want of. I treat the matter quite seriously you perceive.

I have been *cantering* all over the country this morning and am going to town to order a habit—how grand!

The other day I had a curious meeting with the Duke of Richmond. I had quite forgot he existed even and I rushed into Lady Liz's Bedroom expecting to see Caro [St. Jules] trying on her habit. Judge of my

[1] Corisande, daughter of the *émigré* Duc de Gramont. She joined the girls at Devonshire House and lived with them till her marriage to Lord Ossulston in 1806.

surprise when instead of Caro I beheld his grace erect with both arms stretched out and a little thin taylor running round and round him with a measure, and Lady E. with a look of agitated interest, unfolding a book of patterns. Taking it *all in all*, it was the most ridiculous thing I ever saw.

We are very magnificent in trains and such long ones. Adieu my dearest sister. I am going to Town.

We were going on much in the same dull way as usual when Mr. Hare arrived . . . " The scene is changed, we're altered quite." He is in very low spirits indeed about Charles, who he has just parted from. He seems I think to regret having sent him so far from him.

Pray write to me again soon, my dearest dearest sister.

To Lady Georgiana Cavendish

Monday morning, 1801.

Papa and Mama are quite well, we are all packed up and tomorrow, grace à Dieu, we set out. We stayed *at home* last night and Mr. Hare, Lord Granville, Monsieur de Lima and Jules [de Polignac] came. Mama put Lord G. into a fine passion by beating him 2 at chess. It is so funny to see her play as it is very common for her to attack violently and carry off triumphantly one of her own men. Duncannon [the Bessboroughs' eldest son] has made me the most delightful present ; a chess board and chess men with screws to play with in a carriage. I mean to play all the way to Castle Howard. How do you come on ? I have a presentiment that you do not know a pawn from a queen—oh disgrazia !

I expect to see you about Saturday, allowing for St. Albans, Woburn and Hardwicke. My dear G. JE NE ME POSSÈDE PAS. . . . Adieu, adieu, I am summoned to Philip the 2nd and cross-stitch.

ever with the truest affection, yours, HARYO.

To Miss Trimmer

AT CHISWICK

HARDWICKE HALL, *October 10th, 1801.*

MY DEAREST SELINA,

I know you hate me to be in a bustle and hurry, and therefore I am impatient to do off the impression you must have had of my being in a very great one from my note at Welford.

We arrived here last night in very good time for dinner. Augustus deigned come with us from Nottingham, but indeed he has grown so very grand that this morning when he rode I expected him to make Papa hold the stirrup, while he got on. This morning, after a night passed in (I need hardly tell you) very sound sleep, I jumped out of bed the instant I was called, and Caro and I explored the park, which is very much improved from some trees which have been cut down. I have since been examining the pictures in the gallery with the catalogue. The pictures have been cleaned and look very well. I have also wrote to my grandmama as I promised.

We set out again tomorrow morning and sleep at Feny Bridge. On Monday we stop at York to see the Minster, and as it is not far we shall arrive at Castle Howard in time for dinner. I will be particularly careful about calmness when I see my dearest G., and I trust you know me well enough to believe that I would not, to gratify my own feelings, cause the slightest unnecessary pain to her, especially now when it would be so bad for her to be agitated.

I am rather *invalidish* with a little sore-throat and a bad headache, but I have been managing myself famously—taken Rhubarb, ordered gargle etc. and I feel better already.

Lady Newark and Miss Pierrepoint are just arrived here to take Corise to Thoresby. She is so very loud that Miss P. and I wish she was gone for she does not cure my headache with her tongue.

The Cholmondelys are, I hear, at Castle Howard. I hope they will be gone, as that great goose, Miss C. engrosses G. most unconscionably, indeed she never is much troubled with her conscience, if she has one, for some of those two legged birds I sometimes suspect. I have no patience with her, for she unites what is disagreeable in a clever person with the capacity of a foolish one.

I am very sorry not to be able to go to church tomorrow. I think it very wrong to travel on Sunday. However, Car and I go alone in the chaise and we shall be able to read together. I am making a great reform in some things. I hope you will find me improved. Pray come soon with my grandmama, for I think she is determined to come for the benefit of *my* instructions. I wish it was in me power to make her as much happier as it is in hers to make me better, but the latter, I hope, will conduce to it in a great degree and I hope also no exertions will be wanting on my part.

Adieu, my dearest Selina, my head aches very much, and it rather encreases it to stoop.

ever yours most affec[ly], HARYO.

To Miss Trimmer

HARDWICK. *October, Tuesday the 20th, 1801.*

We are all quite well and just going to set out, dearest Selina. I shall keep my letter open to add a line from Feny Bridge where we sleep tonight. And now let me thank you for your kind letter. I am indeed very careful of myself, for it would be dreadful to have another sore throat at Castle Howard.

We hear very constantly from Corisande who seems very happy at Thoresby.

By the bye are not you rather indignant at the *violent honours* bestowed upon Saninton [?] and the inscriptions " Buonaparte saviour of the universe " ? Are we not the only nation who have checked his conquests, did we not drive him out of Egypt in the most glorious manner, and I do not see that even by our own countrymen, we have half enough honour for it. I think the peace seems a sad one, however, peace in any shape almost, I think was necessary. I never heard of anything so delightful as Mr. Fox's behaviour, with his superior talents and abilities, he is with all the nature and simplicity of a child, in real high spirits at the happiness he sees diffused over his fellow creatures ; he says, " I thank the ministers for the peace because I think it was necessary but I gave them credit for a better than they have made." How true it is of Mr. Fox " on his heart we may rely even should his judgement for a moment fail him."

Exit in a transport of universal philanthropy !

Here I am, *cooled* at Feny Bridge. It is a delightful inn and I feel quite well, and have been eating a very good dinner.

HARRIETT.

To Miss Trimmer

CASTLE HOWARD, *Thursday morning, Oct. 1801.*

MY DEAREST SELINA,

We arrived here last night and found dearest G. very well and looking beautiful. The Carlisles, Lord Morpeth, Lady Gertrude, Frederick and Henry [Howard], who are the only people here, seem quite to idolize her and she, herself, seems perfectly happy. It is a beautiful and comfortable place. My room is a little one à la Française with a tent bed in a recess, a couch etc. and delightful. The Carlisles are all kindness and I love them for their affection for our dear G. Indeed if they did not adore her they would be brutes.

Lady Gertrude and I are very good friends and her reserve will, I hope, decrease very much. The weather being so bad is a great mortification to us all as we were as anxious to see, as they were to shew us the place. It appears to me beautiful or as the amiable Bunting expresses herself about it, " Heavenly ! ! Adorable ! ! " Those were her words this morning when she called me.

I was much amused with your adventures in the stages. Pray write to me soon. The post is going, excuse this hurried scrap but I was determined to write, if only a line.

ever yours, HARYO.

I need not say G. is going on *perfectly well.* Lord M. and her seem the happiest of human beings.

To Miss Trimmer

CASTLE HOWARD. *Saturday. October, 1801.*

I cannot tell you, my dearest Selina, half how happy and comfortable we are here. I am just returned from a tête à tête with, I give you 12 guesses ? Lord Carlisle. And besides I have been all over the Park with Frederick and Lady Gertrude.

G. is almost all the morning in her own room and I go and sit with her every now and then. Poor Lady Carlisle has a bad headache today, which is unfortunate as it is finer weather than I ever saw any where, and she wished so much to walk with us. I never knew any body so good natured.

Lady Gertrude *improves* very fast but even her *connoissance* is a work of time, and anything more seems to me *so* tedious that I cannot even look forward to it. Frederick is a charming boy and Henry is . . . spare my blushes, my favoured lover. He is a little bit of perfection and Caro and I are both captivated.

We have heard from Corise that the eldest Mr. Pierrepoint is dead at Thoresby. They are all in the greatest affliction, and it is very melancholy for her.

Papa is just gone to shoot with Lord Carlisle and Frederick. I never saw him so well, and I wish to my heart he would adopt these hours for Chatsworth. I never knew the charm of regularity till I came here.

Adieu, dearest Selina. I am going to the mausoleum. My love and duty to my grandmama.

HARYO.

To Lady Georgiana Morpeth

HARDWICK HALL. *December 3rd. 1801.*

Here we are, my dearest G., after a most adventurous day. We travelled very comfortably till Worksop, when Papa chose with his gout to ride here in pitch darkness and the most jolting roads in the universe. However he arrived safe, and so did Caro and I in our equipage, but with somewhat more difficulty. Our poor postilion was thrown, and while he was getting up, mama's carriage left us and we remained with neither of the postilions knowing one step of the way. We soon discovered that we had turned wrong and we found ourselves in a narrow lane with seemingly no method of turning round the chaise. Madame Aubert, who was in the chaise with us, with exclamations, " Oh, la pauvre femme, oh, là ! " which threw me into fits of laughter. And when we got out of the chaise and found ourselves perched on a high stile, with my shoe off and papa's cocked hat, which Mr. Brown had put under our immediate protection, rolling down the lane, we all three screamed, à force de rire. We all arrived here as tired as you may imagine, and I am very good to write to you. Papa seems much the same tonight and not the worse for his ride.

Lady Melbourne wrote mama word that she was going to dine with Mr. Crawfurd, where the Prince is to meet Mr. Pitt and Fox. How odd it seems to hear of their inseparability.

I am racking my poor brain to find something more to say, but it only procures for me the torment of " apellare e non venire," for two long letters [which are missing] have informed you of all our proceedings between Londesborough and Hardwick. Miss Berry would expatiate on every jolt, and Miss Seymour would flourish about how her heart dragged a lengthened chain, but I had rather not bore you with either, and I flatter myself you know the state of my heart towards you without quotations from "the Traveller."

I hear poor Miss Berry is very ill indeed. What poor health she has. [She lived till she was ninety.]

Most affectionately yours, HARRYO.

III

THE VISIT TO RAMSGATE

1802

IN August " the younger branches of the family " set out for a holiday at Ramsgate under the charge of Miss Trimmer, who disapproved strongly of the association between Devonshire House and the Melbournes. Her disapproval was not to prevent the two Caros both marrying Lambs, for Caroline Ponsonby married William Lamb and Caroline St. Jules, his brother George. But these marriages did not take place till much later.

The marriage of the moment was that of Charles James Fox to Mrs. Armistead, or rather the announcement of their marriage. She had been one of the most celebrated courtisanes of the time and Fox's recognised mistress for many years. Her devotion to him (and his, in his own strange way, to her) was very real, but once their marriage was announced, she was dropped by many people who had received her when she was only supposed to be his mistress. The same thing had happened to Lady Holland after her divorce from Sir Godfrey Webster and her marriage to Lord Holland, though the Devonshires and Bessboroughs were among her most intimate friends. (The consternation described by Haryo in her early letter must be attributed to the presence of the " young fry.") History was to repeat itself when Lady Elizabeth Foster married the Duke of Devonshire in 1809, though the whole world knew she had lived at Devonshire House as his mistress for more than eighteen years and that their two natural children had been brought up with the little Cavendishes.

However, Lady Elizabeth was also the friend of Georgiana, Duchess of Devonshire, and of her sister Lady Bessborough, and was loved and trusted by them both.

But the Devonshire children hated her. In the letters she appears as Lady Elizabeth, Lady E. F., Lady Liz and as a " certain lady " etc.

Her two legitimate sons, Augustus and Frederick Foster, had also been largely brought up in Devonshire House.

Lord Granville Leveson Gower is often mentioned. Both Georgiana Morpeth and Harriet appear to have known of his long liaison with their aunt, Lady Bessborough, and to have disliked him. It must be confessed that he sounds patronizing, rather priggish and conceited, and it cannot be denied that in the long correspondence between him and Lady Bessborough he does show himself to return her selfless devotion with a rather heartless egotism.

Sir Walter Farquhar was another of Harriet's *bêtes noires*. He was the family physician, and, it would appear, a very bad one.

Mr. Luttrell was a constant visitor at Devonshire House and known as the last of the conversationalists. And Mr. Hare kept them in fits of laughter.

To Lady Georgiana Morpeth

DEVONSHIRE HOUSE, *August, 1802.*

MY DEAREST SISTER,

We set out for Ramsgate the latter end of next week and then Papa means to determine about Paris, but I have no doubt that when once he moves at all, we shall find no difficulty in persuading him to go abroad.

My darling little love's [1] letter put me in transports and I saw wit and genius in every cross line. I shall be quite mortified if he drops the correspondence so kindly begun.

I have seen all the little now to be seen in London. I could not give your message to Lord Granville, as I did not see him. We were at Vauxhall last night; indeed we live there. It was very pleasant. All the Melbournes were there with us, Henry Pierrepoint and Harry Wynne, who is as constant as ever. Sir Sidney Smith and Miss Rumbold inseparable, it is reported they are to be married. Thank heaven, here is a piece of real news to enliven my paragraph. Charles Fox has declared that he has been married eight years to Mrs. Armistead. I hear the Hollands and all his friends have taken it amazingly well.

Ever your most affectionate HARRO.

[1] The "darling little love," was her nephew George, the Morpeths' first child. He was born on April 18th, 1802, and was barely four months old.

To Lady Georgiana Morpeth

CHISWICK. *Tuesday.*

Thank you, my dearest G., for your letter.

Mama, my aunt, Corisande and Caro Ponsonby have been spending 2 or 3 days at Brocket Hall [The Melbournes' country house]. Corisande says she liked it for that time, but that if she had staid a day longer, she would certainly have returned sourde ou muette, for that "les rires des Messieurs Lambs" quite stunned her as it was.

There was an extraordinary flirtation between William Lamb and Caro Ponsonby, and they seem, I hear, mutually captivated. When the rest were at games etc., William was in a corner, reading and explaining Poetry to Car., and in the morning, reading tales of wonder together on the *tithertother*. When she played at Hunt the squirrel, Hunt the Slipper etc., he did; always sat by her etc. In short she *roared* all the way from Brocket to Roehampton and came here the next day, the oddest compound of sentiment and oddity, of 50 and 5, that I never was so amused in my life. Pray do not let her hear that we know it, for nobody has mentioned it to her for she is already as vain as a Peacock about it. He did not captivate anybody else, for he does not look cooler or nicer than of old, and they say is grown very vociferous and boisterous.

Of Frederick [1] they can only judge of his snoring, as he was scarce awake the whole time. They sent Lord John Townshend into Corisande's room, and assured him it was his own. She woke and was not a little astonished at beholding him standing by the bed.

I have made acquaintance with a person I am much in danger of being captivated with, John Ponsonby—I think him so beautiful and delightful. However, even there my case is not despairing.

Dear methodic sister! I can see you with a little scrap of paper on your table:

9 to 11, musick. 1 hour Patrick.
11 to 12, Novelle osave. [*sic*]
12 to 1, Miss Seymour and Miss Berry.

Arduous task; in one hour to write to a fool and a prodigy! Have I not guessed aright?

Adieu, dearest G., ever yours most affec^{tly}, HARRIET.

[1] Lamb, who became a distinguished diplomatist and was created Lord Beauvale.

Corisande desires her best love to you. I love her more and more every day, though as we are a little tenacious of our opinions, we have violent quarrels. Par example, she thinks Miss Pierrepoint has a pretty chin ; I do not. Judge how learnedly we argue on so important a subject. We spend a day at Woburn [The Duke of Bedford's] on our journey. I shall like to see it as I have quite forgotten it.

We were at Wimbledon [the Spencers' house] yesterday, and I think the house like a bad inn. I cannot bear it, it is in the shabbiest, most inconvenient style you can imagine. Corise begs me tell you that she wrote her letter quite of herself. I see it is full of *Mistre Jonn Ponsonby*.

Mrs. Ellis is at Claremont. Lady Liz came from her in raptures —" Dear Eliza, I found her in a darling gown covered with little Rosebuds." If I had known nothing about it, that speech would have told me where she had been. I daresay those little Rosebuds cost herself and the poor shopkeepers as much trouble as the Canterbury schawl which fatigued you, or the chair which let Lord Morpeth into the secret of her capacity. Dear Charles Ellis was in high croak or spirits.

To Lady Georgiana Morpeth

DEVONSHIRE HOUSE. *Saturday morning, August 14th, 1802.*

MY DEAR DEAREST SISTER,

We, for a wonder, have not yet changed our plans, and the *younger branches* of the family set out on Monday, but Papa and Mama not till Thursday sennight.

We are as Gay as London will now permit, but the Melbournes, who have been quite living with us, go to Brighton today. We had a turtle dinner yesterday. Mr. Hare, Lord Thanet, General Fitzpatrick,[1] etc. It was *rather* pleasant, and we walk in the garden every evening before supper, which is delightful this fine weather.

Today Lady Liz, Caro, Corise and I are going to dine at Claremount

[1] General Fitzpatrick was the second son of the 1st Earl of Upper Ossory by Lady Evelyn Leveson Gower, daughter of the 2nd Earl Gower. He is best known as the intimate friend of Fox. He served with credit in the American War of Independence. He was subsequently twice War Minister, first under Lord Rockingham and afterwards under Fox. He was a prominent member of society and celebrated for his charm and wit.

and tomorrow we all sleep at St. Albans and Friday we have the *remains* of the *poor turtle* for the Bessboroughs, Lord Cowper, Mr. Luttrel and Henry Pierrepoint, which I shall like better than yesterday's *witty* party.

I give you this "*fashionable arrangement for the week*" that you may not despise our attempts at gaiety, and to compleat the Vauxhal manner of spending our evenings, on Friday the Pandeon pipes are to be posted in the portico. We shall soon rival Mr. Barrett.

I hear the Duchess of Gordon sets out for Spa in 2 or 3 days, and that it is quite schocking to see Lady Georgiana, she is so altered and grown so thin and pale. Henry Pierrepoint was there the other day and was quite schocked at the Duchess's behaviour to her, so riotous and cruel.

How does your darling boy do ? If you could know how I long to see him again. He is the celebrated person of the present age. Everybody talks to me of his amiability and beauty—Lady Sefton especially, odious, tiresome woman ! Do you not see her with her fan tight up to her face, peeping through the sticks—" sweet child, often catch a glimpse, lively woman the nurse "—and all her little detached commendations, nodding her head about like Hart's Muscovy ducks. Oh, I *do* hate her. I am out of sorts today. I don't like to go and be fretted over at Claremount. Lady Hervey was here last night, more odious than ever in a bright purple gown, telling stories of " little Tommy Turpentine."

Addio, carissima sorella, HARYO.

If Lady Caroline has any new fashions from the Archipelago you shall have them.

To Lady Georgiana Morpeth

HOLYWELL. *Sunday morn^g^. August 15th, 1802.*

We have been moving about so much since I wrote to you last, my dearest sister, that I am afraid you must have thought me very idle, for I have hardly had a moment's time to give you an account of our *gay* proceedings. We went to Claremont on Wednesday and found Mrs. Ellis looking *quite* well and I think as pretty as I ever remember her. Her frightful child was well too, but anything so very ugly I never beheld, and we could hardly help laughing whilst Lady Elizabeth talked of " the *strain* of seeing such perfect beauty." Augustus [Ellis, then 2 years old] I think very pretty and engaging but Charles [1] was so dreadfully shy that I could not once see his face. The Singletons were there, Lord Villiers [2] and a disagreeable man, Mr. Manby. How very handsome and aimiable Lord Villiers seems, but I think he has acquired a little too much of the Hervey whine and the Ellis Croak. There are two or three Claremount ways that put me out of patience; how silly it is to hear Charles Ellis ask "when is Ma——a expected?" he is so like a tiresome over*gwown* baby. Mrs. Ellis was in very good humour; *we* sung "Lady Fair" and my extensive and fine base notes were displayed to advantage. So much for Wednesday as we returned to town and went to bed directly.

On Thursday we passed an evening that would have delighted Lord Morpeth; we formed 8 of the 14,000 people assembled at Vauxhall in honour of the prince's Birthday, and after having been nearly squeezed to Death, sat 2 hours and a half in the carriage without a possibility of moving one way or the other. Mr. Hare, Monsieur de Calonne [3] and Frederick Foster were our only attendants and Mr. Hare said he really never could have believed that any public amusement could have had the power to make him so completely miserable. Frederick really *angry* and *affronted*, has been *sulky* ever since, and Lady Eliz, *nervous*, so you see our expedition was not very successful.

On Friday we had a delightful supper at D. House. The Pandeon Pipes [4] played on the portico, which sounded excessively pretty. Henry Pierrepoint came. I like him very much indeed, he is so very gentlemanlike and amiable.

Yesterday we arrived here to take leave of my grandmama, who we found quite well and alone. We certainly set out for Ramsgate on Wednesday and Mama a day or two after. I hear it is as full as possible. The Jerseys are there, Lady Southampton and Miss Fitzroy, Alas! The Melbournes mean to join us, and Lord Cowper and Mr. Luttrel came in their way to Paris, where they go in a fortnight.

[1] Charles Augustus Ellis, born 1799, afterwards 6th Lord Howard de Walden.

[2] Son and heir of the 4th Earl of Jersey.

[3] Had been Minister to Louis XVI. He returned to France in October 1802 by Napoleon's permission.

[4] Pandeon pipes were a form of the Greek Pan's-pipes or syrinx. Probably those mentioned were a larger kind, very possibly played by the wind; hence the portico.

John Ponsonby and H. Pierrepoint mean to come too. Have you heard any thing of Lord Granville lately? I have not for ages. Is Lord Ossulston sporting his little form at Paris?

Corise and Caro desire their best love to you; Corise is in the greatest beauty, though in very deep mourning for her great grandfather, which does not become her.

We have got a new branch of the Hare family *living* with us—Colonel Hare the eldest son, ugly and stupid, but very good-natured and *after all a worthy creature.*

Mama comes here today and we return to town tomorrow for a farewell supper. Is William Howard with you yet; mama wrote to him to beg him to come to D. House but I suppose he was gone, for we saw nothing of him. Will you give my kindest love to Lady Gertrude? Is dear little Henry [Howard] grown and is he as *warlike* as he used to be?

I wish you would write to me, dearest G. and talk about yourself and darling beautiful Boy, to whom I send a hundred thousand loves and Kisses. How I envy Castle Howard the happiness of having him and you. Goodbye, my best, dearest sister. I am going to the Abbey.

Yours ever most affec[ly], H. CAVENDISH.

To Lady Georgiana Morpeth

RAMSGATE, *Thursday morning, August 26th, 1802.*

Here we are, my dearest sister, to my great happiness and I must say, astonishment, for in our unsettled plans that a scheme so lately made should be so speedily executed seems quite incredible.

We arrived here last night, very late, Miss Trimmer, Corise, Caro, Hart, Clifford and I, and have established ourselves in the smallest of the two houses taken for us. They are at Chatham Place, about half a mile from the sea and joining to one another. A very ugly situation and the views are the flat side of the Isle of Thanet without one object to enliven it, except that where in other places you would hope to see a tree and in more cultivated parts of this Island, a bush, you discover a red house or a windmill. The pier we cannot go to as we have no horses, and it is too hot to walk. Clifford is quite wild, and in spite of the heat has been to the sea already three times. Hart is in a violent passion because Caroline has taken his room. He vows vengeance, and Miss Trimmer and he are seated on a couch eloquent almost to blows.

We do not expect Papa and Mama, Lady Elizabeth and Sir Walter (for he alas ! comes to make us sick when we are well) till Saturday. The Prince is returned from Brighton and living at Devonshire House. The disgusting turtles are still rolling about the garden, Mr. Crawfurd and Mr. Crowles still in Town to eat them and therefore Heaven knows when Mama will get away.

To Lady Georgiana Morpeth

RAMSGATE, *August 27th, 1802.*

Though since yesterday my stock of ideas cannot have acquired much interest or variety, I cannot resist thanking you for your letter.

Ramsgate does not abound with incident, and now you shall judge if your way of spending your time is not more dissipated than ours. We get up about seven, and today for the first time I bathed. The sea was very calm and delightful, and Mrs. Harry Greville appeared to me tripping up the cliff, not more discomposed with her dip than she seems to be with any other common occurrence of life, her colour so brilliant and her dress so precise. We breakfast at nine, and then I write, read and practice till dinner at four. We then walk on the pier and cliffs till nine. In the evening more walking and musick till half-past ten, after which reasonable hour Miss Trimmer would not have one of us up for worlds.

You ask me who is here and alas ! I have not a General Phipps to boast of. I have not, except Mrs. Greville's, seen one face I ever saw before. The pier is full of an evening but most of the people on it are dreadfully vulgar. The Uptons are all at Broadstairs.

The Duchesses of Newcastle [1] and Chandos are here, and Lady Ramsden and Sir James de Bathe. I have never seen any of these fine people, but Hart assures me they are all here. I hope my next letter will be better worth the trouble of reading it.

Ever your most affectionate HARYO.

[1] She was the second wife to the 8th Duke and after his death, in 1795, she married Lieut.-General Sir Charles Crauford, whom she cared for devotedly, he having been severely wounded in 1796.

To Lady Georgiana Morpeth

RAMSGATE, *August 28th, Wednesday morning, 1802.*

MY DEAREST SISTER,

I am delighted to hear of your still intending to go to Paris, as I certainly think we shall.

They all arrived here last night, papa and mama both looking remarkably well, and the former is now (between 11 and 12) *taking a walk*, which you know, for him, is next to a miracle.

The sea looks so beautiful and one can see Calais so well, that I should not be surprised in a week to set out for France ; especially as Sir Walter and Lady Elizabeth, two people of great consequence when *we* are to be moved, both go at any rate and are so very anxious to persuade us.

I cannot tell you how sorry I am Sir Walter is come. It was bad enough to have him *going his rounds* every day at Devonshire House, but really to be " unis à jamais," is too insupportable. I see, too, we are all to adore him, and it begins already to be a crime to mention him with disrespect. Lady Eliz^th^ idolizes him and I see Corise begins to think " que cela sera une partie excellente et fort convenable."

I do not envy you your horsemanship, not even the quiet little poney.

I bathe every day and it is quite delightful. The sea was dreadfully rough this morning, but I went in notwithstanding and with the greatest courage.

How I wish I could see George's new hat and his beautiful little phiz.

I have just heard that the Melbournes come on Saturday. I dread their arrival as if I was only to see them once a month, Miss Trimmer would keep up a constant reproof ; she is at present perfectly kind and good-humoured, but you know how she hates Lady Melbourne, and just before we left Town she was angry with me for a week, because I happened to take Frederick's arm at Vauxhall.

John Ponsonby too comes on Saturday to Margate, but means to be constantly here. The Bessboroughs do not come till the 10th of next month, and then bring Duncannon,[1] who they expect from Wales immediately.

Though this place is entirely full, I never see a face I know, which

[1] Duncannon was the Bessboroughs' eldest son, born in 1781. His brothers were Frederick, born in 1783, and William Francis, born in 1787 (created Lord de Mauley in 1858). Their only sister was Caroline Ponsonby.

I think is pleasant in some degree, but here goes rather too far, as I think this is a place that requires a good deal of society.

To Lady Georgiana Morpeth

RAMSGATE. *No date, probably Sept., 1802.*

I am very glad to be settled here, and the only reason I have the *least* wish to go abroad is that there would be more probability of your joining us there.

Mr. Sheridan and Lady Liz had a violent quarrel at Devonshire House the other night. He told her that she went to Paris as most ladies did, under cover of [seeing] the Apollo Belvedere but really to display all the tenderness of her nature. He said he would bet anything that she would faint 7 times running when first she saw Buonaparte, if nothing else would attract his attention, and in short, thoroughly provoked her. Mr. Hare joined, and both together tormented her all the supper time.

The tide is full and we are going down to the sea. I pray not to meet Miss Fitzroy and Lady Southampton. Addio, my dearest dearest G. I hope you *have* written to me, if not, pray, pray do. Perhaps a promise not to teize you with so many of my stupid letters would be the most persuasive argument I could make use of.

Corise is half out of the window to examine some *fashionables* and I must leave off to go and walk. Adieu once more, most truly and affectionately yours,

HARYO.

I wish you could have heard old St. Albans [1] and Mrs. Jones talk of Lord Morpeth. She never saw anybody so perfect, and his beauty and amiability are her constant theme. He is almost as delightful as Lady Mary Howard, though she never tried his patience at Whist as she did that poor old Lady's.

To Lady Georgiana Morpeth

RAMSGATE, *Friday, September 3rd, 1802.*

How wrong of you not to write to me, dearest sister ; if my letters were not the best punishment I could devise, you should not ever

[1] Wife of the 8th Duke, daughter of John Nelthorpe of Little Grimsby Hall.

Lord Granville Leveson Gower, Aged 8,
afterwards 1st Earl Granville
From a Sketch by John Downman

receive another ; it is ages since you have written to anybody—in short you are a wicked unkind G.

We are growing very gay here, and if you and Lord Morpeth had any virtue *in you*, you would come to us. The Melbournes arrived last night, at least some of them, for Lord M. and George do not come till Sunday. Pen [1] and Frederick stay in town, and William is at the Duke of Athol's in Scotland. Mama has just heard from my aunt Bessborough, who comes next Tuesday. John Ponsonby is at Margate, and dined with us the day before yesterday. I believe he is not a favourite of yours, but he is a great one of mine. He is chiefly with Lady Asgill and Mrs. Wilmot, who are at Margate. I have seen them very often, as they come over to Ramsgate every day on Horseback to the great admiration of Hook [the coachman] who is quite smitten with the latter. He does not admire Lady A. so much, as he is much schocked at her showing her legs, which, to be sure, she does freely. Lady Young and her are great friends. I think poor Lady Young has entirely lost her beauty. She is grown very fat and as pale as death, though she is a great deal recovered, Sir Walter says she is obliged to be constantly watched, and I think she looks rather ODD. Miss Talbot is grown much thinner but dresses in such an extraordinary manner that it is impossible to look at her without laughing.

I cannot give you an Idea of the magnificence or abundance of the Mannerses. The Dutchess of St. Albans, Lady Heathcote and Mrs. Duff drove over the other day with 6 Out Riders and in short they fill the Island with equipages. The Dutchess looks beautiful but very melancholy, Mrs. Duff as usual and Lady Heathcote has taken a violent affection for Corise and I and came to see us in *our house* the other day. Now for

An Extraordinary Event—

I *rode* to Margate and back this morning, and Mr. Hook and Mrs. Bunting are erecting statues and rending the skies with my praises. I am bruised, jolted, hot and tired and yet obliged to second all Hook's account of my charming ride and cry Amen to all Mrs. Bunting's hopes of my delightful temper of mind continuing.

We are all going to the play at Margate tonight. Mrs. Jordan is here and it is her benefit. " The Way to keep him " and " the spoilt child," with songs and lutes and Harps to keep us awake between the acts.

[1] Peniston Lamb, the Melbournes' eldest son, who died in 1805.

I am going to Lady Melbourne's with Lady Elizabeth, so adieu dearest, dearest sister.

Yours ever, HARRIET CAVENDISH.

To Lady Georgiana Morpeth

RAMSGATE, *Friday morning, September the 10th, 1802.*

Thank you, my dearest sister, for your letter which I have this moment received, with an account of George's musical powers ; does Lord Morpeth approve of so early and decided a propensity to a talent he does not approve of ? How sorry I am to hear of his gout. I hope it will soon go off.

I must now give you an account of yesterday, as we were gay *to dissipation.* A Mr. Foresight [Forsyth ?] who lives in a magnificent house at Broadstairs, gave a Breakfast, in honour of Lady Heathcote, as he is Sir Gilbert's agent, and all Margate and Ramsgate were assembled. It was excessively pleasant and as the garden is large there was not the least crowd. The Mannerses were all there, en chignon as usual and it looked too ridiculous on rather a cold day with the sea air blowing on their poor defenceless heads. The Duchess [of St. Albans] looked beautiful, but more melancholy than ever. Mrs. Greville and I are great *friends,* (tho' I must confess it is rather profaning the title) but she is very good natured and Lady Melbourne insists upon it that she is clever, which I, in spite of my friendship, must dispute. She is so *circumventing,* minute and winding up in her conversation that it almost makes me laugh and sometimes tires me so it almost makes me cry. She told me yesterday that she played upon the harp " by way of a sort of a something " . . . Capisce ? No, no.

I have also made acquaintance with Lady Young whom I like very much. I think she is recovering her beauty very much, for since I have been here she looks a thousand times better than when we came.

I think George Lamb is very much smitten with Miss Talbot ; they are quite inseparable.

We went in the evening to an exhibition of young ladies' talents which was excessively tedious.

My aunt Bessborough is stopped at Sittenbourne by poor Caro having a disorder in her bowels, but they mean to arrive tonight. Duncannon came last night, looking better than I ever saw him, and with him Willy [Ponsonby], looking terribly pale and thin.

I have now given you an account of all our beau monde, excepting that I did not tell you we see a good deal of the Uptons. It is very delightful here of an evening as we all meet after dinner and walk on the pier till very late ; we then come home with the Melbournes and sup at 11, but I am almost always too much tired with the walking not to go to bed as soon as I come in.

Sir Walter Farquhar is gone to town to meet Lord Lucan, but comes back on Monday. Lady E. F. talks of leaving England the beginning of next month. I shall hate Caroline [St. Jules] going, though I hope it will not be for any length of time, otherwise the sooner the better, for she is so low and nervous, otherwise so cross and difficile à vivre that it quite *discomposes* all our proceedings.

How I wish you were here. I cannot accustom myself to being so much away from you. I know you hate professions but I hope you do not hate to hear how sincerely I must always be

yours most affectionately, HARRY O.

To Lady Georgiana Morpeth

RAMSGATE, *Tuesday morning, September 14th, 1802.*

I have just received your delightful long letter, my dearest sister.

Duncannon comes tomorrow, and I will take care to deliver your messages. I thought he had certainly been at Castle Howard, as they expected him sooner if he had not.

I see you will grow as fond of the nymph-like Julia [Lord Morpeth's aunt] as Mr. Hare is, who says he does not know so sensible or so *charming* a person. Your good graces are easily gained if admiration of George is enough to secure them, as I know nobody who does not express and feel it for the darling boy.

A certain Lady complains of low spirits ever since her séjour here, and thinks nothing but Parisian air will restore them. "Blow, Blow ye winds and waft her swiftly o'er" . . .

Lord Melbourne and George arrived last night but I have not seen them yet. Frederick is, I hear, shooting in the Fens of Yorkshire. Emily is grown prettier than ever.

I have made acquaintance with Lady Young and Miss Talbot. The latter is the oddest of human beings ; I saw her swim this morning, with all Ramsgate assembled in crowds on the sands to see her. She does not mind tossing her little round body about in the least, but floats and swims and kicks about like a fish. She walks almost every day to Margate and back.

I am now going to make you *very very* jealous. Brook [1] is so fond of me, that Mrs. Greville says his only reward and punishment, is either to come and see me when he is good or stay away when he is naughty. You may be sure this is an expensive Friendship, as the Toyshop is its cement.

Adieu, my best beloved G., love me as I do you with all my heart and soul. When I think how long it *may* be before I see you again cela me casse le couer [*sic*]. Adieu, dearest.

To Lady Georgiana Morpeth

RAMSGATE. *Sunday morning, September 19th, 1802.*

Thank you, my dear dearest sister, for your letter and I will answer *all* your questions immediately, though I confess it is an *undertaking*.

My beauty is, I recollect, the first interrogation, and what writer could help being eloquent with so productive a theme. It is, alas! much in the same state as it has been for some time past, and I fear (though Sir Walter and mama are very sanguine) I shall never be rode or bathed into a beauty. Tant pis, but there is no remedy.

We have had Lord Cowper and Luttrel, but they are gone again, and as they were only here one night, they did not make much impression on my mind. The former looked pale and ill and the latter not worse than usual. Indeed, how could he?

Duncannon, when he is at Margate, is desperately smitten with Lady Elizabeth Villiers,[2] but sticks to me here with an astonishing good grace. In short at present Captain MacHeath could not be more easy, "the other dear charmer away," though not quite so bad as Frederick Foster, who says when he is with two of us—"How happy could I be by myself, if both the dear charmers——"

I saw Lady Fanny Villiers yesterday, and think her very beautiful, but not much prettier than Lady Elizabeth, who is in the greatest

[1] Mrs. Greville's little boy, afterwards well known in society. He was involved in the De Ros affair, but not dishonourably, although his conduct was criticized.

[2] This is the first mention of the great Haryo-Duncannon-Villiers triangular flirtation. Lady Jersey was George the Fourth's favourite and the mother of the Ladies Elizabeth, Fanny and Harriet Villiers.

beauty, or Lady Harriet, who, although as black as ink, is uncommonly pretty. I am very angry with John Ponsonby, who is desperately in love with odious Lady Jersey and never leaves her side.

We have been and are to be excessively gay ; balls, plays, Dandelion etc. I am just waiting for Lady Heathcote who is coming to drive Corise, Mrs. Duff and me in her curricle.

My aunt disapproves of this very much, but there is here, you must know, a great rivalité between Lady Heathcote and Lady Asgill, and my aunt *abuses* the former and *protects* the latter on every occasion.

Lord Coleraine is in love with Mrs. Wilmot, who is in very great beauty ; *he* displays his green coat and white horse all over the Island.

I like Lady Young better every day, though I must confess that I think " many honest souls are sent to Bedlam who are not half as mad." She is sometimes so odd that she quite frightens me, though nobody thinks so but myself.

Adieu, my best dearest G., I must go and dress for this dashing expedition.

Yours ever, HARYO.

To Lady Georgiana Morpeth

RAMSGATE, *Wednesday evening, September the 22nd, 1802.*

MY DEAREST SISTER,

Your intention of coming here in your way to Paris quite enchants me, as indeed to look forward to a longer separation than we have already had, is not to be borne. Does mama give you any hopes of our going abroad with you, as I am convinced the people who live with her, know less of her plans than any others, and I very often receive a letter from some *well informed* correspondent who knows much more about myself than I do.

My uncle Bessborough heard from Lady FitzWilliam today, and Lord Milton has been very ill but is already recovered.

You cannot have heard too much of our gaiety. We have been at two balls this week, both very crowded, hot and disagreeable, and at a grand Breakfast at Dandelion. The chief producer of all this dissipation is papa, and he is in love with all the Mannerses. Their chief attraction is that they save *him* the trouble of speaking, as I defy the most determined chatterer to *edge in* a word, especially if Mrs. Duff takes him in hand, and therefore Papa, who does not quite come under that denomination, may be silent, not only conveniently, but necessarily.

Lady Heathcote drove me in her curricle the other day and I was really *stupéfaite* so volubly and without respite did her Ladyship run on. However they are very goodnatured and all excessively kind to me, so I will not abuse them.

The Duchess of St. Albans is in very great beauty, and, what I confess surprises me, seeming perfectly happy. The Duke is the most hideous, disagreeable little animal I ever met with.

I always forget to tell you that Duncannon desired me to make a thousand apologies to you for his seeming incivility in not going on to Castle Howard when he was in Wales. The *families* are rather in alarm at a violent flirtation of his with Lady E. Villiers, as the connexion would not be desirable. He will not speak even to Miss Fitzroy (though she is in the greatest beauty and I really think seriously in love with him) and never leaves the other, who seems, though not so pretty as Miss F. much more amiable.

My aunt and Lady Asgill are at present *violent* friends, and sit cooing over Lord Granville's perfections by the hour. I always guess the subject by the screwing of their mouths and different attitudes of admiration they display.

We expect Frederick Lamb here tomorrow. I am glad as I think him very clever and entertaining. Miss Trimmer looks paler than usual at the thoughts of " un agneau de plus." You cannot think how drole and amiable George is. He has been making us laugh till I am quite fatigued.

We have made a delightful acquaintance here, Mr. MacDonald, a violent admirer of Corisande's, but he goes on Saturday, alas ! He is the best mimick I ever heard and Kemble and Mr. Skeffington he does to the life. He sings, dances and *talks* à la perfection and we shall miss him most excessively. He only came here to see Corise and calls her his *divine*, *adorable* Madlle de Gramont, and is *almost* a Mr. Percy.

Goodnight, my dear dearest sister, if I have time I will add a line tomorrow.

Thursday morning.

I am now going, my dearest G. (depending upon your secrecy), to transcribe for you some of George's verses, which he gave me last night. Some lines are very good and some very bad, but it will give you a good idea of our proceedings and I think them very amusing. It is a parody on Burns' Tim [*sic*] O'shanter, and called John O'Thanet. The beginning is long and tiresome, so I shall not send it you. You must know that *John* is making a tour round the Island, and arrives at Ramsgate just in time for the master of the ceremonies' ball :—

When now the moon shot forth her gleams
And ocean glistened in her beams,
When winds blow cold and loud and drear
And Ladies 'gin to walk the Pier,
When chattering teeth by Luna's light
Just stammer out "a charming night,"
When wiser Young and Devon's Duke
Prefer the chimney corner's nook,
When Talbot clad in thinnest coat
Laments 'tis not the time to float,
When Lloyd, now Cunningham is miss'd,
Hunts round the town in vain for Whist,
Or, if she find a party willing,
The Prodigals will stake a shilling,
When Trimmer follows to and fro
To watch each ill-designing beau,
Then carelessly went honest John, etc. etc.

I send you these merely because they give a faithful account of our evening walks.

I think you have had quite enough of John O'Thanet and Harriet Cavendish. Your reproof, you see, had effect, though not perhaps exactly the effect you desired, but I thought it best to show you by this enormous letter that my repentance will be rather worrying, as you must expect volumes from me.

Adieu, my dearest, best beloved G. The thoughts of seeing you soon drive me quite wild, and I only wonder how I can have supported being away from you so long.

yours ever most truly and affectionately, HARRIET CAVENDISH.

By the bye, Brook told me, even at the moment of receiving a toy, that he loved Lady *Jee* Morpeth, *quite* as well as me. Mrs. Greville is very goodnatured and lets him come to see me very often. My affection for children though, is sometimes rather inconvenient, as we are over-run, and 2 days ago Lady Heathcote called and left her 3 boys with me. C'est trop fort.

To Miss Trimmer

RAMSGATE, *Tuesday morning, October the 12th, 1802.*

I must keep up my character of being a good correspondant, my dearest Selina, though I have very little to tell you.

The weather has quite damped all our spirits, mama and Caroline have very bad colds and papa is a little threatened with the gout. To add to all these discomposing events Duncannon arrives tomorrow —my uncle and aunt, neither of them expecting him to be so very rapid in his motions, are in the greatest fuss imaginable about it. It is quite entertaining to hear the former, though I really pity him, as papa insists upon asking the Jerseys to dinner tomorrow and my Uncle says he shall certainly *dine in his own room.* I think it is wrong to have them, but papa is really so very gay it is in vain to hope for any thing like quiet, and if we do go out, it is difficult to avoid them.

Mama heard from my sister today who leaves Castle Howard on Friday, stays a few days in town and then comes here.

Sir Walter, ever since you have been gone has lived on the joke of putting on Miss Trimmer's dress and is always visiting us, and as he confesses, *searches* every room in the house.

I went to see Miss Farquhar yesterday. We talked a great deal about books and she seems very much and very well read, but rather too fond of sentimental poetry, and romantic histories, and, I do not know why, romance does not suit Cherry's appearance, and I could not help laughing when, talking of "Cecilia," she exclaimed with uplifted eyes, "Oh, that one could but find a Delville." I gave her a lesson in Chess which she is most excessively desirous of learning, and then we walked with Sir Walter and Eliza to chaperone us.

We were to have gone to the play tonight, but the weather is so bad that mama was afraid of encreasing her cold.

Caro Ponsonby behaves very well and does not give us as much of her company as I was afraid she would. Fanny and her dine with us and Caro was yesterday in one of her ways and turning her back the whole time.

The Duchess of St. Albans dined here the other day and it really was too ridiculous to see papa and her flirting the whole evening, and as she is terribly deaf, he was obliged to repeat all the little galanteries and small talk two or three times, and to the amazement and amusement of us all.

Corisande desires her kindest " Loaf " to Miss Trimmer. Her and Mr. Mac. go on at a fine rate.

Adieu, my dear Selina, the post is setting out.

Yours ever most affec. and sincerely, H. CAVENDISH.

To Miss Trimmer

RAMSGATE, *Monday morning, 1802.*

I should have written to you yesterday, my dear Selina, but my morning after church was quite occupied in paying *civil visits* to Miss Lloyd, the Miss Farquhars etc. and you will think I am gone quite civility mad when I tell you I am expecting every minute to be called to walk with mama to Broadstairs and go and see Lady Pembroke, Lady Templeton etc. They are *departing virtues*, for I do not think we shall stay above 4 or 5 days longer ; I am sure I do not wish it, for when Lady Elizabeth and the Farquhars go there will not be a person we know in Ramsgate. Corise would be very angry, for her beloved Mac[donald] stays as long as we do and to her great delight, has a general invitation to Devonshire House when we return. I think she has behaved much better about it lately, though sometimes, her situation considered, her coquetry puts me quite out of patience, and I could beat her when I hear her complimenting Mr. Mac. in broken English.

Mr. Foster has been ever since your departure (I do not know if that was the cause) in a humour not to be described, and last night put himself into one of Hart's passions, because George Lamb mentioned his old hat, which you must know is a sore subject, as Duncannon brought him from town a magnificent new one, for which he has as much respect and admiration, as he had affection for the other. I really am quite glad he goes on Wednesday as his ill humour is really unbearable.

I am very glad G. leaves darling little George in England for several reasons ; first for the sake of his health, and then it will hurry her back to us, to accomplish which anything would be desirable.

Sir Walter continues his *Miss Trimmer* joke, and laughs at it with the same heartiness and delight as when he first blest our ears with it.

We go on bathing though it requires some courage, as the sea feels like ice, especially this morning, when I hardly dared venture in, it was so bitter cold.

Mr. Hughes has ceased persecuting us, for he has taken some violent affront into his head and will scarcely bow to us. Tant mieux, for it was never an acquaintance much to be desired.

Cherry and Eliza teaze us with extasies, romances etc. and they really would be amiable if they would not doat and delight so on every body and every thing. They go on Thursday, but we shall probably see a great deal of them as they spend the whole winter in Town, and I should like to have them now and then at Chiswick as they hate London and *doat* on the country. I wish Cherry was not so highflown ; yesterday in the sociable she had left something behind, which on recollecting, she exclaimed " All gracious Powers ! " and we all burst into laughing. She is, tho', uncommonly good humoured and very sweet.

My bills are most of them come in and much less than I expected. I hope the £10 will be sufficient.

Sir Walter has just been in with his *lively sally* about you and I am called so I must bid you Adieu.

ever yours most affec[ly] H.C.

I hear we are going to have a Duff and Manners dinner, which of all things I hate most.

IV

HARYO IN LONDON AND GEORGIANA IN PARIS

JANUARY AND FEBRUARY 1803

THE years 1801–3 were those of the short-lived Peace of Amiens. A number of English people flocked over to Paris and to France, from which they had been excluded for some ten years, some of them to their great discomfiture, as when Napoleon denounced the Peace in 1803, he arbitrarily interned all British subjects in his dominions, in contempt of international law and diplomatic usage.

Lady Bessborough and her daughter Caroline, Lady Elizabeth Foster and *her* daughter Caroline and the Morpeths were all junketing in Paris.

Meanwhile in England both Lord Villiers and Lord Granville Leveson Gower were laying siege to Lady Sarah Fane, the great heiress. There was much speculation as to which would be successful and it is hardly surprising that Lord Villiers should prove eventually to be the favoured suitor, as Granville was but a laggard lover despite the constant spurrings of both his mother and Lady Bessborough. Lady Sarah married Lord Villiers in 1804 ; she was better known as Lady Jersey and died in 1867.

Haryo went to her first performance of amateur theatricals at the Priory, Lord Abercorn's house at Stanmore. Many more were to take place later. Lady Cahir, who often took the chief rôles, was detested by Harriet and admired by Lord Granville. Cahir is pronounced Care and the Lady used to look at her husband and sing the old song :

> " Begone, dull care,
> Begone for ever from me,
> Begone dull care,
> You and I can never agree.
>
> . . . . . .

For I hold it one of the wisest things
To drive dull care away."

Mrs. Billington, whom Harriet heard at Lady Sutherland's, is said to have been the greatest singer England has ever produced. She made a large fortune, amounting, it is said, to £65,000 and retired to live in princely style at Fulham.

The Morpeths and Bessboroughs were back in London by March, very wisely, as they were reported to be anti-Bonapartists. By May England and France were again at war.

To Miladi Georgine Morpeth

HÔTEL DE L'EMPIRE, RUE DE CERNUTTI,
SUR LE BOULEVARD ITALIEN, PARIS

DEVONSHIRE HOUSE, *January, 1803.*

Lady Emily Wellesley [1] has not yet made her appearance, as Gerald is so anxious that she should be admired that he will not let her stir out because he does not think her in good looks. She is not quite so protecting to his beauty, as when mama mentioned the beauty of the Wellesley family to her one morning, the first time she ever saw her, she stopped her by exclaiming, " Oh ! as for Gerald's looks, I cannot boast much of them."

Pray write to me very often, and never mind how short your letters are, for I like them better than none.

Lady Cahir is going to Ireland, which I am not sorry for, as, in spite of Lord Granville's remonstrances, I cannot think her the amiable, *friendly* being he represents her. However, as I have not £60,000 a year in prospective,[2] and even in that case should [not] chuse Lady Cahir for my confidante, I shall never be able to judge as well as him of the *friendly* part of the story.

I am now going for 2 or 3 hours to experience that most delightful of pleasures ; solitude in Devonshire House, for Miss Trimmer and Hart, the only inhabitants, are now occupied, one in reading to George Ridgeway [a footman who became the Duke's steward] in an audible voice, and the other in writing a love letter with much difficulty and

[1] Lady Emily was a daughter of the 1st Earl Cadogan. She married Gerald Wellesley, a brother of the Duke of Wellington.

[2] Lady Sarah Fane's fortune.

consideration to Miss Berry. He has received an elaborate performance from her, complimenting the dear soul on his epistolary powers, which has quite turned his brain.

John Ponsonby's marriage [1] is at last fixed for next Wednesday, as the papers are arrived from Ireland at last. Lord Villiers is, of course, come to town. To show you how the Abercorns are of the opposite faction, he had been repeatedly asked to go there any day with Sir John Shelley. On the day before the play, the latter wrote to ask if they might come and return to town the same night, to which Lord Abercorn's civil answer was he had rather not.

Once more, good-night, and pray pray let me hear from you soon.

Ever yours, HARRY-O.

To Miladi Georgine Morpeth

HÔTEL DE L'EMPIRE, ETC. PARIS

[The letter bears an English and a French post-mark, the former with "1803," the latter with "an 11," of the Republican calendar. It cost 10*d.* to send to Paris.]

DEVONSHIRE HOUSE, *January the 15th, Tuesday morning, 1803.*

I cannot thank you enough for your letter, my dearest sister, or for your kindness in writing to me so soon. I have had no opportunity till today's post of writing to you, or I certainly should not have delayed it so long.

Your boy is quite well, he is every now and then a little *uneasy* about his teeth, but otherwise en parfaite santé. I spend a great deal too much time with him; as I am very seldom away from him he begins to know me and I flatter myself that I am a great favourite. The only time when he misbehaves most shamefully, is when he goes to Grosvenor Place, and I believe in consequence, his visits there are to be put a stop to. He roars from the moment he enters the house till he goes out, and nurse told me yesterday that the young gentleman *shouted* and *hooted* so loud for *joy* when they got in to the carriage to come away, that she was sadly afraid grandpapa Carlisle would be offended. He comes down every day to desert, and has unfortunately taken a most violent fancy to papa, who though very *civil* to him, will neither play at *Peep bo*, or *Creep Creep*. So much for the boy.

[1] John Ponsonby, eldest son of the 1st Baron Ponsonby, married on the 13th of January 1803, Lady Frances (Fanny) Villiers, daughter of the Jerseys.

I have made you a *silent* promise to devote one page to him, and now for our own gaieties.

On Saturday I went to the opera with Lady Charlotte [Greville] and Lady Mary [Bentinck, daughters of the Duke of Portland]. They were as disagreeable as possible, talking loud enough for the whole house to hear, and when they chose to listen, crying *Hush*, with the voices of ballad singers. They had very few men in the box, only Mr. Stopford and Gerald Wellesley.

Lord Granville supped at D. House ; he was just returned from Trentham looking better than I have seen him for a great while, in very good spirits and no thoughts of going to Paris.

On Sunday we went to a sort of Assembly at Lady Melbourne's ; it was not pleasant. The two Lambs, William and Frederick, had dined out and were very *drunk*, and the former talked to me in a loud voice the whole time of the danger of a *young womans* believing in *weligion* and *pwactising mowality*. Miss Talbot was there doing the honours of her caricature, and without the least mauvaise honte, talking of it to every body.

Last night we went to hear the famous ventriloquest Fitzjames. It was very wonderful and entertaining.

It is quite determined that we are to go to the Priory Friday. They are to act 2 farces ; "Who's the dupe ?" and the "Wedding day." Lady Cahir, the chief characters, "Lady Contest" and "Charlotte." There are to be a great many people at it, some return to town at night, and others sleep at Stanmore, as the Priory will not hold half of them ; our party, consisting of papa (who has changed his mind and means to be present), mama, William Howard, 2 maids and myself, are allowed only *one* bedroom ; How we shall manage, Dio sa.

Shall you be glad to hear that Lord Granville heard of Charles Bagot[1] at a great dinner, en belle convalesence ? He came to town on Monday.

I am glad you *admire* Juste [de Noailles]. *Have ye given Savardet yer picture yet ?* and is *Adrien to write to ye ?* How I long to have you, safe and *une Parisienne* in England again. Pray give my love to all and believe me yours, more than I can express, most truly and affecly,

HARRIET.

[1] Harriet fancied herself in love with Mr. Bagot at this time.

To Milady Georgine Morpeth

HÔTEL DE L'EMPIRE, ETC. PARIS

DEVONSHIRE HOUSE, *January 20th, Thursday morning, 1803.*

MY DEAREST, DEAREST SISTER,

It is so particularly good of you to write to me often when you have so many other things to occupy you, but I think you would be rewarded for it if you could know the happiness it gives me to hear from you. I know no pleasure that comes at all near it, excepting hearing *of you*, which I have from both Harriet and Caroline, and they can talk of nothing but your *beauty* and the admiration you have already excited. The only thing that is not approved of in your conduct, is your selecting Lord Boringdon for a partner. It was much discussed last night, some were of the opinion that you did it to attract more attention, and Lord Granville was quite in a rage and said, "I thought Lady Georgiana had more patriotism than to expose her countryman before so many frenchmen." You see you must take care for you are very much and minutely investigated.

Your darling's *successes* are wonderful; he is in the greatest beauty and very much admired. Even Miss Lloyd says "he is worth all the rest of us." He does not yet make any progress in MAMA, though Mrs. Grant insists upon it that he always talks when she comes to see him. He is more coxcombical in his dress than ever and we want colours to vary his cockades and sashes. *Aunt* is the prime personnage in the nursery, and I hear as I pass that "He must *tell* Aunt he knows" etc. etc.

I tremble when I think of the Priory tomorrow. There are to be crowds and the Prince certainly goes.

The Westmorlands have been in Town 3 days and one already sees more *Beaus* in the streets.

Lord Granville's arrival in town s'explique. He is gone to the Priory today where he will find Lady Sarah [Fane] and he is in such tearing spirits and seems so well pleased with himself, that I think he must have great hopes of success. I put him in a fuss last night by saying I dreaded Lady Cahir. He says she is perfect in every way and the word *friendly* was brought in more than once.

My little Lord O. [Ossulston] is really comical. He has taken the hint from the newspapers and is quite *tender*.

We had a great many people here last night. Lady Essex, but not my dear Mrs. St. John, who is ill in bed.

The 24th [the day she is to go to the Priory] will never come, and I begin to think we are going backwards.

We go on Monday, *the* day, to Lady Sutherland's to hear Mrs. Billington and Viganoni sing, accompanied by Cramer. Cherry Farquhar has just been, telling me it will be a *little Heaven*, and *I* think it will be very pleasant. Lord Gower's [Granville's half-brother] passion for Mrs. Billington is *not a joke*. I played the Duett to him last night and he was quite overcome with tender recollections; we none of us dared say *one word* against her, as the Baron de Rolle, after one of Lord Gower's effusions of delight, ventured to begin with "Cependant je ne trouve pas . . ." and was silenced with a look of horror and indignation.

Frederick Lamb supped here last night and both his sisters. Emily looking paler than ever, but very pretty, and Mr. Lewis making up to her violently.

Did you see the all-captivating Mr. Doyne before he left Paris? He is coming here tonight I believe, and I want to know what you think of him.

Adieu for the present, dearest dearest G. I will finish this letter either tonight or tomorrow morning.

Friday morning.

We are just setting out for the Priory, dearest G., et je tremble. Pray give my love to every body, and especially to my aunt, with a great many thanks for the *pin* she sent me; it is excessively pretty. Now for a piece of Intelligence which will *enchant* you. Your darling has cut 2 teeth and is quite well and does nothing but feel them himself and laugh at the good joke. I dare say he will have another today as the gum looks swelled and red.

To Miladi Georgine Morpeth

PARIS

DEVONSHIRE HOUSE, *Tuesday morning, January 25th, 1803.*

I hear nothing but your *charms* and *conquests*, my dearest sister, and I begin to be sick of all the compliments *you* receive. I have very little to tell you, and therefore I shall send you some of them.

Camille Jourdain says, "qu'elle est fraîche, qu'elle a de jolis bras, qu'elle a une expression de physiognomie." This account you may depend on, as it is from the very best authority.

Lord Whitworth [our Ambassador at Paris] says you are beloved and admired by everybody and conduct yourself, *as you always do*, with a prudence beyond your years. Lastly I have just received a note from Lady Charlotte Greville, who says she has just received letters from Paris, that her correspondents are in raptures and say you are like "une Vierge de Raphaël." This, in case you should not be made vain enough without my assistance.

And now for my sufferings and misfortunes. I have been to the Priory and live to tell you of it. It was formidable, disagreeable, uncomfortable and *royal*, for to compleate the misery, the Prince was there. We arrived to dinner there on Friday, an hour too soon, as we waited for the Westmorlands, who, after all, dined in their own rooms. Lady W. is really as mad as it is possible to be. Her clear and connected reasons for not dining with us were—"We lost our way dreadfully; that is, we came quite right, but I fancied we should, which was as bad. I then *spilt* a *cup* of *milk*, and so it was quite impossible!"

Lady Sarah [Fane] looked as well as she could with a very swelled face which she got by a fall at Apthorpe. Lady Augusta[1] is not altered, her face looked beautiful, but her figure bad and very high shouldered. Lady Sarah had only three adorateurs on her hands: Tom Sheridan, who acted despair (by the bye, he bid me remember him most respectfully to you. He then added, "to that most charming, most lovely, most perfect of human beings." Is it not excusable in me to be tired of your perfections?), Lord Craven, who seemed to think it the best joke that ever was and ready to die of laughing, and Lord Granville, seeming to have made a vow that he would take everything for the best, smiling with self congratulation when she turned her back, and walking about the room with looks of complacency and satisfaction when she was too much surrounded for him to get near her. She treated the three exactly alike, and weighed her words and smiles in the most exact proportion.

Lady Harriet Hamilton was in great beauty, but I hardly spoke to

[1] Lady Augusta Fane, who married first Lord Boringdon and then ran away and married Sir Augustus Paget.

her. She seemed to me to be making a desperate attack upon Lord Foley, whom she talked and sung to from morning till night. Lady Charlotte Hamilton looked ill, pale and very much out of spirits.

The acting was excellent. Lady Cahir was good as Mrs. Jordan, and what surprised me, perfectly original. She looked beautiful, magnificently dressed and covered with diamonds. George Lamb and Lawrence acted uncommonly well, and Pen Lamb spoke an epilogue of his own composition with a *very* little degree of animation more than usual, hoping the audience would find Pope Joan the only dupe tonight.

The Prince seemed pleased, and said, " My dear Abercorn, I never enjoyed such perfect happiness in the whole course of my life."

Lady Asgill was present and more ridiculous than ever. I sat next to her during the performance and in the Epilogue there was, à l'ordinaire, a compliment to the Ladies of the House. Lady Asgill, of course, took it to herself, and covering her face with her schawl, sunk upon the arm of my chair, quite overcome with modesty.

Lady Abercorn was in very good looks and sent quantities of messages and loves to you.

In the morning we had a royal breakfast, at which I sat near three hours, only kept awake by dear delightful Lady Charlotte Lindsay [daughter of the Prime Minister, Lord North]. She was funnier than anything I ever heard.

Mrs. Kemble is the great favourite and she seems very pleasant and good humoured. Lord Abercorn was more endurable than I had expected, excepting that he gave me the headache with proclaiming each separate dish at dinner, and when he wanted to ask me a question, hollowing after me so loud that I was some minutes recovering the stun and my senses. He gives a great dinner at the Priory to-day to Mr. Addington [the Prime Minister] and the party he has asked to meet him are the Melbournes, the Sheridans and Lord Granville, who are all gone, expecting much amusement.

Your dear pretty darling is quite well; he has only two teeth as yet, he has more colour than ever and is very proud of his first pair of red shoes. There certainly never was so beautiful or so engaging a child. Nurse continues to amuse me in her *maternal* character, and on Sunday I found the *Scotch* nurse walking about the room in a passion, exclaiming—" It does not signify one bit. She's as pratty a child as ever was seen, she has *ten* teeth, and you are a naughty unnatural woman."

God bless you, dearest,

Ever your most affec[ly], HARO.

To Miladi Georgine Morpeth

PARIS

DEVONSHIRE HOUSE, *Jan[y] 30th. Sunday evening, 1803.*

MY DEAREST SISTER,

Mama caught cold last night at the opera and is now in bed with one of her bad headaches. She desires me to tell you this, and begs you will *proclaim* it as her reason for not writing.

To answer your first question ; your boy's teeth are as pretty as possible, and he thinks them so, I assure you, for he does nothing but *feel* and *shew* them. You would be quite jealous of me, if you could see how fond he is of me ; he is growing and when he is bid, " *love aunt*," puts his darling little arms round my neck and kisses me.

Lord Granville is in great spirits about his *proceedings*, though nobody can very well tell why, as he has not seen Lady Sarah since the Priory, which I am sure was not a very encouraging meeting ; however he likes just as well talking to Lady Cahir, Mrs. Bouverie, Lady Abercorn etc. etc., who all encourage him about it, à l'envie l'une de l'autre, and I begin to think he *mistakes them* for Lady Sarah, if one may judge from the looks of self congratulation which always follow an interview with any one of these Ladies. Lord Villiers and him met in our box last night, and each looked like the favoured lover, and the least successful was certainly the most triumphant, in manner at least.

And now I am arrived at the end of your letter, which to use my *Phrase* of old " est beau, *mais* il est fort petit." Really, dear sister, you suffer your handwriting to expand in such a manner that your last letter is about equal to 10 lines of close writing. However it was so welcome that I will not abuse it in any manner.

We had a good many people to supper the night before last. Tom Sheridan and William Lamb came very drunk and disputed till they almost fought.

I am tired of hearing Presentations and *non*-presentations to Buonaparte discussed and begin to be of Lord Abercorn's opinion, who only wishes "he may never hear his name again as long as he lives." As *he* is sudden and despotic in his notions, I am in daily expectation of hearing the name of Buonaparte forbid to be mentioned in pain of death 10 miles round Stanmore. Mrs. Huskisson said the other day, twisting her little body into every sort of shape, "I should like to go to Paris, merely to *pique* Buonaparte by not being presented to him."

Lady Anne Smith was here on Friday, looking wretchedly and thinner than any thing I ever saw. Culling [1] was very tipsy, which indeed they all were (I do not mean Lady Anne), *but* looking very well and in tearing spirits.

Lady Charlotte Greville does nothing but envy you for going abroad and wishing she was there too. I always sympathize with her last wish, in the most eager and sincere manner, and my regrets at its not being accomplished encrease every time I see her.

Lady Mary comes every now and then to lay down upon the couch, and I believe sleeps very soundly, at least she never speaks or seems to know anything that is going forward. They bring *BEAU* Lascelles and Mr. Greville with them, who does nothing but lament it is quite impossible to be comfortable either in France or England. He told me that some french man said "Milord Henri Fitzgerald loue tout, Mounsieur Greville dit mal de tout et Mounsieur Lascelles achête tout." Certainly *he* at least keeps up to his character.

Lady Hunlocke, Charlotte, Ann and Jimmy are this moment departed, and Charlotte, who is furious at your not having written to her yet, desires me to give you the enclosed. They have all been during their two days' séjour here as disagreeable as possible; Lady H. worse than ever, Charlotte very cross and looking ill, Ann all day; "Do you love your mother? does your mother love you? do you think me pretty?"—baiting me with *distressing* questions, and Jimmy but one degree removed from Marmaduke. I believe never departure caused more joy than theirs this morning.

Lord William and Lord Frederick Bentinck come here some day this week. I hope we shall go early in the next. Corise insists on writing to her "chère *Dgi*"; Augustus (little o.) is, I think, more in love with her than ever and I hardly dare walk from one room to another for fear of *disturbing a tête à tête*.

[1] Lady Anne's husband, Mr. Culling Smith. She was a daughter of the 1st Earl of Mornington and widow of the Honble. Henry Fitzroy.

Caro P. writes to me very constantly. She is delighted with your being (as she tells me) "so very good to her" and says you are looking beautiful and as big as a house. You know I always wished the latter.

To Miladi Georgine Morpeth

PARIS

DEVONSHIRE HOUSE. *February* (*no date*). *Friday morning. 1803.*

I have not heard from any of you for ages, my dearest sister, and I cannot tell you how *gloomy* and *uncomfortable* the time of your absence seems to me when I do not.

I saw a letter from Madame de Coigny to Lady Melbourne in which she says you *astonish* them with "your beauty, fraîcheur and amabilité." And Camille Jourdain says that you, Lady E. and my aunt, have all the *cleverness*, *vivacity*, and *piquante charms* of what he fancies the ancienne noblesse of france to have possessed in their perfection, united to all the *truth*, *candour* and *solidity* of the English character. This is only an *abrégé* of a letter of his to Mr. Bennet, which I have been at some pains to *sober* down to common English from the "languidly energetic and pathetically sublime" language in which it was delivered to me by Mr. B.

Your little boy grows prettier and more admired every day. Papa shakes hands with him without much persuasion and says now and then "he looks well."

I gave your message to Lord Granville, whose only answer was, shrugging up his shoulders, "How odious they all will be when they come back." I am afraid, my dear sister, it is not in human nature for you to come back without a great deal of conceit and vanity, and if *I* hear in Devonshire H. of your visage angélique, jolis bras, your *virtues* and *agréments*, what must *you* do, who are the object of all this admiration? And I tremble with awe and humility when I hear mama exclaiming at supper, "Oh, its astonishing what G. has been seeing and doing, and nobody ever dared say or hear what my sister does to Moreau and Berthier etc. etc. Strange things will happen." Then Lord Granville and her look mysterious. . . . Now, wonderful G., I dread your treatment of us poor ignorant beings when you return loaded with these miraculous doings and sayings, and mama really talks of you all, as if you were not the same order of beings as you were before this eventful journey.

Well, to talk of *easy* and *comprehensible* matters : we had a sort of assembly here the night before last and a few new people. Mr. Doyne, the Paris Hero, who I think hideous to behold ; Mr. Burrell, remarkably handsome, who is just setting out to join the Cholmondelys. I have made acquaintance with Mr. Harbord, I think him very amiable and pleasant. Lady Asgill and Mrs. Bouverie were here ; the former entirely occupied with Mr. Adair and the latter altered and looking very old.

We have a good many people coming tonight, Lady Charlotte Greville, who came to see your boy yesterday and was delighted with him.

I must tell you by the bye, something that surprised me very much—there is a most violent flirtation *now* between Lady Gertrude [Howard] and Mr. W. [Wynne ?]. He came here last night and I saw them together several times lately. He never leaves her, never takes his eyes off her and speaks to nobody else. She looks very much ashamed of it and as if she wanted to sink in to the earth. Is not it very odd ?

I had a very long letter from Corisande yesterday. *She*, Corise, has been acting, as she tells me " parfaitement bien," in a play given to the Duc de Berri.

Adieu, dear, tres chère Georgine. I have been crying my eyes out over " le Nouveau père de famille." I wonder I did not hear more of it, as it seems to me quite beautiful ; the 3rd volume heart-breaking. I believe I am going to read " Amélie de Mansfield." They are all *dying* over it and it is the general opinion that as I have read " Delphine " [by Madame de Staël] I may read anything. Have you read " Les quatres femmes " and is it good ?

Ever yours truly and affectionately, HARRIET C.

[This is the last of Harriet's letters to Paris as the Morpeths must have returned shortly afterwards (the Bessboroughs left on February the 15th).

The Duchess was quite right when she said that Lady Bessborough had had intimate conversations with Moreau and Berthier. Her (Lady B's) letters from Paris at this time are most interesting and give all her conversations in full. Perhaps this is the place to give a note on the two French Generals, though it is impossible in a short space to describe Moreau's remarkable and varied career. He was alternately the friend and the deadly enemy of Buonaparte. At this date he was living in Paris in friendly relations with him. Two years later

Moreau was put on his trial for an alleged conspiracy against the Government. He made a splendid defence and was, as a sort of compromise, sentenced to a two years' imprisonment. Shortly afterwards this sentence was commuted and he was allowed to go in exile to America. In 1813 he returned to Europe and joined the Allied Sovereigns. He was in company with the Emperor Alexander when he was struck by a cannon-ball and mortally wounded.

Berthier was better known as the Prince de Wagram. He was nominated a Field-Marshal by Buonaparte and was his confidential adviser until 1814, when he adhered to Louis XVIII. Upon the return of Buonaparte from Elba, being uncertain which side to take, he fled to Bamberg, where he met with a tragical end at the hand of some emissaries of the secret societies.]

To Miss Trimmer

Wednesday, April 23rd. 1803.

MY DEAREST SELINA,

Mama and G. go to court tomorrow and I am to be presented the drawing room after [Thursday, April 28th, 1803].

I *think* I have behaved well since I last saw you and as you would approve. I do not know that a happier person than myself would exist if I always acted as to ensure your approbation, and though I do not always express it, you cannot know what I feel when I do not·

yours ever, my dearest dearest Selina,

most affec[ly] and truly, H. CAVENDISH.

To Miss Trimmer

[Written on quite different paper than usual ; a small double-sheet, with an embossed " classical " Empire border, edged with yellow.]

MY DEAREST SELINA,

What must you think of me—but indeed I have been, since I saw you, in so constant a bustle, hurry and worry that I have not had a moment to do anything right and been wholly occupied with endeavouring not to do any thing wrong, which I assure you, considering the life we are now leading, is having les mains bien remplies.

I am now in a room with the monks [Moncks] Tom Sheridan, Mr. Craven etc., practising French country dances. My sister waiting to take me out and my head turning every different way, so you must excuse this dab—tomorrow I will make it a point to write you something better worth the trouble of reading it.

We are all quite well but so tired and knocked as never people were before. Will you give my love and duty to my dearest grandmama and believe me when I tell you, that often in the most crowded assemblies your idea comes to my mind and prevents many giddy or foolish things I should otherwise do or say.

ever yours most affec[ly], H. CAVENDISH.

To Miss Trimmer

DEVONSHIRE HOUSE [*May*] *11th, Wednesday morning.* *1803.*

MY DEAREST SELINA,

We have all been very anxious about my dearest mama ; she was taken ill this morning with a violent attack on her bowels, and was for about 2 hours in the most dreadful pain. Sir Walter does not know exactly what it was, but she is a great deal easier now and has had a little sleep, which I trust will do her a great deal of good.

I see 2 letters for her from my grandmama and you, unopened on the chimney. I am quite vexed at having behaved so ill to you about writing, but I think if you knew the life we have been leading, you would in some degree excuse me. I think I can promise safely to be a better correspondent now, for we probably shall not stir out for some days, and knowing how anxious you must be about my dear mama, I will not fail sending you regular accounts of her.

I will add some more to this scrap later.

Sir Walter has been here again. He says she is certainly better, but as he has given her quantities of Laudanum, he must wait till she has slept it off before he can do anything further. Adieu my dearest Selina. I must send this without a frank, as papa is not well either and I must not go in to him. This has been a very melancholy day.

Ever yours most affec[ly], HARYO.

[There are two letters to Miss Trimmer written in August 1803.

The first is from Devonshire House. " Mama " had one of her bad headaches, brought on by a very hot and crowded visit to Vauxhall, and Georgiana Morpeth had recovered from her second confinement and all the party were shortly to leave for Castle Howard.

The second is dated August 24th and is written from Castle Howard. Mr. Harbord, Mr. Delmé Radcliffe and Mr. Marsh were the only visitors beside the family. The baby girl was thriving. Lady Gertrude amiable. Hart very deaf and silent. Corisande was staying at Thoresby with the Newarks and finding it very dull.]

V

GOSSIP FROM LONDON

1803

HARRIET was engaged in a whirl of social gaieties. Miss Berry writes that " three or four balls at Devonshire House kept the young people in motion ; there have been also, several morning dances, followed by a breakfast, by way of practising quadrilles. Lady Elizabeth Foster brought some pretty music from Paris, and some of the young ladies just come forth, proved themselves excellent dancers."

Among the young ladies were Harriet, Caro Ponsonby and Caroline St. Jules.

There was also the burning interest and anxiety caused by what Harriet calls the " most desperate attack upon Mary le Bone," alluding to Cavendish Square where the Bessboroughs had their town house. This attack had started the summer before and the protagonists were Duncannon, the Bessboroughs' eldest son and Lady Elizabeth Villiers, daughter of Lady Jersey, the Prince of Wales' favourite. " Odious Lady Jersey " evidently thought Duncannon a good match for her daughter and he was nothing loth, Lady Elizabeth being extremely attractive. The Lambs encouraged him ; his mother was dreadfully worried at the prospect of what seemed to her a most undesirable connection but feared to make matters worse by taking them seriously. Finally she had spoken to him and advised him to drop the flirtation unless he was in earnest. When he realized how strongly his mother disapproved, he promised her to drop the whole affair, but he was a weak young man (how weak will appear later) and could not stay away from his charmer or the flatteries of Lady Jersey. Haryo was especially interested as there had been an understanding from their childhood, which indeed still existed, that she and her cousin should eventually marry.

To Lady Georgiana Morpeth

CHISWICK, *Tuesday morning, August 21st, 1803.*

MY DEAREST G.,

I am sorry to tell you that mama has one of her headaches, yesterday there was a dinner here and she was not able to be at it. It was not a very pleasant one; the women were Lady Melbourne, Mrs. H. Greville, who is rather pretty, and the men, Lord Cowper, Pen and William Lamb, Harry Dillon, Mr. Maddocks, W. Spencer, a Mr. Mitford, Jules [de Polignac] and Mounsieur de Lima.[1] We walked in the garden till half past one, it was very pleasant. Mr. Maddocks is not altered but " my good Lady " as usual. I have made acquaintance with Lord Cowper and dislike him very much, he seems so very heavy and stupid. There was a master Smith here who sings beautifully.

Wednesday.

Mama is quite well, dearest G., today and gone to town till Saturday (a happy and fortunate day, the (18th) anniversary of my birth) when there is to be, I believe, a dinner and Fireworks, etc.

I hear nothing of removing and papa seems quite contented with London and will not even come here; oh misera me! how long it is now since I have seen you, my own dearest sister. It is very hard; how cross it was of Lord Morpeth to marry you, however I am *very, very* glad. Pray remember me to him.

I hope you do not leave my epistles about as they are not the most delightful that ever were written.

Adieu, pray write ever yours, HARYO.

To Lady Georgiana Morpeth

DEVONSHIRE HOUSE, *September 10th, 1803.*

I hear that you complain of my idleness, dearest sister, but I wrote you a very long one the day before yesterday, read it over, and would much rather have died than send it, I was so schocked by its stupidity.

We are fixed in London, I very much fear, and my principal occupation is lamenting it. I scarcely know one person now in Town excepting Mr. North, whom I see now and then in the streets. We are going tonight to see that new thing, " Pizarro " [Sheridan's

[1] Monsieur de Lima was a distinguished Portuguese diplomat and Jules de Polignac became Charles the 10th's Prime Minister before the July Revolution of 1830.

tragedy]. It is melancholy to have winter amusements before we have left Town for the summer. I must fill the gaps with moral reflexions ; quoted from Miss Trimmer.

We were much alarmed by a schocking fire breaking out in Berkeley Street, opposite our windows. It was quite dreadful and if it had been a windy night, Devonshire House would have been in the greatest danger. I will not say more about it as Incidents are so scarce that I have no doubt but you will have it from every branch of the family for the next fortnight to come.

John [Ponsonby] and Lady Fanny arrived in Town from Woburn a few days ago. They neither of them seem to like the Duchess [of Bedford] and I believe she is too riotous, all things considered. As to poor Mr. Adair, he seems quite stunned (and like the man who would not look at his wife's picture for fear it should strike him) looks all round the room before he dares mention her name. I shrewdly suspect she calls him *Bobby*, as he complains most pathetically of the nick names she bestows. She calls the Duke, Johnny, and goes up to him, slapping his back and pinching his cheeks, upon which he has been heard to say, " Pray let me alone." But these, dear G., are secrets of state, and the overawed Bob says before company that she makes herself very popular. She eats comme quatre, 2 fowls and Egg sauce for Luncheon to grow fat. Oh ! happy state in which such endeavours are laudable, and how much more pleasant to confess oneself forced to stuff, than condemned to starve. Oh ! in Pity . . .

The Jerseys are just arrived in Town. I am more afraid of them than of Buonaparte, and expect a most desperate attack upon Mary Le Bone.

Lady Fanny [Ponsonby] is much handsomer than ever, the Egg sauce etc. has been doing miracles. John sighs and says to Duncannon, " If you do not wish to be miserable, never marry."

I must tell ill-natured stories faute de mieux, but I do not much mind, as I trust to your not leaving my letters about.

I have just received a letter from Corisande who complains that there are so very many clergymans staying at Thoresby. She writes to me in English, which is too diverting. She says Henry P. is gone for a week to Lord Bagot's, nasty little man. I would rather he would have gone anywhere else.

Yours ever most affect^{ly}, HARYO.

To Lady Georgiana Morpeth

HOLYWELL. *Saturday.* [*No date, probably Sept.*] *1803.*

Mama has just arrived here, my dearest G., but not very well, as she has the remains of a headache hanging about her.

My letter will not be very bright tonight, as I am sitting in a little cold room without a fire, and my faculties as well as my fingers are freezing.

I have dazzled all beholders with my skill at billiards and making cannons and strikes at a great rate. Is there a billiard table at Castle Howard?

We go to town Tuesday for two days, and Tuesday evening to Drury Lane for "Richard the third." Lady Liz, of course, goes to receive the homage of the Kembles. Kemble has promised her not to let appear one good play till she returns. I wonder whether the audience will be so gallantly inclined and wait for her with as much patience. Then the cant about looking up to the boxes to see if my aunt and she are there and being inspired accordingly, and then the two Ladies say they cannot support being out of town while he is acting.

Kemble—When your box is empty I feel depressed. My energy fails and every contending muscle sinks to rest.

Lady Liz—After all, I don't see why we should go into the nasty country. I shall envy all the dear, good quizzy people and cits who stay for dear Pizarro.

Lady Bessborough, in a titter—One wishes one could contrive to hear you notwithstanding the distance. I always think of Prince Jolie, who had a magical pipe contrived.

Kemble—Well, Ladies, when you reappear the atmosphere, till then clouded and dark, will re-assume its wonted splendour, and Rolla, your grateful Rolla, will assume again that animation of which your absence will have deprived him.

This, dear G., is the sort of conversation that passes between this trio and it is very comical.

I am rather crackbrained this evening, as you may perceive by the tenour of this epistle.

Good night, dearest G.,

ever yours, HARY. O.

To Lady Georgiana Morpeth

ROEHAMPTON, *Tuesday morning. Oct. 1803.*

MY DEAREST KINDEST SISTER,

I am delighted at your questioning me as subjects of letter writing are so scarce that I am very glad to have them prompted.

Mr. Bagot is confined with a *fit of the gout* to Blithfield, but I hear, if he is well enough, means to return to London early in November. Lord Granville told me he had been living within 3 or 4 miles of him for several days, but had avoided him with the most scrupulous care, so I could not gain much intelligence from that quarter.

Lord G. himself was in town but 3 days, not agreeable—and very *Fane-ish*, exulting over (I believe) a very small degree of success.

You could not ask me any question that would puzzle me more than " how Duncannon continues," for there never yet was created so inexplicable and *unaccountable* a person. We dislike Lady E. [Villiers] from thinking that she has been very artful and making great advances to him. In short, if he escapes them, I shall think a little of his good sense and a great deal of his good luck.

I believe the Bessboroughs mean to come to Bath, but I am not sure. Lady Elizabeth Monck will be there, alas, alas, with all the Saltram Corps, I conclude. This will make our séjour there Periguadinish which I shall not be able to bear. The Cholmondeleys I believe are going there and I foresee Bath will be a bad edition of town, of which, by the bye, I am at length heartily tired and wish almost never to see again. Oh ! time has changed me . . . it really has in some things and sobered a great many foolish ideas.

Adieu dearest G., I wish I were with you.

I forgot to tell you that mama has borne the fatigue of coming here very well and has been much better these last 2 days than she has been yet.

To Lady Georgiana Morpeth

DEVONSHIRE HOUSE, *Thursday morning, 6th of October, 1803.*

MY DEAREST SISTER,

I should certainly have written to you during mama's illness without waiting for an *answer* had I not known that you had regular accounts of her from everybody in the house.

I went to Madame Sapieha's yesterday, and found her and my "cher petit amant," as she calls him, full of delights and regrets about Castle Howard and praises of you. She is, I think, looking very well despite a terrible cold and headache. We are going with her to the play either to-morrow or Saturday, as she is extremely anxious to see Kemble and Mrs. Siddons. I did not see "il caro sposo," and she complains of his passion for "des emplettes" and says he spends his whole time making them.

London is more gloomy, dismal and uncomfortable than ever, and fewer people in it than when we first came, which I thought was almost impossible. Do you think you shall join us at Bath? Oh! that you could and would.

We have been spending 3 days at Roehampton. It was very pleasant and comfortable, though the weather was dismal and the sunshine of my uncle's temper somewhat cloudy, though we discovered not the cause, but he abused us all under the significant appellation of *people*. He is really foolish beyond permission, and when he adds to his natural defects vociferous or noisy mirth or, as during our last visit to him, childish ill-humour, quite insupportable.

Duncannon has been seeing a good deal of the Villiers's lately, but I cannot make out what his plans or intentions are, and most likely if it were possible, the découverte would not repay me for the pains, as he seems boyish and uncertain to the most worrying degree, and, I am convinced, changes his mind and inclinations in the course of the day as often as the clock strikes. You may think by this guess that we have not interchanged one syllable for these last 4 days, and I am so tired of his folly that I do not look forward to a speedy reconciliation.

How are the two perfections of darlings? I am sure my niece ought to be obliged to me for after a stout battle of about half an hour, I have consented to accompany Miss T. to *Houndsditch*, to buy the little lady some caps.

Will you, my kindest best and ever dearest sister, write to me and forgive me, and I *promise* to bore you as often as I can with my epistles.

Yours ever, HARRIET.

A sudden tightness about my head and oppression at my heart proclaims Miss Berry's approach. No, thank Heaven, it is only an epistle, left for me from her. As it takes all my faculties to read and comprehend her, adieu.

To Lady Georgiana Morpeth

DEVONSHIRE HOUSE, *Monday, October 31st, 1803.*

MY DEAREST SISTER,

I heard yesterday great *rumours* of Bath, and I think Sir Walter seems to think it absolutely necessary both for papa and mama. This puts a stop to anything like complaining and regret upon the subject, or else for many reasons I should have preferred not going so late in the year and in this gloomy weather. However if you join us there, all other objections will vanish, and I know not the place that meeting you in it would not make a paradise in spite of Monks [the Monck family] and Pump Rooms.

Do you remember the advice you gave me as we went to Castle Howard? It has *done* me much good and often cut short a decided opinion or made a full stop in an eloquent harangue, to the utmost surprise of my auditors, who could not know, and if they did, would perhaps not understand, how far the influence of a sister may extend, when admired as one of the most perfect, and loved as the dearest friend on earth.

I saw your friend Madame Zamoiska, last night. She supped here, looking beautiful in a black velvet gown with her head and neck *covered* with Pearls. She had been at an *assembly* at Lady Harrington's to meet *Elfi Bey*, who, I hear, is the most beautiful person that ever was seen, with a look of dignity, mildness and intelligence about him that gives him the appearance of a superior being.

Pac appeared for the first time, not the least more dégagé from the English tour. The whole set of Petits Maîtres are flocking to town. Henry Pierrepoint, Dick Bagot, Mr. Brummel and Pagets without end, are already here, and Charles Bagot expected in a day or two. This is what I hear, as I have not seen one of them.

Adieu, my dearest G., the Post is going.

Ever yours, HARYO.

You seem to think Mr. North's fickleness would grieve me. Indeed no, he is one of those persons really so completely forgot when out of sight that till your letter it was some weeks since he entered my head.

Lord Abercorn has been supping here almost every night, no, only about 4 times, but he makes so much more vociferation and bustle than anybody else, that I forget I have seen or listened to anything else.

I think we treat him too much en maître absolu. My aunt is servile, prostrate, and though she abuses him behind his back, with him is toujours à ses genoux. Lady Abercorn is staying at the Priory.

To Lady Georgiana Morpeth

DEVONSHIRE HOUSE, *Tuesday, November 1st, 1803.*

I believe I told you in my letter yesterday that we are to go to Bath the beginning of next week.

I am sorry to hear of the fever at Malton, though I suppose it will be very easy for you to guard against infection.

London seems every day to have less in it to make one regret leaving it. Not that I believe for the last 2 months there has been one inhabitant more or less, but the dismal darkness and thick fogs make it appear unusually dreary. I think and trust if we are at Bath when you arrive, there will be no attractions here to prevent you joining us immediately.

Of course you have heard that Lady C. Greville has got a little girl, heir to all its mother's—I cannot find a short word that will take in all I want to express—of folly and affectation. She wrote me the strangest note 2 days before she lay in to ask me if I knew whether there was any foundation in the report that Lady C. Hamilton was to marry Lord Waterford ; what other person she was supposed to have had in love with her, and then questions innumerable as to Lady C's conjectured disposal of her own heart. I don't know which was more foolish, the persecuting any person about such nonsense or chusing for that person one so little likely to know anything about the matter as myself. I have just been writing a most ungracious and most unsatisfactory reply and she must catechize elsewhere. I hope for her sake with better success.

Did I tell you Mr. Bagot is expected in Town in 2 or 3 days, and conceive, though I do not require you understand, the caprice that makes me look forward to seeing this much thought of and talked of person with just enough degree of impatience to enable me to say with still less a degree of pleasure. Perhaps present, his beauty and wit may again create admiration, but he is one of those people who do not do upon reflexion, and to bear the test of absence there must be less effeminacy and frivolity to disgust, and a little more variety, to dwell upon.

Our evenings at present are rather dull and triste. The Fosters, Polignacs, and now and then Mr. Adair or Mounsieur de Lima, do not possess the art of enlivening, and I do not know which is most depressing, Mr. Adair's mock sorrows and, I am tempted to think, Ideal woe; or Mounsieur de Lima's " Bon jour, belles anges," and little hops and dances about the room. I forget our most constant suitor, Mr. Crawfurd, who I hope does not feel all the complications of vexations and torments he is always describing. At least I wish he would mourn over them anywhere than at Devonshire House.

Berrina [Miss Berry] is fixed at Strawberry Hill, we have now and then a thundering letter from her, but otherwise are tolerably free from the effects of your Ladyship's early friendship. It is hard that " Mama and Harry-O " as she calls us, should suffer because you were a goose at Cheltenham. I saw Ag. [Agnes Berry] looking a most deplorable figure and ridée and *hagged* to the ugliest degree.

Madame Zamoiska sups here tonight to meet Lady Jersey. Duncannon is gone to the Priory, and the opportunity was seized to ask her, [Lady J.] though even under that circumstance Lady Elizabeth [Villiers] *is* left out. I pity *her* very much, and more so as I think his passion, which was never very deep, is certainly overcome. However in this weathercock cousin of mine's disposition, it may soon be revived again, and one cannot trust to the continuation of any one thing about him for above five minutes.

The Duchess of Bedford is just left Town, but I did not see her. I hear she is with child and looking very pale and thin.

Adieu dearest beloved sister. Pray write to me often and long letters, and believe me ever and most truly yours,

HARRIET CAVENDISH.

To Lady Georgiana Morpeth

DEVONSHIRE HOUSE, *Wednesday, November 2nd, 1803.*

Haryo going to be married? La Comtesse Jules de Polignac or Lady Harriet Adair!! Consider, my dearest G., before you reproach me for not being entertaining, when we can find incidents in this immense Townful of nothing to enliven our epistles. Will it make you think better of our gay proceedings, to tell you that your dear Madame Zamoiska supped with us last night, sans mari, sans Pac, in short without any appendages, and was quite delightful? She played to me a great deal on the Piano forte, which I think she does better than anybody, and talked to me of you, which I like to hear better than anything. Her favourite topics, (les petits paquets excepted) are how Lady Morpez and she used to "danse des reels" and your well known ejaculation of "poor pretty me," which will spread over a great part of the known world. "Oh, what a pretty love I am!" I suppressed in pity to your modesty.

Lady Jersey came all rolled up in schawls, gesticulating and squeaking in the most ludicrous manner. "Lady Harriet, you must have thought me a beast when I wrote you that note." "My dear Madam, if you could know how utterly impossible it was I could ever think you a greater one than I do now," was really au bout de mes lèvres. I did not think Madame Zamoiska very gracious to her.

Bath seems settled for Monday. I trust in your coming there or otherwise quite hate the thoughts of it.

Have you heard any more of Saltram? [Lord Morley's house] and are Bisso's conquests spreading? I heard of one beau who was sadly ungracious; Lord Ebrington, the moment he arrived, laid down on a couch and the dancing began. He *lay* in motionless astonishment till, turning round, he asked how long it was to last and several questions savouring of extreme ennui, which so offended the fair performers that I have heard of nothing but their indignation since. Have you heard that Caroline Upton's marriage is broken off? Pray communicate the Intelligence to Delmino [Mr. Delmé] as I was partly the cause of his hearing the bad news, do let me be the first to acquaint him with the good. How does he do, is he grown, or is my darling chicken of a nephew near as tall?

Tell me more of your domestic concerns. Are you still decked in those little sprigs, and how does that miracle of a woman, that model of her sex, Nurse! do? I am sure Aunt has sunk in her nursery importance, and nothing could grieve her more.

Once more, G., I cannot do much longer without you, and therefore you had better make haste and come, as I have seriously had thoughts of setting out for Castle Howard by myself. I wish I could make you understand the necessity and happiness of my seeing you soon. At least I mean as far as my wishes are concerned. Je m'embrouille, ainsi adieu, ma soeur bien aimée. Pray, pray love always

yours most affectionately, HARYO.

To Lady Georgiana Morpeth

DEVONSHIRE HOUSE, *Nov. 4th. Friday morning. 1803.*

May I ask from whom you receive accounts of London Gaiety? From no inhabitant of this house, I dare swear, and Lord Carlisle's animating powers when at a distance, lose their effect entirely on a nearer approach—and often and often when in the silence of the middle drawing room, I have heard no noise save his drowsy hum, I have wished the climate of Yorkshire more salubrious, and that he would be tempted to try its vivifying powers. You ask me if I get on with him—and what still more offends me—wish I would, for what purpose in the world, unless as Sir Hugh says " on account of the mortal dislike they have to one another."

Mr. Adair is the only one of OUR *young men* that is going to Woburn. Mr. Crawfurd and Sir Walter are, I believe, otherwise engaged.

Sister, you make me angry and I begin to suspect you talk of our gaiety and *youth* as a cut at our total want of both. However when that sprightly lad Bob [Adair] returns, I'll make Mounsieur Zamoiska enquire about her Grace's *petit paquet*, as he is still more eloquent upon the subject than his wife.

" My sister dear and children three." " Basta " indeed with a vengeance and " hush " I promise you. Take care of yourself, my beloved G., and do not by any imprudence hurt a health so very, very much valued. I am enchantée; the more the merrier and I look forward to 38 at least.

My feeble friends are neither of them in town at present. The helpless Dick [Bagot] is gone to Oxford and Charles [his brother] expected in a few days. Mr. Brummell has been seen at the play and Henry [Pierrepoint], I believe, wastes his sweetness on the desert air, for though in Town nobody has seen him, or heard of him since his arrival.

Duncannon's love is just returned to Town, to what purpose and with what effect I know not. He seems to forget her entirely when she is absent, but there is no security, if one considers the art of attack and I am afraid, weakness of the defence. The *from* and the *of* lost not their effect for want of proper emphasis and I admired them very much.

Does Delmio's ill-luck at Pope [Joan] continue? If it does you must quite miss the poverino.

How I wish sometimes I could transport myself into your pretty room, with the most darling of Children seated on the floor ; even Nurse Davies and Anne would be delightful sights, and *nurse*, something to fall down and worship.

I dread being at Bath when you return. However we are to be in London after the first week.

We are all going to Drury Lane tonight to see the " Wife of two Husbands " translated from the French. I pray for some incident to enliven my next letter though I fear a stupid play and empty box, will not conduce much to your entertainment. Have you heard anything of the Westmorlands lately ? I wonder how soon Lady Sarah [Fane] will decide the fate of millions. " La femme à deux maris " would be a happy contrivance, and I expect to see Lord Granville and Lord Villiers tonight, arrived at the Theatre to see if it would be practicable. Perhaps they would not object to sharing her affections, but I doubt whether the division of the rest of their acquisition [her fortune] would be borne as quietly.

Do, dearest sister, write to me very soon again. I shall be very unhappy if you cease writing, as soon as you have excited my industry.

Mr. Green has just arrived. I will go and listen. I hope he won't talk of furniture. I have been down to the dear youth but could not make any thing out excepting that Buonaparte sent to Jérôme, Mr. Green's great friend, and said ; " Défiez vous de Mr. Green." So the poor frightened cause of alarm hurried back to England. He says they certainly will come, and talks of the conquest of England as a thing not admitting of a doubt—nous verrons, nous verrons—

Adieu, much dearest of G's.

yours ever ever, H. CAVENDISH.

To Miss Trimmer

DEVONSHIRE HOUSE, *Wednesday Morning, Nov*[er]. *9. 1803.*

MY DEAREST, KINDEST SELINA,

We set out, sans faute, tomorrow morning. I cannot like the thoughts of this expedition, but if it is essentially necessary to both papa and mama, all regret must cease, and if we stay there more than a month, my sister has promised to join us, which will be a great happiness to me.

Mr. Hare I find is going at the same time as we do and Duncannon and the two Fosters [Augustus and Frederick] come in 10 days ; we shall therefore not be a small party, and I am glad, as I think Bath must require a large and cheerful society to make it tolerable.

I have at present a *Johnson* mania upon me, which I hope you will allow is better than a *novel* one. I have been *re*-reading Mrs. Piozzi and Boswell. The latter I think very entertaining, and it is so long since I read it that I had almost forgotten it. I have hardly patience with Boswell's conceit and pride and wish he would fancy himself a secondary *personage*, as he almost always prefers telling one what he thought and did, to Johnson, and he is too uninteresting to make it ever excusable.

Yours always and most gratefully affectionate, HARRIET C.

VI

THE VISIT TO BATH

NOVEMBER 1803–JANUARY 1804

AS we have read, Sir Walter Farquhar decided that a visit to Bath would benefit the Duke and Duchess's health. The Duke suffered much from the gout and the Duchess had been in poor health for some time. Her eyes had given her trouble since 1795, and she had undergone several ghastly operations on them which she had borne with the greatest fortitude. We continually hear that "Mama has one of her bad head-aches" and by 1803 her health must have deteriorated greatly. But always her vitality and charm made her carry on when others, less unselfish than she, would have given in.

It is in Bath that the great Duncannon-Villiers flirtation reaches a climax. Harriet is nearly worried out of her mind, for while Duncannon courts Lady Elizabeth, he equally courts Harriet. What is she to do? Luckily there is always Georgiana at Castle Howard in whom she can confide and who will give her advice. Finally she tells her mother of her perplexities and doubts. But somehow I do not think she told her mother of her "tendre" for Mr. Charles Bagot. Poor Haryo! Despite her assurances to her sister she cannot quite deny him a place in her heart.

In one of her letters she mentions that Miss Trimmer may "accept the situation." Probably there was already talk of her being elected to the establishment of the little Princess Charlotte, the only child of the Prince of Wales. In a letter of Lady Elizabeth Foster's to her son Augustus on this subject she says, "I believe Miss Trimmer will be sub-preceptress," and Lady Bessborough mentions it too. But nothing came of it and Selina remained with the Devonshires to point every moral and adorn any tale.

Corisande de Gramont and "little o" (Lord Ossulston, son and heir of the Earl of Tankerville), were just embarking on their youthful love-affair, she having apparently forgotten her violent flirtation with Mr. MacDonald at Ramsgate the year before. The courtship was to be a long one and anything but smooth, as Ossulston's father was strongly opposed to the match, for he was a cantankerous, temperamental old man, always changing his opinions and his likes and dislikes.

The Duke of Bedford, whose marriage Doctor Randolph deplored so strongly, was the 6th Duke and had succeeded his brother, "Loo," the pet of Devonshire House, after the latter's death following an operation. "Loo" had been engaged to Lady Georgiana, daughter of the Tory Duchess of Gordon, and on his death-bed he commissioned his brother to go to Paris to console her. Devonshire House had been much upset by the prospect of their favourite's marrying into the opposition camp, but when Lady Georgiana cast off the mourning that had scandalized them and married the new Duke, their horror matched that of Doctor Randolph.

To Lady Georgiana Morpeth

SALT HILL. EN ROUTE FOR BATH. *Thursday evening, 10th of November, 1803.*

I write you one line from hence, my dearest sister, to let you know that we are at last on our way to Bath.

London has been filling provokingly these 2 or 3 last days and last night we had quite a brilliant assembly amongst whom, to my great astonishment, was Charles Bagot. He came with Henry [Ponsonby] and had only been in Town 3 hours. He is looking very handsome and much improved by growing fatter and wearing his hair out of powder. Henry, the gentle Henry, was received with such freezing coldness by the whole house, that I think he will have good courage if he ever comes in to it again. It was quite comical to see him; looking frightened and abashed, first attempting to "aborder" one and then another, and I was transported to see the extreme mortification with which he perceived the general antipathy. Mr. Bagot stayed but a few minutes and I had hardly spoke to him. He leaves town in 3 weeks for ever. Sometime ago this would have required a considerable degree of philosophy on my part, but now *scarcely* any; you see I am honest. I saw him this morning at a distance, and Duncannon told me he had just been to a hatter's with him, where after trying on every hat in the shop and keeping him waiting above an hour, he walked off complaining that none of them *became* him; c'est un peu trop fort. I am rather triste tonight.

I am disappointed more than I can tell you at the thoughts of not seeing you again soon and dread the thought of Bath and all its appendages. The *main spring* [Lady E. Foster] of our action is, luckily, now more discomposed at her performance than any of us. Mr. Hare cannot come, at least yet, and I have the satisfaction of seeing her more discomposed and out of humour than I had given her credit for.

Travelling makes me think of my last happy journey, with you and the dear children; oh, that I could be with you again, my ever dearest sister, and I look forward to seeing you, in a month perhaps, with happiness that makes me forget that Lady . . . [E.F.] is sitting next to me, and that there is any grievance in the world except being away from you.

Now will you be the kindest and most discreet of people, and I will own to you, that one great reason for my wishing to see you so much is that you are the person in the world in whom I have most confidence and it makes me quite unhappy to be obliged to conceal anything that instructs and occupys me very much from you. This is at present the case and must be till I see you again, as I dare not risk your leaving my letters any where and every where.

Adieu, dear dear G.

yours ever and ever, HARRIET.

To Miss Trimmer

BATH, *Sunday, November the thirteenth, 1803.*

We arrived here last night, my dearest Selina, after a slow but very comfortable journey. Mama has borne it without even seeming the least fatigued and though she was once threatened with a little pain, is now quite well. Papa has been better than I almost ever knew him, both in health and spirits, and I trust I shall be able to continue these good accounts of both of them.

We are in a good hotel, but Caroline and I are both extremely anxious to get in to lodgings, as our bedrooms are small and cold, and but one large sitting room in which we dine. I am sorry to say the anxiety to remove is not general, for both papa and mama are contented with this *Inn*, and do not mean to leave it for a week at least.

Bath, especially the part of the town where we are, is much more *Londonish* and noisy than I expected, but it is hardly fair to judge yet, and the badness of the weather would make any place gloomy.

In my last letter I told you of my Johnson Mania, but my volage disposition has already a new object of admiration. I have been reading M'Cormick's life of Burke, a violent and abusive book, but chiefly composed of extracts from his works and speeches in parliament. These I think in eloquence and brilliancy of talent quite unrivalled and in the beginning of his life, his sentiments delightful. I hope you will approve in my choice of a *hero*. Though I fear the change in his sentiments, towards the latter end of his life, will not appear so *blameable* to you as it does to me. But every body must feel indignant at his behaviour to Mr. Fox, even putting aside all political considerations and only blaming it as a most dreadful breach of Friendship. I do not allow myself to dwell upon his faults, for in comparison to his other virtues and talents they are very small. How good Goldsmith's character of him is in "Retaliation." I have been reading more (at least more to the purpose) in this last week, than I have for a good while before, and I cannot express to you how much pleasure it gives me, and the difference to me in making my time pass quickly or tediously is inconceivable. Indeed here in bad weather and the very small party we are, it is necessary not to make our séjour here very disagreeable. I am just going to begin Belsham's memoirs of the House of Brunswick. It is good I believe, though very democratic, and I wish to guard against any constantly keeping to authors prejudiced on either side, as it makes it very difficult to keep free from it oneself.

We are going to the Pump Room as the day is clearing, and I hear of an excellent house in *Poulteney* Street which I believe we are to take. This is consoling news.

I will add a line when I come in, Dearest Selina.

We have been in the pump room, which is more bustling, vulgar and noisy than any place I ever was in. We have since been walking with Doctor Randolph [the famous preacher] and I think the situation and lower part of the town beautiful. We then went to evening service at the Octagon chapel. The service was short but very well read and the singing more beautiful and affecting than any church musick I ever heard. I only hope I shall always come away from it, feeling as much the better for it as I do tonight.

Yours most gratefully and affectionately, HARRIET CAVENDISH.

To Lady Georgiana Morpeth

BATH. *Monday morning. Nov. 14, 1803.*

We have been this morning to see our house. It is beautiful and very comfortable, and I hope we shall get in to it the day after tomorrow. The weather is very fine today, in short, I am better reconciled to our plans and hope we shall, at least, be very comfortable here.

Forgive me, dear G., but in spite of your advice I do hope that man of sense, Lord Cowper, will keep away, and why when there are so many instances (yours amongst others) of finding what is good, should one not only put up with, but seek what even you can find no better recommendation for (with all your prejudice in his favour), than being better than most *young men*. And how far that may be considered as a compliment let a list of our youthful acquaintances (not excepting those in the diplomatic line) determine.

Thank you very much for laughing at Lady Liz.

What are Delmio's muscles made of, or rather his heart, that he can bear all the ons and offs with such perfect composure? Does he improve upon seeing him so constantly? He cannot have a more trying test of his amiability, I should think, and I shall give him great credit if he comes off victorious. The objection I have to him is a constant significant smile and little nodding, and I hate to be constantly watched, which I think he does. In short, I consider it a mercy that he is only about 4 feet, for if he was a tall man, it would be insupportable to have him trot about as he does.

Miss Trimmer is still uncertain whether she shall accept the situation or no; she is with my grandmama at Holywell.

Corise is impatient to return to us, though very indignant against the "perfide Auguste" [little "o"]. If I was her I should do nothing but bless Heaven for the happy escape.

Lady Bathurst is with mama. Do you know her? Odious Lady Clare too is in Bath, and nobody else.

Adieu, my always and most dear and kind G.

ever yours, HARRIET.

My love and hundreds of kisses in defiance of roars and cries, and nurse's, "he should beg Aunt not to kiss so very hard" the adored boy, and my respectful compliments to little Miss [the new baby] whom I must not treat with the familiarity of an old acquaintance.

I do not know whether mama writes to you today; she seems better than ever this morning and in looks she is certainly at present better than I almost ever saw her. Great weakness and nervousness is all that now remain of her illness and I trust change of air, and careful management, will soon give her more health than she has for a long time enjoyed, and that this illness will have proved most essentially beneficial to her constitution.

Once more adieu. Will you remember me in *proper terms* to Lord Morpeth, who does not, I believe, know half how much affection and admiration I feel for him. A hundred kisses to darling George and the little Miss.

To Miss Trimmer

BATH, *Wednesday, November the 16th, 1803.*

I received a letter from you, my dear Selina, just after I had sent you my last. Thank you very much for it.

Bath does not increase in charms and if it does not improve wonderfully upon acquaintance I shall be as happy to leave it as I was sorry to come to it, which is saying a great deal. It is remarkably empty and not one person we know here. The weather till today has been remarkably pleasant and we have quite lived out of doors. Our House (which we shall not get in to till the beginning of next week) has one very great advantage—it is at the end of Poulteney Street and opens on every side to beautiful hills and fields, and a walk of two miles along the side of a canal. This will prevent our ever being obliged to go into the Town, unless now and then to shops or the Pump room with mama, and that I hope will not happen often, as the former will not at all suit the state of my fortune, and to the latter I have a most decided aversion, and the walks I have mentioned are as retired and quiet as possible.

Your opinion of Johnson agrees perfectly with mine, and I am impatient to hear that you partake of my Burke enthusiasm. I have begun Belsham's History of England. It begins with Charles the second, and comes down to the present reign. I mean to confine myself for some time to the history of England as it is a shame not to be well acquainted with it, and I certainly am not.

Doctor Randolph has just been here, mama and him are great friends, and he seems very sensible and good humoured.

I think the good hours and exercise mama takes have already agreed with her very much, and she looks uncommonly well. Papa too is well and in excellent spirits. I believe he thinks Chatsworth and Chiswick much inferior to this Hotel, and though I am sorry for the consequences of this admiration, I am glad he is pleased with it.

It is quite melancholy to see the quantities of lame and sick people that are wheeled and carried all about the Town, and it is impossible to walk a hundred yards without meeting some dreadful object.

There is a very delightful repository here which we went to see yesterday. It is conducted by a committee of Ladies, with the greatest care and charity, and Mrs. Randolph told me she has given *3,000* guineas out of it to the poor. The poor people themselves make most of the things, and when Ladies do them, the work is dedicated to some particular purpose ; on a pair of screens was written " 15/– towards clothing a poor day labourer." The Duchess of Yorke [*sic*] has been quite a benefactress to it and sometime ago sent 50 guineas worth of her own work to it.

Adieu my dearest Selina,

yours gratefully and affectionately, HARRIET CAVENDISH.

To Lady Georgiana Morpeth

BATH, *November the 16th, Wednesday evening, 1803.*

In general I hate apologies, but I have not the impudence to write you so many stupid letters, without at least attempting one. The fact is I could bear being away from you *tolerably well*, when I thought it would end the 22nd of this month, but now that I do not look forward to seeing you again for a tedious 6 weeks, or perhaps 2 months, il n'y a point de patience qui tient, and I really should not be able to bear it without writing to you as you perceive I do every day and all day.

I have not been out of the house today as the weather was schocking, but I do not find the day pass heavily, as I am grown a very *studious, diligent* person, and you would be edified to see me surrounded with books and papers. I am afraid surprise at the novelty would not be the least predominant sensation. I do not know indeed what I should do with myself if I did not, or how occupy the many hours I am alone in a little dirty parlour, but Caro and I after about half an hour every morning spent in watching the rain, and sighing over the future on my part, and a petit jeu de morale about patience etc. on her side, begin reading and writing with a perseverance and courage worthier two steadier and more exalted characters—you and Lady Gertrude. This will make our séjour here, if not very agreeable or entertaining, very useful, and I am really ashamed when I approfondis my ignorance upon many subjects, and instead of repining at being here for 2 months, I am tempted to wish them years, that I might regain some of the shamefully lost time I have spent so uselessly both to myself and others. You will think amongst other qualifications I have been learning to preach of Doctor Randolph, but alas, my indolence and follies furnish so many good texts, that the sermons must follow of course.

You will be kinder than you have ever been yet if you will write to me often. The Post arriving is the great event of the day and it damps the remainder of it when that does not produce one any pleasure. Your letters must always be interesting to me, but never so welcome as they are now.

Send us Mr. Delmé in a parcel by the mail. He would be very acceptable. I do not invite any others of the party for reasons best known to people under 5 feet.

Kiss my darling 1,000 times for me. Could not you by some ingenious sigh or grunt recall me to George's memory?

I am in great hopes that Duncannon and Frederick Foster come here on Saturday. I shall soon even wish for Lord Cowper, and Bath could have no worse compliment paid it.

Lady E. Foster has been unwell these 2 last days and kept her room. She is much improved by it and is *meek* and *amiable* tonight. *Sidney* [Lady Liz's dog] the person treated with most égards here, I am happy to inform you is in perfect health, only " a little nervous and could not eat above two mouthfuls of chicken at dinner. Seriously, do you think he should drink the waters? I am contriving in imagination a little shawl for him and the drapery on his fore leg might be quite Grecian." After all, my love, why should not a silly affected dog be draped like a silly affected woman?

I scarcely dare hope to hear from you tomorrow. Dread my gratitude or my reproaches. I do not know which will be least troublesome.

Thursday morning.

I trust implicitly to all your promises of secrecy, indeed you will see how much from every circumstance it must be important to me that you should not, even to Lord M., repeat what I am going to say to you. My dearest G., you must advise me ; I will therefore try as clearly as I can, to put you au fait.

You will be surprised, after all you have been hearing of Lady Eliz. Villiers, to hear that Duncannon is the cause of all this worry and uncertainty to me. I must begin by telling you that on our journey *from* Castle Howard, the quarrel that we had there, was of necessity made up, and we were, as you have so often seen us, *friends* with a vengeance, but I was so thoroughly impressed with the idea of his attachment to Lady E. that, though his manner and even expressions often surprised me, I rejected the idea of my not being perfectly indifferent to him as at least a very erroneous, if not a very vain and foolish idea. We arrived in Town ; he saw her, did not seem in the least altered, and went to St. Albans with us, where he told Caroline that he was undecided and unhappy, and hinted to her that he was entangled in this affair with the Jerseys, and wished extremely to get off from it.

I then first thought seriously about it ; his manner to me was such as really hardly to admit of a doubt. When we returned my grand-mama and Miss Trimmer dined with us at Roehampton and the latter on my return to London, gave me a most furious lecture that my coquetry was dreadful and that, without caring for my cousin, I had made him in love with me, merely to enjoy the triumph of having supplanted Lady E. Is not this, dear G., an unkind method of giving advice, and do you wonder at its alarming me ?

The next day (as I must often act foolishly and always in extremes) I begun one of our tacit quarrels, and for 10 days at least, we did not utter. He was, for a few days, really wretched and neither spoke nor looked at any body, till suddenly he went off to the Jerseys, saw *her* twice every day and, even when we made up, was very cold to me. During this time I once or twice met them walking in the path and he joined us. He did not seem in the least in love with her, but tearing about in the most buoyant spirits and extremely flattered, evidently with her manner to him, which, though she has more excuses than most people, was certainly a very wrong one. (You will be tired to death, my dearest G.)

Soon after this, my aunt knowing he was always with her, wrote him a letter, which he answered as if he was dying for her—Lady E.—but agreeing to leave off seeing her. Instead of depressing his spirits this seemed to take a load off his mind, and though before my aunt il jouait le Désespoir, with us he was gayer than usual. One night at supper soon after this, he told me all at once, à propos de Bottes, that he made a serious promise to his mother, only to break it, and meant to marry Lady E., *immediately*. This I *immediately* saw was partly to make himself a héro de roman, and partly to try my sentiments. Angry at this *ingenious contrivance*, I told him I thought him very weak and foolish. He fired up. (Do not laugh) I told him I never wished to speak to him again, he assented and for *6 weeks*, we again by a word did not break this agreement. This was very foolish but very decisive ; he really was miserable the whole time. It rather amused me as my aunt thought his sorrow was caused by Lady E., and often consulted me about it, but it *touched* me much more, and it is the *only* time that I have ever felt the slightest *penchant* for him, but the constant and *steady* melancholy for a length of time in this weathercock cousin . . .

[*The end of this letter is missing.*]

To Miss Trimmer

BATH, *November the 19th, Friday morning, 1803.*

MY DEAR SELINA,

I am growing a very early riser (forgive my singing my own praises) amongst other improvements, and this morning was up at a little past 8. We have been walking since with Miss Keating [the Duchess's personal maid] who although not very tall, is a *really* very respectable little Chaperone, and as we do not walk in the gay parts of the Town, and that every part of it is now empty, I think there can be no impropriety in it.

We rather expect Duncannon and the Fosters tomorrow, at least if their military duties will permit them to leave London. It will be a great addition to our society if they can come, but I am rather afraid they will not be able.

The *Caquet* of this Town is inconceivable, and as you say, its being the great trade of all the inhabitants to watch and be watched, makes one alarmed, and ought to make one cautious.

I have only read 2 of Belsham's lives ; Charles the second and James the second. Charles the first I feel pretty well acquainted with, from our old friend Clarendon. I do not mean to go on with Belsham till I have finished Madame de Sévigné's letters, one volume of which I have read. It is a great undertaking to read them through, but they are so very delightful, and I have so much time for reading here, that I do not find it at all too tedious. I do think her letters and most of her sentiments quite incomparable, and the endless variety of anecdote and wit, assure their never tiring or boring. I mean then to—but I forgot you do not like Le Futur, and indeed you have good reasons to mistrust my *visions* of it, though I hope the accounts I give you of the *present*, will make you trust more to my resolution than you have done yet.

Mama is amazingly well. It is hardly possible yet to judge whether the waters do her good, but they certainly do not do her any harm, which is a great point gained.

Adieu, my dear Selina. Indefatigable people that we are, we are going to take another long walk, and then return to dinner. In the evening we all read and oh ! the pleasures of Ignorance. Madame de Sévigné is to me much more entertaining and to my shame I confess, much more *new*, than any novel I could read.

Yours, my ever dear Selina, most affectionately.

To Lady Georgiana Morpeth

BATH, *November the 19th, Friday evening, 1803.*

I just this moment found these lines in one of Madame de Sévigné's letters : "Il faut avouer que nous sommes à une belle distance l'une de l'autre, et que si l'on avoit quelquechose sur le coeur, dont on attendit du soulagement, on auroit un beau loisir de se pendre." The tedious 6 days before it is possible that I should receive your answer to my last letter are indeed enough to tempt one to some tragical deed, and I know not how I shall go through them with patience.

Since I sent you my letter I have been in one continual state of anxiety, regretting one moment that I wrote it at all, and the next that I wrote it as it was—— I dared not read it over and am afraid I did not make you understand what I wished, as I wished. You may trust to the confidence I really have in you, and believe me when I assure you, that I really am not in the least, and am disposed to receive your advice whatever it may be, with an *unbiassed* and free mind, and to follow it, whatever it may be, without difficulty or a moment's hesitation.

With regard to my cousin [Duncannon]—I believe that at present he is, or fancies himself, in love with me. (I must speak sans détour, or you might dread another 11 pages.) Whatever other faults he may have, I believe him to be perfectly free from deceit, and he could have no motive for saying he was, if he did not at least think so himself; but you know my opinion of his boyishness [he was 22] inconstancy and, alas, fickleness of every sort, and it would scarcely create in me surprise, if I was to hear of his making desperate love to Lady E. tomorrow; at least it would create both surprise and sorrow in me to find that a human being could carry those faults to so great an excess. But if I heard it was Duncannon I should absolve the poor human mind and think of him as I always have done.

My poor sister, to what endless and confused epistles do I doom you.

Our mode of life is not diversified. We are still in this Hotel, Papa thinking it, I believe, Paradise regained. Lady Eliz. and Sidney both unwell, both whining and both finally as agreeable as you know I always think them. Mama, in an hotel, as everywhere else, kinder, more indulgent and more unlike the Lady or the Dog, than I can express. I should think Mr. Hare must be coming by the éclats de rire, mended health and great spirits.

Oh, I forgot, *incendio* ANTICO, in every sense of the word! You question me about Mr. Bagot very narrowly. I heard he has left Town again, and "for ever," meant till February.

Papa is at this moment relating a flirtation he had with a very pretty housemaid here. The Duchess of St. Albans should be uneasy, (I wonder if she could?) not about Papa's being volage, but about anything from a cat to a king.

You see, dearest G., I obey you and am not triste. I have indeed no cause to be so. I am in constant alarm for fear Mama should fancy me so, which I think she is inclined to do. I sometimes, I know, appear so, but it is impossible not now and then to think, and anxiety to act right in this affair and to listen to nothing but the sensible part of my composition, make those thoughts naturally serious. I will add a line tomorrow night. I believe Duncannon will be here—though I wish, I am sure, not. The " embarras " is really dreadful, for figure to yourself a dinner of 6, with papa's *naïve remarks*, mama's anxiety, Caro's significance and the waiters all looking, à force d'imaginer, like spies. Ah G., c'est trop d'avoir à craindre !

Saturday night.

I must write you a few lines before I get into bed, dearest dearest sister, though I have been walking about since 8 this morning, and am half dead, but as I have often told you I do not like a day to pass without something that *seems* to connect me with you.

Today has been a dull visiting thorough Bath one, and I have seen nothing but Randolph's minchen [Mrs. Minchen] and all those *Pump* kind of people. Doctor Randolph is thought very delightful. I never knew anything like his attachment to the present Duke of Bedford ; it does not extend to his bride, and when her bonny mother is mentioned, he says he either stops his ears or runs out of the room.

Mama heard from Madame Zamoiska ; she regrets our absence very kindly, and says my dear little Constantin said with a sigh as he passed D. House, " C'est là où je m'amusois avec Henriette." This is delightful, but nothing to my own Brooke's, " I can remember you, Harriet Cavendish, though I shan't see you." And what is that to my most adored George's, though only by compulsion, giving aunt a pinch of snuff? I begin to wish all my acquaintance were under it and I am sure you will by the time you have toiled through these epistles of mine.

Duncannon sends no word he shall be here tomorrow. Write my own G., and love me near as much as I love you.

To Lady Georgiana Morpeth

BATH, *November the 22nd, Wednesday night, 1803.*

Thank you, my dearest sister, for the best and kindest advice and the plainest and most unperplexing directions that ever were so well given, or so thankfully received. You have made the only way I can pursue so easy to me that I am ashamed of ever having hesitated about it, and should feel mortified if I had not, ever since I can remember, acknowledged and loved you for your superiority to me in everything.

Duncannon arrived here on Sunday, and the embarrassment and gêne that I felt gave me a manner to him that I now feel was wrong ; great coldness and avoidance, and we never were, to all appearance, so little Friends, though I have not yet formed my opinion of his sentiments.

This morning your letter brought back just in time, my faculties, ideas and reflexion. I was walking with him at Bristol (but chaperones by dozens) and from the moment I read it, I have felt relieved from a hundred difficulties and (you will hardly believe in your magic dealings) have since felt as much at my ease with him as before all this happened. His manner, though, makes this difficult, and this evening I have been repeating your letter almost alta voce to keep clear of the caprice in looks and manner, that his makes it hard to avoid.

We heard today that the Jerseys have taken the box next to ours at Covent Garden—this coup de main will not, of course, remain unknown—and that Lady E. V. looked in to our box, all over it and then was for the rest of the evening in a deep melancholy. This is not affected ; by all accounts " ce petit conte est joué trop au naturel."

You ask me for his conversation with Caro. It was exactly this, but after the broadest hints. " I do not believe you are much in love with Lady E." No answer—(you know he is laconic). " I believe you are inconstant." A very reluctant smile. " If you were though in love with another person, you would not tell me." " Why not ? " " Good Heavens, would you ? " He only looked at me—I was at the other end of the table. Caroline says she did not believe her eyes and repeated the question ; he still looked and she says she almost screamed " What do you mean ? " He ditto, ditto, ditto, till she ended with a sort of frightened and very (for I heard it) extraordinary, *demi-shriek* and we *rose*. Dear G., how very novel-lish. This you must understand, for I cannot, I have puzzled it so. This by itself, though, would not be convincing, but you would be tired if I was to relate all the similar scenes that have passed. You see there has been nothing yet that does not leave a boyish, giddy person perfectly at liberty. An older and a steadier man, the whole of this would be very different with. We are now going on.

But I forgot to tell you that I do not know whether he suspects that Caro has told me, but I think by his manner he must—he is so suspicious of her that she almost sits with her eyes shut, to avoid an appearance of watching.

We have just been having a very long conversation, at the shadow of anything almost beyond la pluie I stop short. He told me that he leaves Bath on Monday and comes back on Friday, and perplexed me extremely by repeating over and over again, and waiting for an answer.

I hear all London is in the greatest astonishment at my being here, and wonder why I came ? Que dire ? and I feel much as H. Pierrepoint says he does when Miss Fitzroy tells him he is a very delightful man, "I must not say, am I ?"

But, G., all this and more that I should kill you with fatigue if I was to relate, will be easy for me to keep off. I am constantly with mama or Caro and really pursue them as if they were my mind and body. I am sure he does not think of Lady E. at present. To me, if I joke him about her, he disclaims—tonight with such vehemence that I was obliged to run and sit Bodkin between Doctor and Mrs. Randolph.

But I think much less seriously about the whole thing since I have heard from you. I feel quite sure I never should like him, and very possibly his liking me may never be a bit stronger, or go off entirely. If either of these things should not take place, Time, and a long time too, can do no harm, and unless any *very interesting event* should take place, you shall be troubled with no more of the didactic and descriptive.

I saw Mrs. Bouverie and Mrs. Wilmot at Bristol today ; the former much better in health, but altered in beauty to having none at all, I think. Mrs. Wilmot's bark and wit as usual, but she is too constantly and evidently employed in flattering the one and sharpening the other to be very delightful. I do not either admire those riding habit courageous ladies. If you think it will give you the head ache puzzling to find out the reason, pray do not trouble yourself. We also met Francis and Georgiana Palmer. He is a handsome spirited little Duke, for I never saw anything so distingué, but she is by far the most beautiful creature I ever beheld.

I have been laughing myself sick with a specimen of dear good Doctor Randolph's honest pieces of tact. He wrote to the Duke of Bedford to Paris, "I hear a strange report that you are going to marry a daughter of that Duchess of Gordon's. It cannot be true. *God forbid.*" If the Duke makes the same use of his grave as you do of yours, Heaven help poor Doctor Randolph.

Corise is still at Thoresby. Miss Trimmer, I believe, accepts the situation. Caro P. writes us very entertaining letters from London and it seems very gay. Madame Zamoiska was at the play with the Jerseys 3 nights ago. Lord Granville, Mr. Brummell and C. Bagot in our box. Lady Abercorn and Lord Hamilton have both the scarlet fever; I have not heard whether favourably or no. This I suppose will retard the juvenile match. Bath news: Mr. George Glass is going to marry Miss Blacquiere. Messrs Tully and George, shoemaker, no 1 Orange Grove, is making me a pair of half boots. Bristol news: General Tarleton is very unpopular—makes the volunteers wait—won't visit Mr. Pennyman the master of the ceremonies, to whose house I went today, took it for an inn and him for the waiter and behaved accordingly. General and Mrs. Tarleton are thought too conjugal, as they always sit on the same chair and eat out of the same plate. Doctor R., my oracle you see, saw the fact. Is it not going too far and quite nasty, to allow themselves but one plate?

I just now hear the watchman cry, "Past 2 o'clock, a starlight morning." I have not begun undressing. Oh fye!

To Miss Trimmer

BATH, *November the 24th, Tuesday morning. 1803.*

I am quite ashamed, my dearest Selina, of having so long delayed answering and thanking you for your long and very delightful letter, but do not from my idleness conclude that I am insensible to your kindness.

Thank you very much for your admiration of my admired Burke, and more than all for excusing in some degree, the fault that I had so very unwillingly taxed him with. Indeed, thorough conviction of being right would only justify his political conduct during the latter part of his life.

I lament the reason I am going to give you for keeping to one book at a time. I find from the long habits of inattention and unsteadiness in reading to which I have accustomed myself that I cannot remember or connect what I am about as well if I vary the subject, as when I keep steadily to one, and in fact, I gain as much information from constantly having my book *near* or *about* me, I get on very fast. I am now in the 5th volume of Madame de Sévigné's letters, and I own myself to be quite captivated by her style, wit and variety of sentiment. I think people are much mistaken who only dip into this book, as it is impossible to do her, or one's own judgement of her, justice without reading it through with attention and I am sure then with delight.

You will be glad to hear that Laura Chapel, or at least our pew, is as quiet and free from all fashion and etiquette as we could wish it. Doctor Randolph's sermons are (to use a favourite expression of his own) Thunderers, but like other storms, they awe without alarming, or at least alarm that can best mend the heart and raise the thoughts to God. His voice is very fine and his manner impressing and *rousing* to the greatest degree. We (that is, Mama, Car and I) receive the sacrament on Sunday.

We heard the other day that Anne Hunlocke is given over and in the last stage of a consumption. It is hardly to be believed, her appearance was that of such great strength and health.

Mama seems to gain health and spirits every day and the waters to agree with her perfectly. This reconciles me to Bath, though indeed nothing else would, but we pass our time very quickly and as pleasantly as can be expected.

Duncannon left us today. He has been here a week, very amiable and good humoured and we miss him very much. He returns the 9th of next month with the two Fosters and perhaps my aunt.

Have you heard of Mr. Heaton ? [the Duke's lawyer]. I think the bride must be either as deaf as a post or as patient, else how will she bear the sleepy monotony and never ending hum of her sposo's voice. Do you remember his " giving the young french lady a short history of the nature of fens, *marshes* and damp grounds ? "

I must tell you some wit of darling George's. When he is asked what gentlemen do when they shoot, he answers " *Pop*," and the other day when he was shown a print of an eruption of Mount Vesuvius, he exclaimed " Pop ! " again, I leave it to you to judge with what effect.

I think this promises future jokes of equal brilliancy and I flatter myself in a few years his witticisms will be less laconic.

She takes immense walks with Lord Morpeth, and does not think of leaving Castle Howard till about the 12th of next month. I think we shall remain here, perhaps, till the middle of January, in that case I hope they will join us here.

We were at a great Ball last night and are going to a concert tomorrow. This is to shew you that we are not quite Hermits. We saw at the Ball figures worthy of the Bath guide, and Sir Bonas and Blubbers and Lady Bunbutters at every step.

We know nobody here but Lady Clare and a niece of hers, Miss Beresford, a pretty, good natured girl, excepting *wonderful* Mrs. Minchen and a few more whom I will not tire you by naming.

The Tankervilles and Bennets in shoals are coming here next week. Little o I fear not, as he is playing at being a soldier, or rather a bit of one, in the north.

There are, too, *16* Fosters in Bath, most probably 16 too many, excepting John Leslie who is really a sensible gentlemanlike little man.

Hart will be here next week. I think he will enjoy the amusements and novelty of this place and be much amused with the Theatre, which is a very quiet and early one, and generally good plays well acted.

We breakfasted the other morning with dear good Doctor Randolph. Mrs. Randolph is a very nice good sort of woman—a little too much of " my dear creature " and all that—but otherwise worthy her husband which is saying a good deal. Car and I go to church twice every Sunday, and it is so easily done that I am ashamed of never having done it before. The musick here is quite beautiful and we have learnt some Hymns that I am sure my grandmama will like. Will you, if you are with her, give her my love and duty ?

[*End of letter missing.*]

To Lady Georgiana Morpeth

BATH, *November the 29th, Tuesday night, 1803.*

This has been a busy week, my dearest sister, and though I promised you in my last letter not to torment you any more with details and perplexities, I find that whilst I have anything to say, and you have the kindness and indulgence to listen, I cannot answer for my silence or your peace.

Duncannon left us after supper last night—but first I must tell you that I have confided entirely in mama, and that she is all goodness and kindness to me, and what I own surprises me, as anxious as myself to keep my secret. Do not therefore, by mentioning it to her, make her think it less sacred, for si elle éternue je suis perdue. I do not think she has been prudent, but I suppose she knows best. The whole time he has been here, she has let (what she alone could have hindered) us be constantly together—that is, walking at least 4 hours every morning and then the rest of the day, as you know, *even* by experience, it is impossible to avoid being with him—inseparable. I dislike this from its putting me constantly in the most awkward situations, and unavoidably hurrying and increasing, what my only wish is to retard and check. You will say, perhaps, that I might have put a stop to all this, but how can I, " en cousine," act any part but ignorance, and I could not keep that up, even as much as I do was to act differently to what I have done before. The grand answer to every thing is —seeming persuaded of his purpose for Lady E., but this cannot go on for ever, and he returns here the 9th.

I am *almost* sure (I have a good mind to leave out the *almost*) that I could never like Duncannon. I think him uncommonly handsome, good-tempered and affectionate and feeling in his heart and manners to everything that belongs to him, but I *do not* think him clever and I *do* think him trifling, inconstant and inconsequent to the greatest, most dreadful, and even unparalleled degree, and unless a woman is convinced, not as a manière de parler, but as a positive fact that she is the handsomest, cleverest and most fascinating woman that is, or ever can be, produced, how can she have any happiness with a man whom caprice attaches to her, and who has no principle to confirm, or character to secure him to her? I am convinced of his present attachment to me, but in the state it now is, 5 minutes might transfer it to some other object, and it is, on my part, so little valued, that in 5 minutes my vanity might recover the schock.

Another thing to be considered is the good-natured world, and if this could even go on in its present state, when I have heard almost every servant in the house remarking it, how can I hope that it will long be a secret? You say in your letter you fear my being engaged or entangled without knowing my own heart, and how can I go on for a year, *swearing* and vowing to him that he loves Lady E. when he denies that he doth ; me assuring him that he is constant when he declares till he is black in the face that he is not, and as to talking on any other subject for the *10* hours in the day when we are together, quite impracticable, and my last resource was sitting on the couch with mama, stopping my ears. This would be laughable if it was not cryable, and when I think of the possibility of being hurried on to decide either for or against him in a hurry, I am half wild. Perhaps this may stop here. It is a mercy that he had not an inclination to rob on the highway, for I am convinced he has no more command over himself than—— I do not know anything strong enough to compare to him.

But why should I not entirely and at once put a stop to the whole thing ? If I do not like him now, what should ever make me, and to a shuttlecock, who could not be a battledore ? I might easily do it without assuming the air of rejection or the pride of repulse, and really I have been contentedly his cousin so long, that I do not see why I should ever be anything else.

Do you remember Charlotte Hunlocke writing for advice whether she should refuse Lord O. before she had ever entered his head, or occurred to his little capacity in any light but as Charlotte Hunlocke ? Have you made the odious comparison ! But, my dear G., indeed this is a different case. I do not know what changes may take place before the 9th in the fickle administration of my cousin's ideas, or if it ever was in agitation to be more than a gay deceiver ; like wicked Captain Smith. But enough has passed to make me at least cautious, and I should not forgive myself if through mauvaise honte I was to lose your advice or my title to your confidence. If I was but with you, if you could come to Bath, or if we could meet you in London, I should be too happy. But why should I hope, what I am afraid, cannot for a long time be realized.

Do not be surprised if you see in the papers that he is married to Lady E. I hear *they* are making greater preparations than Buonaparte. I would bargain for losing Mary La Bonne if we might keep England.

To Lady Georgiana Morpeth

[*Beginning of letter is missing.*]

Mr. Bagot is in London, very ill and confined to his room. The Westmorlands at Apthorpe, but Lord Granville *hoping* from good authority that they will soon be in town—by the bye he talks of coming here for a day—my aunt, in the Metropolis, perhaps she will come *for a day*. I have not said anything and you cannot blame concatenation of ideas. I wonder I have the courage to talk to you of men and manners when I saw your letter to M. [the Duchess] how political the whole turn of your thought is grown.

Write to me, even on the tiny sheet, though I am obliged to read them as one goes up stairs—2 steps forward and 1 back not to have done too soon. May I be remembered to Lord Morpeth?

I forgot to tell you in the list of our acquaintances of a Mrs. Pennington, a bergère of about 50—her dress, person and conversation are impayable. The latter is eloquent and incessant beyond all powers of description and she talked mama and I the other morning into a sort of stupor; of how Mrs. Randolph has a hand to execute what her head performed and her heart conceived; and about Mama's illumined smile, vivifying all around and beaming the rays of a mind . . . je m'y perds—but imagine this under a flaxen wig, gipsy hat, *miminey* voice and, as she expresses it, a frame all nerve, delicately alive to every call of sensibility, and I defy you to produce a pendant.

By the bye, I am delighted to be reckoned like mama. "A very bad edition though," as an honest man said of me at Mrs. Somebody's ball.

To Lady Georgiana Morpeth

POULTENEY STREET, BATH. *December the 11th, 1803,*
Sunday night.

How very much the letters I received from you this morning made me laugh, and Lady Julia's Blue Ribbons nearly choaked me. I will certainly take the hint, as my arms are, I think, redder and rougher than ever, though I own it is hardly possible. I hope I am not grown fatter, though *certainly* not thinner, and yet I wish it so much and persevere in exercise etc. with so much laudability that I think I deserve success.

As you seem rather behind-hand in the way of news, it may possibly be interesting intelligence still that Buonaparte is "alive and merry." I believe Lady Liz would have mourned if at least the thoughts of Mr. Hare's arrival on Tuesday had not acted as contrepoison.

The Tankervilles are arrived and "little o" coming. Duncannon and Augustus Foster arrived here tonight. The former is furious with me. I believe I told you of my letter. But he cannot even be angry with any degree of consistency, and is vexed at my having formed an opinion of him that every moment confirms. In short, "on n'as pas encore trouvé le moyen de lier le vent, ou de fixer Mercure."

Kiss 19000 times the *sliding* darling of a George for me. Does little Miss begin to be witty?

We are going to Balls and concerts without end this week. You seem anxious about our partners; Jules [de Polignac], Cugino [Duncannon], Hart and Apothecary are the great variety and we shift these valuable youths from one to the other, without regret or rivalité, and resume them with sighs that we have not better.

We are going to meet the Duke of Bedford, Lady Bath, etc., tomorrow at Doctor Randolph's and some musickal people. I am learning of Mrs. Miles and fagging very hard at it. *She* was so astonished at Lady Morpeth with two children that I had a good mind to add "and a half."

I hear London is very gay; Jerseys in every shape and nook—Lady Fanny [Ponsonby] looking very pretty. The Cholmondelys improving in wisdom and Miss Seymour in sense every day. I wonder how Lady "*Holmonly*"'s wonderful talent for Geography goes on.

We go on in the same regular and quiet manner I at first described to you, and I am grown so used to it that I look forward to dinner at 8 and supping at 12 quite as tremendous events.

God bless you dearest G.

ever yours most affectly.

To Lady Georgiana Morpeth

POULTENEY STREET, BATH. *Friday night, Decr. 30th, 1803.*

Thank you very much, my dearest sister, for your letter. We return from Bristol on Wednesday and I trust you will not delay your journey any more. I need not tell you with what impatience I shall expect you, or with what happiness I shall feel having you here and my darling George, who I hope will survive the first transports of our meeting and bear my embraces with tolerable patience.

We hear from Mr. Foster's servant, Quin, who arrived here yesterday, that Duncannon does not return here at all. I am glad you think him incomprehensible, as it justifies my opinion of him. Do not talk of his ever being a *nearer relation*. You do not know me if you ever for a moment think it possible. I told you some time ago that it would not surprise me if he returned to Lady E., but after what passed the last time he was here, I own it does. It was not only manner, for that with him is nothing at all, but declarations, though not positive not to be misunderstood, every 5 minutes. I am happy that he is not coming here, as it spares me the difficulty of an alteration in my manner, which, though necessary, would be extremely distressing to me. I had determined it before his Lordship's fickleness spared me all further trouble.

I hear Charles Bagot is certainly coming here immediately. I like Bath better every day. We are very very *gay*, and pleasanter gaiety than at first, from having a great many agreeable acquaintances. But my *adoration* at present is dear little Mrs. Tarleton. She is *perfectly* delightful and so kind to me that that alone would almost make me love her. I was with her yesterday from 2 till 5, and she is so entertaining, merry and goodhumoured that it seemed like 10 minutes. I was quite ashamed coming home *loaded* with presents, for whatever I looked at, she gave me and she lent me the most beautiful books to read. It is delightful to have her too at the stupid rooms and I am quite delighted with her being here. The only *flaw* in her character is her great admiration of Miss Seymour, but that I am doomed to meet with. She [Mrs. Tarleton] is rather pretty, I think, but so original, so remplie de talents, *so* fond of her husband, so good and so giddy. In short, pray agree with me in all my praises or I shall be quite vexed. She is coming to see me tomorrow morning.

Another of my new acquaintances is Miss Dixon, the Bishop of Down's daughter ; she is pretty and sensible, but not to be *named* in the same day as Mrs. Tarleton. Another, a Mr. Beresford, a Leech sort of a man, upon whom a title acts as a magnet and who sticks to a Ladyship with laudable perseverance. He is handsome but very conceited. General Tarleton's nephew dined here one day. He is a little like some of the Lambs, but near 7 feet high, I should think. I like what I have seen of him very much, and I love even the General's dear red face.

Pray answer this scrawl, my best, dearest of pretty G's, and tell me you love me and do not forget me. I am glad Cugino has the *face* to keep away. He could not indeed come, all things considered, and he had better stay where he is prosperous, as no Bath gales could blow him into my good graces. And I shall feel my conscience acquitted towards Lady E., as she is (excepting a little too much giving into her dear Mama's plans) a great favourite of mine and too amiable and pretty to be discomposed by the jerks of a weathercock. By the bye, did you ever hear that the weathercocks in Ireland are all sign posts? This is very like D., who, I suppose, thinks that tant qu'il *chante* la même chose, that it does not matter much which way the wind blows it. Send me word if Lady E. is in beauty and admired and above all attribute the question merely to curiosity.

Addio, cara carissima.

31st, Saturday.

I forgot to tell you that Mama's headache is a great deal better tonight and I hope she will be quite well tomorrow. Pray tell Delmio to come here, we want Beaux sadly and he would be a very useful one.

Will you tell Duncannon from me that I am anxious to know whether he would not like me to send him some *Cocoa nuts*, as I fear the *extreme* WEAKNESS of his constitution will not be able to go on prosperously without them. Pray do not forget this message, as it is, to use a favourite expression of Mr. Foster's, *an exquisite gibe.*

Addio, chère soeur. Je te souhaite une année remplie de tout le bonheur que tu mérites. Kiss your *large family* for me. I am glad you bring Mr. Marsh. If all Bath does not stare you out of countenance when you come, it will not be for want of practice.

To Miss Trimmer

POULTENEY STREET, *January 19th, Thursday Evening, 1804.*

I am sure you will be glad to hear, my dearest Selina, that I have just got rid of my sore throat, and a little weakness excepted, am quite well again. I must again claim your kind indulgence to forgive me my long silence; you may conclude that I have been in a *whirl.*

I wanted a little illness to sober me, and it has had the desired effect, as you may see by this epistle.

We are so perfectly comfortable here that I shall be almost sorry to return to Town, though you know how anxious I was for it a little while ago.

I think my grandmama very well and in good spirits. She seems to enjoy being here with us all and I need not say how happy we are to have her.

G. is not quite well, at least she has cold and languor hanging over her and complains of the air of "*Odious Bath.*" George is more beautiful and delightful than even my partiality had pictured him. I long to see the little girl. I do not think my sister occupies herself enough about her.

Mr. *Marsh* and Mr. Delmé are here. The former *perfect* and Papa and Hart delighting in him, which is *delightful*, though I fear that is all. He really contrives to make himself beloved by every body. I believe one of his great charms is totally forgetting himself, and it is an *oubli* that one does not meet with very often.

Little Mr. Delmé is perfectly harmless, and seems very much pleased with being here, which prevents one's *grudging* it him. Lord Boringdon is not as convenient, body or mind considered, but he will leave Bath in 2 or 3 days. They are all gone to a Cotillon ball tonight where Hart and Caro are to perform ; he dances very well and with an amusing degree of solemnity in his face and feet.

I believe I have not talked to you of my dear little Mrs. Tarleton, she is a delightful person and I do not know which to admire most, her good or her brilliant qualities. She has certainly a greater share of both than generally falls to the lot of mortals, and what is perhaps more uncommon, a perfect *command* over them. That is she never gives you too much or too little of them and employs her talents as the embellishments, and not the object of her existence. Do not you think this requires sense and judgement and deserves admiration ? I think so more perhaps from having lately *heard* Lady Eliz. Monck and *seen* her daughters.

Adieu my dearest Selina. I am very easily tired and will write you a better letter in a day or two. I do not deserve it, yet perhaps you will write to me.

Yours most affecly, H. CAVENDISH.

To Miss Trimmer

DEVONSHIRE HOUSE, *Monday, April 4th, 1804.*

I need not tell you what I felt for you and all your family on hearing of poor Mrs. James' death ; what you say of both piety and your brother's resignation is indeed an awful lesson that I hope I shall not soon forget. I think when we meet again you will find me more what you wish me to be than when we parted.

My dearest Selina I must leave you, to perform a melancholy duty —to write to my poor Corisande, from whom I have just received a heart breaking letter with an account of her mother's death. Poor Madame de Gramont.

Ever most gratefully and affec[ly], HARRIET CAVENDISH.

To Miss Trimmer

April, 1804.

I have had another melancholy letter from Corisande. Poor little thing, she has not the consolation you all derive, my dearest Selina, for though very well meaning, her religion is, I fear, very faulty and misguided, and it vexes me to see how totally she gives herself up to despair, instead of attempting even to seek for comfort in religion.

My sister is waiting for me, my dearest Selina, Adieu.

Yours ever most truly and affec[ly], H. CAVENDISH.

VII

CASTLE HOWARD

1804

GEORGIANA MORPETH, after rejoining her family at Bath, lay-in of her third child in London and therefore we have no letters from Haryo until she went to Yorkshire in the autumn.

Just before she set out on her visit to her sister at Castle Howard, she mentions Lady Hester Stanhope and Lord Granville. Though he was still wooing the heiress, Lady Sarah Fane, he had also become involved with Lady Hester. She was Pitt's niece, older than Granville, eccentric, plain and brilliant. Lady Bessborough had recognized for some time that Granville should marry, but she could not help feeling relieved when Lady Sarah made up her mind between her two suitors and married Lord Villiers. But she was now distraught at the new turn in Granville's affections ; Lady Hester had a will of iron and though Granville made light of the whole affair he might easily have found himself in a position where marriage was unavoidable. However he left for Russia in October as our Ambassador, and though a terrifyingly cryptic letter from Lady Hester followed him, she soon had the good sense and good breeding to renounce any claims she might have upon him.

Harriet left for Castle Howard in September, travelling with her uncle and aunt, Lord and Lady George Cavendish. Lord George (the Duke's younger brother) was later created Earl of Burlington, and the Dukedom eventually passed to his line, as Hart never married. Lady George was the only daughter of the Marquis of Northampton and, both her parents having died when she was a child, she had been brought up by her grandmother, the Duchess of Beaufort. They were a dull, kind, rather provincial couple.

Castle Howard was another family stronghold. Not only did the Morpeths and their children live there, but also Morpeth's aunts, Lady

Anne and Lady Juliana. The latter, who figures largely in the letters, died in her 100th year and at this time was fifty-five years old. There was also Morpeth's sister, Lady Gertrude Howard (who married Mr. Sloane Stanley), and several of their brothers. And, of course, Lord and Lady Carlisle, he as cross and dictatorial as she was sweet-tempered.

Haryo also found there Lord Gower, Granville's half-brother, the eldest son of the Marquis of Stafford. He subsequently became the first Duke of Sutherland (his wife was Countess of Sutherland in her own right), and he had been our Ambassador in Paris at the time of the Revolution. His wife had sent Marie Antoinette linen and other necessities for herself and her children when they were imprisoned in the Temple. Their daughter, Lady Charlotte Leveson Gower, afterwards Duchess of Norfolk, was also at Castle Howard.

Miss Augusta Byron was another guest. She was the half-sister of the poet, a niece of Lord Carlisle and subsequently married Colonel George Leigh. Her unhappy story needs no comment here.

Tommy Wynne who came to stay later on, was a candidate for Parliament ; he stood for Knaresborough against the Duke of Devonshire's interest, a crime in the eyes of Harriet and her mother.

Thomas Grenville was George Grenville's second son. He did not share the politics of the family and for most of his public career was an adherent of Fox. In 1807 he withdrew into private life and devoted himself to the formation of a splendid library, which he bequeathed to the British Museum.

Harriet was wrong in her dislike of Lady Stafford, who though she fussed over her adored Granville, must have been a " perfect dear."

Harriet's letters to her mother leave no doubt of the great love she bore her. The Duchess's health was again precarious, and largely attributable to the worry that her huge debts were causing her. Haryo evidently knew that her beloved mother had other anxieties than those caused by the yet unsolved problem of Duncannon, which was still perplexing her.

To Lady Georgiana Morpeth

CHISWICK, *August the 18th, Saturday morning, 1804.*

I must write you one line, my beloved sister, though I have very little to communicate to you, chiefly to remind you that I *cannot* do without hearing from you, and that if you do not let me hear from you very often, you do not deserve to be *adored* as you are by Mr. Marsh and I. I must put in his name as he is the only person digne de moi, when affection for you is the theme.

I have but two ideas in my head at present—that I can't live in Middlesex and must go into Yorkshire.

We have nobody here but Lord O. [Ossulston] and Mr. Adair. Corise is in very good spirits and he seems so seriously and really attached to her, that I begin to hope she may be happy They have long silences as usual, though more conversation than dans les commencements.

The Bessboroughs come here tomorrow for a few days. Lord Granville too, I believe. I have seen him once or twice. I hear Lady Hester is in despair and vents it at Roehampton—is that policy or ignorance?—and that "il bel Uomo" sits at dinner bodkin, with "decent triumph and a look serene." Oh, how many fair Germans, Poles, Hungarians, Livornians, Scavonians etc. etc. will rue this gay deceiver's soft looks and broken vows!

Adieu dearest of all human beings; much, much.

yours ever most affectly, HARRIET.

To Lady Georgiana Morpeth

CHISWICK, *August 23, 1804.*

[*Beginning of letter is missing.*]

Our party here is very much decreased, we all meet, however, on Wednesday at a turtle dinner at Roehampton. By the bye, it is my birthday and pray drink my health. Mr. Foster and I have great disputes about my age and he wants me to recite a sweet thing beginning "Of years I have now half a century past."

And now addio, my beloved G. If Lord O. would grow tall, Corise clever, Caroline bad or myself!—[scratched out] I would write you longer letters, but whilst we all remain in statu quo, what is to be done?

Yours ever most affect[ly].

I am glad you spare me the description of Naworth, though I wish you would write a little pamphlet about it, as people enquire me mad about the soil, situation, shape etc.

Lady Hester dined again at Roehampton the other day; she sat next to Frederick Foster and told him, sans cérémonie, that she could not bear his brother, and that his cousin, John Foster, was like a great fat dictionary, which, by the bye, is very true. My aunt has thoughts of going to Lowestoff to see *Willy* embark.[1] *It may be*, as the miller says in the tale of mystery.

We are very comfortable here. I sit out of doors the whole morning *reading*,—do not insult me by looking surprised—and in the evening we go on the water by moonlight and walk till supper. I have just recommenced my starving system and *begun* leaving off rouge. As Hart said the other day when somebody said Corise and I blushed, in his slowest way, " Yes, the girls blush Madlle Martin, Rue St. Honoré."

Addio, much the dearest.

To Lady Georgiana Morpeth

CHISWICK, *September, 1804.*

I cannot believe I shall see you in 4 days, my dearest sister.

We set out at ½ past 9 tomorrow morning, and I am afraid we shall not arrive at Castle Howard till Sunday. My little darling boy—La testa mi gira—and I am too happy.

My joy is only diminished by my leaving my dear mama, but as it will not be a very long absence, I will only look on the beau côté. I have a hundred things to tell you, but they shall be deferred till Sunday, a day the fairest sure that ever rose.

Addio, dear, dearest G.

H. CAVENDISH.

To her Mother

BARNBY MOOR, *Friday evg. September, 1804.*

MY DEAREST MAMA,

I have but one moment to tell you that we are arrived so far on our journey without delays or accidents, and it has been as pleasant as any that takes me from you can be. We came 85 miles today, and have about as many tomorrow, as we do not mean to be another day on the road. Nothing can be kinder than my companions and I quite love Lady Betty[2] and think her much prettier than Lady Essex. C'est tout dire, you know.

[1] Willy Ponsonby accompanied Lord Granville as his secretary to Russia.

[2] Lady Elizabeth, Morpeth's aunt, married (1) Peter Delmé, (2) Captain Charles Garnier, R.N.

Our étiquette is surprising, and my civility has hitherto been à toute épreuve. We have disputes at every stage about the order of our procession and at the inns spend almost as much time at the doors of the rooms as we do in them.

Tell Mr. Foster upon these occasions I long to say—" *Bless my soul,*" which I practise all day.

Good night, my adored, own mama. My love to my dearest papa and to all of them.

I will write to you the moment I get to Castle Howard.

Yours most dutifully and affectionately, HARRIET CAVENDISH.

To her Mother

CASTLE HOWARD, *September, 1804.*

How shall I ever thank you enough, my beloved M., for your delightful letter. It makes me think myself with you all, which is the only thing qui me manque.

I have scarcely left my sister and the darlings for a moment. George is more improved than I could have thought it possible and he is really intelligent and witty. He calls himself a *little tiny romp* and says, " *Aunt Harry-O spoils George.*" Caroline is beautiful, but her mental accomplishments are not great and the little baby almost the prettiest of all.

I suppose you know that the Staffords [Granville's parents] are here. I do not *adore* them, but they are very kind and good natured to me. Lady Charlotte [Leveson Gower], Lady Gertrude [Howard] and a tall, reserved, alarmed lady, called Miss Byron, are inseparable, which leaves me more time to be with G., but it is a formidable côterie, as the intrusion of a fourth person, even for a minute, causes such panics and tremors that one suffers more from their shyness and gravity than they do themselves.

Lord Gower and a Mr. Murray, a friend of Duncannon's, are coming here. I am very sorry to hear of his [Duncannon's] sore throat. Will you ask him if he will bring two or three things for my sister when he comes, and if he is *so gracious*, I will send you word what they are.

Pray write me the little french song you said one day on the portico was like me—Clorinde or Jacinthe.

Castle Howard from the South

To her Mother

CASTLE HOWARD, *September, 1804.*

Thank you, dearest mama, for a dear long letter I received from you yesterday. Lord M. and my sister are riding, but desire me to tell you that they will write tomorrow.

I am afraid you have been very much worried lately about different things, my beloved M. I am sorry that I should have contributed my share, but I hope I shall for the future occasion you no more anxiety, at least not any that my own exertions in different ways can keep from you.

I had a note from Corise, to whom I wrote 3 days ago, this morning. I hope her affairs are going on better and that they will at last, in spite of all Impediments, turn out happily.

My sister and I finished the 3rd volume of Cowper yesterday. I am enthusiastic about him, and if there was anybody like him alive, I should certainly be *very poorly*, as Sir John Shelley calls it. He is one of the few persons who have as much heart as head, and more of either than dozens of *existing* men, who dispute his having at least the latter. Lord Carlisle is one. He is jealous of his head and does not understand his heart, and thinks " the Father's Revenge " [a tragedy written by Lord C.] and " the Task " not to be mentioned in the same day. No more do I, for they are things as distinct as an Earl and a Poet, and I was nearly telling him so at dinner, when he talked nonsense about it—that if it had been Henry, he would have been whipped for.

Adieu, my beloved M.

Yours ever, HARYO.

To the Countess Dowager Spencer

CASTLE HOWARD. *September, 1804.*

[*Beginning of letter is missing.*]

We expect the Duke of Rutland, Mr. Norman his brother-in-law, and Colonel Throughton his toadeater, to dinner today. His visit has nothing interesting in it, but he may make it formidable by publishing it in his next tour and giving us some share of the ridicule of appearing in print, whether one was hungry at dinner or tired at supper etc.

The Staffords go tomorrow and I am sorry they do. He is a very good person to have in a house in the country, as he goes on quietly his own way and has a hundred little pursuits of his own, such as poking into all the ponds for weeds, and examining all the Cobwebs for insects, and when he is wanted to take a share in those of other people, he is goodhumoured and ready to oblige.

God bless you, my dearest grandmama, most dutifully and affec^{ly}

yours, HARRIET CAVENDISH.

To her Mother

CASTLE HOWARD, *September, 1804.*

Your letter, my dearest mama, made me very uneasy and unhappy, not only for poor dear Corise but for you, as I am afraid this sad affair must be very bad both for your health and spirits. Lord Tankerville must be a *monster*, but yet it is difficult to go against such terrible threats. Has Lord O. told you the cause of the last delay? If this redoubled violence proceeds from his Father's thinking he was hesitating, I think there is still hope if he shows him that he is firm and determined.

I am delighted to hear that Duncannon is so much better, but I will not worry him with commissions, as they are of no consequence, and some French books, which was the principal one, I find I can procure in York.

The babes are quite well. George rather conceited and repeating all day, " George Howard is a very beautiful boy, a very good boy and a very *clean* boy."

The Staffords left us this morning to my great joy, as I cannot bear *her*. Mr. Delmé and Mr. Grenville are arrived. The latter seems a great favourite with all here, but Lord M. and G. quite *adore* him.

Addio, dearest best of M's. I cannot bear to be away from you when I fancy you anxious and worried. Will you tell Corise how much I love her and all I feel on this occasion?

G. is looking quite beautiful and more angelick than anybody ever was. Lord Carlisle is pretty well but not in very good spirits.

My dear mama, I am up before any of the family, ready for dinner the first, and Lady Julia says I am the most exact person she knows. This is not *qui dab*,[1] though it may appear strange.

My sister is almost as bad as Mr. Pierrepoint and insists on my cutting off my trains and wearing pockets.

[1] Abbreviation of " qui dabit recipiet " ; he who shall give will receive.

Tell Mr. Foster I shall really be a "worthy woman with very good points about me," when we meet again.

Yours, my own M. a thousand times.

To her Mother

CASTLE HOWARD. *September 26th, Wednesday, 1804.*

I have just received your delightful long letter, my best, my dearest mama and if it was not quite impossible to give you any idea of my gratitude to you, I would at least attempt it. I am very sorry that you have another of your nasty headaches. Happy as it makes me to hear from you, pray do not write if it tires or worries you.

I like to feel I am doing what you approve, therefore pray send me some more commissions of the same sort. I will be particularly careful about my behaviour at Church. Indeed I feel most seriously the necessity and propriety of it, even if I did not feel, what I trust I do, the greatest devotion and real piety, though I often must appear as if I did not.

I am glad Lady Stafford has some good about her to compensate for the very great share of bad. Mr. Grenville I now *love* for myself, and he is almost the only person I know that in so short a time I could like so much; so *steadily* would be a better expression, as I do not mean my flashes of admiration and dislike, neither of which ever last beyond 5 minutes.

How vexatious that Duncannon should have caught cold again. About what day do you think he will set out if he goes on well?

Tommy [Wynne] comes on Friday, which is really a monstrous unpleasant circumstance. I am most angry with him for his impudence in daring to appear here, nasty little upstart.

George is delighted with your message. Caroline roars without ceasing and the little thing is a prodigy of intelligence and good humour.

Mr. Marsh goes in about 10 days, which puts us in despair and his "Toho" is in full force.

Addio, my adored mama. I cannot tell you half a quarter what I feel for you. My love to the *Pusses* [the two Caros and Corise], make them write and a hundred messages and kisses to dearest Hart. I shall be most anxious to hear how he is. When does F. Foster set out? He would laugh if he could see how well *Tybald* [her own nickname] can behave, where there is no *simplicity* to corrupt her.

Yours ever, ever, HARYO.

G. sends her love and George kisses "Danmama Dutchess with lips," which is a great distinction.

To the Countess Dowager Spencer

[Note.—There is a small sidelight on Harriet's character and on those of her correspondents, in the way her letters are written and dated. The letters to her grandmother are tidy, and neatly dated. Those to her mother are very untidy and are never dated. Those to her sister show the handwriting of her mood of the moment and are sometimes dated and more often not. Those to Miss Trimmer are obviously "duty" letters and the post is always just about to go.]

CASTLE HOWARD, *Sunday morning, September the 23rd, 1804.*

MY DEAREST GRANDMAMA,

I have been so occupied with my dearest sister and her children since my arrival here, that I have not performed my promise of being a good correspondant, but now that we have begun great regularity and exactitude in all our occupations, I mean to become a most diligent one.

Your advice on the subject we discussed in the berceau walk, I have no difficulty in promising to follow, as it [is] the only way of uniting what I ought, and what I like to do, and it relieved me from that most painful state of mind—indecision and suspense.

I was very sorry to hear how seriously ill Duncannon has been but we have much better accounts of him this morning. I cannot tell you how happy I am here. I found my sister in great health and beauty and looking very like her picture—as happy and *paisible*. George very much improved both in body and mind, and the two little girls grown and livelier than they were. The former is a little conceited and pays "George How-ard" most extravagant compliments, but otherwise he is as good and amiable a child as it is possible to see.

I was delighted to see Mr. Marsh again, and to see him *himself*, in every sense of the word. He is delightful in every character but that of a Strephon and I think he has the grace to think so as well as I do.

Mr. Grenville is here. I scarcely know him but he is a most amazing favourite both of Lord M. and my sister, which is a good lettre de recommendation.

The Staffords went yesterday and Mr. Delmé arrived, who is too insipid to be offensive and too quiet to be bothersome, which, I think, is the most one can say for him.

Adieu, my beloved grandmama, we are just going to chapel and I will delay giving you an account of my early rising and industry till I write again.

Yours most dutifully and affect^{ly}, HARRIET C.

To her Mother

CASTLE HOWARD, *September 29th, 1804.*

If I was not extremely sorry, my dearest and best of M's, that my doubts and difficulties should have given you a moment's trouble and anxiety, I should hardly regret anything that procured me your good and kind advice.

Believe me, there is no one on earth whom I would so willingly consult on any and every subject, and it is merely from fear of taking up your time uselessly that I have not before mentioned this subject to you since I left Chiswick. I believe I am wrong about Lady E. [Villiers] and yet I think you will do me the justice to own it is natural I should have a thousand scruples about her, that I even would not forgive myself if I had not. Her situation (whatever may have been blameable or excusable in her conduct) is a most particularly delicate one, and whatever may in future may be decided on to try and prevent its being either mortifying or injurious to her, I not only consider a duty, but really one of the first wishes of my heart.

But I do not believe I differ in my opinion on this point from you, for all I ask is time, and you tell me it is all you must require. Another doubt I have is that if a year hence or more, I should have altered my mind, I shall be blamed by everybody, accused of being unfeeling, coquettish and other faults, if that is the case, I am now as much bound as if I actually was engaged.

But I will not torment you any more upon this subject. There is time enough to be in no hurry, I trust, to decide upon any plan and for the present your advice about good humour and steadiness of conduct I will implicitly follow.

Tommy Wynne arrived to dinner yesterday alone, as Lady Charlotte is ill, but he returns in about a week, nasty little creature. I was obliged to be by him at dinner but contrived not to open my lips.

Addio, dearest, best mama.

Yours most affectionately and dutifully, HARRIET CAVENDISH.

To her Mother

CASTLE HOWARD. *Monday morning. 1804.*

Thank you, my own dearest mama, for another letter I received from you this morning. We expect Duncannon tomorrow, I hope that the journey will not make him ill again.

Mr. Grenville left us yesterday. I love and admire him very much, indeed I have quite a hopeless passion for him. I put my sister quite in a fury by insisting upon it that Lady Julia H. has one too, and as they sat together at meals and at Pope Joan, I never could look at her without laughing, and I am afraid she must have seen it, as her eyes are quicker than anything I ever knew, her ears excepted ; and she talks, listens, hears and eats all in a breath and all with the same impetuosity. I remember John Ponsonby saying once, when I asked him whom he thought pretty, "anything and everything except Lady Julia Howard," and I really think she does defy all ugliness that ever was seen.

Lord Carlisle and I have a quite "*suivie*" flirtation, and I don't dislike him *more than can be expected.* William Howard and I quarrel from morning till night. He is as hard and impenetrable as a stone, and no warmer, and all that every different attack of mine produces is either—" Don't be troublesome " or " You disturb me."

Frederick is good natured and civil. *Therefore* I let him alone. Mr. Foster might profit by that consequence.

Dearest Emma, how much nonsense I have talked in five minutes.

Will you give my love to all and believe me yours with all the love and duty you can think.

Aunt Hary O, which George dwells upon with peculiar emphasis.

To her Mother

CASTLE HOWARD, *Sept. 1804.*

I did not write to you by Duncannon, my dearest mama, as my sister did. He is much better than when he came here but I think he still looks very ill and ought to take care of himself.

I have just received a long letter from Corisande, she seems in spirits and delights me by telling me that he behaves perfectly to her and she ends with " so we *will* be very happy after all."

My sister and the children are quite well ; she is going to ride which prevents her writing this morning. Little Georgiana is a perfect beauty, she is a mixture of Frederick Howard and G. Her complexion and intelligent countenance are wonderful in so young a child and she is to be as clever as she is pretty, for she takes more notice than *Miss Howard* already.

Mr. Marsh is still here. He has quite recovered his spirits and is delightful. W. Howard is a little more civilised, but Mr. Delmé, quiet, cautious Mr. Delmé, was obliged to own yesterday that " he was as rude as a bear."

The aunts are in high feather, *literally*, and if you were to see them come down to dinner, Lady Betty ghuirlandée comme une Flore, and Lady Julia looking like all Peru, you would, by the bye, be too good natured and kind to laugh at them as your wicked daughter does. But I really like them both, and am very grateful to them for their kindness to me.

Adieu, tout ce que j'aime, chère adorée maman, HARRY O.

To her Mother

CASTLE HOWARD, *September, 1804.*

MY DEAREST MAMA,

I have been very idle these 3 or 4 last days, but you are so kind and indulgent that I do not despair of your forgiveness.

Duncannon is already a great deal better. I cannot tell you how vexed I was at the paragraph in the newspapers, or how I wish it might be contradicted, but that of course must be entirely left to you. If it is not, as there are so many additional circumstances that seem to confirm it, it will be universally believed, and I am every day more anxious that it should not. I think it will be the greatest disadvantage to me if it is, as I will own to you that I feel more *uncertain* about my sentiments every hour. However I may decide I have the comfort of feeling sure that whoever (especially his own family) may be inclined to blame me, they must feel that it would be kinder of me to make *him* unhappy for a week or two, than for life, and as on ne voit plus mourir ainsi d'amour, and if one did, it would not be the Lord in question, I think at the end of the fortnight you would all rejoice, and him more than any of you, if he had common sense.

Do not, my own Mama, worry yourself by thinking about this. There is no hurry, and I promise while he stays here to make no alteration in my manner, and remember, though these are very towering Castles, they are at present only in the air.

To her Mother

CASTLE HOWARD, *September, 1804.*

Thank you, my dearest, dearest mama, for your very kind letter and for a few lines I received this morning. I hear of nothing but your good looks from Selina and Caroline. I am jealous of everybody that can be near you, and I mean when I return to lock you up for a week and not let anybody have access to you except myself.

We are all quite well and in the most perfect *peace* and harmony. Lord C. is in better spirits and better *humour* than he has been for some days, and of course so are we, for he is *par force* the mainspring of every smile and frown that *publickly* appear upon our faces. This, I think, the great inconvenience and fault of the system here. Il règne en despote ; his gloom or gaiety are not, as in other individuals, " en particulier," and one is, of course, almost always stifling a laugh or forcing one. His sons, at least William and Frederick, are at times perfectly mute, and conversation is *managed* too much to be agreeable or even easy. Charles Bagot once told me that he went to a dinner and found a most formal circle established round the room, from which the lady of the house advanced and said to him, " The subject is Lord George Gordon," which method of conversation is a little in the style of ours here, and, without being very impudent, I am almost the only person here who does not blush at the sound of my own voice.

The regularity I am now accustomed to (through the clock in the hall being put on five minutes) is announced to the whole family, as a journey into the Peak would be among *nous autres.*

I like them all though, People and Clocks, for they both do well when one's used to them.

To her Mother

CASTLE HOWARD, *Wednesday.*

I have again to ask your pardon, my beloved mama, for having been so very idle, and it shall be for the last time that for the same fault I will claim it.

We are going on here very well and happily. I am treated so kindly by everybody here and so affectionately by dearest Lord Morpeth and my sister, that I have no one regret, and have no wish ungratified (that of being away from you always excepted) I could reasonably indulge. And if you and one or two others could be transported here, I should be perfectly happy. The degree of form and over-precision that used to make this place more *tedious* than disagreeable, is entirely worn off. A book is no longer a miracle, and a chair out of its place is looked on with no more horror than when in it. G. may take at least a great share in this reform to herself, as you may recollect when first we came how different everything was. *They* are, too, all more "dégagés," as the dancing masters call it, and in short we are sometimes not only merry but noisy, and Pope [Joan] and Cribbage contribute not a little to both.

Lady Julia is quite a clock, and her regularity and rapidity are wonderful. Lord C. has very gloomy fits, mais au milieu de la tempête on peut entrevoir des beaux jours, during which he is pleasant and tells some funny stories—amongst others of a man whom nothing could put out of his way, or dérouter in the least. To try him one night Lord Somebody and a large party at a house in the country made him dead drunk, rubbed him all over with sirrup, rolled him in a feather bed and then hid themselves in his room to watch his recovery. When he woke he walked slowly up to the glass, and, upon beholding himself, quietly said—"A bird, by God," and went and sat down again. I tell you this because I nearly expired when I heard it and though it does not do as well par écrit, I like to fancy I see you laugh at the same things that I did.

Addio, adored Emma.

Yours ever most dutifully and affectionately, H. C.

To her Mother

CASTLE HOWARD, *October 8th, 1804.*

[*Beginning missing.*]

And now let me explain to you how I adore you. I never knew thoroughly what I felt for you till I left you. I cannot think of you, I cannot mention you, without crying like a fool, and when I think of the happiness of seeing your dear smile, of hearing your beloved voice, I am almost mad with joy.

I am sure you alone could inspire what I feel for you, it is enthusiasm and adoration, that for anybody else would be ridiculous, but that to deny it you would be unnatural.

I have you so present to my mind that it is almost painful, as I feel already as if I had been parted from you for years, and I think when once again I see you, hear you and feel you, I shall never be able to leave your side for a moment.

Adieu, my mama.

Your HARRY'O.

To her Mother

CASTLE HOWARD. *October 15th, 1804.*

MY DEAREST M.,

Your letter today was very short and a *little* obscure. Whose perfidy do you mean at Knaresboro', for I conclude you mean Knaresboro' tho' you do not mention it. I hope papa has enquired in to the whole affair, because, tho' there appears to be no danger to him, one can hardly believe that even Tommy Wynne would be such an idiot as to make the attempt without any possibility of success.

I believe Lord M. wrote to you about the *Houses* you mentioned and the Boxes for the theatres. I am very glad we keep the Covent Garden one, and get Mr. Ogilvie's at the Opera.

Pray tell us the Weymouth news when you hear it. Lord C. is very inquisitive for news always.

I am very glad Corise's affairs go on better. I hope she got my letter and knew that I wrote it before I received hers. You can have no doubt of Lord M's always being kind to her and little o. and wishing me to be so.

We have finished Cowper and have begun to read Charles the Vth. I am afraid Duncannon intends to go soon. We shall all be very sorry.

Addio, carissima madre.

yours ever and ever, H. CAVENDISH.

To her Mother

CASTLE HOWARD, *October, 1804.*

Your kind and indulgent affection, my beloved mama, leave no sorrow, no regret to your happy *Chimène*, but that of not being more deserving of them. You have made my situation with regard to Duncannon just what I wished it to be, and if *he* will now have the goodness to be *volage*, for the only time in his life perhaps when it will do himself and others no harm, all will go well. I do him the justice to believe that his faults proceed more from his head than his heart, and I am sure you will agree with me, that those of the latter are much the least easy to forgive. If Chimène chose to be candid, she would perhaps own that her caprices are not a few, but at the same time I think that the person who changes her mind is always condemned before the reasons for her doing it are even thought of. Whilst you meet every day with people who vary by the hour, and appear in that hour perhaps in two or three different characters, how can you be more steady in your opinion of them, than they are in justifying it. It would be like the Irishman who chose a weathercock for his sign post.

But that you should not for a moment suppose that I am defending the *thing*, whilst I think Caprice too general a word for the *twists* of opinion that I among others have every day, I think it much too slight a one for inconsistency in real friendships and attachments, and I hope I am guiltless of what I think a fault of the first magnitude. I am sure I do not know a person I think ill enough of to accuse of it.

In short, my dearest mama, if I have been ever unsteady in my friendships, it is because they were too hastily formed and too slightly cultivated to deserve the name; and if I have been supposed to change my *attachments*, it is because I never *really* had one. At the same time I blame and feel the necessity of moderating the enthusiasms and aversions of the moment, which often both ways appear greater than they really are.

It is a pity that in a world where one finds so little, one should expect so much, and I do not know whether it is the privilege or misfortune of youth to fill up the gaps of reality with such very bright imaginations as I often do.

It is very delightful to conjure up a spirit and imagine him a deity, but if, as you were giving the finishing stroke, you were to see a thin, rouged fop appear with a snuffbox in one hand and to hear him "talking like a waiting gentlewoman," the disappointments would overbalance the pleasure of the illusion.

You will ask me as the man in the Bath guide does Tabitha, "what is my drift?"—and as you must be tired of my prosing long before now, I will wish you good bye, my own mama, and you must accuse your own goodness and kindness to me.

To her Mother

CASTLE HOWARD. *1804.*

[*The beginning of this letter is missing.*]

I have heard much praise of the girl [Lady Elizabeth Villiers] since I have been here, and I believe whatever we may have heard to the contrary has been dictated by prejudice or policy. Do you know what part *dear* John Ponsonby takes? If he now protects Lady E. I shall think everybody else ought, for he was not inclined to do so, and I think would not, unless he had strong reasons for it.

Does my aunt blame me? I think she *ought not*, but conclude she *will*, but from the most amiable if not the most just motives; therefore far from resenting it, my only endeavour will be to soften whatever anger she may feel against me.

Though I am perfectly decided as to my own sentiments, whatever happens I neither wish them to be known or hope for his marrying Lady Elizabeth.

I think he might make some woman happy, but not Lady E. after all that has passed, and not Lady H. [herself] whatever might pass.

Perhaps it is a misfortune to have such very high ideas of perfection, especially as I always expect to find them realized, but it is also a safe guard and adds interest to every society, though often great disappointment.

Addio, dearest mama. Believe me ever yours most affecly. and dutifully Harriet Cavendish.

To her Mother

CASTLE HOWARD. *November 13th, 1804.*

MY DEAREST MAMA,

Happy and comfortable as I am here, I look forward every day with more pleasure to the happy moments when I shall be with you again. I hope we shall find you still at Chiswick, chiefly that you may be able to see more of the dear children; you will, I am sure, be quite enchanted with them. George is entertaining to a degree that I did not think it possible that a child could be, and Caroline is a petite originale, and very surly and comical.

We are all going to dance tonight as it is the Duchess of Rutland's birthday, and we really contrive to assemble if not a very brilliant, a very merry set. We had one a few nights ago and Mr. Marsh is indefatigable and dances comme si il n'y avoit pas une Caroline au monde, though I do him the justice to believe that he remembers her at other times, as every body who has once loved her, must. William condescends to perform here and Mr. Delmé's compact little steps cause a sensation that you can have no idea of, unless you were to see a Malton farmer and a Hoffingham milliner gazing at them.

Lady Julia dances away as she may have done some forty years ago, but unfortunately it is the only thing she does slow, and when a little of her usual velocity would not be amiss, she totally omits it.

What can have put Lady Jersey in good humour ? I hope Lady E's spirits are better.

Adieu, my adored M.

ever most affec^ly^ yours, and dutifully, HARRY O.

To her Mother

CASTLE HOWARD. *December, 1804.*

Thank you, my beloved M. for a letter and handkerchiefs I have just received. The latter are beautiful and I thank you for them in both our names.

You would be tired of the endless repitition if I was to tell you how constantly I wish to be with you.

Lord M. and my sister talk of departing from hence in less than a month, when I hope you will still be settled at Chiswick. I must be very different from what I am before I feel worthy of belonging to you, though if to love and admire you, not only as the most indulgent and adored of mothers, but as superior far to every other human being I ever met with, is to deserve it, you would scarcely find anybody that could as much.

Dearest mama, you do not, and cannot know half what I feel for you.

Duncannon goes tomorrow morning and talks of sleeping one night at Chiswick. I have had a letter from Hastings this morning and a dear message from Hart, to whom I am going to write immediately.

I have been reading a great deal of Italian, there are a thousand beauties in Metastasio that I had never observed and I had never read some of the best parts of it. "Isacco" is I think, almost more beautiful and affecting than any of them.

To her Mother

CASTLE HOWARD, *December, 1804.*

MY DEAREST MAMA,

We leave this place on Saturday, and if I could think of anything but happiness in going to you, I should leave with many regrets.

I feel an affection for Castle Howard that the happiness I have felt in it fully justifies. The very sorrow that I have for the first time experienced from being separated from you endears it to me, and it may sound paradoxical that your absence has consecrated this place in my memory more than the presence of any other being on earth could have done. I have thought of you more and, if possible, loved you better than ever, and in short one cannot feel what it is to be without you, before one can be worthy of being with you.

Lady Carlisle received the melancholy news of the death of the Duchess of Rutland's little girl this morning. I believe she has been for some time in a very hopeless state.

To her Mother

CASTLE HOWARD, *Wednesday, December, 1804.*

MY DEAREST MAMA,

We shall certainly be at Chiswick on Wednesday, but I am not sure whether late, or for dinner. The children will arrive with us. We have had snow today for the first time since we have been here and it is less cold, but very dismal and dark. I say this to account for my stupidity, which must be more melancholy to you than sleet and rain is to me. Lord C. is more influenced by weather than anybody I ever met with, and one can tell by looking out of the window before breakfast, what humour he will be in at dinner.

How are the O's going on? I had a long letter from Corisande in high spirits, and a great deal about him, "*tel qu'on dépeint les Dieux*"; it seems odd to me to find them going on so exactly the same as when

I left Chiswick. I should not mind if there was any distant chance of its not being just as odd some months or years hence.

Does Mr. Hill *spare* them, or is he more spluttering and satirical than ever? Corise says Lord Cowper is " maigre, triste, beau et un peu plus causant."

Have you heard any more of the Jerseys? I hear Lady Anne has been dangerously ill.

Adieu, my dearest mama.

ever yours most affct[ly] HARY-O.

George is incessantly talking of grandmama Duchess.

VIII

A YEAR OF MARRIAGES

1805

1805 started with a tragedy ; the Melbournes' eldest son, Peniston Lamb, died of consumption. Lord Melbourne was fonder of Peniston than of any of the other children, probably because " Pen " was the one child that he knew was his own. Though it was a terrible blow to the Melbournes, it was to change William Lamb's whole life, for now he was the eldest son and heir to the title. For some time he had been in love with Lady Bessborough's daughter, Caroline Ponsonby, but had hesitated to declare his affection for he had nothing to offer this delicate, brilliant creature. Now, however, he was free to woo her and he did so with the greatest tact and feeling.

There is a wonderful description in a letter of Lady Bessborough to Granville dated May the 8th, describing the engagement, when she announced to William at the Opera that Lord Bessborough had given his consent to the marriage. The scene must have been very comical, for on her telling William the good news, he flung his arms about her and kissed her. At that moment Mr. Canning and Mr. Hammond appeared and she was forced to tell them of the engagement for fear of William's demonstrativeness being misunderstood. On their return to Devonshire House, there was another scene, but a painful one this time, for on the news being made known, Hart, who was then fifteen, went into violent hysterics, " reproached Caro bitterly saying he looked upon her as his wife, that no plan of future happiness was separated from her, that she might think it hard to wait for him, but that he would have waited any time for her and had always been in hopes his Papa would let him marry her when he was 18—in short, it ended with his being so ill we were obliged to send for Farquhar." Poor Hart, who was cursed with deafness, blessed with charm and died unmarried.

Lady Caroline Lamb

Corisande de Gramont,
Wife of Charles, Viscount Ossulston,
afterwards 5th Earl of Tankerville

Caro and William were married on the 5th of June and Harriet gave her cousin a burnt topaz cross.

In May Emily Lamb married the "maigre, triste et beau," Lord Cowper.

Lady Bessborough must have had a very trying year for Duncannon continued to give trouble. The Duncannon-Villiers-Harriet affair is now further involved by Lady Maria Fane taking Lady Elizabeth's place and by the introduction of Lord Abercorn and Mrs. Payne upon the scene. We will let Lady Bessborough explain it to us herself. She writes to Lord Granville on the 26th February as follows: "Yesterday I dined and stayed the evening at my Sister's, which is quite an hospital; her son is ill and her daughter (to whom Lord Abercorn pretty near makes love) is also confined with a bad cold. It really is quite unpleasant and Lady Abercorn begins to dislike it. I think both my sister and Harriet wrong to suffer the kind of marked and familiar attention he shows her. It is a foolish story altogether and began with pique on all sides. Duncannon was angry with her and I believe merely to pique her, flirted very much with little Mrs. Payne who, being very coquetish, as well as very pretty, encouraged him till I am afraid he is now seriously in love with her. Lady Abercorn did not discourage the flirtation, because she was jealous of Mrs. P. and Lord A. who, extremely angry at Dun's attentions, after many remonstrances told Mrs. P. Dun should never be invited to his house again if she did not immediately cut him . . . She, indignant at this prohibition, told him she should go on exactly as she had done but that if Dun was banished on her account, she should think herself obliged to make him amends, which Lord Abercorn would have to answer for and that from the moment he ceased coming, she should also. Whether this threat, half joking and half earnest, frightened Lord Abercorn, I know not; he has suffered Dun to be invited as usual, but never speaks to him and immediately after this conversation, seeing Mrs. P. and Dun talking together, he began the most marked flirtation with Harriet and the same thing seems to have befallen him that did with Dun—beginning from anger and continuing from liking."

Lady Elizabeth Foster also commented on the Duncannon-Payne flirtation and then on September the 21st Lady Bessborough writes to Granville: "Duncannon has involved himself in a variety of scrapes

. . . I told you all his history with Mrs. Payne ; it had been going on violently till within this three weeks. A little before I left London I found out there was some coldness between them. . . . The year was almost come round again and the time approaching when Duncannon and Harriet, who have been quarrelling the whole twelvemonth through, were to decide whether they liked each other well enough to marry. Ca (the Duke) and my Sister, as well as Lord B., were anxious for it ; and to me, had they liked each other, it would have delighted me. . . . They seemed to like each other and my Sis told me H. owned to her she should like it, but he must promise to cure himself compleatly of flirting, for she could not bear it ; and, nommément, Mrs. P. and Lady Maria Fane must be given up. I asked him about the latter one ; he only laughed and said 'what nonsense !' He added that he liked his Cousin extremely, but was not over anxious to marry at present and above all would not bear rules to be prescribed to him '*by any woman living.*'"

The letter then goes on to say that she hears from her sister that Duncannon and Lady Maria are engaged and that she had received that very morning a "letter from him telling me he had proposed and was accepted by Lady M. F." and so on and so forth.

Duncannon and Lady Maria were married on November the 16th, 1805.

To top all this, Lady Elizabeth Foster writes to her son Augustus in April 1805 that "Your friend Lord *Aberdeen* braves the Duchess of Gordon" (whose daughter Lady Catherine Hamilton he subsequently married in July 1805) "and flirts with Harriet more than ever ! I admire his spirit, but I am sorry the papers have got hold of it and amiable and delightful as he is, he would not be a good match for her" (Harriet).

If further diversions were needed, there was always the infant prodigy "Roscius" acting at Drury Lane and what more could you want ?

Georgiana Morpeth came to London to lie-in of her fourth child, Frederick, who was born in June, so there are only two letters early in the year when Harriet was being, to use her own word, so "volage." She probably spent August and September at Castle Howard.

To Miss Trimmer

End of July 1805.

MY DEAREST SELINA,

I have indeed behaved most shabbily to you about writing, but as we have now, I hope and trust, entirely done with the odious dissipation that I am heartily tired of, I hope for my own sake, as well as that of my friends, that I shall not for the future give them so much cause of complaint against me.

Mama, though still suffering a great deal of constant and worrying pain, has been gradually amending for the last 3 days and Sir Walter and Phips give us hopes of her speedy recovery. She is in much better spirits about herself, though this complaint has been calculated in every way to make her low and uncomfortable.

My sister is much better and has been so all through her confinement than she ever was before. The child is terribly thin and she has 20 troubles about wet nurses as she is obliged to change the one she has at present and cannot find one that seems likely to suit her. Its nose distresses me very much as it is already nearly as prominent as Mounsieur de Sivarot's, but Newson consoled me last night by assuring me it is a "very respectable feature."

Caroline *Lamb* arrived in Town last night, amiable as possible and already most amazingly improved by being as gentle and posée as if she had been a matron in the country for 20 years instead of days. It is impossible to believe that she is a wife and it seems quite like a dream to have her here again in that capacity. He is not well and she frets about it, but I believe it is only cold and toothache.

I hope you have heard of Lord Aberdeen's marriage that you may not fancy my coldness or caprice as you call it, had any very desperate effect. It seems to be a very happy match and he looks almost blooming upon it. I hear Lady Catherine is very much attached to him and from Miss Humphries' account of her she will make a most excellent wife. Hart wrote word that he "pitied Tybald [Harriet's nick-name], indeed, for he supposed she was involved in a hopeless passion."

Mr. Lawley has left Town and I have nobody left to behave ill to, so that poor Mr. Foster bears the whole weight of my torments and he has not romance enough about him to "feel all this, yet think his sufferings sweet."

Adieu, my dearest Selina.

Yours, most affec[ly], HARRIET CAVENDISH.

To Miss Trimmer

DEVONSHIRE HOUSE, *Friday.*

I have seen very little of my tormentor, Lord Abercorn, and hope to see still less, for however I may *storm* at the time, I generally come round to your opinion at last. He is a dangerous friend and a most unprofitable acquaintance. I do not think in that light he would do one harm, but I am quite sure that he would never do one good.

The only reason I ever liked his conversation was that I thought him entertaining and, luckily, even that inducement to listen to him, wears off when you find it confined to one subject—himself.

To Lady Georgiana Morpeth

HOLYWELL, *Wednesday October 9th. 1805.*

I have so much to thank you for, so much to say to you, so much to ask you, that I scarcely know how to begin.

I went over to Brocket Hall on Saturday. Caroline Lamb looked very pale and ill in health, but pretty. I think her grown very fat, but not at all from her situation which, from her appearance, I should not have guessed excepting indeed from her moving about and walking, which she does with caution as if one quick step would be fatal. She was more gentle and amiable than I could ever have imagined her and she seems the happiest of human beings, without thinking it necessary to prove it. I saw William for a moment. He looked very ugly and was as cold to me as she was kind which, as I really do love her, and don't care a fig for him m'était à peu près égal. Lady Cowper was there. The first thing we were told was that she was very anxious as it was just barely possible that she might be going to be with child. They really do announce any events of that sort very soon in the Melbourne family ; but I hope this will prove true as she is very anxious about it.

Lord Cowper seldom appears in the course of the day. Caro told me Emily says she is so extravagantly fond of him that he sometimes appears a little cold to her, but that she supposes all men to be so and does not mind it in the least.

To Lady Georgiana Morpeth

HOLYWELL ? *October 1805.*

MY DEAREST SISTER,

I need not say anything about my sorrow at your having left us.

I *pine* for you as children and dogs do after their nurses and masters and I am sorry to say with no more power to struggle against it than either of these beings would exert. By the bye, your little Frederick has just been here, looking blooming. I love him dearly and now he is quite a personage. I hope he will bear his unexpected successes as well as Lady M. Fane does hers [her engagement to Duncannon]. Caroline Lamb tells me she has received a very pretty answer from her and seems much pleased with the match. She talks of your good looks and so does Lady Melbourne.

We are rather triste, past, present and future. I know nothing more of my grandmama's plans excepting that I have mama's leave to go to Lord Harcourt, if they will receive me. I have some scruples on that head as I suppose I should be one of the last persons they would ever dream of seeing at Nuneham and people of their age are not fond of such unexpected pleasures.

Mama is quite well again. Frederick will be the handsomest of you all; he begins to take a great deal of notice.

I wish you could see my fretful french face.

To Lady Georgiana Morpeth

October 10th. 1805.

[*Beginning missing.*]

. . . Saturday we set out by break of day to arrive at a 5 o'clock dinner at Nuneham as I have had a very kind *consent* from Lord Harcourt. Do you see me there?

I have forgot all this time to tell you how very much I like Lady Maria Fane. She came to Chiswick with Lady Villiers and her appearance and manners met with general approbation. She is certainly not a beauty but she has something so pleasing and feminine about her that nobody would think of regretting it. I hear the servants all thought her very pretty and Miss Keating [the Duchess' dresser] was in raptures about her elegance. Her manners must please—she was very shy, very kind and amiable to us all—to me she was perfectly so and said 2 or 3 little things that marked a wish to prove to me that there could never be, on either side, the least obstacle to our being very good friends. Duncannon was in high spirits and extremely attentive, too, and anxious about, her. Lady

Villiers abated much of her usual loquacity upon the occasion and she ought to know what a blessing it is when she does.

Miss Byron used to abuse Duncannon's looks to me rather, at least said she was surprised at his appearance as she had heard he was handsome. She used in her tiresome way to joke me to the last and say "it would certainly be—but what can make you ask—pray let me know."

I see you all and heartily wish myself listening to the little jokes, nodding over a book, playing to Lord C., in short, doing everything or anything to be but with you. The country dance seems to me right and is beautiful. It recalled many eventful hours; often and often have I dragged Lord Aberdeen down the middle to it and witnessed the "delectable look of suffering" with which he performed the footing. By the bye, where can my grandmother pick up the strangest, falsest piece of intelligence I ever heard? Yesterday, after a long pause she said to me, "So I hear Lord Abercorn liked you. Did you like him?" A minute after when I had denied that likely fact she asked me if I was not "desperately in love, a sighing and dying sort of passion, a concealed, sentimental affection for somebody?" I never was more astounded. I ventured to say, "I suppose you heard this from Lady Essex or some other Gossiping person in her set?" She said, No but that she had heard it *30* times from a great many different people; that it was a person for whose dear sake I refused *everybody* and several *eligible offers*. Can you conceive such a pack of falsehoods and nonsense? This must make me doubly careful of my conduct though I do not fear detection but misrepresentation, this is not calculated to raise my spirits in the way I described to you that they were depressed.

I shall probably write to you once more before Nuneham. When I am there, do you wish me to be descriptive about flower gardens and landscapes etc.?

Ever yours most affectionately and gratefully,

HARRIET CAVENDISH.

Have you heard that poor Captain Price has been taken up for attacking his landlord and beating him and breaking his windows? Nothing can be more interesting than the papers and things found in his room, all expressing the greatest misery. If he was to kill 20 landlords I should think him an angel still.

1000 kisses to the darlings.

To Lady Georgiana Morpeth

HOLYWELL, *Friday morning October 11th. 1805.*

We are just setting off, my dearest sister. If I have a moment's time I shall write to you tomorrow from Nuncham before I go to bed to give you a little Chiswick news and to tell you how I like my début. I am half frightened, now the time approaches so near, a little for fear I should not like them and a great deal for fear they should not like me.

I have had letters from Chiswick this morning. A friend of Captain Price's went to them yesterday and told them his story. He was sent to India without a suspicion of his insanity, rose quick to be a Captain, was his General's favourite, and esteemed as a most excellent officer, till one unlucky morning he chose to *shave* his horse in the presence of the whole army. When he returned to England he behaved very well till he was taken up for impersonating the Ghost we heard so much about last year in Hyde Park. Three months ago he was released from a private mad-house, where he is at this moment.

Corise writes in despair—"I must be obliged to shut myself up in my room for 3 days." She congratulates herself upon Duncannon's not being at Chiswick as she says it is a little more quiet without him. I do myself confess that if I had chosen throughout the year, there is not a moment I should have preferred for being away, though I suppose the Bessboroughs will live with us now. When does Lord Granville come? I ask it next because of Willy [Ponsonby; in Russia with G.L.G.]. I wish people would never announce themselves so long beforehand.

I play the country dance all day. I do not think it is quite right, but I do not know where it is wrong. Tell Mr. Delmé to show you my "H.C." as he performed it. It is on my favourite Tree in much the prettiest part of the whole wood. You do not say if Frederick Howard is with you. I am glad Lady Gertrude has banished the bows [drawing of little people bowing] it must enliven the whole place. What do you do with Lord Coleraine quite en famille? I wish he would marry Lady Julia—no, she is too good for him.

God bless you, much the dearest of people.

Ever yours, HARRYO.

To Lady Georgiana Morpeth

CHISWICK. *Monday morning October 21st. 1805.*

I was beginning to be extremely unhappy at not hearing from you, when I found your *little* letter and I am now only rather angry and very jealous of your children, though George was an angel for saying "Bo" at Lord Cranley.

We arrived here the day before yesterday, but I must go back to Nuneham, from which I wrote last. [*Letter missing.*] Mr. Vernon was with us the two last days and we both liked him very much, not only for himself, but because he put us so in mind of Lord Morpeth in his manners which are, if it is possible, as gentlemanlike and good as Lord M's. He went with us to Oxford, where we saw only inanimate beauties, of which I will give you no description, no more than I did to Lord Harcourt who expected me to come back like an old antiquarian.

We left Nuneham on Thursday for St. Leonard's Hill, a second edition of Harcourt's, which is the most delightful place I ever was at. General Harcourt is very gentlemanlike and Mrs. Harcourt seems the most kind-hearted, good-natured person that ever lived and to exist only for the happiness of everything about her. All form is entirely banished from this place as it is *cherished* at Nuneham and nothing can be more comfortable than the whole way of life. We found my dear Mr. John Talbot there who is quartered at Windsor and dined with us both days. In the evening we had musick, looked over Mrs. Harcourt's drawings, which are beautiful, and some excellent caricatures. Friday morning we all went to Windsor, walked all over it and breakfasted at the Barracks in Mr. Talbot's apartments, where we heard the Staffordshire band play. It is the second best in England and really beautiful.

We left St. Leonard's Hill for my part with great regret and found Chiswick swarming with Bessboroughs looking like a gala, uncles, aunts, Cousins, children and dogs. The Lambs are here, but go tomorrow. They seem very happy and, contrary to custom, at peace. She [Caro-William] looks very pale and thin. Lady B. is to dine today tête-à-tête with Lady Westmorland [Duncannon's future sister-in-law], which does not seem le comble de ses voeux. Lady Bessborough is in ill looks and worse spirits. I have heard nothing of Duncannon since I came, but I hear they go on in great harmony. They say Lady Maria watches and listens to Duncannon as if he was an oracle. I am so afraid of not being asked to the Priory that I do not know what to do. Do you think the " Oronooko " and " Faulkland " are great undertakings ?[1] How he will writhe !

To Lady Georgiana Morpeth

CHISWICK, *October 24, 1805.*

As a play is quite an event to me now, I must begin by telling you that we went to Covent Garden last night with Lady Bessborough to see " the Fair Penitent "[2] and " the Bravo." The only merit that the latter has is owing to Kemble, who has spared neither pains nor expense in the decorations. The Dialogue is flippant and tiresome and one's attention only kept up by claps of thunder and Pistols firing. My head aches so much from this that I can scarcely see to write.

You will be surprised to hear that Lord Aberdeen was in the next box as we all thought he was by the sea—he came from Twickenham. You will be still more surprised to hear that I now almost grant him all the perfections I once denied him, beauty not excepted. He is more improved than I could have believed it possible. The Abercorns have quite cured him of shyness and " embarras," which is as advantageous to his manners as to his person, and he no longer dresses his hair so—[Drawing of hair " en brosse "]. He must be very happy, for his countenance, voice and smile are all as animated as they were once dolcful and one can almost believe in the spirits Lord Brooke expatiated upon.

We met with the most perfect cordiality and are very good friends—he sat next me (in Lord Abercorn's box), as I had the Chaperone's place in ours, the whole night and took me out. He asked after you and when you are to return. They are to be asked to dinner here on Friday, which delights me, as I am tired to death of F. Foster's jokes and Mr. Vigoreux's buffoonery and want to hear something *Terse* from the Bravo, [Aberdeen's nick-name].

Duncannon sat by me at the play on the other side. Lady Maria is gone to Brighton and he follows today. Caroline and I were very much amused at his hating my talking to Lord Aberdeen more than

[1] The two plays chosen to be acted at Christmas.

[2] *The Fair Penitent*, by T. Rowe, published 1703, taken from the *Fatal Dowry*, by Massinger.

ever—(I was going to say "now that we are all married") and scolded me so for it that I was in terror all the time. I could have fancied myself a year back with much ease, but thank Heaven, no satisfaction.

The Lambs were at the play in Lady Holland's box, talking considerably louder than the actors. I wish I could transport myself to you at this moment—never would it give me more pleasure and comfort. My head is racking. God bless you ; Frederick is beautiful and Nurse Sherlock and I are intimate friends.

ever most affec[ly].

I have read my letter over—it is like a tragedy queen's—incoherent soliloquy.

To Lady Georgiana Morpeth

CHISWICK [*after October 25th*]. *1805.*

Thank you, my very dearest G., for your kind letter and for the beautiful lock of hair. I wish you would send me a small bit of George's and tell him it is for Aunt Harryo.

Papa is not quite well and I should not be surprised if, as soon as it is possible, we were to go to Town.

The play (do not tell Lord Morpeth) is, I own, a great inducement to me, as they are reviving all the good old plays and give one the chance of pleasant society.

William [Lamb] is to act Falkland, which we all think ill judged as Lord Aberdeen would have done it 1000 times better and from his manner to me the other night, gave me the idea of being hurt at its being thought of for Mr. Lamb and I think will be much more so at its being accepted by him. Falkland ought also to be the most gentlemanlike of gentlemen, ainsi jugez !

Corise is low about her little fatuosity and God knows it is no private calamity and I condole with her from my heart, and when she talks of constancy through years of delay, I am nearly in Hysterics. If they were more interesting, more in love, taller even, it would be more supportable, but to see their little forms from night to night—Dio mio !

God bless you, my beloved sister. My love to Lord M. and the darlings. Frederick grows more beautiful every hour.

Ever yours most affec[ly], H. CAVENDISH.

To Lady Georgiana Morpeth

CHISWICK. *1805.*

[*Beginning missing.*]

Corise is, as she always is during the absence of le cher Charles, paler and more ghastly than anything I ever saw before. I wish she would wear rouge merely to keep up my spirits, for her sepulchral appearance depresses me strangely ; she writes to him all day and he is as exact a correspondant.

This is all certainly very good and lucky but I am not sure what it is that makes it so extremely ridiculous.

Mr. Ellis has not been here since you left and thank Heaven, not his ugly uncle or whatever he is.

Lord Aberdeen's—servant only, was seen somewhere near here yesterday. I wish they would come here again.

God bless you, dearest G., your little boy is grown beautiful and laughs and begins to take notice. I am afraid Mrs. Sherlock is dull, for she wanders about in the most doleful manner. I see Maby courtesying about in her green gown sometimes but how I miss dear Nurse Pin and 3 angels.

To Lady Georgiana Morpeth

[*October 26–28 ?*] *1805.*

I have no more news to *agitate* you with, my dearest sister. I have not seen the Bravo's Bride [Lady Aberdeen] since she became so and himself only that one night at the play. Mama promises continually to ask them to dinner, but as often puts it off. Caroline and I go to Covent Garden on Thursday. If they are there, I will certainly deliver your message and tell you what I think about them.

I went to see "Jane Shore" since I wrote to you last with Lady Bessborough and Caroline Lamb. Mr. Adderley was the only man in our box and he was any where but with the company in it. He looked very ill, very wild and seems in short, more fit for a private mad-house than a Theatre.

Caroline was very gentle and amiable to me but in the beau milieu of a violent quarrel with her husband. They had disagreed in the morning whether Betsey (her maid) should go to the Priory in an open or shut carriage and so violent was the contest that he went out upon business and sent word he should not come home till late in the evening. Upon this, she came and dined with us; covered herself with all my aunt's Trinkets; rouged herself up to the eyes, sent home her wedding ring and went with us to the play. She cooled a little there and I set her down at Whitehall, half indignant and half frightened, but begging me not to communicate these details—which I should not do if, with their usual consistency, both herself and my aunt had not made it known even to Our servants, through Mrs. Peterson [the Bessboroughs' housekeeper]. I hear it is all made up now and they are gone to the Priory.

Abellino [Aberdeen] they say, took a sudden alarm 3 or 4 days ago and said he would not act till he had seen William [Lamb], who is consequently to undertake Falkland. We tell Caro she will die of jealousy of Julia.

I do not wonder at your feeling much interest about the dear Duncannons at Brighton. One hears much more of their furniture than of their love, of their home than of themselves and it is all so comfortable, proper and uninteresting that until you reminded me of them, they had nearly escaped my memory. I do hear every now and then—"Well, Duncannon has fixed upon a Cook." "Poor fellow, he could not afford to buy the salt sellers [*sic*]." "Lady Maria says she will give up the curtains being blue if he prefers green!" For love is still the Lord of all!

You delight me by telling me that mama praises me, and above all that she does not feel as much regret as Frederick Foster does, at my not having met with the *person*. He has just been telling me that he is in utter despair—"Why am not I like the dear old girl in the north?" to whose darling Mice he begs to be remembered. I am afraid they have quite forgotten me.

I am miserable at the prospect of your not returning so soon. I shall be quite jealous if Lord A. talks to you more than to me, now that he has done being a match.

To Lady Georgiana Morpeth

CHISWICK. *Monday morning* [*November 4th, or 11th*]. *1805.*

Dearest and kindest of all people, do not talk to me about the witty darlings as it makes me long too much to be with you all.

Caroline Lamb is still at the Priory, quite recovered but not yet able to leave her couch. As Lord Abercorn's edict is, "no pain to be felt at *My* house," it was unlucky her being obliged to prove its inutility, but I hear they were all very kind to her, and William being necessary as their chief actor, will receive their continued indulgence.

They talk now of acting Miss Baillie's "Count Basil"; William Lamb to be Basil; Lord Aberdeen Rosenberg and Lady Cahir Victoria, but vide Lady Bessborough, so do not spread the news.

I hear Duncannon is to be married about Wednesday week and that it is to be very private.

I am afraid that Ratisbon was a trap for interest with a dearly beloved of mine, but I fear the failing to excite it will be of no avail and we shall have his nasty headaches and the old aunt in Shropshire all next year.

Mama has desired me to join her in the garden, so I must have done—I will write tomorrow. Pray continue to write. Pray remember me to all, but especially to my dear Mr. Howard. Frederick and Mrs. Sherlock grow fatter and more prosperous every day.

To Lady Georgiana Morpeth

[*Trafalgar was fought and Nelson killed on Oct. 21st* 1805.]

CHISWICK. *November 6th. 1805.*

MY DEAREST SISTER,

The last letter I received from you was a violent complaint against us all for not telling you of mama's illness.

I trusted to the rest of them, which is always my plan and always a foolish one and she was well before I had time to repent.

I conclude, however, that I am safe in supposing you have heard all the details of the great events that have roused even me from my usual apathy upon those subjects. Poor Lord Nelson. The universal gloom that I hear of from those who have been in Town, is the strongest proof of the regret he so justly deserved to occasion, as otherwise I suppose such a victory at such a moment is every thing, both for our honour and safety and would have driven us half wild.

I wish to heaven something would take us, as we have the enemy's fleet and put us out of our dawdling element for a short time.

Lady Villiers was here the other morning and nearly lost as she returned to Osterley from the thickness of the fog. She was remarkably amiable from being more silent than usual. I hear Lady Boringdon is with child. Lady V. burst into tears when she heard it and coloured like fire when mama asked her about it. I hope this is not proof of what Lady Westmorland told you, but only regret, that in her situation is very nearly allowable.

The Jersey family are all in Town, furious at Mr. Wyndham's riding about in the lightest and gayest colours he can find. They seem to think that Lady Ann [Wyndham, née Villiers] has become the model of a patient, resigned wife and when I think of that injured excellence in her blue Landau, I am tempted to send him a pink coat with orange buttons.

Mrs. Sherlock is all this time bidding Frederick wonder why aunt won't look and such sort of hints, so I must stop to shout and crow.

George's hair has been in constant contemplation from one or the other of the family ever since it came. What did you mean by refusing it at first? It is *redundant.*

Corise and Lord O. go on famously for them. He is always here, very sulky, but she says "Il m'aime trop," as cold as an icicle, but she says, "Sais tu, ma chêre, je n'aime pas ces charactères fougeux," longer but less every day, but she says, "Vraiment il grandit et embellit tous les jours."

The God of Love a bandeau wears and when . . . !

God bless you dearest of G's. I beseech you to write or I cannot go on making mountains of mice.

To Lady Georgiana Morpeth

CHISWICK. *Sunday morning November 10th. 1805.*

Duncannon is to be married on Saturday sans faute. Lady Bessborough was with me near 3 hours last night. I do not think she seems to like the marriage much ; at least she talks of it en victime, praises her in rather a languid way, says she thinks her very ugly (which is, I think, both ill-judged and ill-natured), and hopes he will be happy and constant, with shrugs and reveries. Then says with a sigh, it is fortunate that from mixing in so new a set, he will be very little in our family. If she fancies this to be gratifying to me, which by her manner I suspect, she pays no great compliment either to my head or heart and only gives fresh proofs of how very little she knows of Duncannon. She complains indeed of his want of confidence in her, but I think she has done enough to justify it. (I must quote Lady E. Monck, "God bless you, don't tell.")

Lady B. has just been at the Priory of which, allowing a little for her usual exaggeration, she gave me very entertaining accounts. She went there intending to sleep, but was so coldly received by Lord Abercorn that she returned to London at 12 o'clock, which I think was perfectly right. He is more despotic and dictatorial than ever, has absolutely forbid politics being mentioned and seems willing to impose the same fetters upon the understandings of his guests that he does upon their actions. Lady Abercorn is dreadfully low, says that life is not worth living and wishes hers was at an end.

My aunt says there never was anything so conjugal as all the rest of the party. That she found Caroline and William reading out of the same book, sitting on one chair; Lord and Lady Aberdeen on another, also reading in the same manner, or playing at Spillikens, with their arms round one another's necks—this is her account remember—Lord and Lady Hinchinbroke sitting on the couch very civil and simpering; Mr. and Mrs. Hooley and Mr. and Mrs. Huddlestone finished the group.

Caroline Lamb is, in fact, going on well but Croft says she must not be moved for 6 weeks, therefore she is to remain there till after the play at Christmas. They are all extremely kind to her and Lady Maria, whom my aunt says it is quite melancholy to see, adores her and sits watching her for hours, but says it is quite impossible she should ever have a child, that it will be a little thing with wings that will fly away as soon as it is born and nobody be able to catch it.[1] I think it is a very good idea.

The Aberdeens are happier and more in love with each other than ever married couple were. William and him are inseparable. Lady B. says Lady Aberdeen is always beautiful but looks very ill for her. She calls him *boy*. Lady Hinchinbroke is gravida again. Lady Aberdeen is not. Lord Aberdeen is to act Falkland so you may go back to your first reading. So much for the Priory.

To Lady Georgiana Morpeth

CHISWICK, *Saturday November 16th. 1805.*

Lady Harriet Cavendish is not so easily appeased—but 1 little scrap did I receive all last week and that full of reproaches, though I had written you volumes almost every day.

[1] Which was sadly prophetic, as the baby died at its birth in January 1806.

I never was angry with you yet, for about 5 minutes, but I do really think you a little unreasonable and very idle about writing. (This I have learnt from my aunt George [Lady George Cavendish], who sent me a scold last week beginning " I do think, dear niece . . .")

I am sorry to say all my interest for Lord Aberdeen is vanished since I have heard that he is a good husband, an amiable member of society and sits in one chair with his chère moitié. He must look hideous " en groupe."

I believe we are going to the Priory for one night. Pray send me word how to behave. I am like an old person who meets in her latter days with those who formed the little histories of her youth and does not know what she is to seem to remember and what to forget.

Fred is quite well ; give my love to 3 angels.

Duncannon is to be married this evening and the Bessboroughs come to us tomorrow.

Alas, dear G. (I forgot I ought to be glad) we are settled here for ever. Papa, I am sorry to say, has the gout and has determined to be confined here. He sent yesterday for all the apparatus of flannel shoes etc.

Adieu, my dearest G. I cannot write more as the post is just going.

To Lady Georgiana Morpeth

CHISWICK, *November 17th. 1805.*

Papa has the gout settled in his knee and he says it is the most painful fit he ever had. He is confined to his roon and of course we are all very triste and uncomfortable. Mama stays almost entirely with him.

The Bessboroughs came here last night. They say the wedding went off very well. Duncannon was the most nervous of the 2 but the rest of the party so very much comme à l'ordinaire, that they were soon quite calm. . . . *Lady Duncannon* seemed more affected at parting with her governess than with anything else and when she saw her, threw her arms round her neck and cried very much. She had told mama the day before that having lost her mother and seeing nothing of her father, she had already experienced more kindness from Duncannon's family than from anybody else, so I am afraid your crazy friend gives up a little too much of her time to Theories and Discussions.

My aunt was obliged to put her nerves entirely out of the question and if Lord Bessborough has any, they did not make their appearance.

I gave up my ci-devant true love without a sigh and even Mr. Foster congratulates me upon my wonderful command over my feelings.

Lady D. sent me some beautiful bracelet clasps and rings to Corise and Car. with magnificent favours which you will, of course, already have seen.

I tremble to think what my letters must inevitably be for the next month ; we expect nobody but Lord O.

[*End of letter missing.*]

To Lady Georgiana Morpeth

CHISWICK, *Friday morning November 22nd. 1805.*

Is Lord Aberdeen's conjugality all conducted in Pantomime then ? I no longer wonder at its being so striking to all observers. I can fancy him chattering more easily than attitudinizing.

Mama went to see Lady Duncannon yesterday and was quite delighted with her ; she says nothing can be more perfect than her manner or more amiable than her whole behaviour. He has had a fall from his horse that might have been very bad as it was on his head, but I hear he is not at all the worse for it.

Caroline and I mean to walk there [Roehampton] tomorrow or Sunday and next week they come to establish themselves here.

In the morning I read by myself for two hours, and this though not a large portion of time to devote to reading, if persevered in will lighten at least—if it cannot remove—the heavy burthen of ignorance that on many subjects I often feel.

Caroline and I take very long walks and find out very pretty ones, when we have courage to go far enough for them.

Lady Westmorland and Lady Villiers came here the other morning. The former is thinner than I imagined it possible to be as I fancied bone by itself would have looked more substantial. Her face looked pretty well, but that constant fever and irritation of spirits must destroy any health and the worry she puts herself into to decide difficulties of her own starting is enough to make two people ill, without complaint.

She made Lady Bessborough almost as wild as herself by tormenting her to know (and she set about it the moment she arrived !) which she had rather have ; a beautiful child who was very unhappy or a deformed one who was in a state of perfect health and my poor aunt had no sooner taken breath than she again flew at her to insist upon her deciding upon a hideous lover, very much attached, or a delightful one extremely volage. You may judge whether poor Lady Bessborough did not lament at that moment one consequence of Duncannon's marriage.

Lady Villiers was just then detailing the pantry, scullion-room, out-houses etc., of her sister's new house, so did not join in the debate.

I believe we shall not go to the Priory. Caroline and I go to the play tomorrow with my aunt to see the new prodigy, Miss Mudie ; it must be an invention of Kemble's to throw ridicule on Roscius but God bless him for anything that sends us to the play tomorrow, though upon second thoughts cela m'est a b s o l u m e n t é g a l.

Adieu, dearest and best and kindest. Give darling George a message that I love him, kiss him and I will send him a tiny Toy in a letter the first day I go to London.

To Lady Georgiana Morpeth

CHISWICK. *Monday evening November 25th. 1805.*

The Play was not all that I expected. Miss Mudie was ridiculous and disgusting and if she is 9, which from her extreme *littleness* I suppose she is, it is melancholy to see how much conceit and impudence (with no talent to justify it) can be attained at that early age.

We were left undisturbed to make these moral reflexions and we saw nobody but Frederick Byng and Lady Holland. Lord Holland was laid up with the gout. She was in high spirits and beauty and rather entertaining, but too much in her way, which you must call to mind, for I do not know how to describe it. She was furious with Kemble for bringing out this little lady, but more so when he addressed the Audience he only said " Gentlemen." I am sure you can hear her saying—" Where are the ladies ? "

We went to Roehampton yesterday, my first visit [since the Duncannons' marriage]. I shall not easily find words to tell you how much I approve of our new cousin in her new situation, unless indeed that yours excepted, I never saw any manners that pleased me so much. She has all Lady Villiers' *self-possession* with a gentleness and modesty that I never saw equalled. Perhaps this praise is not quite disinterested, as I confess I am extremely delighted with her great kindness to me. She was just come in from a long walk when we arrived, had a great deal of colour and really looked excessively pretty. Her figure, from being better dressed than when we saw her before, certainly deserves Philips' encomiums and, in short, she seems to me, as far as 3 interviews justify my decision, a most delightful person. They seem as comfortably established as if they had been married a year instead of a week; nothing can be more attentive and good than his manner to her. But I shall be able to judge more of them both in a few days, as they come here Wednesday or Thursday. She seems anxious to see a good deal of us and much pleased with the thoughts of coming. I saw a very pretty seal he had given her; a gold dog and the stone a ruby with "Fidate" written on it. I was delighted at this as it proves his anxiety to give her reason to trust him and I hope this marriage will make him as much better as I trust it will make him happier.

Have you heard of the Woburn Plays? The Duke, Major Sturgeon; Lady Holland said to me, "The Duchess in performing Mrs. Brudgrudding will scarcely depart from her own character." If you remember the landlady of the Red Cow in John Bull, you may judge of the severity of this speech.

Papa's gout is still very bad. They seem to think he will go to Town the first moment he is able.

Lady Elizabeth is still in despair for Lord Nelson and really her private affectation is enough to destroy the effect of a whole nation's public feelings, for she has so much grimace about her grief that one can hardly prevent one's disgust of her operating upon one's pity for him. She sobs and she sighs and she grunts and she groans and she is dressed in black cockades, with his name embroidered on every drapery she wears. She is all day displaying franks to Captains and Admirals and heaven knows what—and whilst she is regretting that she could not "have died in his defence," her peevish hearers almost wish she had.

God bless you, my dearest sister. It is near 2 and as I walked above six miles this morning as hard as I could go, I hope you will excuse my being very sleepy.

To Lady Georgiana Morpeth

CHISWICK. *No date.*

And what is the great difference in point of variety, that you are graciously pleased to compliment me upon for the last week, unless whether I eat meat or fish for dinner, or walked in the village or the garden with the agitating transition of the Baron de Rolle to Mr. Vigoreux and back again? I do not know that the days have had one inch of difference; you know it is *this that makes me dislike Chiswick.* (I feel getting in to a passion) and yet you talk to me as if writing with such a wonderful fund of inexhaustible variety, was a pleasant *and easy task.*

Lord Ossulston is returned, in one of his sulky fits, but she is satisfied with his being tired and low, so it don't signify.

I hear Lord Granville returns in a month.

Ever most affectionately yours, HARRIET CAVENDISH.

To Lady Georgiana Morpeth

CHISWICK, *Dec. 1805.*

The play at the Priory is to be tomorrow and we are this morning to leave Chiswick for good. I am more miserable than the occasion justifies but it is really a sorrow to begin London with the Cowpers, Melbournes, Macdonalds and Frederic Byng—which I hear is the sum total of our acquaintances in it.

Roscius acted better than ever and was received with great favour—Henry Bennet was the only person I saw in the box. The Duchess of Bedford was in hers, with Johnny looking so like a writing master that I had no patience to see him. She looked very cross and grand—Lady Holland must have Mrs. Sneak. I have heard of no Priory play-bills but as far as I can recollect—Falkland—Lord Aberdeen; Capt. Absolute—William; Sir Anthony—Mr. Jack Maddocks; Acres—George; Sir Francis—Lawrence; Mrs. Malaprop—Lady C. Lindsay; Julia—Mrs. Hesseltine; Lydia—Lady Cahir; Lucy—Miss Butler.

In George's Opera [1]—which is most uncommonly good—Tom Sheridan and Mrs. Hesseltine are the Hero and Heroine, for the sake of their singing, as they are undoubtedly the worst performers.

[1] "Who's the Dupe?" by George Lamb.

William, the Captain of Banditti (reckoned very fine but I think too violent and ranting); George and Miss Butler, Andrew and Phyllida—she very much in love with him, and Mr. Maddocks one of the principal ruffians, but I shall write you volumes on Wednesday.

[*End of letter is missing.*]

To Lady Georgiana Morpeth

No date.

Lord Henry Petty dined and slept here last night. He is in very good spirits, "comme si il n'y avoit point de Maria au monde," very amiable and, of course, sensible to an alarming degree.

He is at this moment in raptures with Lord M's verses; repeating different lines over in transports—he says he cannot imagine any thing better—uncommon fine—(I shall never keep pace)—the last line finer than anything he ever heard.

He winds it all up with this eulogium—he never knew anybody who had such excellent parts with so much good sense to direct them, such good abilities or so clear a judgement. Do not you hear it all winding up, reaching the highest tone and then rushing down, fine by degrees and beautifully less?

[*End of letter is missing.*]

To Lady Georgiana Morpeth

DEVONSHIRE HOUSE. *Thursday December 18th. 1805.*

Mama desires me to write to you, my dearest sister, to tell you there is no news; that she is impatient for you to fix the day of your departure from Castle Howard and that she would have written to you herself if her eyes had not been very weak from a cold caught at the Priory the other day.

I have no intelligence of any sort to communicate to you as I did not go with mama to Lord Abercorn's and have not stirred out of the house, or seen a soul in it, since I last wrote.

The next Priory is tonight, but we go on Saturday I believe to sleep there. I am a little tired of it—I dare not say *very* as you will have judged by my having avoided the last representation.

They are all going to see Roscius in Macbeth tonight. I am lazy and sick of acting, so stay at home.

I should tremble at the prospect of London till August if I was not sure that your arrival will thaw me.

I am sorry your *paquet* is conspicuous, though I rather admire it. I met 5 children at Lady Garlies's today, to comfort you and I dare say she has quantities, for these were quite old people.

Lady Cunningham is in Town. I saw her one night at the play, looking dreadfully out of spirits and very ill.

Tell my George I wish him a merry Christmas and that I mean to kiss him much too hard when I see him. Nurse Sherlock lives upon the hope of your raptures at the improvement of your boy, and she deserves to be gratified, for he is at times a beautiful creature and her attention and care of him has been unwearied. She is almost as impatient of your return as I am and as angry at Mrs. Gibson's silence upon the subject as I am at yours.

Caroline and I had entirely relaxed from our system when first we arrived in Town, but we have begun again our three first rate virtues—reading, walking and fasting, with redoubled vigilance—she is grown considerably thinner but it agrees so well with me that I believe that I am fatter than ever. Christmas dishes for luck, have occasioned great excuses, and mince pies are quite fatal.

Lady Bessborough came to Town yesterday; she is in a terrible state of lowness and sent Lord B. to say she had so bad a cold in her eyes as not to be able to stir from her room.

They prepared for her being very unhappy tonight and "poor Willy" is proxy for all the public and private grievances of Russia. Mama is unwell and of course in a very unpleasant, anxious situation, but she has little command over her feelings—and has a most unfortunate knack at making everything into a scene.

God bless you, my dearest sister,

Believe me most affec^ly^ yours, HARRIET.

I beg you to write and do give civil messages for me to the heads of the family.

[At this time the Duchess was more than usually desperate about her huge debts and her health was very bad.]

To Lady Georgiana Morpeth

DEVONSHIRE HOUSE. *Dec. 1805.*

The play was very fatiguing but very entertaining and the acting excellent. George's play went off perfectly and William is reckoned an excellent actor. He is too much occupied with his beauty and expression of countenance and makes crooked smiles to the audience, when he ought to be attending to his companions. He is also rather tame as a lover and looks much alarmed as Caroline sits and watches him and would probably go into fits if an expression or look of well acted tenderness was to escape him.

Tom Sheridan looked very handsome with rouge and sang well, but his tragedy is too comic to be very unlike buffoonery. George, incomparable and must have enjoyed the double satisfaction of the roars of laughter that his good jokes and good acting excited. Mrs. Hesseltine and Miss Butler both looked and acted well. The " Bravo " looked hideous as a ruffian. In the farce, which was " Cross Purposes," he was rouged, which made his face look worse than ever in my opinion, but mama was in raptures. His acting is slow and sure, but otherwise has no merit and Falkland will be a melancholy business. Tom Sheridan as an old man and Lady Charlotte Lindsay as his sposa were excellent. The audience was chiefly composed of Stanmorians and Harrow youths.

The Rumbolds and Lady Glenbervie were very conspicuous. Lady Charlemont looking so ill that I should scarcely have believed her the same person I used to admire so. She sent many insipid messages to you, is more Irish than ever and says she is going *to Christmas* at the Priory. Lady Cahir is grown absolutely ugly and very disagreeable. Lady Aberdeen looked ill and was very cold to us.[1]

Believe me most affec[ly] yours, H. CAVENDISH.

To Lady Georgiana Morpeth

DEVONSHIRE HOUSE, *December 1805.*

[*Beginning of letter missing.*]

I saw the Duncannons yesterday, in a broad grin—they are the gayest of the gay—and walk about the room arm in arm, with their mouths open from ear to ear, in the style of the Clonmells.

They are both ill with colds and both very fanciful about themselves ; she thinks him the greatest wit in the Kingdom and he thinks her the greatest beauty.

[1] Because of Haryo's flirtation with Lord Aberdeen.

She really is a most engaging little person and is so unaffected and sweet tempered that I should think it impossible to live with her without loving her.

God bless you, ever yours most affec[ly].

God bless you ; we dine early as I am going to see Gustavus Vasa. The Hollands are all to be there. Remember me to everybody ; my love to dear Mr. Howard or if that is wrong, my respects.

To Lady Georgiana Morpeth

DEVONSHIRE HOUSE, *Friday morning December 1805.*

I do not know why I write to you today, for you might as well hear from one of the patients in St. George's Hospital, but I believe it is to excite your pity and prove to you how particularly acceptable your letters will be.

Corise has been in bed for some days with this odious influenza. Caroline can hardly speak with a wretched cold. Mama has a little inflammation in her eye and I have got a sore throat. We are all very much out of temper but I am in a continual fury.

I wish you would come in a hurry, for if you do not, the snow will stop you.

We expect my grandmama in a few days. I believe she is coming to settle in Town. My aunt is confined to her room ; mama went to her last night. I hear there are very long letters from Willy [Ponsonby] in Russia but only 3 lines from Lord Granville—but mama will give you details of course.

The Lambs stay at the Priory till Friday and then go to Brocket, instead of coming here as they were to have done.

The Duncannons are like dormice, so quiet and comfortably settled for the winter. I have not seen them for ages and I fancy they never stir from the library at Roehampton. Lord Bessborough, on the contrary, is become a most active member of society and he is by far the gayest beau we have amongst us at present.

Lady Cowper is in Town still. I went to see her the other morning ; she looked very pretty and interesting and in good spirits. He is never with her and affects the greatest indifference and neglect, though I believe he really cares for her as much as he can for anything and she seems tolerably contented, though I hear she is reduced to rejoice when he comes home drunk, as he talks more to her then than at any other time. Mr. Luttrell, who is his inseparable companion, talks in raptures of her and says it is impossible to know and not adore her.

Lady Cowper says all the stories about Lord Henry Petty's admiration of her were put about by Lady Holland, to make people believe he does not care for Lady Maria ; that woman is certainly a blessing to her friends. I shall be very sorry if she succeeds in diverting Lord Henry's thoughts from Lady Maria. I think her a very delightful person. I do not mean in manner, but all I have heard of her, gives me a very high opinion of her heart and understanding and her very great melancholy and yet strength of mind in getting over all foolish display of it, make her very interesting.

God bless you, dearest sister,

Most affec[ly] yours, H. CAVENDISH.

To Lady Georgiana Morpeth

[*End of December*] *1805.*

MY DEAREST G.,

Mama desires me to tell you that she had just finished her letter to Lord Morpeth when his arrived and is now so hurried that she had not time to tell him how very sorry we all are for poor Mr. Marsh's affliction.

Lady Duncannon was here on Sunday to dinner, she is as gentle, good, proper and amiable as mortal thing can be but Caroline and I tremble that she is a little insipid—at least we sat in a select groupe all night and were so bored and put to it for conversation that I thought we must have cried. She looked ill ; her figure is very pretty but her face was paler and more squinney than any thing I ever saw. She watches him incessantly, obeys him implicitly and they sit hand in hand. She is a grande rieuse and ready to die of his wit. I, who never much admired it, out of égards for her, expired in chorus, which seemed to surprise him full as much as it did me. He is more of a baby and a tyrant than ever and having a sweet smile—the two things she thinks irresistible—she boasts of her " good men " at the opera but, as we agreed the other day, her love of the world is perfectly harmless and she is really and sincerely attached to her husband.

God bless you, own dearest sister,

Ever yours, H. C.

What can have possest me! I have cut a wise tooth! Don't be agitated, my dear G., it was attended with no pain and indeed not even a consciousness of this event till this morning. Do not be hurt with me or suspect me of want of confidence; my gum rises a little on the left side of sapiente; if anything it has moved my chin a little more to the right; my upper jaw remains in the same place; the under one projects about a quarter of an inch more, but nothing to signify. But you will be able to judge better than I can of all these little niceties.

I am very sorry to have got another, but man was made to mourn!

To Lady Georgiana Morpeth

December 29th. 1805.

I am so very much tired that it is one of the greatest exertions I ever made to write this letter, but you will be glad to hear that "The Rivals" was acted even to satisfy Mr. Sheridan who was forced to laugh at all his own jokes and applaud all his own sentiments. Lord Aberdeen was what the newspapers term respectable. The opinions were very divided; he looked ugly and awkward, his action is very bad and his countenance even at that moment of receiving Julia's pardon, deplorable and embarrassed; but his voice is clear and distinct and he certainly acted with a great deal of feeling and a perfectly just conception of his part. In short, all that one heard was good and all one saw bad.

Mrs. Hesseltine was an excellent Julia and looked pretty with rouge; Lady Cahir was not near so good as I expected. She looked old and absent and has not a look of nature about her. William [Lamb] I thought excellent, so perfectly natural but still his two great faults, one that he can't help and the other that he can, are the most ungraceful carriage and action I ever beheld and too much *sympathy* with the audience.

But now for the wonders. Mr. Maddocks Sir Anthony; George [Lamb] Mr. Acres and Lawrence Sir Lucius, were better than any actors I ever saw on the stage and Mr. Sheridan said Lawrence was the first person who had represented Sir Lucius as he had intended him to be. Mrs. Malaprop was very good though she might have been better.

For the audience, Lord and Lady Abercorn are like Turtle Doves and she in tearing spirits. Lady Aberdeen looked ill in health, but of course classically pretty, but she is grown more cross and grave than any person ever was. It is not only our remark, but everybody at the Priory. I hear they are as conjugal as ever, she never leaves him an instant and follows him behind the scenes. Lady Charlemont looks ill but beautiful and Lord C. and I are dear Friends, as we compare notes about Lord Abercorn, who is in a quarrel with him.

Lady Villiers looked so very ill that it was quite melancholy to see her. She is quite a skeleton, pale as death and seems dreadfully out of spirits. Lady Harriet was with her with the Jersey complexion and arrived comme une bombe, looking beautiful. She is very amiable. Lady Aberdeen sat by Lady Jersey at the table where I was. They seemed great friends, but she talked very little and seemed so very melancholy, it made me quite unhappy. I think it must be sorrow not to be with child, and I do pity her from my heart.

God bless you, the only person I love, the only person I wish to see and the only contrepoison to the misery with which I look forward to the little suppers that begin tomorrow with Lord Cowper and James Macdonald. God bless you.

Is it the map of Europe I see before me? Dear G., all George's hopes of geography are on my dressing table. Oh! careless maid! I will mend it myself this instant. [George had "dissected" maps, like modern jig-saws.]

To Lady Georgiana Morpeth

[*End of December*] *1805*.

MY DEAREST SISTER,

We had quite a great dinner here yesterday; Bessboroughs, Lambs, Ossulstons, Mr. Motteux, Mr. James, Mr. Delmé and Sir Walter. Caroline Lamb was very amiable but looked extremely ill. She worries herself to death about a pain in her chest, which she will fancy very alarming, though everybody she consults (which is in other words, every soul she sees) assure her that it is nothing but a muscular pain in her back and that her fears are all fancies. William was very grave and disagreeable. Lamb, I mean—for William Ponsonby is in every way as much improved as possible.

My aunt was in very good spirits but did not mention Lord Granville or anything about Russia.

Little Delmé in high feather and full of the Dow. Lady Jersey, who in the solitude of London in December cultivates him and Frederick Byng and has them always with her.

Mr. Foster wrote a long letter to Car and I today without mentioning Frank [Lawley] esprit bouché that he is.

God bless you, my dearest G. We have more people to dinner today.

To Lady Georgiana Morpeth

DEVONSHIRE HOUSE. *December 1805.*

MY DEAREST SISTER,

Your letter arrived at a most acceptable time and the news of your having fixed the day of your departure did me more good than all Sir Walter's physic. I do not know how to put my happiness at the thoughts of seeing you into any shape or measure. Lord M., too, has an amazing share and each of the darlings a quantity not to be expressed. But I fear the latter are the only people out of Austria for the moment and from a part of one of your letters to Caroline, I am afraid I ought to have been writing you political pamphlets instead of private nonsense for the last fortnight. But I always think that to re-echo the substance of what you must so certainly hear in detail, would be but a melancholy occupation for both of us. I hope that you will be so kind as to take for granted, without receiving packets of " ohs " and " ahs " to illustrate my feelings, that I compassionate the miseries of the human race.

I do not wonder at Mr. Howard's remark, as I think several things at Castle Howard must be offensive to his independent spirit. Is Grand [Lord Carlisle] as dictatorial to him as ever? and has he the same slight degree of rebellion I used to think very entertaining?

God bless you, HARRYO.

IX

DEATH OF THE DUCHESS

1806

AS 1805 had been a year of marriages, so 1806 was to be a year of deaths. In one of the first letters of the year Harriet mentions that she is glad she cannot go to Nelson's funeral, chiefly, I think, because Lady Elizabeth Foster's vapourings on the subject had so got on her nerves.

Hardly had the nation recovered from the loss of its hero than it suffered yet another staggering blow in the death of Pitt. But these losses that meant so much to the older members of Devonshire House, did not touch Harriet and her contemporaries very closely.

She is much more occupied with the doings of her friends and relations; "little o" was at last to be married to Corisande de Gramont; in January Caro-William Lamb had her first baby, which died at its birth; Emily Lamb had blossomed out into Lady Cowper; the theatricals continued at the Priory; Georgiana Morpeth had a new baby and a new house in Park Street and Harriet had her own flirtations.

But in March a blow fell in truth upon Harriet and indeed upon them all. The Duchess was taken ill on the 17th. She had had recurrent and severe attacks of illness for some years previously, and if she had not lost her charm, vivacity and sweetness, she had lost her health and her looks. She had undergone those ghastly operations on her eyes and suffered them with heroic courage.

On the 21st of March she was worse, and though all her family, who surrounded her, were anxious, and Lady Bessborough sat up with her night after night, her condition was not regarded as dangerous, though for once, Sir Walter Farquhar seems to have realized the gravity of her condition.

On the 25th Charles James Fox wrote to Lord Granville that she was out of danger, but she endured five days more agony and died on the 30th of March.

She was only forty-eight, but a whole age died with her. Luckily for Harriet her sister and her brother were in London at the time. The Duchess' death completely shattered not only the entire family and household, but all London. The letters of Lady Bessborough and Lady Elizabeth Foster are quite heart-rending, and we may realize, to some slight degree, what her adored mother's death meant to Harriet, for she never brings herself to refer to it in her letters, nor even mentions her by name. There is just one pathetic little reference when she says she hopes she will always be worthy of her.

The whole of Harriet's life was to change for her with her mother's death, but this is not immediately apparent.

Life begins again; the Ossulstons get married; politics begin to interest her; there are parties and expeditions; Mr. Motteux and the "little men" of Devonshire House come to supper and to play chess, but nothing will ever be quite the same again.

But let us start the new year with Harriet in her happy ignorance of what is to befall.

To Lady Georgiana Morpeth

CHISWICK, *Thursday morning. 1806.*

A thousand thanks for your letter, my dearest sister.

Mama and Caroline went to the Opera the night before last, and London is still very empty, though it is expected to be fuller in the course of next week than ever. The Boringdons are just arrived. [She was his first wife, a daughter of Lord Westmorland and a sister of Lady Duncannon.] I hear she is in the greatest beauty, but immense for her time, and that he is grown fat and blooming and never out of a broad grin. The Duncannons leave Town today. She is an amiable person and I am sure you will like her very much. I met Lady Charlotte and Lady Mary[1] in the Park yesterday. I hate the former with so much bonne foi that I cannot allow her to be in good looks, though everybody else does. She overpowered us with affectionate abuse and looked like a sour lemon.

You are very naughty to have told William [Howard] all I said about Mr. Harbord, who happens at present to be always at my

[1] Daughters of the Duke of Portland. The former married Mr. Charles Greville and was the mother of the writer of the delightful journals and of his brother, who also wrote pleasant memoirs.

Georgiana, Duchess of Devonshire
From the Painting by Thomas Gainsborough, R.A.

elbow and will think it very treacherous of me to have laughed at him. Do you remember his saying that whenever he was left for a minute by himself, he grew so wearied that he *always* fell into a profound sleep of some hours? What am I to say if Mr. Howard asks him who bores him most, and refers to me for an explanation? I am sadly afraid you have lost none of the openness of temper I used to complain of.

I am sorry to tell you that Mr. Cavendish is a constant inmate of this house, and that I suspect he is employed by Lady Cahir as a new attempt to edge herself into it.

Lady E. and Caroline talk of going to Brocket. Mama has, I believe, some thoughts of taking me there for a day. How they will crow and shout over us when we are so entirely at their mercy. I am sure they trod on Lord Morpeth's foot and I dare say they will knock out my tooth. It is like getting among savages, there is no knowing how far their vivacity may carry them. This is my idea of Brocket in the lump from my knowledge of its individuals. If I am mistaken, tant mieux for all parties.

Papa is still well but I think he is very much afraid of gout. Mama goes to Town with commissions, which will probably make us dine about 10, which is particularly cruel, as she has asked all the Vigoureux and we shall have them fainting for want of food. Caroline is with her; Corise writing to my "dearest *Charles*," which is "une bonne idée nouvellement découverte" [because she used to call him Auguste], and Frederick Foster hiding because he knows that I am the only thing to be found in the house. I have fitted up your little room beautifully and I mean to forget then that it is possible to be happier. Mama is too good to me. She tells me she shall like to read with me. We have begun Paley's *Theology* and we are going to read Sarche's *Herodotus* together. I want to take exercise, but it requires courage to toil over Kew and Hammersmith.

Pray remember me to dear Lord Morpeth. I hope he suffers less than when he left Chiswick. Kiss the dear children and Caroline too; though her goodness now is not more flattering to us than her naughtiness was before.

Believe me ever most affec^{ly} yours, HARRIET CAVENDISH.

dy Georgiana Morpeth

DEVONSHIRE HOUSE, *January 7th, 1806.*

The "Exquisite Dose" did wonders and my cold is almost well, hough I have not yet left my room, I shall miss many gaieties by it. Lord Ossulston's supper is tomorrow, the thoughts of which have made him and Corise for the last 10 days the happiest little beings in the creation. He is to have Arioli and La Carina, all Devonshire House, of course, the Melbournes and a few men. I am really glad to be forced to stay away, for I know he will be in a painful state of agitation and hesitation, if it is only from excess of delight.

Lord Nelson's funeral I rejoice at escaping, for it would have been the greatest fatigue and exertion and most likely to be able to see very little after all.

They all go to the Priory Friday, and there is to be a ball after the play, but strange to tell, to miss all these united pastimes cost me not a sigh, and I do nothing but think of the 15th, wish for the 15th, and shall probably go mad on the 15th.

George Lamb is in town. He seems tired of the Priory. He says Mrs. Hesseltine is reckoned there very like me and a little like Car. We agree in being very much vexed at it, for the only thing that can create a resemblance is her being very fat and thick, as her peculiar countenance, which is her only charm, we neither of us have a trace of.

Lady Charlemont and I had a very long conversation about Mrs. Payne one night at supper at the Priory. She says she was very much in love with Mr. Payne when she married, and it was chiefly from jealousy that she parted from him, of which Lady C. said, he was continually giving her cause; but that he now wishes very much for a reconciliation and, that though she declares at present against it, Lady C. is sure it will end by it.

[*End of letter is missing.*]

To Lady Georgiana Morpeth

DEVONSHIRE HOUSE. *Saturday.* [*January ?*] *1806.*

MY DEAREST G.,

We went Thursday to the Priory and I was more amused than I had been before though it was "Whistle for it" again and "Sylvester Daggerwood," pretty well acted by Mr. Dawkins and Tom Sheridan.

The Audience was more brilliant than usual and considerably more animated, perhaps from the addition of Mrs. Damer and Miss Berry in transports. By the bye, *B.* seems most extremely delighted with her visit to Castle Howard, she says you are in greater beauty than she ever saw you and you say " the drollest, oh, the very drollest things about your situation."

The Bravo and I had a short conversation, but his sposa is so constantly on the watch, that I, out of consideration, walked off, upon which he went to Lady Jersey, which redoubled her watchfulness, especially as the latter was making her fine eyes and really looked quite beautiful; but the tenaciousness of Lord Aberdeen's attentions is quite as great on the Abercorn part as before the marriage, and you would imagine that they were still trying to gain him. He is constantly surrounded with some part of the family and Lady Maria never leaves him a moment.

With so good a husband I do not see why this prodigious care is necessary, however I dare say it flatters him and as it does nobody any harm, peu importe.

Lady Aberdeen was dressed in a pink gown, her hair entirely off her face with a topaz crown, paler than a sheet, her nose a little red, her cheeks hollow and her countenance doleful.

Caroline and I agreed in a whisper that she looked ugly— pas du tout. Lady Jersey, Lady H. Villiers, Lady Castlereagh and a long train came up to us in the course of the evening—" Look at that lovely creature, did you ever see any thing so beautiful? Oh, she is the most beautiful creature I ever beheld," and we, pour cause, were obliged to be in raptures!

Such is the triumph of Grecian symmetry, gems, antiques, stamped by Lord Haddo's taste.

Lady Cahir was " petite insupportable " indeed. William says she is more plague than the whole home put together, and it was owing to her whims that, three weeks after, marriage was delayed till next week. George Lamb says she is the most odious little d——l that ever breathed and I tell you all this to sanction my cordial detestation of her.

Caroline Lamb was confined to her room with the influenza. Lady Abercorn is still very sore about Mrs. Hesseltine, but in high spirits and Lord Abercorn seems to behave very well to her. Mrs. Hesseltine is not the least like any of us, I assure you—unless that she is very fat and [has] light hair ; her only pretty look is one like Mrs. Ellis', when she lifts up her eyes in singing.

We had a supper here last night ; 2 tables and not one fool excepting Lady Fanny [Villiers]. Lady Melbourne, Lord and Lady Holland, Doctor Allen [the Hollands' Librarian], Mr. Horner, Lord Archibald, Mr. Ward, Lord Cowper, Miss Berry, little Ward who sung quite beautifully, and Lord O.

Mr. Horner, to whom I never spoke, has enough sense in his eyes only, for half a generation and I hear he is the most delightful and eloquent person that ever lived.

Lord Holland, who is grown more fat and rosy than any body I ever saw, was giving them all puzzles, such as " malaga raisins are good " etc. and really roared with laughter. Lady Holland would every now and then tell the joke and once I thought he would have cried because she helped Lord Archibald find out why the miller wore a white hat. He is the greatest love certainly in the world and enters into every thing de si bon couer [*sic*].

Mr. Ward was too ridiculous, he is grown even more chirping and affected than ever, and mama will ask him here every night.

Lady Cowper is very unwell, with a bad cold, and I am afraid he is very inattentive to her. She says he loves her excessively but he is always away from her.

[*End of this letter is missing.*]

To Lady Georgiana Morpeth

[*Beginning of this letter is missing.*]

January, 1806.

. . . and when Lord Abercorn comes to her, will scarcely answer him, or only with the bitterest reproaches. The object of this strange jaealousy is, by all accounts, and indeed I saw her at the play one night, a very short, fat, quiet little woman, scarcely pretty, very fond of her husband and very much distressed at the ridiculous part she is forced to perform, as Lady Cowper says they do not flirt much and only sing together sometimes, which is the great cause of contention, as Lady Abercorn cried out the other night, in an hysterical voice, " You never sing with me ! "

Lady Cowper is quite indignant with Lady Aberdeen, but one must allow a great deal for the difference of systems throughout in these two brides—her expression was that she never saw anybody make such a fool of herself; that he never walks across the room that she does not follow him; never sits in a chair she does not squeeze herself into it also; that he is much graver and more doleful looking than before his marriage and never has the least share in the display—but she said, "Poor man! he cannot help it, she forces him to it all."

I think there must be a little spleen in this account of Lady Cowper's, though I do think a little backwardness to "groupe" more in character than what we first heard of him.

You cannot conceive how anxious Lady Cowper was to make Caroline discreet—how far her endeavours have hitherto succeeded you may judge, but I entreat you not to spread the evil any further.

The Duncannons, of whose existence I am sometimes near losing all memory, are at Roehampton living in Clover.

Adieu dear, dearest sister.

Believe me, ever yours, HARRIET CAVENDISH.

They say Lord Primrose is going to marry Lady Augusta Greville, the Beauty; what a family party Warwick Castle must boast.

To Lady Georgiana Morpeth

CHISWICK, [*January ?*] *1806.*

I am quite ashamed of myself, my dearest sister, but it is but today that I have at all recovered the terror, fatigue and bustle of the Priory. I suppose you will have heard from mama that it was one continued scene of prompting, rehearsing and managing, and as all the men and women merely players, I have every little to say about them.

The Abercorn tracasserie is so totally at an end that I could not discover any trace of it. Mrs. Hesseltine is quite a gooddy—a harmless inoffensive woman, thinking of nothing but her hideous husband, and Caroline Lamb says that if Lady Abercorn had not had an unusual fit of irritability on her nerves, she would have been no more thought of by any person in the house than a chair or a table.

They say there never was anybody so altered—that she was very handsome, and she is now, I think, ugly. Mama and Lord Abercorn and George allow her the remains of a very fine countenance.

I scarcely saw the Aberdeens and could not judge of their manière d'être. Miss Humphries, though, rather confirmed Lady Cowper's account, and blamed Lady A. for her manner to him at first, which she says she has lately altered. I scarcely spoke to him. The morning we came away Lady Aberdeen looked perfectly beautiful and with rouge, which I hear he insists upon her wearing next year ; I think she will be the handsomest woman in London.

He is silent as the grave, but looks very happy and contented.

Caro and William go on exactly the same. She was very amiable ; his attention to her is unwearied—he never leaves her a moment and seems to love her more than ever, but she is too exigeante and with so good a husband might spare herself the trouble. She is so jealous of him, that her maid told mine that when he goes to the *piccola*, which is the only moment he is away from her, she sends her to watch him and find out where he is and if he comes straight back. This would be terrible with any other people, but I really believe it succeeds in this case, for they seem the happiest of human beings. She looks very ill.

Lady Cahir is very much altered and I think her (with all possible precaution) the most odious little woman in the world. She besieged me with her usual weapon—the most fulsome flattery—I was the person she had always most longed to know, I was exactly the person she should most love and admire. Then a string of praises, to which I answered so very like the Miss Trimmers when we shake hands with them, that she did not speak one other word with me. And so this much wished for moment ended. Caro seems tired of her and disgusted with her flattery.

God bless you, dearest G., I have sent George a map of Europe, more for your sake than his, as I suppose he will not think it a very amusing present.

We go to see Roscius on Monday and to the Priory on Tuesday. It is whispered that we settle in Town next week. I do *not* know what I have been writing. I promise I will be a much better correspondent for the future.

H. C.

To Lady Georgiana Morpeth

CHISWICK, *Thursday, January 30th, 1806.*

You ought not to be so kind, my dearest sister, for I have been most shamefully lazy.

Lady Abercorn was even affectionate in her manner to us, but she seems unhappy, fretful and irritable and irritated to the greatest degree. She is grown very thin and without rouge I hear she is very much altered. Lord Abercorn was cross and grand and we were on common civility terms.

Lord Aberdeen was for one 10 minutes on our old terms of friendship, but that excepted, *comme la glace*.

I hear Lady Cowper is in the greatest beauty and that Lord Henry Petty admires her to so violent a degree that Lady Holland says if she was unmarried he would certainly propose to her immediately. So much for modern fidelity.

The play at the Priory is to be Friday and then Monday. The Melbournes dine here today. I am not *too* glad. Pray look at my seal [the impression of a cat]. It was given me yesterday and is going to have written upon it, "Je caresse, mais je trahis."

Addio, cara carissima. I love you better than anybody and anything and admire you more than any thing except my new seal.

Your ever affectionate, aunt HARRY.

Kiss those three angels till nurse says "I must tell mama not to kiss quite so hard," and then say it was aunt Harry, and then make him say, "No, no," and "*dearest aunt Harry.*" Oh, the pleasures of imagination.

X

THE NEW RÉGIME

JULY TO DECEMBER, 1806

THERE are no letters between January and July as the family had all remained together in their great sorrow, and when the letters recommence there are no signs of the loss that was every day more apparent to Harriet. Indeed while she writes from Chiswick she appears quite happy, but things were to be very different when she returned to Devonshire House in November.

Harriet, indeed none of the three children, had ever been at all intimate with the Duke. In London she did her best to become better acquainted with her father and is touchingly grateful for any sign of affection, or even of recognition, from him. Lady Elizabeth was where she had always been, in Devonshire House at her father's side, but instead of ceding to Harriet her proper place as mistress of the house, she usurps the position and shows even greater want of tact by plaguing Harriet to go out into society with her.

There was a question of the Dowager Countess Spencer coming to live at Devonshire House, or of Harriet's going to live with her in Jermyn Street, but the old lady, so worldly-wise and so supremely tactful, solved the problem in her own quiet yet decisive way. Under the Dowager's guidance and with her sister's advice, Harriet achieves maturity.

On November the 29th she mentions the possibility of the Regent of Portugal going to the Brazils. The facts were briefly these; M. d'Aranjo (whom she wrongly describes as M. D'Aranjuez) was the only man of ability, decision and experience in the Portuguese Cabinet. He was suspected of being a partisan of Buonaparte, who was known to have designs on that country. The British Government were forced to intimate to Portugal that, whilst that country could rely upon British support if their government either resisted invasion or withdrew to Brazil, if they did neither Great Britain would be forced to seize their fleet. The danger was temporarily averted by Buonaparte's intervention being distracted by a new Northern Coalition against him.

She also speaks of Madame de Genlis. This lady was governess to the children of "Philippe Egalité," Duke of Orleans. She was extremely high-flown and always preaching moralities. This did not prevent her being the Duke's mistress and she was the mother, though she did not admit it, not only of the Casimir mentioned by Harriet, but also of "la belle Paméla," who married Lord Edward Fitzgerald.

To Lady Georgiana Morpeth

CHISWICK. *July the 8th, 1806.*

You are too good to me and I do not know how I shall ever thank you enough for another long letter I received yesterday.

I suppose you have heard that the little pair [the Ossulstons] are to be married in about 10 days. They have not yet settled their plans and proceedings, but they seem very happy and the silences are much shorter and less frequent, which is as great a relief to the lookers-on as it is to themselves.

Mr. Marsh, Caro and Miss Trimmer have been forming the underplot, but this you must, if you please, keep to yourself.[1] Miss Trimmer was confidante and never was anybody so pleased or so proud as she has been of this rôle. It gave her, what is all I am afraid she must ever expect, the *appearance* of a flirtation, and she makes mystery more mysterious and silence more silent. Caroline was obdurate and dear Mr. Marsh is in a state of love and despair, I hope too violent to last. I think he ought to receive the reward offered for the discoverer of perpetual motion, for never has a muscle been at rest since he arrived here, and the money might serve to pay for the furniture he has spoilt by dint of stumbling, falling flat, spilling, tearing, etc. With all this he flatters himself that his passion has not been discovered to anybody, therefore pray do not appear to be in the secret. I wish I could think or talk of it seriously, as I am really very sorry, mais c'est plus fort que moi.

[*End of this letter is missing.*]

[1] Mr. Marsh was then in love with, and shortly afterwards proposed to, Caroline St. Jules.

CHISWICK. [*21st of July 1806.*]

Another letter—you are too good and I am too happy.

It is my turn to hear of poor dear Mr. Marsh's weal and woe. Pray do not forget!

We all dined at Roehampton yesterday to meet the Duke of Sussex. Lord Granville and Mr. Adderley were there. The former gracious beyond the power of caprice, but too playful and gay to be agreeable. The latter I could not fix in any sense of the word, for one moment. He was at dinner between Mr. Foster and Willy [Ponsonby], looking wilder and more agitated than I ever saw anybody in any situation, and so impetuous in his looks and gesticulations that I really think his next visit ought to be to Doctor Willis [the Alienist].

Lady Cahir is very unwell with her face. Caro raves about her still, but in so foolish a way that I wish for her own sake and it, that she would drop the declamatory part of her friendship.

Papa is at last come to settle here, though I fear not for long. He has not yet pronounced my asset. [Probably her allowance. The Duke gave her, in 1807, £400 a year.]

Lord O. and Corise are to be married, I believe, this day week. They trot about all day together and make very pretty bird's eye views in the boats, temple, etc.

Lady E. F. has taken up drawing and places herself in all the most romantic spots. Thank heaven and summer she is obliged to leave off the mud coloured shawl.

Have you read of the little French girl in Kotzebue who one day, before company, pulled all her petticoats over her head and when her mama scolded her, said, "mais, maman, c'est que je me drape."

To Lady Georgiana Morpeth

DEVONSHIRE HOUSE, *Wednesday evening, November 5th, 1806.*

You must not expect me, my own dearest sister, to say that I am not unhappy at your having left me, but indeed I am very reasonable. I must awaken your regrets by telling you a Basket of Pears arrived for you from Mr. Motteux at 6 o'clock, that he followed them close, and is at this moment vociferating Election songs about "Sammy Hood and Dicky Sheridan."

All Caro's Heros are assembling; George is just arrived fuming about votes and canvassings. Lady E. fancies she is to carry Mr. Sheridan's election; she has just left the room proclaiming that she is going to thank some Voters and assure them of Papa's anxiety and gratitude, and she must heighten her Knight's Fever by the number of notes she writes to him.

I must tell you before I go to bed a Joke of Mr. Sheridan's; he said at the Crown and Anchor dinner, "I hope at least if the Mob knock out my brains, Mr. Paul will find them."

Thursday morning. Nov. 6th.

I miss you very much, my dearest G. This is darling George's dinner hour and I cannot accustom myself to find your rooms deserted. Hartington goes on Saturday. He is tearing about in his light blue bedgown, and begs you will not mention the scrape he got in to about a letter to Lord Carlisle.

God bless you, my dear dearest sister, ever most affec[ly] yours,

H. CAVENDISH.

I hear Mr. Sheridan is going on better today. Lord John is come to Town and things are to be better managed.

To Lady Georgiana Morpeth

CHISWICK, *Friday morning, November 7th, 1806.*

I am quite happy now with all the darling people [Lady Morpeth's younger children had been left in London]. Papa brought me here this morning and I found them perfectly well and delighted to see me. I think Nurse resents your departure and talks of George with pique and affected indifference; she says the young ladies have quite forgot him and were not at all offended at his leaving them. Georgiana is more brilliant than ever and Caroline more amiable and affectionate, but has taken this expedition ill and says *she* will never go to Castle Howard.

I cannot help thinking also that papa has been particularly kind to me these 2 or 3 days, which encourages me to exert myself and repays me for it at the same time.

After I had finished my letter to you yesterday I went to see Miss Berry, where I found Comte Potocki. Agnes [Berry] and her seem quite to "have marked him for their own," and he is treated as

L'enfant de famille. He is uncommonly handsome and has very much the manners of an Englishman, only still more grandeur and indolence. He talks English more like a child than a foreigner and very like little Henry Fox.

We had quite a large supper last night, but entirely composed of the Melbourne family. Lady Cowper proposed coming in the morning and I was afraid papa might not like my having said they might; however he supped with us and seemed pleased and amused, with George especially, qui ne se possède pas when he talks of the election, and storms at the ill management and worse success of all Mr. Sheridan's friends. They all stay in Town a week longer and Lady C. takes Caroline [St. Jules] to the play tonight.

God bless you, dearest sister. The women want to be one upon each knee, which must effectually put a stop to my writing any longer.

Most affec^{ly} yours, H. C.

We all send 50 kisses to George. I have been trying to compel them to be sentimental, but Georgiana will say nothing but " Buy me new doll," and Caroline is in one of her obstinate fits and does nothing but nod. Pray give my love to dear Lord M. and remember me as it is most proper to Lord and Lady C. and Lady Gertrude.

To Lady Georgiana Morpeth

DEVONSHIRE HOUSE, *Friday evening, November 7th, 1806.*

I stayed some time with your dear children after I finished my letter this morning. Fred was very gracious to Papa, gave him a Pear and made him laugh. Nurse did not seem to approve of my plans about Caroline, but she says *both* the young ladies may come and dine in town whenever I please.

When we returned to Town we found that Mr. Sheridan had gained near 400 upon today's poll. Lord John Townshend dined here. The agitation of the election does not make him agreeable; he seems verging upon madness and gets so bewildered in his accounts, that it is difficult to gain any information from him.

Lord Thanet and Mr. Motteux arrived about an hour ago. I had never seen Lord Thanet, and am very much captivated with him. He was very entertaining and his voice in speaking is so delightful that I should think that alone would make him a pleasant Companion.

Saturday morning, Nov. 8th.

MY DEAREST SISTER,

Miss Berry has just gone and has been, for a wonder, gentle and amiable. She really has excellent feeling and principles and I regret that I do not like her quite as much as I ought.

Caroline saw the Bagots at the play. She must be an odd woman ; she sent for Lady Cowper's lying-in nurse to engage her for her own, which is to be in about 7 months, and gave this old woman the whole history of her marriage. She raves about Lady Cowper and will have patterns of everything she wears and the young coxcomb is to wear. She told the nurse that Charles was just like Lord Cowper, beautiful, clever, delightful, the best of husbands, but not foolish before people as most men were. In short she was communicative to the greatest degree. Car says she seems desperately in love with him, so you see fops have their votaries.

Yours most affec[ly], H. CAVENDISH.

To Lady Georgiana Morpeth

DEVONSHIRE HOUSE, *Sunday, November 9th, 1806.*

DEAREST SISTER,

I am better but a good deal of Laudanum I took last night for my cough, has made me so sick and giddy I can scarcely write.

Mr. Sheridan is going on ill today and George Lamb is very desponding. I have just seen Lady John who seems to think he will lose the election.

I wish you would write circular letters to all your correspondants who, in a happy state of ignorance, continue to direct to you here, as I do not know how to convey these Epistles Free.

The Bell rings. You may depend on my not missing one day, though it should sometimes condemn you to such a scrawl as this.

Ever yours, H. C.

To Lady Georgiana Morpeth

DEVONSHIRE HOUSE, *Monday morning, November 10, 1806.*

Your letter was more acceptable to me than I can express, and I almost forgot I had reason to be unhappy. I am afraid that you are very low and that your feelings upon arriving at Castle Howard have been too painfully awakened.

Hartington left London at 7 this morning ; and Miss Trimmer was going, but I persuaded her to stay with me till tomorrow. My aunt sleeps in Town tonight. I wish she could remain for a few days, as my cough is so bad that I shall not be able to go to Roehampton for a week.

The Melbournes and Cowpers come here almost every day and, strange to tell, I am very glad of it, for they help disperse the gloom of a long evening with Lady E., and are much more gentle and comme il faut than usual.

My mornings I like extremely. I am as regular as clockwork, and though " morning " means from 9 till 8, I do not find them at all too long.

Miss Keating [who had been the Duchess's personal maid] has just been here to tell me that 50£ a year is at last settled upon her ; she means to set up as Milliner and Mantua Maker at Christmas. I shall be very anxious about her and I hope it will be a good deal in our power to make her succeed well.

Hartington has behaved much better to papa ; he complained I took up the thread of your lectures as soon as you were gone, but it is indeed a subject upon which too much cannot be said to him.

Most affec[ly] yours, H. C.

Tell me when I may frank !

To Lady Georgiana Morpeth

DEVONSHIRE HOUSE, *Tuesday, November 11th, 1806.*

I will begin answering your letter before I go to bed, my dearest sister, as I had not time to do it this morning. I will not be too sanguine about your returning sooner than you intended, but the hope of it, however slight, does a great deal towards reviving my spirits.

Your joke about Colonel Leigh is the drollest I have heard for a long time, but not to poor Miss Byron, I fear.

Is Mr. Sloane " quite neat and tidy " still, and does Lady Gertrude feel very happy, and as pleased with him as ever ? You mistake when you think Cumberland news does not interest me. For example it made me the person of importance at dinner today, and though it rather amuses them at present, they will soon grow accustomed to my being Head Politician.

My actions since I despatched my letter this morning, have not been many or interesting. My aunt dined here ; we played 5 games at Chess. Lady Melbourne, George and Lady Cowper came to supper and I talked the remainder of the evening with Lady C. who improves very much indeed upon acquaintance. George is thinned by the energetic support both of body and mind that he gives to the *Popular* Mr. Sheridan and Caro has been flirting with him, to recruit his spirits for tomorrow's canvass.

Caroline Lamb is in great tribulation I hear. She has been copying a picture of William by Cosway and out of over care, had it put up to an amazing height after every hour of drawing. The consequence was, that in one of these mountings, the top of a ladder was thrust through it, and the Devil of a hole, to quote Lord Melbourne, made in it. This is very unlucky as I do not think she is in favour with them now, and this was a very favorite picture. Lord Melbourne said, " I have written to her not to be so over careful another time, so now we shall have some damned accident happen t'other way." Lady M. is dry about it, and George shakes his sides with laughing. They talk of William rather like a jerry sneak and as Caro both shoots and hunts, I expect to hear of him modelling wax at home.

Wednesday morning, Nov. 12.

Caroline is the greatest comfort to me, and now that both Miss Trimmer and Hartington are gone, I do not know what I should do without her. Lady Bessborough leaves Town today and I go to Roehampton tomorrow to stay there till Saturday. Nothing can be kinder than my aunt's behaviour has been to me and I like the thoughts of being with her in the country very much.

I do not know exactly what Lady E. means—excepting dinner at Holland House, my aunt does not mix more in society than I do, and that, even if it was in my inclination, would not be in my power. She will, I am afraid, worry me about going to the play with her, as she has already before Papa, which prevented my saying much against it at the time. I did not think she would propose it to me for some months at least and pray send me word what answer will be the most civil and most conclusive.

How your account of the little wit entertains me. Is there any prospect of Miss B. [Byron] and him joking into a mutual attachment ?

Lady Jersey is still at Osterley and remains there a month. Lady H. Villiers' example seems to have roused all romantic passions that had lain dormant for want of precedents. Miss Fitzroy is going to marry Mr. William Ponsonby, and Lady Mary Hussey, Mr. Wodehouse, a young Norfolk Clergyman who has not a penny, unless his two elder brothers (in the true spirit of the times) promise him never to marry.

You will be surprised to hear that Lady Cowper has grown so very fond of me, that she has been here either morning or evening every day, wanted me to go to Brocket, and upon my refusing it, insists upon my *writing* to her while she is away and promises me long letters in return. To quote Mr. Lewis's quotation I say like the little old woman cut shorter, "Can this be I?" I think Lady Cowper much more amiable than I did and much better; she has taken coming to St. George's Church and talks to me of nothing but morality, the misery of being with people of bad character etc. But I feel scarcely to know her and I am grown *old* and cautious and should prefer omitting correspondence till we are better acquainted. It will also, I am afraid, put Car Lamb in a fury, yet I do not know how I am to manage not to affront one way or the other. I have also many doubts about Lady Cowper's sincerity. I will tell you what I think of doing and you must send me your opinion and advice. She is to be away 3 weeks. During that time I will write to her twice, merely any news I can collect, which is what she likes best. Then today I am going to write a very *kind* letter to Caroline to thank her for having asked me to Brocket, and to tell her how my aunt is, where you are etc. This will prevent her saying, if she should hear that I have written to Lady Cowper, that I have neglected and never written to her.

I must now apologise to you for troubling you so much about such trifling concerns, but you know how I wish not to give any cause for Lady B. or Caro to talk of my *cruelties*, therefore I beg you will answer this long history.

Believe me most affec^ly^ yours, H. C.

[Harriet was right to suspect Lady Cowper of insincerity. Lady Bessborough wrote to Granville in Dec. 1806, "she does not seem to me good natur'd or sincere. She flatters Harriet violently to her face and takes every opportunity of cutting at her."]

To Lady Georgiana Morpeth

DEVONSHIRE HOUSE, *Wednesday evening, Nov. 12th, 1806.*

After I had finished my volume to you this morning, I wrote to Caroline Lamb as I intended, a very kind letter and a still kinder message to William, without which I knew everything else would be nothing worth.

Lady Bessborough came in her way to Roehampton to promise me the warmest room in the house tomorrow, but to announce that antidote to all comfort, Doctor Wynne; I do not however mind him as much as she seemed to think I should, and I really like the thoughts of going there very much indeed.

We are a smaller party today than I think we shall be again; Papa, Lady E., Car and I. Frederic Foster arrives on Tuesday and Miss Trimmer will return some time next week. I do not regret Mr. Motteux or Mr. Robinson who are at length gone, and only wish that Mr. Crawfurd would compleat the desertion by following their example.

The Ossulstons have left Brighton and are at the Oaks. Corise is better, but she has been obliged to relinquish the Pills she had so much faith in as they weakened her to a great degree and made her quite ill. I conclude she is not with child, as she never could have kept it so long a secret and her letters are more desponding than they would be if her wishes on that point were accomplished.

Mr. Foster is coming to Town in a Flame about Sir Francis Burdett. He will certainly lose his election, but I hear that he means to hold out to the last, though all parties are equally determined to oppose him.

Mr. Jones is just arrived and announces Mr. Crawfurd, so we shall have the two extremes of contradiction and compliance. I quite regret the Melbournes, who are all gone to Brocket.

Thursday morning, Nov. 13.

I had a letter from nurse this morning. She desires me to tell you that the children are all perfectly well, but she will not let them come to Town till the Middlesex Election is over and the roads quiet again.

My aunt is just arrived in Town. Lady Westmorland is very unwell and going to Lisbon for her health and wished to see her before she goes. Lady Bessborough says she sets out tomorrow. I shall hear more about it probably before I finish my letter. I go back to Roehampton with my aunt and return here to dinner on Saturday.

I hear Lord Lauderdale and Lady E. Monck create much scandal; Lady Cowper says her behaviour is grown so very bad that she thinks People will soon be quite ashamed speaking to her. As we are happily related to none of the reigning favorites, she never comes near us.

I hear Colonel Leigh is going to take Richard into his service. I hope this increase of establishment may be favorable to poor Miss Byron's hopes.

Caroline has had a letter from Caroline Lamb today, begging her to go to Brocket Hall. I do not know what she will determine about it, but she does not seem much disposed to go. She dined at Whitehall the other day. They were quite en famille and perfectly at their ease and nothing ever was equal to the jollity. Lady Cowper sat singing all dinner time, and Lord Melbourne and George quite stunning her with their noisy gaiety. I do not wonder at Car Lamb affronting them by escaping too often to her own room.

most affec^{ly} yours, H. C.

To Lady Georgiana Morpeth

ROEHAMPTON. *Friday morning, Nov. 14th, 1806.*

[It is typical that the letters from Roehampton are written on black-edged paper, but not those from Devonshire House.]

It is very quiet and comfortable here, and my dear aunt is so good and kind to me that I only regret not being here for a month instead of a day. I should not, however, like to leave Papa for any length of time and am well satisfied to have recruited my spirits and to return to him tomorrow.

My aunt is in tolerable spirits and very good looks. She was hours with Lady Westmorland, who sets out for Lisbon on Monday, with nobody but Peggy Hunlocke and Doctor Fellowes. Lady B. does not seem to think her quite as ill as this journey would make one fear she was.

My dearest G., The Post is all but going.

God Bless you.

ever yours, H. C.

To Lady Georgiana Morpeth

ROEHAMPTON. *Saturday morning, Nov. 15th, 1806.*

I am quite ashamed of the letter I sent you yesterday, my dearest G.

I did nothing but play at Chess with Doctor Wynne last night and this morning him and I are the only people up in the house.

I had a great deal of melancholy conversation with my aunt yesterday. I do love her most sincerely and pity her still more, for she seems more miserable than ever.

I had an answer to my letter to Caroline Lamb today—she says nothing about herself, but seems in good spirits, and is as usual, very kind and affectionate in her expressions to me.

I feel sorry to leave Roehampton today, for it has done my cold and spirits both good to be as perfectly quiet and comfortable as I have been here.

Miss Trimmer has written me word that she is ready to return to D. House and I think of sending for her on Monday. I hope Papa cannot dislike it, and it is an unspeakable comfort to me to have her with me when you are away. Dearest G., you may return in little more than a fortnight and perhaps much less.

I hear Frederic Ponsonby is going on very well in his election, and when he last wrote to Lord Bessborough was not going to give a Ball and Supper.

Tell me if I do wrong in enclosing to Lord Carlisle, as I cannot always procure a frank.

Believe me most affec[ly] yours, H. CAVENDISH.

To Lady Georgiana Morpeth

DEVONSHIRE HOUSE, *Monday, Nov. 17th, 1806.*

I heard of the paragraph you mention from Lady Bessborough; she says she was startled by the name at first, but otherwise it could not give a moment's uneasiness. I have heard nothing of Lord Morpeth that has caused me a moment's pain and I think you will believe this has not been from want of interest in what concerns you both so nearly.

I only hope your sickness is as *uninteresting* as mine; my head is full of *sirrup* of *Poppies*, and I live upon Magnesia and Bread pudding. This is to cure my cough which I began to be afraid would remain with me all the winter.

Lady Westmorland and Peggy were to set off this morning. I hope Doctor Fellowes is fond of conversation. Lady Westmorland is with child and I hope not dangerously ill, as her friends do not seem much alarmed about her.

I had a letter from Corise today ; she is with Lady Derby at the Oaks, recovering her beauty and in raptures with Lord O's unceasing affection and attentions. She is not gravida and they seem to bear it as *well as can be expected.* Lady Derby is in great favour with them, and never did people like going to Country houses as they do. No wonder Lord O. resented Lord C's behaviour about asking him to Castle Howard. They are beginning to be *surprised* at not being asked to the Priory, and going to Brocket in the hopes of receiving an invitation whilst they are. I have sent your message about Park Street. I begin to fancy you in Town again.

Lord Granville comes to Town Tuesday or Wednesday in his way to Saltram, I believe. London is emptier than ever. Miss Trimmer is here for one night but is obliged to return to Brentford tomorrow. I do not so much mind as the Bessboroughs come to stay 3 or 4 days. My poor aunt is very, very low. I heard the most extraordinary statement of things today. Lady Jones told Miss Trimmer that Lady Mary Fitzgerald, an old relation of Lady E. Foster's,[1] says, " What noble sacrifices Elizabeth is making ; she is an angelick creature and it is 10 thousand pities that she should be in such a family, amongst such people ! "

I do not think our characters will injure hers. Lady Mary talked of her as ruined by being thrown amongst us.

George Lamb supped with us on the night before last and was very entertaining in describing his canvassing. The Actors are all very active for Mr. Sheridan, and Munden carries all before him. I heard of a Taylor saying to be sure Mr. Sheridan did owe him 5 hundred pound, but he was such a good sort of man he could not refuse him his vote. He must have Lady Mary Fitzgerald's notion of things.

I am quite unhappy at being kept from your darling children. 76 kisses to George.

[*End of letter missing.*]

[1] Her aunt.

To Lady Georgiana Morpeth

DEVONSHIRE HOUSE, *Tuesday morning, November 18th, 1806.*

The Bessboroughs come today, Lord Granville in the course of the week, and the Ossulstons at the latter end of it, so that our extreme quiet is over, and I rejoice at it. Your letter to Lady E. about my going out is, I suppose, the cause of her never having a second time said anything about it. It was painful and distressing to me when she did, and to your kindness do I owe this, as I do every other comfort I ever enjoy.

Lady E. has just been up to see me. She is going tomorrow to see Mr. Sheridan chaired. Corisande is coming to town for it with Lady Derby, but returns in the evening to the Oaks. Lord O. is in high glee at Mr. Bennet's being returned for Shrewsbury ; really their successes are beginning to be Tiresome. Mr. Hill is, I conclude, chosen the other Member ; some people say now that he is certainly to marry Lady Esther and that he always was inclined to like her. He had an odd way of showing those *dispositions*.

Lady Elizabeth says General Fitzpatrick is very ill indeed, that his complaint is a Carbuncle ; they are afraid it may be something worse, but do not like to say anything decided about it till they have ascertained more. Lord John Townshend seemed in the greatest anxiety about him.

I cannot tell you how sorry I am at what every body else seems glad of ; General Tarleton's having lost his election. I hear his affairs are in a dreadful state and I am sure poor Susan must be very unhappy.

William Ponsonby has been at the Priory. The Aberdeens are still in Scotland, and nobody there but the Castlereaghs and Hinchinbrokes. Lady Maria is in great beauty and greater spirits, so I conclude Lord Henry [Petty] is faithful.

God bless you, dearest G., I promise you a better letter tomorrow.

most affec^{ly} y^{rs}, H. C.

To Lady Georgiana Morpeth

DEVONSHIRE HOUSE, *Wednesday, November 19th, 1806.*

I am glad your spirits are better, my dearest G., and it consoles me for your being left with Miss Byron and Delmio, which in point of insipidity must be cosa da morire.

I received George's Geographical Galantine with delight. No

little women yet—I cannot go to them and nurse will not bring them to me during the Election.

I am happy when I think I contribute in any degree to dear Lady B's [Bessborough] comfort. She dined here yesterday and we played at Chess all the evening. They are gone, I believe, to see Mr. Sheridan chaired.

I am glad that my cough is an excuse for me, as it is one of the things Lady E. F. would have compelled me to do for a quiet life. I do not think there is any difference in her conduct, excepting that I always *fancy* her perhaps more at her ease and laying down the law when Lord M. and you are away. Whilst I kept my room, she paid me the most unconscionable visits, but as that is one of the things that must be meant kindly, I will not complain of it. She is in one thing very tiresome to me ; constant *controversies* with Miss Trimmer, who really endeavours to keep out of them, always talking to her on some religious subject and forcing her to say things that she may dispute them. Caroline began last night, before the Bessboroughs and all of us assembled, reading *out loud* a letter of Madame de Maintenon, in which she excuses her conduct towards Louis and says, " si je ne vais pas dans sa chambre, à qui pourrait il confier ses secrets," or words to that effect, and describing in short scenes too like what we are so often witnessing. This was to lead to every sort of question to Lady E., whether Madame de Maintenon was right in her conduct, whether she was ambitious or only making generous sacrifices, etc. I fancied Lady E. was embarrassed. I was at Chess at another table and could not see her face, but she hardly answered and only made *little noises*.

I hear Mr. Sheridan is to be chaired, through this Court. Papa says he cannot refuse. I cannot tell you how sorry I am. I suppose it will be a most riotous Mob and I hate any uproar here. They are to come about 4.

I have heard no more of Lord Granville. It was today I heard he was to come.

God bless you, dearest sister.

most affec^{ly} yours, HARRIET CAVENDISH.

My dearest G., I have just time to tell you that the procession has past. There was musick and much shouting and Hurrahing. The Post is just going.

To Lady Georgiana Morpeth

DEVONSHIRE HOUSE, *Thursday, November 20th, 1806.*

Many thanks to you and Miss Berry for the letter I have just received. I am sorry my admiration of Comte Potocki was so evident as I do not remember saying anything about it to her ; and I fear he must be equally impressed with the idea of it.

I hope I have never said too much to Miss Berry upon a subject [Lady E. F's presence at D. House] I perhaps had better not mention at all, but the two last conversations I had with her, she drew me into it by so much kindness and above all, so much moderation, that I did not feel the self reproach I do when I have allowed myself to enter upon it with any other person.

Miss Trimmer is here and received your letter ; she stays with me a few days longer.

I have just been interrupted by a long visit from Miss Berry and have felt the full force of your observation, " she *prevents* one's liking her as much as one wishes to do." She was not in an agreeable humour, in outrageous spirits and to the heighth of familiarity and *Hail fellow well met.* She has been really very ill and I expected a weak invalid, which added to my disappointment.

Yesterday was not a pleasant day. It began with what was to us most melancholy ; Mr. Sheridan being chaired through the courtyard. My aunt was very much overcome by it, as the noise was very great and anything like a procession going out of these gates, recalled most painful scenes to her mind.

Just before dinner Lady Elizabeth came up to see me, with a significant smile, a look full of meaning and a note in her hand. " I suppose you know who is coming tonight ? " I said with great *naïveté.* " Who ? " " Lord Granville." Will you tell me, my dear G, why she always talks of him to me as if I was so very much interested (to say the least) about him ?

But now for La Montagne accouchée d'un Souris—Lady Bessborough sent Lord B. and Willy to dine here, as she was too much tired to come till afterwards. We waited the whole evening but in vain ; nobody appeared. Lady E. kept watching and winking at me till 12, and then became most terribly out of humour, wondering in rather an illnatured way at my aunt's not coming, till just as we were going to Bed, a note arrived to bid us not expect her. I think after what you know of my altered sentiments about my aunt, and the real love and admiration I feel for her, you will not suspect me of being actuated by anything like illnature or unkindness, if I *to you* regret the imprudence of her conduct. Neither Lord B. nor Willy knew that Lord G. was in Town, as Willy told me, when I said he was, his mother had told him it was quite impossible for him to come now. She had left Willy here, depending on her to carry him home, and he was extremely angry and very sulky all the evening. I dread his taking any fancy in to his head, and it is impossible not to lament that my aunt, with the best intentions, the most exemplary change of manner and a heart quite broken, should, by a little imprudence, expose herself to the suspicion of others ; for by what even Lady E. and Caroline say, one may judge of what others less indulgent will.

Perhaps I have said too much on this subject, but you must allow for the extreme solitude in which we have been, for any little thing one hears much talked about, making an impression on one's mind. You have often told me that Men consider it as illnature or frivolity when women dwell much upon such subjects as that of the latter part of my letter. I therefore hope for the sake of Lord Morpeth's good opinion, which it is not exaggeration to say I value more than almost anything upon Earth, you will not let him see, hear or *find* any part of what I have written. There is one thing to be said for me, that when trifles act upon the reputation or happiness of those we have a regard for, they ought to cease to be called so, and what would be wrong to say to other people, may not be so in confidence from me to you. The reason I am writing so upon the defensive, is that I remember when Caroline wrote to me at Aldwick, blaming Lady B. for much the same thing as I have. You said they were fancies and rather illnatured ones.

Remember, my dearest G., I shall not be happy till I hear from you that you do not blame me for anything I have said.

Believe me most affec[ly] yours, HARRIET CAVENDISH.

To Lady Georgiana Morpeth

D. HOUSE. *Friday, November 21st, 1806.*

Lord Granville and Mr. Robinson supped with us last night. I played one game of Chess with Lord G., but had no conversation with him. Lady B's behaviour was so perfect that I would have given the world to recall my yesterday's letters. She is gone to Roehampton. Lord Granville dines at Holland House today, but I do not know if he will sup here afterwards. He will probably think it too select.

Miss Hunlocke, George Lamb and Mr. Robinson dine here. I am glad we have something like Beaus for her and I hope we are not responsible for their brilliancy. I do not mean to abuse dear George, as I am *become* one of his admirers.

I have a visit from Kitty Monck hanging over me. They are going into Norfolk the latter end of the week to be present at Lord George Beresford's marriage with a Miss Schutz. To compleat Kitty's disastrous destiny, the Bride is her old friend and the Bridegroom is her old lover.

[*The following is written in another hand.*]

If it had not been for the lucky circumstance of my being present at the composition of this letter, she would have exposed her ignorance of the common rudiments of grammar ; both she and Miss Trimmer have formed a conspiracy against my writing to my cousin G. Harriet has just cut a good joke.

Dearest G., Willy [Ponsonby] has been tormenting me till I let him put in the above nonsense, and it was at that price alone, I could prevent his reading my letter, which would not, for many reasons, have been agreeable.

Lady E. and Caroline were at the play last night. The house was crowded. Lady H. Villiers and Dick were there ; she looked very pretty, which must have been more than he did. Mrs. Beauclerk was with Lady Holland, very immense but in Brilliant beauty. Lady E. had seen Lord Lauderdale and I suppose he was galant, as she came home most amazingly elated. Lord Granville sat in front between her and Car, which, I conclude, pleased her, and they had George, Mr. Lutrell and Mr. Robinson, which was better perhaps in quantity than quality.

Le Fidèle Robinson seems perfectly happy and contented here and I should not wonder at his proposing himself as steward during our absence, for he seems quite established here and so very gay that I do not see a probability of his removing.

I am sorry to hear that you have been worried about a nurse—I do dislike Lady Westmorland's, she seems to me always to be doing disagreeable things.

Adieu, my dearest sister, love me but a quarter as much as I love you and I shall be quite happy.

Yours most affec^ly, HARRIET.

[Mr. Robinson was created Viscount Goderich in 1827 and Earl of Ripon in 1833. His nickname was "Prosperity" Robinson.]

To Lady Georgiana Morpeth

D. HOUSE, *Saturday, November 22nd, 1806.*

The Frank was the first thing that gave me pleasure in your letter today, as I know what it must be to you to have Lord M. with you again. Pray make yourself quite easy about my cough ; it has been a tedious and rather bad one, but I am now almost well again.

I do not know whether I have said enough to you of my aunt's very great kindness to me since you have been gone. She has lost no opportunity of expressing how much she wished to be a comfort to me, and has been a great one. She returned to Roehampton yesterday morning and did not accept an invitation to dinner at Holland House where G. was going. Lord Granville came from Holland House late. We played 2 games at Chess, which lasted till supper was over. He is in one of his most gracious moods and certainly improves upon the pleasantness of our evenings.

Lady E. F. is very disagreeable in doing the honours instead of me ; which for every reason in the world is painful to me. I believe Lord G. goes to Roehampton today and to Saltram on Tuesday.

I have been enduring Kitty Monck for an hour. She has been gossiping on every subject she could think of. She had just met Mrs. C. Bagot looking perfectly beautiful—but how extraordinary she should be walking alone in Bond Street—she wondered what her allowance was for she was covered with sattin and deep white lace. There is no end to this sort of conversation as with Kitty—Lady Isabella Fitzgerald is going to be married to I do not know who ; Miss Bentinck to Lord Rodney ; Miss Blake to Mr. Courtenay and Lady Elizabeth Villiers to Mr. Irby "by the force of passion driven." If this is so, and Kitty declares her authority is excellent, the capability those Lady Villiers' have of falling in love is extraordinary, considering the objects.

I must tell you that I was in a fever last night. I was talking to George Lamb and Lord Granville was standing by listening just as George said, " I tell you what is nothing new, Lady Cahir was always a little Devil ; she has only been consistent, she cannot act otherwise than in this detestable manner." Luckily Lord G. swallowed this most patiently, but from what you have told me he used to say of the " friendly little woman," I expected every moment the flame to burst.

Miss Berry was very entertaining the last time I saw her about Ernestine de Starhemberg mimicking her saying " n'est ce pas que Mounsieur le Comte Palfy vous a dit que la bouche de la Catalini est plus belle que celle de la Grassini ? " By the bye, I hear the former will oust Grassini in everything but galanterie. Her voice and person are beautiful, but she is devoted to her husband, a Mounsieur Valabuy whom she has brought from Paris, and is quite a *bonne enfant.*

God bless you, my dearest sister, a thousand kisses to George and a thousand remembrances to Lord Morpeth.

most affec[ly] yours, H. CAVENDISH.

[All through the correspondence Harriet spells Monck without the " c." In this letter she first corrects her error.]

To Lady Georgiana Morpeth

Sunday, November 23, 1806.

[This letter is written by William Ponsonby, all except the signature and the last line.]

I am positively ordered by Lady Harriet to write. It is in vain I say I am tired, hungry and exhausted—that I wrote yesterday and mean to write tomorrow. It seems quantity and not quality is to be attended to.

Lady H. will probably not tell you herself that she is in full possession of her talents and spirits—that she rose this morning an hour earlier than common, videlicet at half past one, and will probably amuse herself and her society till tomorrow morning about three. Is not this nonsense enough for one day and one page ?

H. CAVENDISH, victime de la Calomnie !

To Lady Georgiana Morpeth

Monday, November 24th, 1806.

I never said I would copy out the newspapers, especially as I thought you had the *Courier*, and that a second hand edition of it would not be necessary—my excuse for not commenting upon it, is that just as I was going to prepare a letter upon the subject, I received one from you, saying " Lord M. does not mind the attack in the newspapers," and then all his reasons for it—as I have seen but one, I concluded we were talking of the same and was happy to have my arguments (which upon such subjects are never good ones) cut short. As this is the only word I have seen I hope you will retract your scold, and this made so little impression here (which God knows it would have done if there had been the slightest idea of its being deserved), that it slipped more easily from my memory.

I am glad I have had so much to say upon this topic, as I have very little upon any other. Last night we had nothing but the O's and F. Foster (who is returned to Corise's) dining, who had just been convincing me he would never set his foot here again, and he came back with the same surly unconsciousness that he went.

Lord Granville was in Town but did not come.

I am to go out in the carriage today for the first time. This will prepare me for Holywell where I hope to be the 1st or 2nd. Lady Bessborough sleeps in Town tomorrow and goes on Thursday to Holywell, thence to Brocket and lastly to the Priory. Lord Granville, I believe, goes into Devonshire today.

God bless you, my dearest sister.

Believe me most affec[ly] yours, HARRIET CAVENDISH.

D. HOUSE, *Tuesday, Nov. 25th, 1806.*

I open my letter to tell you that the O's, Lord Thanet, Lord Granville, Bob Heathcote and *some other men* dine here today. Oh, what can make papa so frisky ? And how this dinner me pèse.

To Lady Georgiana Morpeth

Wednesday, Nov. 26th, 1806.

DEAREST SISTER,

You take in the *Courier*, so I need not repeat in future whatever nonsense I see there. Caroline asked George Lamb the other day if he had ever heard anybody blame Lord Morpeth's conduct. He said, never ; that he had seen a great many people at Holland House and had, on the contrary, happened to hear him the other day, most excessively praised. I am glad of this as if you should take it in to your head to be worried about Newspaper attacks, you must have at least equal delight in hearing private encomiums.

My dearest sister, I really cannot tell you what delight your return gives me.

Our dinner yesterday went off very well. Lord Thanet did not come. Bob Heathcote was in high feather, mimicking all the actors and Papa very entertaining in laughing at him. Lord Granville was here ; he goes into Devonshire tomorrow but does not stay away very long. He enquired very much about you and Lord M., and I never heard anything like his praise of both of you. I never before saw him *roused* to so much *energy*.

God bless you, my dearest sister.

ever yours, H. C.

To Lady Georgiana Morpeth

D. HOUSE, *Thursday*, *November*, *27th*, *1806*.

Many thanks for your letter, my dearest G. Wednesday seems to me now at a much more immeasurable distance than the end of the month appeared to me when you first went, but my consolation is like Madame de Sévigné's, "il faut que ce jour vient, comme tant d'autres que je ne désire pas."

Those disastrous Duncannons have had another overturn ; in going from Saltram he was thrown from the box, but was not hurt, and she was only very much frightened.

When I saw that angel chicken's large hand I was in extasies not to be described. Will you thank and kiss him and tell him his sisters are coming to stay all tomorrow with me, and I will send him word what they do and say. I am afraid Caroline will not contribute much to the latter article.

I have had this morning a long letter from Lady Cowper and an excessively entertaining one ; not talking about the *Horizon* as she did to you just after her marriage when I am convinced she was a little crazy, but very unaffected and amusing accounts of the Hertford Ball and the people they have had at Brocket. Lady Holland and Antonio seem to have been intolerable. She tells me Lady Georgiana Cecil is very *fond* of Mr. Brand and that she hopes she will succeed in the conquest, as she is a very good-natured girl, and her mother frightens every body else away from her, but encourages him. Caroline [Lamb] seems in great favour with her and I hear from C. St. Jules that she says nobody ever was so improved as Lady Cowper.

Lady B. goes to Holywell today and from thence all over Hertfordshire. Lord G. came very late last night and goes today. My aunt's behaviour never has been for a moment what one could not wish it to be. I cannot do justice enough to her kindness to me.

I was quite distressed last night when Lord Granville went up to take leave of Lady E. He said, " You have no commands for me ? " She answered, " Only to repeat to Lord and Lady Boringdon that I never can be grateful enough for their kindness to my poor dear Clifford, and that I hope they know how sensible I am to their attentions to him."

He actually gave a loud and contemptuous laugh and made a long *Oh*, drawing back as if he said, " indeed, I cannot undertake such messages."

I dared not look at her for some time, till I found I had all the embarrassment to myself and that she, as usual, either did not, or would not see what really made me colour to my finger's ends.

" For some will watch and some will weep,
So passeth life away."

The grave digger said very true ; there are many in England full as mad as he.

Is not the news dreadful, dear sister, and was not Lord M. perfectly right, as he always is, in not encountering such hopeless and unavailing dangers ?

F. Foster is come back full of his jokes, and in raptures with Walmer. He said out loud, before Lady E., that Mary [1] was an odd old girl, for she did *not* like her and was not kind about her. Lady E. must lament this extreme naïvité in everybody belonging to her.

Lady Jones has been with me and talking in the most dismal manner. She says if 5 cannons were shot into Buonaparte's body, she is convinced it would do him no harm, not even give him a moment's pain.

[*End of letter missing.*]

[1] Lady Erne, Lady Elizabeth Foster's sister.

John Charles, Lord Althorp,
afterwards 3rd Earl Spencer

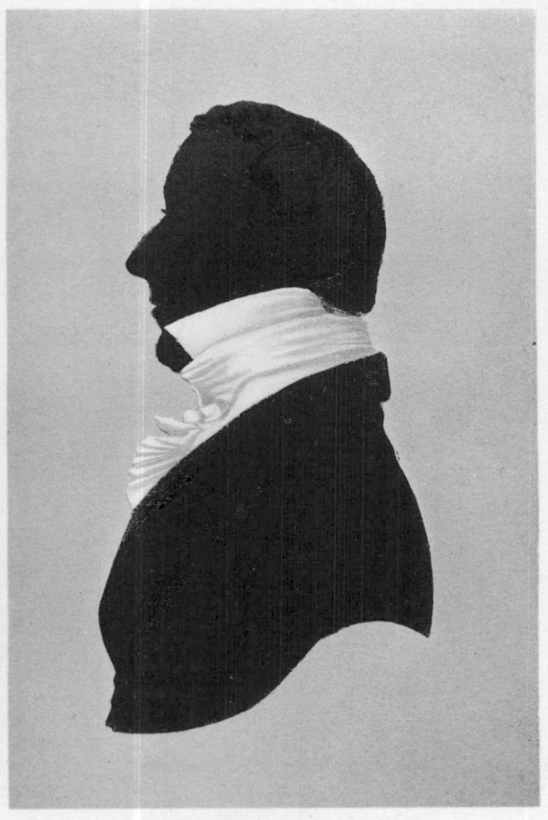

John, Lord Duncannon,
afterwards 4th Earl of Bessborough

To Lady Georgiana Morpeth

DEVONSHIRE HOUSE, *Saturday morning, November 29th, 1806.*

Mounsieur de Sousa is very anxious for the King [1] of Portugal to go to the Brazils. His brother and Almeyda are equally so, and the King's not having done it at first, he attributes to the advice of D'Aranjuez, whose politics are timid, if not treacherous, some fear having gained ground that he was won over to the French Interest.

Madame de Genlis writes constantly to Casimir, her élève, and as is supposed, her son—the wildest, most ill-bred boy that ever was seen, but a most wonderful player on the harp. In one of her letters she says, "Il est impossible d'être plus aimable que le Roi de Westphalie [Napoleon's brother] ; il a passé deux heures chez moi ce matin," just as we should of Mr. any body.

So far is mot pour mot from William Spencer, and not another piece of news, political or private, have I got to send you ; excepting by the bye, that Miss Roper told me Mr. Coke is certainly to marry Lady Townshend as soon as her marriage is over. As she is 54 this is more suitable in point of years than your account. I suppose the truth is that he has no thoughts of either.

My aunt has just been here ; she dines with us on Monday with all the tribe of them and wants me to go to the play with her. If my cold is well by that time I shall not dislike it but at present I am like le feu Boursoufflé, and can neither see nor hear.

The weather is delightfully bad today and all my hopes are mounted upon the fog and frost. I long for your coming more than ever, my dearest sister. I really do think, "Dear Hary-o, will you dine with us . . . Yours affecly, G. M." will set my brain a madding, and to be in Park Street, with the smart crowd of people [the children] coming in to desert, is really too much joy in prospect for one head to have to look forward to without turning.

Sir Walter says Sir Andrew is the pleasantest fellow in the *cra-atian.* Let me know if your opinion of him is the same and again what wind blows him to Castle Howard. I suppose he took some of you out to sea when you were little boys.

Papa's gout is better again and he has not yet seemed ill with it. I hope it will go off for many reasons, but chiefly that I fear if he has it decidedly, it will throw him back into his late hours. Yesterday he

[1] Harriet should have said Regent.

was not up till near 5 and then his earlier dinner must be bad instead of good for him as it comes immediately after his breakfast. There is no Brooks's yet and Mr. Motteux is so good as to devote his leisure hours to us.

God bless you, my dearest dearest sister.

ever most affec[ly] yours, HARRIET CAVENDISH.

To Lady Georgiana Morpeth

D. HOUSE, *Saturday, Nov. 29th, 1806.*

Thank you a thousand times for your politics, dearest sister, and for the future I will never let slip an opportunity of worrying you.

This news is dreadful [1] but it is musick to my ears to hear every body say how *sadly* right Lord M. was in his judgement of things when he left Hamburgh. Miss Trimmer who has hitherto with deep sighs, hoped no blame could be annexed to Mr. Marsh, now is all felicity and says, " Well, *they* were perfectly right after all," and I rejoice that your mind is relieved from anxiety, which I conclude Lord M. could not feel with the conviction he had that everything would turn out as it has done.

Do not write me word again that " my arguments are defective." If I had not seen " dear Haryo " I should have thought I had got a letter from Cobbett.

The dear little girls stayed with me till past 4. Caroline talks more and Georgiana incessantly. When she got her doll she shouted with joy, " See new doll, smart new doll." Pray give George these details. How I wish I was 5 years old. Yesterday conversation never flagged for a moment with the women. I wish I could say as much of those with older people.

Last night we were the usual quartette—Lady E., Miss T., Car and I, and what with the strange topics Car selects and the dread of disputes about the Jews and their Sanhedrin, I never was so uncomfortable in my life. The O's came late ; him from his Mother, who has been very kind and talking of " dear Lady Ossulston."

I hear there never was anything so personal and abusive as the Shrewsbury Mob have been to poor Mr. Hill ; and nothing so miserable as he was, not daring to utter one retort. Will this tame or aggravate him ? I am afraid he will sputter forth with more

[1] Napoleon was then carrying all before him on the Continent.

violence than ever from the constraint he must have been labouring under, and I see Lord O. is in terrible apprehension of being swallowed up in the torrent.

I think my courage would have failed me if the hope of it had been much prolonged.

God bless you, dearest sister.

most affec[ly] yours, H. CAVENDISH.

To Lady Georgiana Morpeth

Sunday, November the 30th, 1806.

If the Post had not brought me 3 letters today, I should be very much at a loss what to talk to you about this morning, for I have been confined to the house since I last wrote, and have not seen or heard any body or any thing of the slightest interest. One of my letters was from Sarah Spencer, to commission me to buy her mother a shawl ; another from Lady Mary Lowther begging me to sell our box at Covent Garden to Lady Monson, and a third and last, from dearest Lady Morpeth, to spin out answers to which is my only hope of filling this small page.

I have no more royal follies to transcribe to Lord Carlisle, but as George, par droit de naissance I suppose, is nearly as much interested about these elderly lovers as grandpapa can be, I shall make it a point to know a great deal more upon the subject before tomorrow's post ; though what is sport to him is death to me, for really when the Hero and Heroines of a Piece are none of them under 50, the main plot, à mon avis, becomes extremely flat to the audience.

Mounsieur de Starhemberg never means to leave England come what may. He has attached himself to it, considers himself as a native and will have nothing more to do with Austria if it finally declares war against us.

The point Lady Holland particularly dwelt on to prove your Angel-ism, was Lord and Lady C's adoration of you and your behaviour to them. If you did not feel the faults of his character and the *weariness* of hers, you would have no merit in bearing with them and the pinnacle of all merit içi bas, is to have the feelings of a mortal and the endurance of an angel. I hope you are now convinced of your claims to Lady H[ds] epithet and that I have not laboured the point in vain. [*End of this letter is missing*.]

To Lady Georgiana Morpeth

D. HOUSE, *Monday, December 1st, 1806.*

I cannot believe it possible that I shall see you next week, my dearest G., and when I heard that you might have remained in Yorkshire till the 15th, I was near fainting like Mrs. Heaton [wife of the Duke's lawyer] when she heard of the precipice she had passed in the night.

I am happy you did not disapprove of what I said about Lady B. Lord Granville has not been at Roehampton and she has not been in Town since I wrote. He supped here last night and if Lady Harcourt had seen us she would have given up her prophetic visions. We were both of us in our Aldwick humours and he seemed so bored, and went off in such a hurry, that I think he will never come again without more attraction. Tant pis, et tant mieux ; when he is agreeable, Lady E. is tiresome and she has power to turn any pleasure into a plague.

The Ossulstons are arrived and supped with us ; he is making up to her amply for these long years of scorn, as I never saw anything so attentive, affectionate and proper as his behaviour to her. She looks pretty well and has recovered from the effects of her rash, which really seems to have been a very bad one. She is not with child but it does not affect her spirits, as she is in des éclats de rire from morning to night, and determined, very reasonably, not to fret about if she is not, or to make it known if she is. It is not in her nature to keep either of these resolutions, but it is something to have made them.

They are both charmed with the Oaks and Lord and Lady Derby. I hear the little Earl calls his wife " my dear sweet darling " whenever he speaks to her and that they are the happiest of human beings. Corisande expatiates upon this little pattern of conjugal felicity and says Lady Derby is so in love with him !

I suppose you will know as soon as my letter could inform you how dreadful the continental news is. I have been to Lady Elizabeth to enquire if there is any thing more known than what you will see by the papers, but she says not. Mr. Hill and Mr. Bennet are coming to Town in a few days. Poor Harry fared ill at the Shrewsbury election —he was terribly unpopular and knocked down twice by the mob.

The Hollands are gone to Brocket Hall for 4 days, to make confusion more confounded. The visit will be laid on poor Car's shoulders and the Melbournes cannot bear it, but I hear Lady M. has written a very kind letter to Lady E. praising her and I hope she is now in favour again.

God bless you, my dearest sister. Mr. Foster has not appeared. Corisande came up to me last night and said very mysteriously—" Tu sais que Fredérique ne veut plus retourner." I must enquire what she meant. He has not character enough for this to be true and it would be late in the day for him to begin being scrupulous. I have no doubt that the Hawkesburys' [Lady E. F.'s sister and brother-in-law] have been making a violent attack upon him.

George Lamb is gone and we wear the willow. We have flirted in the most shameful manner and to all appearance his passion is a desperate one. This is all to enrage Caro [St. Jules] to whom I have read out loud what I have been writing. The truth is, his destiny is, I fear, to pine in hopeless love and Caro is as grand as any Empress. I find the explanation, which I have also read to her, offended her as much as the accusation, therefore I am to say " nothing more at all about me."

God bless you, most affec^{ly}, yours, HARRIET CAVENDISH.

To Lady Georgiana Morpeth

December, 1806.

God bless you dearest. We had the Examiner [1] yesterday. Mr. Hunt's jokes are really wretched. I am more convinced than ever that jokes are the Rocks upon which 9 understandings out of 10 split. When he is serious and impudent his writing often seems to me to be very good, but the Turtle, the sauce etc. in his remarks upon Ld. Ellenborough font Pitié. I wish there was a House of Correction somewhere for people who cut bad jokes. The Motto of it should be another comprehensive maxim of Lady Carlisle's (who I find a very famous Person) and a better than " spell well if you can,"—" Whenever you have nothing to say, say nothing."

[1] Leigh Hunt joined his brother John, in 1805, in writing and editing the *News*. They then embarked on the *Examiner*, a paper of advanced radical views. The appearance of an article in this paper on the Prince of Wales, in which Hunt had epitomized Prinny as a " fat Adonis of fifty," led to his being fined £500 and two years' imprisonment.

XI

THE VISIT TO ALTHORP

JANUARY TO MARCH, 1807

BY the beginning of 1807 Harriet was thoroughly tired of being a pawn in Devonshire House. Her easy-going character submitted to this, but she had a strain of toughness and justice that resented it, while her common sense told her that it was unnecessary.

It must have been with mixed feelings that she wrote to her grandmother to tell her that she had been invited to Althorp, that she appreciated the kindness of her uncle and aunt, Lord and Lady Spencer, in inviting her to stay with them, and she was sure she was going to enjoy herself very much.

But was she ? The Spencers and the Devonshires had never been very intimate. Georgiana Duchess's brother had always been a dull dog and he had married a sharp-tongued shrew. George, second Earl Spencer, son of Harriet's remarkable grandmother and her mother's brother, was very unlike them both ; where old Lady Spencer had been unconventional, he was very conventional, where Georgiana Duchess had faced her physical disabilities with courage and laughter, he had proved himself a hypochondriac. He was extremely handsome. He had married Lavinia, daughter of Lord Lucan, and she had willingly undertaken the direction of their household. To her mother-in-law, the Dowager Georgiana Spencer, she had been ingratiating and " douce," but to her sister-in-law, Georgiana Duchess, she had been impitiable ; she had never missed an opportunity of gently deploring Georgiana's eccentricities, of laughing at the imbroglios at Devonshire House or of deprecating the Devonshire set. But it was all done very delicately, and though the two branches of the family had never been intimate, Harriet accepted the Spencers' invitation with gratitude. Anything to get away from Lady Elizabeth and her royal " we."

Lavinia, Wife of George, 2nd Earl Spencer, and Daughter of the 1st Earl of Lucan

George, 2nd Earl Spencer, K.G.

There was, of course, one great drawback . . . the Spencers' eldest son, Lord Althorp, fancied himself in love with her. Or was it only the prevailing passion for arranging marriages between first cousins that had led to the idea that Althorp wished to marry Harriet? We shall never know. There is no sign that he was in love with her; indeed he appears to have been only wholly in love with fox-hunting.

Anyhow, Harriet sets out in the landau accompanied by her grandmother and arrives at the Spencers', only to find herself in nearly as confused a maze of indecision as regards to Lord Althorp as she had been with Duncannon.

But during her stay there she made a lasting friend of her cousin, Lady Sarah (the Spencers' daughter, who was to become Lady Lyttelton), and she came to understand her Aunt Lavinia, and with her characteristic generosity, to give her affectionate loyalty as well as gratitude for her hospitality.

Dear Hart complicated things a little. He was now seventeen and insisted that his bosom friend, Sir William Rumbold, was in love with Harriet. There appears to have been no foundation to this, but all the players entered into the game with zest and no harm was done.

But greater things were afoot; Lady Bessborough realized that the only way out of Harriet's invidious position at Devonshire House was marriage. She had played about too long, and when she came back to London, her aunt with determination took her out into Society.

But meanwhile she is at Althorp and cannot go out because of the frost-bite.

To the Countess Dowager Spencer

DEVONSHIRE HOUSE, *January 22nd. 1807.*

I am schocked to find that the letter I have to thank you for is dated the 12th, my dearest Grandmama. I did hope that by this time I should have been able to make my apologies to you in person. You have now, I believe, a house nearly, if not quite full, or I would beg very hard to be allowed to go to you for a day or two next week. If this should be the least inconvenient to you, do not think a moment of it and I will wait till you are at least rather a smaller party.

I think my aunt [Lady Bessborough] was the better for her visit to you. I saw her yesterday looking well and in tolerable spirits. Caroline Lamb is not going on in a comfortable way, she is very weak and full of pains and fatigue. Lady Duncannon, whom I went to yesterday, will I trust go on very prosperously. We all think her grown fat and looking well. Corisande is already so big for 3 months that I do not know what she will be before 3 more. She is perfectly well, and both she and her little Lord as happy and comfortable together as one can wish them.

I believe you know that Selina was with me from Tuesday to Saturday this last week, and although I rather hope she has boasted for me, I must tell you (and from *later* authority than hers) that I am become a confirmed early riser as (for the first time, I am ashamed to say) I follow your advice of jumping out of bed *the very moment* I am called, and for ten days I have persevered in it, till it has become as easy to me as before it was difficult.

I do not know whether you will have heard from my sister that she is to present Corisande the next drawing room, which is on the 12th of February. G. was with Mrs. Howe yesterday, who said at first I ought certainly to go, but upon being told the circumstance of my having been there exactly at this time last year and of my not feeling equal to it now, she most kindly said she would say something to the Queen that would prevent her being offended at my not accompanying my sister. Pray tell me if you disapprove of this arrangement.

Adieu, my dearest Grandmama.

Most affec^{ly} and dutifully y^{rs}, HARRIET CAVENDISH.

To the Countess Dowager Spencer

DEVONSHIRE HOUSE. *Saturday, February 17, 1807.*

MY DEAREST GRANDMAMA,

I am sure it will give you pleasure to hear that Papa has in the kindest and most generous manner allowed me to have from the next quarter 400£ a year. With the habit of economy I have, I trust, acquired, I shall feel myself the richest person in the world.

Adieu, my dearest grandmama.

Believe me most dutifully and affec^{ly}, yrs, HARRIET CAVENDISH.

To the Countess Dowager Spencer

DEVONSHIRE HOUSE. *February 28th. 1807.*

MY DEAREST GRANDMAMA,

I have but a moment to tell you that Papa has given me leave to take the landau to Althorp. Will you therefore let me know what day you leave Holywell, as I will be there the day before? I should prefer not leaving London till the last day. It is impossible to say how much I feel my uncle and aunt's kindness to me and the pleasure with which I shall enjoy being there.

Most dutifully & affec^{ly} y^{rs}, HARRIET CAVENDISH.

To the Countess Dowager Spencer

March 19th. 1807.

MY DEAREST GRANDMAMA,

My sister has kept me out so late that I have only time to thank you for your letter. I found my sister and the dear little children all perfectly well. We promise ourselves the greatest comfort in being with you the 28th.

Lady Duncannon and Corisande are both going on very prosperously. I have been with the Spencers today. I did not see my Uncle, but I hear he is well. I leave the *political* department to my Aunt, as I only know they, Lord Grenville's Administration, are out and barely that: God bless you, my dearest Grandmama.

Most dutifully & affec^{ly}, y^{rs}, HARRIET CAVENDISH.

To Lady Georgiana Morpeth

ALTHORP. [*March 1807*].

MY DEAREST SISTER,

I pity you for your dinners past and to come. Lord Granville seems to me to have the art of forming parties of peculiar terror.

What grieves me most is the number of visitors you seem to have in the morning, and you always say "I am interrupted by"—and then a string of fashionables, and all of them so interwoven into family connections that it is hopeless to escape from them.

I received this morning eight pages from Lady Elizabeth chiefly about Caroline [St. Jules], who I am afraid has been tormented by her little thoughtless namesake [Caroline Lamb], as she herself writes to me in a strain of remorse that is always favourable to George and tells me that C. Lamb has been meddling. I am going to despatch as much contrepoison as I can cram into a sheet of paper, but you may be sure that I shall not say a word that can set her against Mr. Lamb (oh ! if you could hear my deep groan) whom I firmly expect will be one of the chosen friends of my bosom before the year is out.

Corise seems to me by a note I received from her today in great glee at the increase of size and some pleasing symptoms. She quite scolds me for having left London and bribes me to return by saying Charlotte Hunlocke will give me some very nice little parties. Without any witchcraft she might have thought of greater inducements.

Lady Spencer continues to be in the most perfect good humour, and when she is, it is difficult to be more delightful. Her conversation is so improving without the least pedantry and so very entertaining and animated that I could listen to her for ever. She laughs at poor Lord Althorp without mercy, and she has no compassion on him when he gets bewildered, which often happens to him in the course of conversation. He, however, bears it all with the most unruffled good temper and bears what very few men at five and twenty would, to be treated by her as if he was the age of one of his little brothers. He sat down last night to solace himself with a game at patience. She immediately said, " Sal, go and take those cards from your brother, I won't have them dirtied." He offered one night to read out loud, as my grandmama was tired—" And who, my dear Jack, do you think would understand you if you did ? " was the answer. When he has been away for two or three days she either pretends or really does never miss him.

God bless you, my dearest G. I am going to venture myself into all the misery of a compleat thaw.

Most affec^ly yrs, H. C.

To Lady Georgiana Morpeth

ALTHORP. [*March 1807*].

I must begin by wishing you every possible happiness, my dearest sister, that every blessing may be secured to you and that if you have any wish ungratified, it may be fulfilled.

I hope it will not really be a disappointment to you, that any prospect of my ever being connected with this family is as far from my wishes as it is from probability, almost possibility. Everything puts it out of the question and anybody seeing the whole situation of all parties would in one half an hour think it as little to be expected and, forgive me for saying it, so little to be wished, as for foxes to hunt hounds or horses to turn Gentlemen. *We* suit so little and could be so little acquainted with one another if we did, that it never enters any of our heads to have any one idea about it, and when you mentioned it in your letter, it seemed quite droll to me. I love and admire my aunt, but had rather be anything but her daughter. I esteem and think highly of him in some respects but had rather be his Cousin than his wife. If I was so, I have no doubt but that I should be a very happy woman. The situation as far as every worldly advantage goes, would be to the height of enjoyment. His temper and benevolence are, I believe, unequalled and would secure the happiness of everything about him, as far as peace and harmony go ; but how could one speculate upon anything but a weary, tedious existence with a man whose whole soul is engrossed with one most uninteresting pursuit, who never speaks or seems alive but when one subject is mentioned, whose family talk of him *really* with despair, even my grandmother gives him up. He attends to no one person, no one thing, is surrounded with the vulgarist set of men, whose only merit, he confesses it, is their eagerness when they come in at the death ; in short a character that might have been distinguished both for all virtues and good sound understanding, dwindled into something less respectable than a groom, for I suppose it is on principle that the latter rubs down the horses and feeds the dogs. Now for a fair summing up of my opinion. Althorp as he might have been, no *reasonable* woman could refuse or help loving or respecting. Althorp as he is, no reasonable woman can for a moment think of but as an eager huntsman. He has no more importance in society *now* (as he is, remember) than the chairs and tables. He neither improves, heeds or values it. It is all one to him if he is amused or bored with pleasant or unpleasant people, listening to musick, playing at cards. He does it all, but as a way of passing through that portion of his time which is a dead weight upon his hands. Evenings and Sundays are to him visible penance and that time and the hour got through them his undisguised and only consolation. But when he appears at breakfast in his red jacket and jockey cap, it is a sort of intoxication of delight that must be seen to seem credible and one feels the same goodnatured pleasure as at seeing a newfoundland dog splash into the water, a goldfinch out of his cage, or a mouse run out of his trap. This is the man that I cannot wish to marry, that I cannot *snap* at and if I did, "nor wish nor snapping would avail."

Good night, my best and dearest sister.

To Lady Georgiana Morpeth

ALTHORP. *Sunday* [*March 1807*].

I like being at Althorp much better than I did when first I arrived and my time does not hang at all heavily upon my hands. Lady Spencer is kinder to me than words can express, and also to my grandmama, who is so perfectly good humoured and delightful herself that it would be impossible to be otherwise to her. Lord Spencer does not allow himself to be as much better as he certainly is. He is rather less of a shadow than when he left London, sleeps tolerably and eats as never man, sick or well, ate before. Lord Althorp who, as my aunt says, cares for neither Father, Mother, brothers, sister or for anything on earth but that noble animal, a horse, went on some hunting expedition early on Thursday morning and is expected back to dinner today. We are all going to receive the sacrament this morning and as I have promised to go and read with my grandmama, I must finish my letter later in the day. All this is happening before breakfast soon after nine, that most delightful time when I find my letters on my plate.

Ever most aff[ly] y[rs], H. C.

To Lady Georgiana Morpeth

ALTHORP. [*1807*].

A thousand thanks, dearest G. I did not dare expect to hear from you today. I had a letter, too, from Caroline. I am ashamed of the letters I write, but it is a moral impossibility to mend them. We are all as regular as clocks; read, work and play on the piano forte all the morning by the rules that are fixed, and play at Speculation all the evening.

I have only been out of the house once since I came, and that was the first day. The cold, which was excessive, gave me a frost bite on my cheek (not a hole like Wm. Ponsonby), and Doctor Carr, who was here the other morning, says if I go out during the Frost it will get bad.

God bless you, my dearest sister. If you have the slightest wish to have more of me, make Car show you all my letters. I never say anything to her that I do not equally intend for you, though I say many to you that I do not for her, of course.

My love to Lord Morpeth and the children.

Ever most affectly yrs, H. C.

To Lady Georgiana Morpeth

ALTHORP. [*March 1807*].

I am beginning my letter to you by the light of my lamp; my grandmama and Lord and Lady Spencer go to bed at about 10, Sarah and I at 11, and I was preparing for a long evening by myself, as I cannot go to sleep so early, when a light was seen in my room from the opposite wing, and Mrs. Scafe arrived, seized upon my candle, and has left me in a state of despair and astonishment not to be described.

Excepting a great deal of German and musick with Sarah, my day has passed exactly like the last I described to you. Lord Spencer is better though still very weak and my aunt in delightful spirits and good humour. Her attention to him is really beyond anything I ever beheld. She is like the most attentive servant and seems to watch every turn of his countenance and does not let anybody do anything for him but herself.

My fire is growing so dim that I must submit to go to bed and I promise you not to send you this scrawl tomorrow if I have time to write another whole letter. God bless you.

Friday morning.

As I have nothing but my thanks to send you, I have no excuse for beginning a better letter. Your letters are the delight of my life. I would not have you yield one inch in your comfort or conduct to the person [Lady E. Foster] I hate to talk about as much as you can. I am quite obliged to Lady Spencer for never having mentioned her to me.

I have had a very long letter from Corise. She is, of course, full of the agitation of meeting Lady Tankerville and says " Lord O. had ever since last night tears in his eyes." It must add more to the interest, than to the beauty of his appearance. She is full of Sir A. Paget and his admiration of you, which I will not repeat, as I suppose she has talked to you of nothing else.

Most affecly yrs, H. C.

I think we shall leave Althorp on Tuesday sennight, but I am not quite sure.

To Lady Georgiana Morpeth

ALTHORP. [*No date. March 1807 ?*]

A thousand thanks for your letter, my dearest sister. I am sorry Lord Granville has said anything to make your prospects more uncomfortable at Castle Howard. My opinion is that Lord Carlisle should be made to feel that he has to do with people who will not sacrifice their time, enjoyments and liberty to him, if ingratitude and complaints are all that they are to receive in return. His health is an excuse for irritability and resentment *at the moment* of what he may *fancy* cold or offensive in Lord M's manner to him, but such cold-blooded undervaluing of such a son makes my blood boil. I am convinced he is jealous of him and venting his rage at finding him attaching friends to him every day, whilst he remains old, ill and spiteful, with nothing but two or three old wives to listen to or heed him.

I do hope Papa is not going to Town. Pray thank him a thousand times for writing to me, no words can say how much I love him.

I am glad Lord Granville thinks I do not like him. It is not his opinion generally of the fair sect, but I suppose he thinks it love turned to deadly hate.

Sarah and I have had several long conversations yesterday and today in which she has done more to make me love and value her than months of the sort of *distant* intimacy we were before upon could have done. This at some future time, which I cannot bear to think of, may add to my misery, but now it gives me in many ways the greatest delight. She has the strongest and warmest feelings and her friendship, interest and anxiety about me and my future fate till yesterday I had no idea of, and to the last hour of my life I shall remember it with gratitude and affection.

I do not quite understand my aunt. I am clear of one thing, that she would *dislike* my marrying Althorp and that she prefers my keeping very much in the background in society and general conversation. There was a moment when I thought all was not quite so kind in her feelings and manner to me, but I became very submissive and silent—more like 3 than 23—and all is perfectly smooth again.

I have heard from Hart today, a long delightful letter. He is coming here very soon and I am to write this morning to desire him to fix a day. He complains that Keddleston is rather dull.

God bless you, dearest G. Pray write *fearlessly* for I have got a Pincushion, and on that Pincushion a pin, and through that pin a gold chain, and on that gold chain a key. This Key locks up a box which is hid under a couch in my own bedroom.

Most affectly yrs, HARRIET CAVENDISH.

To Lady Georgiana Morpeth

ALTHORP. *Sunday morning* [*March 1807*].

Your account of Lady Elizabeth hardly surprised me. "They be used to it," as the old woman said when she skinned the Eels.

Is Lord Granville in or out of spirits? And what do you think about Miss Beckford? [1] I spent yesterday entirely in crying. I do not often make such confessions, but my spirits were tired, "et je n'en pouvais plus." I had a long and melancholy conversation with dearest Sarah, but relating to subjects with which she was in no ways concerned. She has the strongest feelings but she has been taught to check and controul them as if they were crimes. (I need not tell you to destroy this letter.) But Mad^lle Muller told me she thought this had materially injured her constitution. She sang to me for the first time. I can say a thousand things when I see you that I dare not in a letter. She is quite an angel. It is very odd that she never showed me confidence before, and now it is as if she was anxious to lay open to me every thought and every feeling, and to make me thoroughly acquainted with every part of her life and conduct.

I am anxious about so foolish a thing that I have been half an hour by the watch wondering if I could be fool enough to talk to you about it. You know how anxious I am to behave well here and that

[1] Daughter of William Beckford, author of *Vathek*, who built Fonthill. She married in 1810 the Duke of Hamilton. Granville L. G. courted her in 1808.

the audience is Lord Stair, who is all full of Gossip, idle curiosity and ill nature. You also know how particular they are and that they would be rather uneasy if I was to speak for 10 minutes running to Louis Vigoureux or Signor Occhieda. Well, G., I am afraid that Sir William Rumbold, who is rather in the situation of the black Cow who may not look over the wall, will cause bad blood amongst us. Now remember you must not say to Lord M. or Caro what I say to you. I said to you the other day something about La Sorella della Madre, which was that. Hartington wrote me a long letter in which he says—" I resist all William's entreaties and wishes to see your letters. Yet if you knew how he bothers my life out about you ! " I thought from this, what we agreed upon at Chiswick, that he had hit upon the best way of toadeating Hart. I wrote to my brother to tell him that all I assured him was, if he ever showed one of my letters to any one of his friends, it would destroy all my confidence in him and put an end to our correspondence. This morning I received another letter from him, written as if he was drunk with spirits or mad, as you may judge by the style. " William and I shall be at Althorp on Sunday, for William is anxious beyond measure to be there. I only hope you will not tumble as much in love with him as he is with you. It would be a 'dénouement.' Oh but !—Addio sorella del mio cor. Hartington, Sanlo or William, for I really begin not to know which *yet* ! Fear not for your letters ! " My dearest sister, do not think me simpleton enough for a single moment (even if this is not a joke of Hart's without poor Sir Thing ever having mentioned my name), that this is anything but most mortifying to my vanity. If Sir William does pretend after 3 days to be charmed with me, it confirms all the harm we have heard of me and is humiliating to me beyond measure. But whatever is the state of the case, this is not the place for real or sham *dénouements*, and my dread of the remaining part of my stay here is not to be told. They will be here today by dinner time. Pray write and tell me exactly how to behave, only think all that is absurd in the world. There is no place in the world but this where I should have thought twice of this and no person but you to whom I should dare expose myself by repeating it. God bless you, my dearest sister.

Most aff yours, HARRIET CAVENDISH.

To Lady Georgiana Morpeth

ALTHORP. [*March 1807*].

MY DEAREST SISTER,

Hartington arrived last night whilst we were at supper. He is looking remarkably well, and in *outrageous* spirits. He goes again on Thursday, to be at a great Derbyshire ball, and means to dance all tomorrow night at Northampton. We expect Mr. Hanbury and Mr. Knightly today, 2 friends of Lord Althorp's, and Francis Hare tomorrow.

I breakfasted this morning with my uncle, Lord Stair and Mr. Isted and to my great surprise they were all praising Sir William Rumbold to the greatest degree. They are émerveillé at his beauty and think his manners remarkably pleasing and insinuating. My aunt, I expect, ne chante pas dans le même ton—at least, she mimicked his voice all the way as we went to bed, but really her satire is grown so very general that I do not think it in la pauvre humanité to escape untouched upon. The Duncannons went this morning and I feel very differently with regard to her from what I ever did before. I think her merits are really incalculable and attaching to the greatest degree. They are as happy as possible and the little girl is really a darling. Do you know, I suspect Doodle [1] of having confided to Lady Charlotte Greville that I am one of his adorers. I have often told you I am convinced he thinks so of me and half the world beside. I will tell you why when I see you. O Doodle mio, se tu vedessi quel cor che tu chiami fedele! [2]

My grandmother bids me tell you that she does not write whilst she knows that I do every day. She is delighted but I think very much out of spirits. I hear my aunt shouting in the next room. She is in her kingdom this morning, every body but me sitting round her, bouche béante, and it is well worth their while for she is entertaining beyond measure when it is her sovereign will and pleasure so to be.

Poor Lady Jones is confined to her room, in Indian muffles, and Shipley crabbedness, by a most violent sick headache.

I am delighted that Papa does not yet talk of leaving Chiswick.

God bless you, my kind and dearest sister.

Ever yrs, H. CAVENDISH.

[1] The sisters' nick-name for Lord Granville.

[2] "If you could but see the heart which you call faithful."

To Lady Georgiana Morpeth

ALTHORP. [*1807*].

A thousand thanks for your long and most delightful letter, my dearest sister. It has quite *elated* me and your very great kindness makes me happier than I can express.

As to Lord Althorp, my opinions must be at times inconsistent as it is quite impossible to fancy more distinct a difference between what he is and what he might be. He has contrived to make himself so compleat a zero in society, at least in this, that his having dined, danced and slept at Northampton last night never occurred to any of us as something wanting in it. I can conclude this from what I observed in others and answer for it in myself.

For Sir William Rumbold, I believe Hartington wishes his friends to see through his eyes till he fancies they do, and construes the simplest and most commonplace compliments into symptoms of love. I however believe Sir William thinks me (as I do not wish to make disclaiming speeches to you) prettier than Lady Jones and more *coming* than Sarah, but there is nothing in his manner which gives the slightest ombrage. This is a fair test by which to judge it, and a severe one.

Hartington does not talk as he wrote, or at least he says things that prove he was half mad with spirits and did not in the least know what he said. He ought to be pleased with his reception here. My aunt is remarkably gracious and Sir William is liked by them all. My aunt says that she is a miracle of candour in owning that she has overcome all her prejudices against him. They go back into Derbyshire tomorrow, at 6 o'clock in the morning—I am very sorry.

I cannot say enough upon the subject which you so sensibly and so justly lament—my aunt's really unaccountable violence. It is often entertaining, oftener disgusting, but certainly loses its power entirely as to the effect it might have in correcting or reforming the world. It is a lesson that cannot fail to bring conviction with it. To you only will I say, she has hardly left herself a friend. I never will be estranged from her, as well for her sake as my own. There may be a time when she may feel what it is to want the affection I never will withhold from her. To me she is uniformly, I may say *indulgently* kind. God bless you, my dearest love. I am not a moment alone and so afraid of being looked over.

To Lady Georgiana Morpeth

ALTHORP. [*1807*].

I do not know anything that could have vexed me much more than Lord Granville succeeding in getting at any part of that letter. All the subjects mentioned in it, I wish to be confined entirely to you.

The impossibility of hunting has thawed Lord Althorp a little, or perhaps the constant contemplation of the two extremes of madness and dullness, his friends Messrs. Knightly and Hanbury. Mr. Hare is infinitely more disagreeable than when we thought him so very much so some years ago at Chiswick.

My conversation is entirely engrossed by Hartington and Sir Wm. between whom I am *bodkin* the greatest part of the day. Hart, much the most galant and empressé of the two. Their carriage was at the door this morning at 7 o'clock. We had all pathetically parted, but the first thing that appeared at breakfast was ces Messieurs, who now stay certainly till Saturday and perhaps till Monday, which is the day I shall probably be with you at Chiswick, I trust.

Sarah is more improved by living more amongst young and *softened people* (I mean people whose tongues are not invariably two edged swords) than I have time or spirits to explain. She is indeed a most delightful creature, but till I see you I will not talk much about her. Her singing quite overset my poor uncle the other night. It is improved and really beautiful, with something so full and melancholy in the tone of her voice, that it is hardly possible to hear it without being affected by it.

I hear La Chape sung, and steps performing, and of course, Hart coming, so good-bye to you and all hope of quiet, besides a Turkey Pye and a round of Beef.

Remember how much I wish you never to show my letters and believe me

ever ever yrs, H. CAVENDISH.

I wish Lady E. would impress herself with the idea that it is not the gift but the giver etc.

To Lady Georgiana Morpeth

ALTHORP. *Sunday* [*1807*].

The last letter you shall write to Althorp, but pray write if it is only one line to Holywell that I may wake upon tidings of you. I have been very comfortable here and for many reasons a return to Town brings many miserable thoughts with it, but the thought of seeing you again is a charm I have neither inclination or power to resist, and I am this morning in spirits, which the dear and kind people here must perfectly understand and seem not to resent. My aunt does understand more than anybody else all I owe you and all I feel for you. It is one of the reasons that I love her so much better than Sarah who, with much less that is wrong about her, has not near so much warmth and feeling. In short, in what is right I have most esteem for Sarah and most affection for my aunt.

If you cure Mr. Drummond of his satire, you take away his principal recommendation. I think he is quite right in the use he makes of it, as he has neither bitterness nor ill-nature in his conversation and it does not, as in Lady Cowper, attack all equally. I never heard anyone more enthusiastic than he is in praise of his friends, both public and private, and nobody can blame him for talking of the folly of the Jerseys, of the inanimation of Lady Aberdeen and treating with some contempt the little race he meets with at Devonshire House. These are the only objects upon which I have heard him exercise his severity: I am afraid these arguments smell of the shop. I am afraid Caro and Lady Duncannon are both unwell, poor precarious ladies!

Ever most affec^{ly} y^{rs}.

To Lady Georgiana Morpeth

ALTHORP. *Wednesday morning.*

MY DEAREST SISTER,

I went into Sarah's room in the evening and Lord Althorp came and sat with us sometime. Except at odd times like that, I never have any conversation with him, and when I do, I always like and esteem him. He is so very natural and has so much simplicity and sincerity of character that it is impossible not to feel a great regard for him, but he wants everything that living out of his own family would perhaps give him. It is impossible to compare him with Hartington and not feel strongly all that he wants. There is so much sweetness and affectionate attention in that dearest boy's manner to anything that belongs to him, such animation in all his feelings, and kindness in all his intentions, that it is captivating to everybody that comes near him. My grandmother quite adores him and is, I think, unjust to the other, whose unpolished and unsocial manners are particularly offensive to her. Doctor Carr whom my brother saw and consulted about his deafness, said to my grandmother that he never was so struck with anybody in his life and mentioned, what I have done, the sweetness of his countenance, kindness of his manner. He then looked very steadfastly at her and said "Lady Spencer, all this you have in your other nephew, but repressed, checked—not one of you can know it—but if you were to see him as I do, you would know there were few—indeed nobody like him." This, then, is the harm of the system pursued by a mother to her children, meaning well, but judging, I think, most mistakenly. It is impossible not daily and hourly to have its bad effects and to harm the value and the consequence of indulgence and softness in all its branches. One must come into this school—I must again repeat that, for myself, I have experienced much kindness in a thousand ways, that to anybody but you, even saying what I have done, would be blameable to the greatest degree. But to you I must say that from many divided faults in one person, and different reasons that I will give when I see you, there is no house I would less willingly make my home—I love them all, I am grateful to them all, I see a great deal to admire, and to express my opinion of, or affection for. Sarah would be impossible, but on Saturday you will understand many of my apparent inconsistencies—and I have not passed my opinions lightly.

Lady Jones is an uncommonly clever woman but a wolf in sheep's cloathing. She sat by my bedside yesterday, agreeing with me in all I chose to say—but going far beyond—not my thoughts but my words.

God bless you, my sister. On Friday I think there is no doubt of my seeing you, and that is the day after tomorrow.

I beg you will give my best love to Papa, and tell him how I hope he is better—oh, how I do adore him, you and Hart—I would not be daughter or sister to any other people for all this world could offer me. Amami credi mi and hold your tongue, for as the poor people say—I make too free with mine.

H. CAVENDISH.

XII

DEAREST GRANDMAMA

1807

HARRIET'S letters from July to the end of October 1807 are to her grandmother, the Dowager Lady Spencer.

Lady Spencer was a very remarkable woman. She was Georgiana the 1st; eldest daughter of Stephen Poyntz of Midgham and was born in 1737. So vital was her character, so modern were her views, that it seems impossible to believe she was born 200 years ago. She married John Spencer, Esquire, of Althorp, grandson of the great Duke of Marlborough, in 1755, and ten years afterwards he was created Earl Spencer.

She had pronounced views on education and ruled her villagers at Holywell with a benevolent despotism. She started a school there and when her daughters, Georgiana Devonshire and Harriet Bessborough, retreated to the shelter of her house to recover from the buffetings and perplexities of London, they had to submit to a strict and salutary discipline. "Early to bed and early to rise" was the rule at Holywell, and not only that but the great ladies had to obey their mother's commands and go down and teach in her village school. Their children, too, had to attend the school when they were at their grandmother's, which was a remarkable practice of democracy in an aristocratic age.

Lady Spencer was original, decided in her views, filled with the best kind of worldly wisdom and remarkably tactful. Her handling of the incredibly difficult situation at Devonshire House after her daughter's death, is a triumph of good breeding and diplomacy.

Harriet, the daughter of the house, was in a most invidious position; instead of taking her natural place as her father's hostess, she was pushed aside by Lady Elizabeth Foster, saying "we" and "us" all the time.

It was true that Lady Elizabeth, too, was in a difficult situation; the Duke could not do without her. He was genuinely fond of her (as far as he could be fond of anyone) and admired her crisp common sense and sophistication. She had come there at Georgiana's suggestion to act as governess to the Duke's natural daughter " Louchee " in 1782. She had remained ever since, loved by Georgiana (who was grateful to her for undertaking her dull and antipathetic husband) and trusted by her. Had she not been Georgiana's go-between when she had approached the Duke and arranged with him for the settlement of the Duchess's huge debts ? To show Bess Foster, and the world, how much she loved and trusted her friend, had not Georgiana left her all her papers at her death ?

But, in Harriet's word, " the scene is changed ; we're alter'd quite." What had been an arrangement convenient to all before the Duchess's death, became exactly the opposite afterwards. It was most unsuitable and unseemly that Harriet should live under her father's roof with Lady Elizabeth at the head of the table. But on the other hand, Harriet could not live elsewhere without giving rise to even greater scandal and both Lady Spencer and Lady Bessborough realized how necessary it was that the Duke should learn to know and love his daughter. Never had there been a man more detached from and indifferent to his children, and this state of affairs must be changed, at any rate in Harriet's case.

So with the greatest tact, Lady Spencer set about solving the problem ; while Harriet was to remain under her father's roof, yet she must spend the greater part of her days with her grandmother who needed her company. Not only this, but Lady Spencer managed to remain on good terms with her son-in-law while contriving not to set foot within Devonshire House.

We find Harriet relying more and more on her grandmother. Both Lady Spencer and Georgiana Morpeth supported the young girl loyally and wisely with advice and comfort in her miserable situation.

Harriet must have had much in common with her grandmother ; she certainly looked ludicrously like her. There is a miniature of Lady Spencer as a young woman that might be a likeness of the child in the mob-cap when she had grown up, so strongly does it resemble the little Harriet. Lady Spencer is painted dressed in a riding habit, wearing " her own hair " and not powder (when this was almost de rigeur) and her features are exactly like Harriet's.

In the letters of 1807, Harriet's unhappiness at Devonshire House is not immediately manifest. She is still full of gossip, news and entertainments. All her friends, Caro Lamb, Lady Duncannon, Lady Cowper and Corisande are having babies. She goes to a few balls and the "little men" continue to sup at Devonshire House. Life appears to be the same outwardly.

In August she goes to stay with her beloved sister at Castle Howard and leads a happy, healthy life, reading, writing, walking and playing with her nephews and nieces.

To the Countess Dowager Spencer [1]

DEVONSHIRE HOUSE. *July 22nd, 1807.*

Our journey was very prosperous, my dearest Grandmama, but I regretted Tunbridge too much to think it very pleasant. I arrived in Town so tired that I could hardly walk upstairs and found nobody but Papa in the house. He enquired very much after you. I kept awake with great difficulty till Corisande and Caroline came from the Opera, and then found that I should not see my sister as she had gone home early to bed. Corise and Lady Duncannon are both well and we heard a good account of Caroline Lamb, who is arrived in Town. Mr. Vernon, Mr. Howard and Lord Lauderdale supped here but I resisted all these attractions and was fast asleep soon after 12, tho' Lord Lauderdale sent me up word that it was *very impertinent* not to stay and receive him.

I am now going to Park Street with my Tunbridge ware, which I hope and expect will make great sensation amongst the dear men and women there, and the first words of my next letter will be to give you an account of it.

My love to dearest Selina and believe me, most dutifully and affec^{ly} y^{rs},

HARRIET CAVENDISH.

To the Countess Dowager Spencer

DEVONSHIRE HOUSE. *Thursday July 23rd, 1807.*

I went to Park Street immediately after having finished my letter to you, my dearest Grandmama, and made the children perfectly happy with my Tunbridge Toys. George's delight at the nest of

[1] Harriet's way of addressing her grandmother.

GEORGIANA, COUNTESS SPENCER, GRANDMOTHER OF 'HARY-O'
FROM A MINIATURE

HARRIET, LADY DUNCANNON, AFTERWARDS COUNTESS OF BESSBOROUGH
FROM AN ENGRAVING BY BARTOLOZZI AFTER A PORTRAIT BY JOHN DOWNMAN

Boxes is not to be described and I was charmed to find that the surprise continued as undiminished as the pleasure, for the effect each new box produced seemed to me much the same after I had gone through the whole process a dozen times, and if my patience had been as unwearied as his astonishment, we should probably be at it still.

I found my sister well, but as everybody was, quite overcome with the heat of yesterday. She dined with us and we established ourselves at the Portico till near 12 with the Duncannons and my aunt, who came very late from Whitehall.[1] Lady Duncannon does not look ill but she is so much increased in size that I think it cannot be many more days before her confinement. George Lamb, Willy and Mr. Motteux supped here. I do not know if you are acquainted with the latter. I am, only because I cannot help it as he is rather a favourite of Papa's, and upon the strength of that comes here sometimes. He is most particularly disagreeable and has a mixture of insolent familiarity in his manners with a strong and evident partiality for rank and distinction in his heart, which is the more unpleasant as he is always forcing himself into the society of his superiors and then fancying that he makes all even by behaving to them as if he was theirs, and I am convinced that while he is treating Papa as if he was a Macaroni Merchant, he thinks himself little less than a Duke.

This morning I got up between 8 and 9, read 500 lines of Milton's *Paradise Lost*, walked in the garden, played upon a Russian Bilboquet Willy brought me last night, and pique myself upon my candour in confessing this last occupation to you.

I have received your kind and delightful letter, my dearest Grand-mama, and I do not know how to thank you enough for it. I envy you the coolness and the quiet of the grave, and remember perfectly seeing the man you mention and endeavouring to find out by his countenance whether his studies were gay or grave. I think you had better cultivate his acquaintance and establish him as your guard, as I know by experience that dread of footsteps in the Background interferes terribly with the comforts of a romantic situation and I am certain that the Tea and Cowper will have doubled their charms if a protector is seated at the corner of the bench.

[1] Lord Melbourne's house in Whitehall, since known as Dover House and now the Scottish Office.

Friday 24th.

I was at a great assembly at Lady Stafford's last night and the heat and crowd made me feel quite ill. Lord Lauderdale and Mr. Vernon came home with us to supper. Mr. Vernon has been speaking uncommonly well in the House of Commons and I like him very much for the quiet and unaffected way in which he receives all the compliments that are paid him about it. He enquired very much after you and hopes to meet you at Nuneham this year.

Most dutifully and affecly yrs, HARRIET CAVENDISH.

To the Countess Dowager Spencer

DEVONSHIRE HOUSE. *July 25th, 1807.*

I went last night to a Ball at Lady Heathcote's and was less hot and tired than I expected, which is saying all I can for it. It must seem odd to talk to you of Balls and assemblies as virtuous efforts, but ainsi va le monde, and it is not my fault that I am obliged to live in it.

Sunday 26th.

Hartington arrived here last night, to my great astonishment, as I had not heard he was expected. He has almost promised to fetch me the latter end of September from Castle Howard and we have even a grand scheme of going to Bolton Abbey on our way home. But this is quite a Château d'Espagne, and many may be the reasons for not putting it into execution.

I did not go to the Opera last night but the Duncannons and Lord Lauderdale supped here and I did not get to bed till very late. I begin to be afraid that you will think of my frequent mention of Lord Lauderdale quite suspicious, but if you have any fears, " look in his face and you'll forget them all."

Lady Duncannon is still well but I do not think it prudent of her, after the decided alarm she had two days ago, to be out so much and so late.

I was at St. James' Chapel this morning in the Vestry. The musick was beautiful and the sermon good, but the Ladies insupportable and seemed to be assembled there only to gossip and fidget about.

Here comes Corise to talk of what I am sure she thinks is the first accouchement that ever took place.

Tuesday 28th.

Lady Duncannon, Caroline Lamb and Corise were with us last night and, strange as it is to tell, they have as much emulation and rivalité amongst them as if there was a second apple promised to the biggest and I am quite worn out by discussions and comparisons on the subject, which is the only one they ever by any chance think upon or talk about. I hope it will all come to a happy conclusion very shortly and certainly at present no three people ever seemed better.

Poor Lady Frederick Campbell's [1] shocking death is but too true. I have not heard any particulars but it is supposed she must have fallen down in a fit near the Candle, as they say she was always remarkably careful about fire and would not have put it in any dangerous place.

I was at the Duchess of Rutland's yesterday after her little boy's christening. The King was Godfather, Lord St. Helens stood for him. The Godmothers, the Dowager Duchess and Lady George Cavendish, *were in hoops.*

[Haryo left for Castle Howard the next day, in the company of her sister and Lord Morpeth.]

To the Countess Dowager Spencer

CASTLE HOWARD. *Saturday August 1st. 1807.*

We arrived about 7 o'clock last night, my dearest Grandmama, and found nobody here but Lord and Lady Carlisle, William and Henry Howard. Lord Carlisle is considerably better than he was before he left London and it is wonderful how good his spirits are after all he has suffered. This Place is in its greatest beauty and magnificent beyond description. I woke this morning at 6 o'clock, but as nothing provokes Lord Morpeth so much as for people to get up early the day after a journey, as he does not recover from it, whatever they may do, I remained in bed till 8, which I mean in future to be rather a late hour in my day. I walked before breakfast in so high a wind that I could hardly keep my hat and schawl on, and came home with an appetite that can only, I am certain, belong to Yorkshire. They keep very good hours here ; dinner at four and supper at ½ after 9, and I was in bed last night by 11.

[1] She was a Miss Meredith, and was married first to the 4th Lord Ferrers, and secondly to Lord Frederick Campbell, a son of the 4th Duke of Argyll.

Lord Morpeth and little Frederick have got a complaint in their eyes, it was very troublesome to them in the heat and dust of the first day's journey, but I hope a good dose of Physick to both great and small, will cure it in a day or two. G. and the women are quite well and the latter very good travellers and pleasant companions. The Staffords are expected here on Tuesday and the Bishop of Carlisle next month.

I heard from London today that Lady Duncannon has had a second alarm but that it went off and that she is still well. I shall expect, however, to hear of her accouchement every day, as she cannot, I think, have many more of these slight attacks before the great one.

God bless you, my dear Grandmama,

Ever dutifully and affecly yrs, HARRIET CAVENDISH.

I must ask you a few questions before I seal up my letter. Do you recollect Bossuet's discourse " Sur l'histoire universelle " and do you think I shall be as much pleased with it as I am afraid I shall, that is, most excessively ? Do you advise me in my German studies, which I mean to pursue here with great diligence, to read with a dictionary or to do with literal translations ? Pray, do not say what I confess is the obvious answer, " both," as I have only screwed my application up to one and I wish for your decided preference.

To the Countess Dowager Spencer

CASTLE HOWARD. *Sunday August 2nd, 1807.*

We went to Chapel in the house this morning, which I never like as well as the smallest village Church, but as there is not one within two miles and none of the family go to it, I of course must give up my inclinations upon this point. I have taken two long and delightful walks in the course of the day and the variety of this delightful place is as great as its beauty. The hours we keep are if anything too early, as you will judge when I tell you that the clock has just struck 9 and I am expecting to be called down to supper every minute. However, the surprising amendment of Lord Carlisle does credit to the life he leads and I could not have believed that after such dreadful suffering any person could appear in both the health and spirits he does at present.

The little children are quite wild with the joy of running about all day in the woods and garden, and there is a great child who enjoys Castle Howard about as much. Indeed, George said to me yesterday upon my expressing more delight upon some subject than I suppose suited my years and dignity, "Don't be babyish, Aunt." Harriet [1] is becoming a great favourite with us all and she is the most intelligent little creature I ever beheld. She talks more than Frederick already and, to use nurse's expression, *masters* them all.

Monday August 3rd.

I walked an hour and read 50 pages of Bossuet this morning before breakfast, which to a person who gets up at half past six is easy. I hope you admire my triumphant style. Yet my journal has most of the merit of these good deeds, for I do not know that my industry or Bossuet's eloquence had half the weight as the idea of being able to boast in my writing today had with me. So now, as Walker says to Miss Trimmer—"You see my motives."

The Carlisles are in great uneasiness about the Duchess of Rutland's little boy who was taken extremely ill and is thought to be in danger. There is no post tomorrow and we can hear nothing further till Wednesday. Lord Carlisle continues very well and is all kindness and good humour to us all. Lord Morpeth's eyes are much better and G. only a little languid and easily fatigued.

I must leave you now to write to Hartington and beg him not to marry in a fit of irritation till I see him next. I know you have heard of Lord Tavistock. I have written a letter that will put him in a rage.

Tuesday August 4th.

We expect the Staffords to dinner today. Lady Charlotte Leveson is one of those people whom it is not merely difficult but impossible to get acquainted with. This is tant pis et tant mieux, as after the first disappointment, it saves one infinite trouble. Lord Stafford you know and I do not. He wears green spectacles and looks like a bird with a great beak. I used to fancy he had about as much in him as his likeness but my sister assures me he is most well informed and sensible. Is it a pincushion I see before me? ! ! ! I had better not say another word but that I am your dutiful and affect.

HARRIET CAVENDISH.

[1] The future Duchess of Sutherland, but now the latest baby.

To the Countess Dowager Spencer

CASTLE HOWARD. *Wed. August 5th. 1807.*

I walked after breakfast yesterday to the poultry-yard with Lord Carlisle. It is excessively pretty. The animals were all lodged, as I wish more people were, and it is better to be a Pheasant at Castle Howard than most things elsewhere. I then went upon the Lake and angled with a patience that deserved a better fate, for I caught but one small Perch and dropt it into the water as I was turning to exult over my success. My next expedition was to the farm, which is near a mile from the house. I cannot describe to you anything like the neatness and comfort of the whole thing, and the very pigs have an air of cleanliness and consequence about them. To be sure if the farm was like any other farm or the pigs like any other pigs, all the noble blood of the Howards could not walk over every part of it as they do, and it is no common sight to see so much dignity in a Pigstye.

On our return home we found the Staffords just arrived. This morning I was up very soon after 6 and took a long walk, wrote a long letter to Caroline and read Bossuet before breakfast. Can this be I?

Thursday, August 6th.

You do not mention amongst the arrivals at Tunbridge William Cavendish [1] and his bride. They are only to be there a few days, I believe.

I suppose you will see in the newspapers that the Duchess of Rutland last lost her little boy. It must have been a great schock to her, and I hear she is very much overcome by it. He was never healthy, and many people felt alarmed about him from the first.

I expect every day to hear that either Corise or Lady Duncannon are brought to bed and my letters from Town talk of the former especially, as oppressed and unwell with symptoms of its coming on almost immediately.

Saturday, August 8th.

George's reading goes on prosperously and Georgiana is the quickest little creature that ever was met with, but Caroline remains on my knee sometimes (to the credit of the patience both of aunt and niece) with b a, b e before us, till I hardly know them better than she does, and

[1] Father of the 7th Duke of Devonshire.

my sister, who is their great instructress, must have great talents for teaching if she makes anything of her.

I hear that Lady Duncannon has been suffering a great deal for the last 2 or 3 days and that they expect her to be brought to bed every hour. Corisande is still quite well.

I walked nearly five miles this morning before breakfast and to the most beautiful place that can be conceived. How I wish I could see you admiring this place.

To the Countess Dowager Spencer

CASTLE HOWARD. *Wednesday. August 12th. 1807.*

I suppose you will have heard from some London correspondent, my dearest Grandmama, of Corisande's safety and the birth of her little girl.[1] I hear it is a fine child and the image of her, with immense eyes and a quantity of black hair. She suffered for six and twenty hours. Poor Lord Ossulston was in dreadful agitation and has charmed them all with his kindness and feeling about her. Lady Tankerville was with her all the time, and Lord Tankerville arrived just as it was all over. I long to hear of poor little Lady Duncannon's accouchement for I fear all these delays must be bad for her strength and spirits and I believe she has already had to go through a great deal of pain.

I have been, since I last wrote, going on with my *usual* regularity. I do not think I have ever been in bed after 7, and I am half way through the last volume of Bossuet, with which I am quite delighted.

The only thing I have rather overdone has been exercise. I was tempted three days ago by the finest morning that ever was seen and a beautiful ruin of an Abbey[2] at a great distance from the house, and like a great fool walked ten miles before breakfast. The fasting and fatigue quite knocked me up; but it will make me wiser and you shall hear of no more follies in that line.

Ten thousand thanks, my dearest, kindest Grandmama, for your delightful letter, it is much more than I deserve when I think of my past indolence.

Thursday, August 13th.

I do not wonder at Selina's increased eagerness about the Jews. Lady Bessborough says in one of her letters—" All Mrs. Trimmer's

[1] Who became Lady Malmesbury. [2] Kirkham Abbey.

interpretation of the prophecies seem to be rapidly accomplishing." It seems to me that no one can hear of what is going on on the Continent unmoved.

To the honour of pincushions be it known that I retract my unjust assertion that it was an impossibility to become acquainted with poor Lady Charlotte Leveson. I have accomplished that event and find her a very pleasing sensible girl. She seems well informed and anxious to be more so and I never knew anything like the respect she has for Lady Sarah Spencer and all that she has heard of her acquirements. Lady Stafford treats her daughter very much in the same way that Lady Spencer does Lord Althorp, and never were there two people with whom such conduct is more ill-judged. Indeed I do not know anybody whom it would not make appear to disadvantage.

I have just been looking from my window at a most extraordinary person, an agent of Lord Stafford, who weighs seven and twenty stones.

[*End of this letter is missing.*]

To the Countess Dowager Spencer

CASTLE HOWARD. *Friday August 14th. 1807.*

We have had both yesterday and today violent storms of thunder and lightning and it is now raining in torrents. I think a bad day is sometimes not unpleasant in a large house in the country, though people in general lament over it as if it was a great and irrecoverable misfortune. The Gallery here is the whole length of one side of the house and very near the Billiard room, where I am learning to play, so that between the two I am in no want of exercise. I have been almost the whole morning puzzling over one of George's dissected maps—I did not know the names of the departments of France as it is now divided, which made me feel very ignorant, however I took up a newspaper and I have so bad a memory that it is quite a task to me to remember them.

My sister had a few lines from Hartington this morning. He writes from Chatsworth and says "Tavistock and I are both here, luckily, unmarried." He means to meet us at York races next week and will, I conclude, come here with us afterwards. I am afraid Papa has had a good deal of gout, with some fever ; it is now in his ankles and I did not quite like the accounts today. I cannot fix a time for leaving

Castle Howard and though I think this gout of Papa's makes it more probable that he will go somewhere in the Autumn, I have not heard a word of it in any of my letters from Town.

Corisande is going on delightfully and both her and Lord Ossulston half wild with joy at Miss Bennet's strength and beauty. No news of Lady Duncannon yet ; I wish I felt as secure of her doing well and I think my aunt must be quite worn with anxiety about her. The accounts of Caroline Lamb are as good as possible.

Saturday 15th.

My sister had a letter from my aunt Bessborough this morning ; she says Papa is better and his fever gone off. The weather is quite delightful today—the storms have cooled the air and the rain has made everything look so fresh and smell so sweet that I cannot stay in the house any longer and you may congratulate yourself upon it, my dearest Grandmama, for I am in a very stupid humour and wish anything would clear my head as well as the weather.

Sunday 16th.

I got up this morning at 6 and finished Bossuet—I am very much pleased with it and afraid that Russell's Modern Europe, which I mean to begin tomorrow, will sound but ill after the eloquent language and beautiful style I have been accustomed to in the other.

I have had a long letter from Caroline this morning with very good accounts of the different invalides—Papa is a great deal better and Corisande almost as well as if nothing had happened. She had just seen Lady Duncannon, who is constantly in pain, but nothing that seems as if her confinement was nearer than it has done for the last fortnight or three weeks.

To the Countess Dowager Spencer

CASTLE HOWARD. *Thursday, August 20th. 1807.*

Frederick Howard came here the day before yesterday. He is a great addition to our party, as he is a very good-humoured, pleasant person and talks rather more than the rest of his family, which is the great and almost only thing one laments the want of in the society here, as Lord Carlisle certainly keeps his children in great awe of him and they are in their behaviour to each other more like a Prince with his followers, or a General with his Aide de Camps, than a Father with his sons and in conversation with him, those who will not submit their opinions entirely to his direction have no alternative but silence. I think the fault does not lie entirely on Lord Carlisle's side. William, by not drawing any line between independence and obstinacy will yield to him in nothing and Frederick by the same error of not distinguishing civility from servility, yields to him in everything. Lord Morpeth is so reserved and the little boy quite a spoilt child, so that amongst them all there is not one that encourages him to more familiarity or kindness, and they all increase in him the very faults they suffer from.

Saturday August 22nd.

I am glad to find that at the time you sent your letter you were relieved from your anxiety about Lady Duncannon. I hear it is a fine, fat little thing and they are both going on perfectly well. My walks before breakfast have of late been put a stop to, from various reasons. Samuel [her footman] has been indisposed, which began by shortening them and I then found that as I always take long walks with the Morpeths I was not equal to quite so much before and after dinner exercise in this oppressive weather.

I am sorry to hear that there are such drawbacks to what I have heard of Mr. Hare's great talents and acquirements. I know very little of him and only remember thinking him in danger of being pedantic and affected.

August 23rd.

I have only just left myself time to tell you that Papa is so much better but that I hear nothing more of his plans.

God bless you, dearest grandmama,

Most dutifully and affecly yrs, HARRIET CAVENDISH.

To the Countess Dowager Spencer

CASTLE HOWARD. *August 25th. 1807.*

I had a letter from Caroline yesterday with a much better account of Papa but she says they cannot prevail upon him to be moved into the room next his to change the air. This does not look like a journey, at present, at least. My brother is to be at York with Lord Tavistock today and we meet him there tomorrow. He has written twice to us. The first letter began, " Mei cari sorelli," and ended, " Goodbye, my good girls, behave well at York and do not disgrace your brother." This last direction he seems to have much at heart, for again today his letter is full of good advice. He bids G. bring jewels for Tybald [herself], come in a coach and six, bring none of the children and above all treat him with the greatest respect and upon no account call him either " Hart " or " my love." He says one of us must open the ball with somebody of distinction, that he wishes he could unbrother himself for the occasion, as Lord Tavistock is not known in the County and does not dance well enough. They are both going to Scarborough after the races and Lord Carlisle has asked them to come here in their way.

Wednesday August 26th.

We have had another letter from my brother this morning. He means to return with us tomorrow and sleep here one night, on his way to Scarborough, where Lord Tavistock is gone to wait for him. We go to York after dinner today to dress there for the ball.

Today's post brought us still better accounts of Papa. I hear Lady Duncannon has been obliged to give up nursing as they were alarmed at the very great weakness of the child.

I have just been sending invitations from Lord Carlisle to Frederick Foster and William Ponsonby. I shall like their being here very much, if one will talk enough and the other not too much. Either of these extremes would be particularly mal tombé here.

I continue to be a very early riser and am not often in bed after ½ past 6. I read with great regularity and find it the only way to do it with either pleasure or profit. I have got over my very unreasonable terrors upon two subjects, as I can walk through a field of the quietest cows without fainting or Hystericks, and I remain superba di me stessa, perfectly quiet whilst my great enemies the wasps fly close to my face and hands.

Most dutifully and affecly yrs, HARRIET CAVENDISH.

To the Countess Dowager Spencer

Friday, August the 28th. 1807.

" Ah ! le plus beau jour du voyage est celui du retour," was never so applicable as in the present case, my dearest grandmama ; our York expedition has been a most uninteresting one, but now that I am here again in peace and quiet, I have no regret but the impossibility of conveying any amusement to you.

We found Hartington waiting for us at the inn on Wednesday, with the greatest impatience, but more eager about our being in time at the ball than anything else and in a ferment about our dress, equipage and behaviour. I never saw him look so well ; he is grown quite fat and blooming and has more appearance of health and strength than I ever saw him with.

We arrived at the rooms and found very few people there, but it got very full later, and we stayed till near 4 o'clock. I danced with Mr. Thornton and Mr. Ibbetson, of whom I can only say that I hope I never shall look upon their like again. The race in the morning was excessively pretty but the stand was so hot and crowded that we were all quite knocked up when we left it. We brought my brother here and he stays with us till tomorrow, though Lord Tavistock is waiting for him at Scarborough.

Saturday, August the 29th.

Papa has been out on the steps and is considerably better. Lady Duncannon's little girl is quite well again, now that she has given up attempting to nurse it. Lady Jersey is, I find, decidedly with child and though excessively weak and obliged to take great care of herself, likely to go on well.

I find Modern Europe really very entertaining, at least as much as is quite independant of the Author, Mr. Russell, who seems insupportably flippant and conceited, but my ignorance makes much of it new to me and I am continually deeply interested in the dénouement of events that I dare say the rest of the world know as well as their Alphabets. I am now in the beginning of the 16th century, and am rather proud of being a little tired of the three great rivals—Charles, Henry and Francis, but these are symptoms of ignorance that I cannot expect you to enter into.

Hartington is just going and I must bid him good bye—we expect him and Lord Tavistock here before they leave Scarborough, where they both intend leading a very regular and studious life.

God bless you, my dearest grandmama,

Most affec[ly] and dutifully yrs, HARRIET CAVENDISH.

Do you know that I have attained the great age of 22 today ?

To the Countess Dowager Spencer

CASTLE HOWARD. *Sat. September 5. 1807.*

A thousand thanks, my dearest Grandmama, for your letter of the 28th, and for your kind remembrance of my birthday.

Lady Carlisle has been giving me some lessons in driving, and as she has a perfectly quiet horse and only drives in a gig, I am not the least afraid and enjoy it very much.

I am afraid I am too fastidious and I have accustomed myself to *speculate* too much on the characters of other people, which has two very bad consequences ; in discovering their failings, I overlook their perfections and whilst I am discussing their faults, I forget that I might be better employed in getting rid of my own. I will guard against this uncharitable temper of mind and your excellent advice shall be a check even upon my thoughts.

We hear of nothing but the beauty, strength and size of Caro's boy and her rapture at its birth. She succeeds in nursing it and seems to be as well and as prosperous as one could wish her. Lady Duncannon's child, too, is very much recovered and Caroline tells me is grown quite pretty. Corisande writes me whole pages about the perfections of Miss Bennet [her baby] and I hear Lord Ossulston can think and talk of nothing else ; he forgets even his politics and thinks more of the Cowpox than of the Danes, and of nurses than Ministers.

I have just received letters from Town—nothing is mentioned about Papa's leaving it and I begin to think he will end by remaining there the whole year.

Our party here is very small at present ; William Howard is not returned from Belvoir Castle yet and Henry is gone to Eaton. The Dow. Duchess of Rutland is coming and I am so used to see her covered with jewels in the thick of a London crowd, that I feel tempted to say as Horace Walpole did of a french woman whom he had seen "briller" very much at an assembly in Paris—"C'est fort bien içi, mais que fait on de cela à la maison ?" Tempted only, my dearest Grandmama, for I shall not now say it to anybody but you.

Believe me most dutifully and affecly yrs, HARRIET CAVENDISH.

To Lady Georgiana Morpeth

[BOLTON ABBEY] *Monday. 14th Sept. 1807.*

Hartington's account of the wind coming in at all the doors and the beds being damp was only to alarm you, my dearest G. The House, or rather the room, is perfectly warm and comfortable and my sore throat is entirely gone.

I cannot even attempt to give you any description of this place. It really is beautiful beyond what I could have any idea of. I have as yet hardly seen it, except by moonlight ; I do think it much finer than anything I ever saw before.

Hartington is in high spirits, sings a good deal, plays upon the spinet and makes Chance bark to enliven the place. We are going to walk to the strid and I have hardly time allowed me to finish my letter. Our bedrooms are a little like some of the small bedrooms at Hardwick with Casement Windows and Velvet Beds. The room we sit in is really delightful with three large arched windows at one end and a blazing fire at the other and the two arches which were originally the entrance into the gateway are in the middle of it. The Abbey is entirely detached from it and stands upon a steep bank close to the River Wharf. There are two magnificent trees between the gateway and the Abbey and the rocks and woods on the other side of the river are perfectly beautiful. Put all this together in your own head, which is as you see more than I can do on paper, for though nobody admires this sort of thing more than I do, I never can describe and feel when I attempt it, like Mr. Harbord, an intolerable weight upon my brain.

God bless you, my dear G. I mean to persuade him [Hartington] to set out early on Wednesday and hope to be at Castle Howard soon after 4. What shall you say at breakfast ? Pray, remember me to everybody.

To the Countess Dowager Spencer

CASTLE HOWARD. *Friday Sept. 18th. 1807.*

MY DEAREST GRANDMOTHER,

Hartington's raptures about Bolton [Abbey] and all Doctor Whitaker's animated descriptions had not prepared me for the extraordinary beauty and magnificence of every part of the place. We saw as much of it in two days as was possible, as we walked on Monday 10 miles and Tuesday 14, and they appeared to me nothing from the variety of almost every step we took.

I was delighted to find the Bishop of Carlisle [1] here at my return.

[1] Edward Harcourt, afterwards Archbishop of York.

He went this morning before breakfast to my great regret and returns into Cumberland in about 10 days, where he is anxious for my sister to go for the Carlisle races. I do not know what will be done about it, as Lord Carlisle is against it from the fear that Mounsieur [1] will be here about that time and have nobody to meet him. I hear Papa is to be strongly advised to leave Town about the end of this month, and if he does I am afraid I know what I ought to do. If he should remain in Town, I think I might, without scruple, continue longer here, especially as my sister and Lord M. seem to wish me to stay with the Carlisles during the week they are in Cumberland, as my doing so might in some degree lessen the objections to their going.

Sunday 20th.

I wish very much to talk to you about my own plans which are now coming to a *crisis*, and although I hate to torment you with my perplexities, I am too anxious for your opinion and approbation to keep them from you. Papa is certainly going to Bath in a few days and as my sister is to be in Cumberland this day week, it was necessary that something should immediately be settled about my leaving this place or remaining here entirely. My sister is, therefore (after much consideration and I confess some fears and doubts remaining in my mind) to write to Papa today to tell him how much she wished to keep me with her, and to say many kind things from Lord and Lady Carlisle, who really have been all goodness to me about it, but at the same time to assure him that if he has the least wish for me to accompany him, I shall be happy and ready to do it. It is impossible for me to tell you how anxious I feel. I never felt so strongly a wish to act right, or how much the consciousness of having done so may console me under any degree of suffering, or the contrary embitter my enjoyment. I was told when I came here that if my father went into the country, I ought without doubt, to go with him, but now all that I see here give me exactly contrary advice.

I will write to you again tomorrow, my dearest grandmama, when I shall perhaps be able to do it more clearly.

most dutifully and affec[ly] yours, H. CAVENDISH.

[1] Comte d'Artois, brother to Louis XVIII.

To the Countess Dowager Spencer

CARLISLE. *Wednesday, September 30th. 1807.*

I have been so hurried since I last wrote to you, my dearest grandmama, with forming my plans and, as you will see by the date of this letter, putting some of them in execution, that I am afraid you must have begun to dread a relapse into indolence, and I write to you chiefly to prove to you that if you had any fears, they were without foundation.

The high character my sister bears with so much justice is contre-poison to many sorrows and mortifications that other circumstances sadly connected with me must perpetually make me feel, and I do every day find her more excellent and more kind, and there never was a person more formed to contribute to the happiness of everything about her than she is.

ROSE CASTLE. *October 3rd.*

MY DEAREST GRANDMOTHER,

This letter will give you better than I can an idea of the hurried, unsettled life we lead. Our Carlisle gaieties which finished yesterday did not leave me a moment to continue my journal to you. After the bustle of a race ground every morning and a ball every and all night, it is impossible to describe the enjoyment of returning to the quiet and comfort of this delightful place.

I never saw Lady Ann Vernon [1] before. She has been all kindness and civility to us. Of the Bishop, it is hardly necessary to say that to know him better is to love him better and it is delightful to see him surrounded by his family. You know Mr. Vernon and therefore I need not tell you that he improves upon acquaintance more than anybody I ever met with. Leveson, the second son, is very handsome and both he and William, the next son, have the gentlemanlike manners and right sort of civility that for a long time one has seen so little of amongst young men, that it is become almost as rare as it is pleasant. No pins in the family, my dearest Grandmother, and indeed you have blunted all mine so effectually with your wise advice and kind reproof that I begin to find no pincushions into which they will stick. At the balls I danced principally with the Vernons and Lord Lowther,

[1] She was a daughter of the 1st Marquis of Stafford and half-sister of Lord Granville, wife of Edward Vernon-Harcourt, then Bishop of Carlisle.

Lord Lonsdale's son, who is very young and very goodhumoured and seems endeavouring to retrieve by reading and good company, the harm that a neglected education has done him. There never was certainly any creature sent out into the world so unfinished.

Adieu, my dearest grandmama.

To the Countess Dowager Spencer

CASTLE HOWARD, *Sunday Morning October 11th.*

I have not given you any account of the two last days we spent at Lowther, both of which omissions in my tour, I must make up for, before I thank you for your letter which arrived the day before yesterday.

I had often heard my sister say she would like to live at Naworth which I own surprised me when I saw it, as although it is beautiful and interesting to the greatest degree, it owes both these advantages to the very things which to me would put liking to live there quite out of the question. Every step I took within the Castle made me quite grateful that I did not live in times when everything was obliged to be sacrificed to personal security and I should never breathe quite freely in a place where damp dungeons, great Iron rings to chain the prisoners of war down in them ; Walls almost thicker than most modern houses and intricate winding staircases in every part of the Castle still exist and are perpetually reminding you of all the horrors of petty wars, the constant dread of attack, and precautions for concealment and safety that must have occupied its inhabitants and would make me fancy even now, if I was one, that I heard the enemy at the gates and expect to see armed Chieftains in all the dark windings of this most gloomy edifice.

It is rather a falling off to describe our morning there, after this formidable picture of what my feelings might be in the same place, but as the Scots no longer make inroads into Cumberland, excepting indeed with their droves of cattle, which incommoded us so much in the journey that Lord Morpeth was very near turning Quixote and fighting them out of the windows of the landau, and as Lord William Howard's apartments are now occupied by a fat Mr. Ramshaw and his wife, who thought of nothing else but preparing us a most excellent breakfast, I must tell you that we established ourselves in the most modernized room in the house and devoured Yorkshire cakes and hot rolls as if there had been nothing better to see in the place. We then took a beautiful walk round a wood in which the Castle stands, and drove to the Abbey of Lanercost—the finest I ever saw—for Bolton (considering only the Abbey) is far inferior to it.

The Lonsdales are very civil and obliging people and Lady Mary,[1] the second daughter, a good humoured, lively girl with many delightful talents, drawing very well from nature, playing with great execution on the piano forte and delightfully on the harp. I was pleased to find her *as early a riser as myself* (how does that sound, my dearest Grandmother, in Oxfordshire? In Yorkshire my activity is becoming quite proverbial), and we walked all over the place, which is magnificent, before breakfast. I am just now in the most uncomfortable uncertainty about my plans.

October 12th. Monday.

I was interrupted yesterday but must proceed to tell you that my Father talks certainly of going to Bath next week and I am waiting in anxious suspense for a letter from Hartington, who will come for me either before or after a great ball Lord Fitzwilliam is going to give at Wentworth. In the first case I must, I fear, leave Castle Howard next Sunday and at any rate in less than a fortnight. I will not allow myself to dwell even to you upon the change this will be to me, but perhaps if the sacrifice was not so great a one, I should be less able to make it; for as it is, the necessity of it seems to me so strong that for some time a doubt upon the subject has not entered my mind, and nothing is so painful as indecision and uncertainty.

This house is going to be quite full. Mr. Vernon arrived last night and we expect Prince Esterhazy, Comte Potocki and a Major Something who travels about with them, today and Mounsieur with two of his suite, the Baron de Rolle and Monsieur de Puységur tomorrow. I will begin my next letter with some account of our foreign guests.

Adieu, dearest grandmama,

Most dutifully and affecly yrs, HARRIET CAVENDISH.

To the Countess Dowager Spencer

CASTLE HOWARD. *October 18th. 1807.*

I have your letter still unanswered, my dearest Grandmother, from my time having been so much taken up with my undecided and

[1] Afterwards Lady Frederick Bentinck.

uncomfortable prospects. Every day brings me a different account from London, and I am now convinced that my Father will end by remaining there. When he has any return of gout, he is unable to move, and when he is at all relieved from it, he thinks it is unnecessary. At all events, I leave Castle Howard next week. Hartington is to be here Wednesday and wishes me to be ready to go on Thursday. I shall find Devonshire House in the most disagreeable state, as Caroline is gone for a short time to Hastings with the Bessboroughs. But even this makes me glad that I determined to return.

I have often heard of Lady Cecilia Johnston and always with praise of her wit and dread of the use she makes of it.

This house for the last week has been quite full, chiefly of foreigners. Mounsieur is perfectly good humoured and unaffected and puts one entirely at ones ease, but it is wonderful to see what high and childish spirits he is in from morning till night, for I should have *thought* even the constitutional gaiety of a Frenchman would have yielded to as much public and private calamity as I suppose any one person ever had to go through. Madame de Sévigné said of James the 2nd, whom she saw dining at Versailles—" Il mange comme si n'y avait point de Prince d'Orange au monde." I wish she had been by Mounsieur at dinner yesterday. What virtue is it that they flatter themselves they are practising, my dear Grandmother, on their jour de maigre ? I never saw any Protestants feast as these Catholics fast, and they must be desperately fond of roast Beef and roast Mutton, if such dinners as I have seen them eat for the 2 last days have anything to do with self-denial. Prince Esterhazy and Comte Potocki are also here. The latter is very clever and entertaining, but terribly languid and indolent, a little by the bye in the style of William Ponsonby. He is an excellent mimick, but in the most inoffensive manner, as it is almost always general, such as noises at a great dinner and English people footing in a Country dance. Mounsieur de Puységur, whom you have probably seen, is most uncommonly clever and entertaining, but a thorough Frenchman, growing old reluctantly and mixing so much bitterness with his satire that it is impossible in our turn not to mix a great deal of disgust with our admiration of his brilliancy. He seems to me to have less heart than anybody and whilst his countrymen are gay and forgetful from thoughtlessness, he is so from want of feeling.

To Lady Georgiana Morpeth

SCARTHING MOOR. *Sunday October 25th. 1807.*

MY DEAREST SISTER,

Our journey hitherto has been as tolerable as I could think it, having left you with a sorrow and regret that I will not attempt to describe, but you will be glad to hear that I do not give way in the least to low spirits and have begun practising the exertion that I shall have so much need of.

We had, thanks to our supplies from Castle Howard, a very good breakfast at York and both Hartington and I made up for our early rising by sleeping very soundly for the next stage. At Feny Bridge he devoured all Mrs. Hall's jellies and cakes and at Barnby Moor we had a magnificent dinner that I was quite sorry not to be able to do more honour to.

It was rather against Hartington's inclination that I persuaded him to sleep here tonight, but he is now perfectly reconciled to it as our rooms are much more clean and comfortable than those we should have found at Newark and we shall be able to reach Bugden with great ease tomorrow.

We have been looking at the Comet for the last five miles, as it has appeared for the first time to me, very bright and conspicuous. When first Samuel announced it in a loud voice from the Coach Box, I was convinced it was a robber and pulled off my rings in a great hurry as an offering to him. This delighted Hart, almost as much as my afterwards expatiating for an hour upon the singularity of the Comet and the length of its tail, and at last finding out that I was exercising the powers of my imagination upon the evening star.

Prince Esterhazy was here yesterday morning and the waiter when he told me this added " and Lewis slept here the night before." I suppose I looked surprised and he took it for ignorance, as he turned round at the door and said with rather a contemptuous nod, " Lewis the 18th."

Your praise has given me the strongest wish to deserve it and your advice I will endeavour to follow in every moment when I am tempted to act in a way contrary to it. I promise you neither to be *harsh* nor *gloomy* and to think cheerfulness and gentleness almost as great duties in my situation as propriety and firmness. The last without the others may lose half their effect. It would be a sad thing to make the sacrifices

I have made of no use, by neglecting to make smaller ones of my own feelings of discontent and ill-humour.

I love you better than anything else in the world and my confidence in you is as great as my affection, therefore never scruple blaming or scolding me, and above all write me constantly your opinion " tant en bien qu'en mal."

Ever most affecly and gratefully yrs, H. CAVENDISH.

XIII

"DELICATE DISTRESSES"

OCTOBER TO NOVEMBER, 1807

BY the autumn when Harriet returned to London from Castle Howard, she had fully determined to take her rightful place in Devonshire House and so she immediately set about making herself noticed by, and necessary to her Father.

But it was not so easy—Lady Liz was ambitious for her daughter, Caroline St. Jules, who was unofficially engaged to George Lamb. She believed that the Prince of Wales would further the young peoples' interests when he came to the Throne, and as he was then at Brighton, to Brighton they would go. Harriet was in a fever—she could not, would not smirch her mother's memory and her own reputation by haunting the Pavilion and its dubious inhabitants in the company of Lady Liz. Luckily the weather and the Duke's indolence saved her.

Also old Lady Spencer came to settle in Jermyn Street for the winter in order to help and protect her granddaughter, in which project she succeeded with her usual tact.

The autumn offered Harriet the addition of several new admirers. Amongst these were Frank Lawley and William Ponsonby, who proved more of a trial than a pleasure with his boyish and ill-advised attentions. There were also Comte Potocki and Prince Paul Esterhazy who had been staying at Castle Howard. These young foreigners appear from both Harriet's and Lady Bessborough's accounts to have been excessively coxcombical, were in England, accompanied by "a sort of travelling Tutor," and were much patronized by Miss Berry, till she heard that Potocki had been poking fun at her, when she focussed all her attentions on Prince Paul. Miss Berry was also in "a chain" about her first cousin, Robert Ferguson of Raith, as Lord Elgin was divorcing his wife, by Act of Parliament, on Ferguson's account. Agnes Berry had been engaged to her cousin in 1804. Mr. Ferguson and Lady Elgin were married in 1808.

Louis XVIII resolved to join his brother, the Comte d'Artois in England, having been forced to leave Mittau by the Russian government. He landed on October the 29th and established himself with his little court of *émigrés* at Gosfield Hall, lent to him by the Marquis of Buckingham. Corisande's father, the Duc de Gramont, went to pay homage to his King and his son-in-law, "little o," threw all his tiny weight into the royal scales.

To Lady Georgiana Morpeth

D. HOUSE, *Tuesday, October 27th, 1807.*

I have but a minute or two for writing. I found Lady Elizabeth in papa's room, to which I immediately went. I am certain he was glad to see me. He kissed me and smiled very much. I think he looks well and asked after you immediately. I am quite revived, but I really wanted it for I never felt more low, and even agitated, than I have done all this morning, but I am now full of hope and your letter has given me equal pleasure and courage.

Lady E. is in perfect humour and quite *obsequious* to me. She is dying to leave Town and thinks if the weather is good we shall certainly go to Balls [Lord John Townshend's] and Salt Hill. There is also a grand scheme in agitation, which I see would be exactly what she would delight in—to go to Brighton for a month, where the Bessboroughs, Melbournes and Cowpers would immediately join us.

Now that I have left you, I feel a strange sort of indifference come over me about time and place. I do not care in the least what we do, or if we do nothing. I have no object but Papa and that I may be one to him, I feel more possible than I ever did, and I have not one wish besides excepting those *ungovernable* ones that relate to your arriving here.

God bless you dearest.

To Lady Georgiana Morpeth

DEVONSHIRE HOUSE, *October 28th, Wednesday Morn*[g]*, 1807.*

MY DEAREST G.,

I cannot tell you that my regret at having left you is less than it was for it does, and must, encrease every moment, but my prospect of comfort here is much greater than at my first thoughts of returning I allowed myself to think it could be. I do not think I was disposed to look on the bright side of things yesterday, yet I really flattered myself there was more kindness and *cordiality* in my Father's manner than I had ever before seen, and I find the best way to think less of Lady E., is to think more of him, and instead of brooding over her situation and conduct, to devote myself to the duties of mine.

After I had finished my note to you, I went again to her room, and found her so very anxious to leave Town, and backing her anxiety with so many quotations and recommendations from Physicians and friends, that I expect to go for some days into the country, if it is only for the sake of a quiet life. Dinner was ready at half past 6, which I find is half an hour later than it has been for at least two months. I talked so much, that I should be ashamed if my father had not seemed pleased with my doing it. He is amused at Frederic Foster's size and appetite, which he says you told him of first, and I took care to expatiate upon it. He questioned me a good deal about the foreigners and made the most *prononcé* laugh at Puységur's comparison of Lady Perth to a " ramoneur " [chimney sweep]. Lady E. is full of the Duchess of St. Albans, who was with her yesterday morning. She says she has much more mind than could be supposed from her manner, but confirms what we have heard of the disorder or derangement of it. She is full of " Corinne " and studying Italian. These foreign and sentimental occupations gave me suspicions at first, but Italy and Poland are not the same countries, and I am sure Count Potocki and sentiment are not the same things.

Hartington and my father had a great deal of conversation after we left them and my brother was delighted and said, " His Grace was all gaiety and condescension," and woe is me, complimented him on his playing the piano forte remarkably well. Think how this redoubles all the well known Waltzes.

At half past ten Mr. Motteux arrived and congratulated himself in a manner that proved he thought himself congratulating me upon his being settled in Town for the Winter and assured me he never set foot in any house but ours. What a happy distinction !

We had to wait supper for my father till ½ past 12 and I was by that time so excessively tired that I only just stayed to see him begin eating and came away.

Caroline Lamb is settled at Brocket. Lady E., who to give her (reluctantly, I fear) her due, is more fair in her statements than most of the people we have to deal with, gives an account of her something between the praise and blame we alternately heard so much of. Her child has not cured her of her absurdities. She went to the play the other night tête à tête with her Page, and the first thing she saw was Lord Egremont in the opposite Box, who must have enjoyed it much more than the Farce.

Corisande's letter was from Edinburgh ; the given cause for going there, a Tooth wanting Plumbing, but the real one I suspect, what she frequently expresses " the not being sorry of a little excursion."

I found a note here from Miss Trimmer, who proposes coming to me tomorrow for a few days. This is in some ways delightful to me, but I have always the fear of it not being liked by my father. However it will not be for long, and as Lady E. said to me last night, talking of Prince Paul and Count Potocki, " We must go very often late to the play and if we see them bring them back to supper," I am too happy that her being with me will be an excuse, at least till near the time Caroline comes. I shall like to have these people sometimes, for a long evening with Lady E. and Motteux is really beyond my limits of patience.

Grillion's Hotel is taken for the King of France, who is expected in a very few days.

Adieu, my beloved sister. I entreat of you to write to me and tell me which of the expeditions I mentioned yesterday, you should approve of for me.

most affec^ly^ yours, HARRIET CAVENDISH.

Pray remember me to everybody, and tell Frederic Foster that I really do think him, upon the maturest deliberation, the greatest fool I know. If " Lady Morpese " is as douce as the Foreigners think her, how will she ever contrive to deliver such a message ?

I have thought more of Miss Trimmer's coming and really rejoice in it ; for long days, mornings rather, spent quite alone, would prevent me being able to keep up my spirits as much as I would wish to do. God bless you, dearest of G's. How unkind it is of them to torment Mr. Delmé, if he is simpleton enough to dislike it.

Lady E. has been to me just to say that she means to encourage

Caroline's staying as long as the Bessboroughs do at Hastings. This may be 3 weeks longer, but I cannot be selfish enough to regret it. I also hear that papa is likely to go to Balls early next month, and that Lady Melbourne hopes to prevail upon *us* (Lady E. and I) to go to Brocket whilst he is there. Is thy sister a Lamb that she should do these things ? I might as well be a daughter in law at once. If my grandmother is at Holywell I shall settle the difference by going to her ; if not, " to live in the same house, sign the same name, all one large family," may possibly have been prophetic !

To Lady Georgiana Morpeth

DEVONSHIRE HOUSE, *Thursday, October 29th, 1807.*

My great consolation since my arrival here has been the different letters I have received, yours of course the principal. But both my grandmother and Sarah have written with so much kindness and approbation, and Lady Spencer, whose affection and good opinion you know how much I value, has sent me messages so warm and flattering, that I felt if possible more convinced that I have not made the greatest of all possible sacrifices, that of being with you, my dearest sister, in vain, and that in proportion as my conduct is approved of, it would have been blamed, if I had listened to my own wishes and inclinations.

I have just been answering a kind note from Lady Bessborough and one from Caroline [St. Jules] urging her to stay at Hastings as long as they do. It almost makes me laugh, which is but fair, as I am sure it has often made me cry, at my perpetual role of Heroine, and I mean to myself to be constantly occupied in arguing against my wishes.

It is odd to be in a situation where such strange things are difficulties. My greatest at present is how to avoid going to the play. Lady E. worries me from morning till night about it and is always saying " When shall we go ? After all we must go." Miss Trimmer arrived yesterday to my great satisfaction. I thought papa did not seem the least displeased to see her and Lady E. is in the highest good humour. But she redoubled last night her hints about the play, and indeed they are such broad ones that, for the first time in my life, I have felt rejoiced at waking with so oppressive a cold, that my stirring from the house for some time is quite out of the question.

Dinner went off very well again yesterday. Doctor Stephenson prevented all fear of the conversation flagging, and as he is contented to go on like the accompaniment of a song, nobody scrupled occupying themselves about their own subjects. I could not help thinking that it would be an excellent thing at Castle Howard to hire someone to keep up a perpetual hum. It prevents that fear of a long pause and dread of breaking through it, that makes the dinners there so formidable. Lady Melbourne has come to Town and sups here tonight.

My blood boiled at the beginning of your letter (of which I take the most *vigilant* care). Is he [Lord Carlisle] jealous that he can't talk bad French and cut silly jibes? Does he wish no smile to appear on the human face divine, that is not put there by his stale stories and far fetched jokes, or can he really enjoy the mortifications of others and check all enjoyment and humble all vanity but his own, from motives of spite and malevolence? Patience and Pardon, dear G., but there is fire in your room where you may put me and my sins in a blaze in a moment. I am really weary of crying, " Le pauvre homme ! " Oh, Aunts, Aunts ! wherefore are ye aunts !

A packet has just been brought to me from Lady George Cavendish, requiring an immediate answer to a pressing invitation to Latimer. Have I written page after page about my duty in vain? I will send her Edgeworth on the concatenation of ideas, that she may another time put together in her dear head, that after having every inducement to stay and sacrificing every wish of my heart in the necessary and positive duty of coming to Town to my father and explaining all this to her in the longest detail, I cannot the next day set out for Berkshire [Buckinghamshire ?] with no reason at all. Mais comment faire, hélas, pour s'expliquer ?

Hartington met Prince Paul yesterday who said he would call upon him today. I have not yet made advances towards seeing Miss Berry ; but will send this morning to see if she is in Audley Street.

Ever most affec[ly] yours, HARRIET CAVENDISH.

F. Foster consenting to remain till Sunday at Castle Howard, does not look like resentment, but if I hear anything I will let you know. Tell him to write to me, as he would not scruple venting his anger to " la vieille."

Pray tell Lady Carlisle that Bertrand made an immense " Mr.

Sloane " for dinner yesterday and that there was not a crumb left, so great was its success.

To Lady Georgiana Morpeth

DEVONSHIRE HOUSE, *Friday, October 30th, 1807.*

How very happy your letters make me, my dearest G., you do not know how much good and pleasure they bring with them and in this melancholy house, with nothing mended in the prospect I have so long looked forward to with dread and sorrow, I feel myself after receiving them, full of nothing but delight and gratitude to you for your encouraging kindness.

I never in my life saw my father so much at his ease with Hartington and so affectionate, I may really say, to me. He supped with us last night and talked to me the whole time, and though at near two my Yorkshire eyes were like pieces of lead with fatigue, I enjoyed it, " comme s'il n'y avoit point de Lady Elizabeth au monde." I used to do her too much honour in suffering her to have so much influence over my feelings, whilst I prided myself that she had none over my conduct, and my real aim ought to be to make both equally independent of her, at least as far as is possible in my situation.

George Lamb came here yesterday evening and is grown so tranquil and posé that I was quite pleased with him. To be sure there was no being very boisterous with my father, Miss Trimmer and I and he accordingly adapted himself to us with a very good grace. We talked of the Quaker Persuasion and Mr. Boreham's scruples of giving his oath to please Miss Trimmer ; of jugular veins and surgical operations to interest my father, and the evening passed with mutual satisfaction and perfect harmony. He is grown considerably fatter, I am afraid, though it might be from not being used to him that it struck me.

I received a letter from Lady Charlotte Leveson this morning that really made me laugh out loud ; after many apologies for writing again she tells me it is " because I have been so fond of you ever since I left you at Castle Howard (not but that I had a great esteem and respect for you before), but not at all what it has been since that period " etc. She then quite turns my head by telling me that M. de Puységur says he does not know of which he is amoureux fou—Georgiana or me ! Console her for this divided homage by telling her that it would be her if she could play on the piano forte.

Hartington met Comte Potocki in the Park yesterday, all muffled up in great coats and silk Handkerchiefs, and Prince Paul swinging up St. James's Street.

Lady E. continues to persecute me about the play, but my cold is at present an excuse, and will give me time to find another.

I hear nothing more of Balls and Brocket. It is still suspended over me by a single thread, but as that thread is neither more nor less than my dear papa's indolence, I have a tolerably firm reliance on it.

Did I tell you that Lady George [Cavendish] and Anne are coming to town tomorrow, and hope to spend 2 or 3 hours with dear Harriet? I must prepare myself with numberless anecdotes of "my sweet little godchild," to whom, by the bye, and to all the dearest men and women I beg to be remembered in whatever you find the most efficacious manner.

God bless you, my dear dearest.

To the Countess Dowager Spencer

DEVONSHIRE HOUSE, *Saturday, October 31st, 1807.*

Your letter has put me quite in an agitation, my dearest grandmother. No words can say with what delight and gratitude I should accept your kind offer of coming to Town, but I fear I ought to have scruples in pressing you to a scheme, that must in many ways be very painful to you. Yet I cannot resist telling you that the relief and comfort of your society and protection would be to me just now would be unspeakable. My difficulties with regard to Lady Elizabeth (left as I am *at her mercy*), for Miss Trimmer being with me does not in the least prevent her persecuting me from morning till night to go out with her to the park, play etc., would all be done away with the instant you are in Town. And yours, with regard to the same person, might easily be removed by your determining (as Selina tells me you have thoughts of doing) never to dine out.

I think, my dearest grandmother, for a short time you might contrive to be not very uncomfortable in Town. It is so empty that you would not be in so much danger of being worried by visits and acquaintances as you usually are.

The Post this morning has brought me so many letters requiring answers, that I must not give any more time to a subject both my head and heart are so full of, though I am afraid I shall make sad nonsense of any other today.

Most dutifully and affly yours, HARRIET CAVENDISH.

To Lady Georgiana Morpeth

DEVONSHIRE HOUSE, *Saturday, October the 31st, 1807.*

George's green trowsers is a more unpleasant event than upon first reading I thought it. I hope it will be cleared up. One does not see to whom the dear man's little inexpressibles could be object enough to prompt such a daring theft.

Today's post has brought a letter from my grandmother with the kindest offer of coming to Town on Tuesday to stay till Lady Bessborough returns, which will be on the 15th. She means to make her health and a fear of having other invitations an excuse for always dining at her own house. I shall devote my whole mornings to her, but I have told her that from dinner till the time my father usually leaves the drawing room, I shall never sacrifice one moment that I can be with him. Her being in London will be a great protection and her society a great delight to me. It will be an effectual excuse for not going out with Lady Elizabeth, who worries me now so incessantly about it that I should have been puzzled what to do after my cold had left me. The life I now lead is so suited to my grandmother's early rising and love of occupation that I think she will not find herself uncomfortable here, and as Lady B. is away, I have no doubt but that her avoiding Devonshire House may be managed without fuss or tracasserie.

Another comfort that her coming will give me, is that if my father goes alone to Balls (which has been talked of) my grandmother will take me during that time to Holywell, instead of my remaining tête à tête with Lady E. here, or accompanying her to Brocket.

Lord Bessborough and George Lamb dined with us and the latter was, as usual, very pleasant, but a little more unruly than the night before. I will own to you also that he looked so very enormous, his hair and face so red and his actions so uncouth, that I felt more strongly than ever all my doubts and fears about Caroline's present and future prospects, with something so perfectly opposite to herself and what I had always fancied she could love. My relief, therefore, was very great at a letter I received from her this morning in which she says, after telling me they correspond (which, by the bye, is to be kept a profound secret), that her feelings for him are such as would fully satisfy any person who could doubt the reality of her affection.

I had also a long letter from my aunt Bessborough, very affectionate and seeming pleased with my having written her one. George is very reasonable about Caroline Lamb. He laughs excessively at her attempting to deny all that passed at her lying-in, but thinks she had some excuses for her. He says she is very absurd with the child; rides out upon the high road, the Horse or Ass (I do not know which it is) led by the page in full dress, the baby on her lap and her maid and the nurses following on foot, and then wonders why the Turnpike men laugh at her.

God bless you, my dearest G., I long to hear how the Hollands *do* at Castle Howard; if Lord H. is allowed to be agreeable and if Lady H. allows herself to be so.

most affec[ly] yours, HARRIET CAVENDISH.

Miss Berry is at Strawberry Hill, but comes here on Monday for a few hours. She wants me to go down to Brocket with her and Lord Melbourne next week! The deuce is in the people. What do they think I have left you for? I am to think about it and by that time my dear grandmother will come and be my universal excuse.

To Lady Georgiana Morpeth

DEVONSHIRE HOUSE, *Sunday, November 1st, 1807.*

My letter today will not be quite so much couleur de rose as mine have hitherto been and yet I do not know that anything but fancies prevent it being so. I believe I exerted myself too much upon arriving here and the kindness of my reception and your approbation and praise really had such an effect upon me that for the first three or four days I was in the highest spirits. It was not in the nature of things for these to last, and if I have been worrying myself unnecessarily today you must attribute it, as I do now, to fatigue and hurry of spirits.

I told you yesterday with what pleasure I looked forward to my grandmother coming to Town and how great a comfort and relief her protection would be to me. All this I still feel, but I am sure you understand the dread that has seized me, of her and Miss Trimmer doing anything ill-judged or violent that should put me in the most painful and distressing situation. As it is, I must be the bearer of all messages between her and my father and the awkwardness or difficulties that may arise from her never coming into this house must consequently all devolve upon me.

For the other thing that has worried me today, it is so trifling that I hardly know why it vexed me, and so nonsensical I have hardly patience to repeat it. I should have put no importance to it, if the person who had mentioned it to me had not put so much, and I put it in your head to get it out of mine.

My maid, after a great deal of confusion and prefacing, praise of the openness of her temper and the toleration of mine, told me that she had been made very angry and unhappy by hearing my conduct much wondered at and blamed. And what do you think for? My behaviour to Mr. William Ponsonby! My unfeigned surprise and incredulous laugh seemed rather to relieve her, but she proceeded to tell me that there was not a person who does not firmly believe that I mean to *marry him*. Not only every servant in the house, but in every one where she visits, and that George Lamb and Caro are not as much considered as engaged as William and I; that at Castle Howard the servants did nothing but lament it, and that your amiable suivante abused me in a way that almost ended in a serious quarrel. She said that after having set myself up for difficult, from *motives of prudence* (what a consistant account!), I refused Lord Duncannon whom I *loved*, to accept his youngest brother and that you were extremely to blame for suffering it and not *put a stop to it at first.* Walker then ended by imploring me, if I did not think it of any consequence to myself, to reflect how much others did, and that it had been said to her at three different places that no man could ever think of marrying Lady Harriet while she suffered Mr. W. Ponsonby to dangle after her wherever she went!!! She added to my astonishment by saying, " I always thought less of it, My Lady, from knowing that there is another person who would be your choice, if it was not from motives of prudence." She then told me that this was Frank [Lawley]. That Joseph, Duncannon's valet de chambre, told her of it, and that one morning about 5 months ago, one of the servants rushed up to Laure's [Caro St. Jules' maid] room and said to her—" If you wish to see My Lady's sweetheart, Mr. Lawley, you must watch at the window, for they are shut up together in the drawing room and you may see him go." That she flew downstairs to the lobby and supposed at the time she thereby missed him by that means.

Dearest G., was ever unoccupied person so constantly occupied, disengaged person so eternally engaged, proud person so perpetually humbled ? In high life supposed to be promised to Frederick Byng, in low life to Willy ! Seriously, is it not tiresome and pray measure out to me in your next letter the degree of anxiety and impression it ought to make on my mind, and if any change of manner to my poor unconscious cousin would ensure me from all this steward's room gossip. Goodnight, my dearest, dearest sister.

My aunt George was with me an hour yesterday. Anne dressed "en bergère," a stuffed gown bound with blue, straw hat on one side, nothing wanting but Lord Lismore and a crook to compleat the picture.

Monday, November 2nd. 1807.

A letter from you, my dearest kindest of G's., to make everything smooth and quiet again.

I have just had a line from my grandmother and, that I may not weary you with being of the same mind for two pages together, I see her arrival again du beau côté.

Papa is going to take me to Chiswick today and we return to receive the following gay set to Dinner ; Mr. Crawfurd, Mr. Meynell, Mr. Crowle and Mr. James.

I have never mentioned Miss Trimmer to my aunt, nor has Miss T. even told me how long she means to stay here. Papa is excessively civil to her and she is the greatest resource and comfort to me.

Corise did not mention Lady Holland or Mr. Brougham. Tell me more of them all and how they all suit one another. I believe I was melancholy all yesterday morning from no other reason but having neither heard from nor written to you.

God bless you, ever most affec[ly] yours, HARRIET CAVENDISH.

To Lady Georgiana Morpeth

DEVONSHIRE HOUSE. *Tuesday Morning, November 3rd. 1807.*

I had but just time to seal my letter before Miss Berry arrived. She stayed with me near two hours and though she was neither in the best or gentlest of humours, I was very glad to see her. She seems seriously affronted at our thinking Comte Potocki more agreeable than Prince Paul, which she says she sees by your letter you do and that I made no secret of. She says Potocki may drawl out " Elles sont charmantes " (which, by the bye, if he does would fully satisfy me) but that Paul praised us with *sense and spirit.* She is at this moment in the height of worry and anxiety about Mr. Ferguson's affairs, which is just going to be brought forward, and was going to take him with her to Strawberry Hill. I should not like to be in a chain with Miss Berry if my mind was as much occupied and perplexed as she describes his to be and perhaps if the truth was known he does not either, but she has a great degree of perseverance as you and I and Thomas know by experience.

I went with my father to Chiswick and nothing could be more unlike the tête à tête I had just left than the one I had with him. He was, however, very goodnatured and very full of one subject—Lille's puppies which we went purposely to see. He is going to give me one and though I confess to you that I hate the whole race and still more to be possessed of any part of it, he seemed to think I should be so rejoiced at the gift, told me he had refused so many people to keep one for me and above all, so very anxious to have a pretence for admitting another into the family, that I could not refuse and forced myself to appear delighted. It is an odd rage—he really thinks of little else and the whole time of dinner and supper he feeds and watches them, laughs excessively every time they squeak or run and listens to no conversation with half the pleasure as he does when these puppies are the subject. Lady E. who never underdoes anything, of course, overdoes this, and is all the time—" Oh, I must die, oh, look, look ! " whilst I, not willing to be left entirely in the back ground, force out every now and then—" Oh, where is it going, poor little thing, what is it doing with its paw ? " and Miss T. looks on in maiden meditation, fancy free with the courage not to conceal how very much this interesting topic bores her.

Yesterday our young friends dined with us and as there was not one married man amongst them, Frederic would have congratulated me upon my chances. Mr. Crawfurd and Mr. Meynell are really so infirm that I wonder they like to dine out. Mr. James was quite galant and agreeable, seated between Miss T. and me and Mr. Crowle and him made a great many enquiries after Lord Carlisle without seeming to have heard a word of his illness.

God bless you, dearest sister.

Most affec^{ly} yours, HARRIET CAVENDISH.

To Lady Georgiana Morpeth

DEVONSHIRE HOUSE. *Wednesday Morning, November 4th. 1807.*

I have this moment received your long letter, my dearest G., and the next delight to receiving a letter from you is to see that it is a long one. Before I begin answering it, I must tell you that my grandmother arrived yesterday at about 5 o'clock—I was waiting in Jermyn Street to receive her. She seemed very much affected at first coming to Town and I do not think her well in health, but I hear she has had a very good night and she is to consult Dr. Pitcairn this morning who will, I hope, give her something to strengthen her for she appeared to me more nervous than anything else. My father sent her a very pressing invitation to dinner by me, promising to dine exactly at $\frac{1}{2}$ past six. Her being unwell is quite excuse enough and she means to come and see him this evening and tell him that she is desired to keep early hours and will, therefore, dine at present in Jermyn Street. Now that my fears are all vanished, I am enchanted at her being here—she is kinder to me than I ever knew her and we have plans after my own heart of early rising, reading and walking that I trust will give as much comfort to her as pleasure to me.

Lord Holland's situation at dinner was certainly not inspiring and I do not understand (well acquainted as I am with the geography of the table) why he did not par droit de naissance et par droit de conquête seize upon yours. It breaks upon me—he had grandmama Carlisle and in short I understand and pity him. Lady Holland's absurdities are too absurd and as I know Lady C. piques herself upon the coffee, I suppose a discovery of that whim would have been sufficient to have her turned out of the house.

I am very proud of Mr. Allen's [the Hollands' Librarian] praise and happy to find that I have not listened to his histories of Spain and Peru for nothing. I have no doubt but that I shall be Duchess of Argyle before (to me an elegant expression) I have time to say Jack Robinson and as I probably shall never see his Grace, it may easily be arranged without my knowing a word of the matter. I would not swear that I might not be anything Lady Holland meant me to be and I have a good mind to pin my faith upon her and begin inviting my friends to Inverary.

I had a long letter from Corise yesterday—she is quite in love with Mr. Brougham but does not mention his disliking Lady Holland. She says he has quite an aversion to Caroline Lamb and cannot talk of her with patience. I am glad the Hollands approve so much of George and Caro—I begin to do so too—her letters are full of him and when I do not look at him—merely *look*—for listening is all in his favour, I feel great security and comfort about it.

Motteux supped here last night and Lady E., him and I sat up till two comparing the speckled and spotted puppies, consulting what Physick was best for them to take, what regimen as to diet to pursue etc. I am glad of any conversation that never fails or lingers which I assure you is the case with this but how you, with your anti-canine disposition will bear it, I cannot tell.

God bless you, my dearest, dearest sister.

DEVONSHIRE HOUSE. *Thursday Morning, November 5th. 1807.*

My grandmother was a great deal better yesterday and in good spirits again—my father went to see her in the morning and pressed her so very much to come to Devonshire House that it will be very difficult for her, if she continues well, to avoid it. He told her he would dine earlier—exactly at six if she liked it and have a Whist party for her in the evening. Whether she will or no, she is delighted with his kindness and indeed nothing could be more amiable than his manner to her—I never was so much pleased with him before. I begin to be convinced that health has a great deal to do with his coldness and reserve for now that he says he is particularly well, his manner is quite different. Last night at supper George Lamb, him and I were quite jolly and he laughed several times more than I had ever seen him. He made us laugh with saying that whenever he meets a Puppet show, he stops to look at it till he sees a carriage coming and then *hurries* away. The best part of all this is that Lady E. is grown duller than ever, she coo's over the puppies and whines about Louis the 18th from morning till night and last night I really forgot that she was in existence.

Did you hear that Charles Bagot was sent to receive the French

King; how did he go through with it, not speaking a word of French? And how elated he must be at this humble, dubious sort of Embassy thinking himself half a head taller in consequence. I dare say they extasied themselves about his tabathière, praised his tournure, thought his white inexpressibles and pink cheeks, tout ce qu'il y a de plus gracieux, and that he will come back with nothing in his head and mouth but the perfect good breeding of Louis and his suite. I am going to Jermyn Street and will finish my letter when I come back.

We have been reading and working very comfortably, but not without interruptions from the Shipley family. Lady Jones is a great favorite of mine and I think her remarkably equable, but Mr. and Miss Sloper are so tedious and affected that I had no patience with their intrusion.

Lord George Cavendish dined with us yesterday and was as usual very good natured to me and cold, almost rude, to Lady E.—she is particularly much with him and indeed upon the whole I think if there is any change it is that she keeps more in the background than she used to do, excepting in her manner to the servants, which is assuming and tiresome for I would rather she would fly in a passion than argue with them, which she does by the hour.

I think my spirits are upon the whole very good—I keep as much as I can to my Castle Howard regularities and systems and I love you better, if it is possible, every day of my life—

Ever yours, HARRIET CAVENDISH.

To Lady Georgiana Morpeth

DEVONSHIRE HOUSE, *November 6th, Friday morning, 1807.*

Lady Elizabeth went to the play last night and I dined alone with my father. Till desert it was a very rapid and silent performance, but we then talked a great deal and I felt very much at my ease with him. He praised George Lamb and said he thought him very agreeable; questioned me a great deal about Caroline Lamb, whether she was liked and if people were prejudiced against her by hearing of her oddities. He said that men like her a great deal better than women and that she is very entertaining. We then talked about the Edinburgh Review and the Hint to a young reviewer, that I sent you, which he thinks very clever. Upon this subject he was really formidable, for in asking me what I thought of different parts, both of the review and criticism of it, he questioned me so closely, contradicted me so flatly or agreed with me so cautiously, that it was more like a trial than a conversation, and I got up from this cross examination with my face as hot as fire and my hands as cold as ice.

Mr. Motteux and George supped here. They seem very good friends, though George has rather a triumphant, protecting manner with him.

I was with my grandmother for 2 hours in the evening. I should not be surprised if she was to remain in Town for a long time, at least for the whole of the winter.

A thousand thanks for your long and delightful letter. You prophesied right in the beginning of it; my grandmother does nothing but what one can wish her to do. My father and her call on each other and are very good friends, everything about coming here seeming entirely and quietly dropped for the present, though his very pressing and kind invitations may make it difficult for her to avoid D. House when she is known to be quite well again. Jermyn Street is an excuse for me in every respect where Lady E. wants more of my company than I want to give her, and makes my day pass much more quickly and pleasantly, as I go there in all the times that I should here be with Lady E. without my father. He is luckily so regular in his irregularity, that I can manage with perfect ease to be always here when I can see him, and in short, at present, I am going on prosperously and comfortably.

Miss Trimmer is in a gentle conciliatory mood and lives so entirely in Jermyn Street that I do not think my father has seen her once since my grandmother's arrival.

I hear today that the Dean of Christchurch arrived in Town last night and I saw a letter from an Oxonian talking of his being Archbishop of York and his having long built upon it, refusing several bishoprics with a view to it as certain. Pray let me know what you hear about it. I flew in a passion and I am in luck if it is not attributed to a passion for Mr. Vernon.[1]

[1] Edward Vernon (b. 1757, d. 1847) was at that time Bishop of Carlisle. He had married Granville's half-sister, Lady Anne Leveson Gower, and on the death of the last Earl Harcourt assumed the name and estates of the Harcourts by royal licence, in 1830. He became Archbishop of York in 1807.

I lock up all your letters and they are as secret and safe as anything in mortal box can be.

I met Comte Potocki today close by D. House and was very much flattered by Samuel's coming to me with rather a schocked face, before I was well upstairs, to know if I was at home to Comte Potocki. As the dear love was riding the other way and must have exerted himself to turn round, I flatter myself he had a little wish to see me ; however that may be, I had a very great one to see him, and it was all I could do to summon up propriety enough to refuse.

God bless you, dearest G.

most affec[ly] yours, H. CAVENDISH.

To Lady Georgiana Morpeth

DEVONSHIRE HOUSE, *November 7th, Saturday morning, 1807.*

I cannot answer any of your enquiries about the Doghertys, as nothing is known of them but what his extraordinary book retales. Every body has seen her and agree in saying that she is extremely pretty. Lord William Gordon told Mr. James he had met her coming out of the Opera and thought her the prettiest woman he had ever seen. " My ever dear Hugh " seems very much given to friendships and it is strongly suspected that the trial will prove one of the Barouche box friends (said to be Mr. Quintin Dick and his brother) to have had a great deal to do with Mrs. Dogherty's extraordinary change of measures. The gentleman who went to their house, professing his intention of living and dying with them, was Bob Heathcote, the Earl of B., Lord Barrymore and the Honble T. C., Mr. Coventry. This is all I know and all I suppose anybody will, till the trial is made public.

How our wits jumped about Charles Bagot ; the first time we ever agreed sur son compte, I really believe.

I do not think our leaving Town as much out of the question as I did. My father said to my grandmother that he had not given up thoughts of it, and to my great surprise said to Mr. James the other night, " If I go to Bath you had better come there too." Lady E. leaves no stone unturned and says she hopes he will end by Bath or Brighton till the middle of December.

The Bessboroughs will be in Town Saturday. Caroline being here will give me the greatest pleasure. My aunt, I suppose, will be very little in Town at present.

The Melbournes leave Town today, excepting George who is what they call studying.

Tomorrow is the odious day without the post going or coming, however my grandmother seems to me to have formed such extensive plans for going to church at different hours and in different parts of the Town, that I expect my day to be nearly taken up, without any other occupation.

It is said that Lord Henry Petty's marriage with Miss Beckford is certain and Lady Maria Fitzroy's, Lord Euston's eldest daughter, with a Mr. Micklethwaite.[1]

God bless you, my dearest G., Kiss the dearest people for me.

To Lady Georgiana Morpeth

DEVONSHIRE HOUSE, *November 9th, Monday, 1807.*

I will not omit writing today though with little time and less matter, if it is only to thank you for your letter, which after a whole day without you, was doubly welcome.

The little women in their Pasteboard Bonnets perfectly enchanted me and I heard their dear shouts of laughing as if I was happy enough to be seated in the great chair by your fire.

You will be surprised to hear that Brighton is more likely than ever. Lady E. even talked as if we might possibly go there Thursday. She gives me details of the travelling, lodging and *comforts* of the expedition as if her society was my first object and delight. The St. Albans are gone there and (much more attractive) one of Lille's puppies with them. I talk to one who never had a dog, or I would say more of the power of this magnet.

But my chief care and I beg you to talk about it by return of post is the Prince and the Pavilion. She told me last night with great glee, that my father said he should not have the least objection to going there sometimes, and I must tell you, for what reason I know not, all her thoughts at present seem occupied about the Prince ; denying his ill-health, commending his system, praising his beauty, whining about Ragley and Lady Hertford [the Prince's mistress], the subject in the world that interests me the least and her the most. In short if

[1] Neither of these projected marriages took place.

she was old enough or fat enough to please him, I should think she was flattering herself with the prospect of being Heiress Apparent to the Marchioness, and God knows if I could *forward* so desirable a transition as from Piccadilly to Pall Mall, I would so and Chaperon her into every corner of Brighton, live in the Chinese Apartment [at the Pavilion], and never rest till I had fastened her by hook or by crook upon his royal highness ! Ah, si gran sorte non e per me, and I must content myself with endeavouring to keep clear of all the difficulties I foresee will await me if this plan is put in execution.

Plan again ! It is hard that I am not allowed to be quietly uncomfortable, a state of body and mind I had just, with much difficulty, attained to. Pray see me in your mind's eye standing close to the fire between every sentence, with my cap half off, my little eyes opened wider and my eyebrows half an inch higher than usual. Am I to go to Mrs. Fitzherbert with Lady Elizabeth, ten times more commented upon than in London, where I have always avoided being seen with her ? On the other hand, how can I let him and her go without me, and what reason can I give for not going in to bad company (for surely one need not mince the matter about Mrs. Fitzherbert) without her silencing me with, " After all, if *I* do ? " One of those questions that would cover *me* with confusion and gain for her the point she aims at. So much for moral justice and virtue is its own reward. Talk, my dearest of G's., and make Lord Morpeth talk and both of you forgive me for not worrying you the less for being two hundred miles away from you. We may not go, but yet there are dreadful notes of PREPARATION and when it is once settled I may be hand in hand with the Prince upon the Steyne before I receive one word of your advice.

My grandmother wants me to tell my father I had rather, and better not, go to Mrs. Fitzherbert's, which is very true but rather Trimmerian, and alas, it is no easy task to parler de cordes dans la maison d'un pendu. I hate to say this ; it may be very wrong but it is only to you, and I must, submitting as I do entirely to your judgement and guidance, say my objections to this and most other excuses I could make.

I am not satisfied with what I have written, but I cannot write this again, or I would. I may have spoken lightly, but to you I need not say that I feel all this most deeply.

God bless you dearest G. Pray advise me and blame me, for that is a greater proof of friendship and trust than any other.

Perhaps we may not go and I have teized you very unnecessarily. Perhaps too, Lady E. may not think of going to the Pavilion but only mean my father, that however is not likely, as the Prince will make a very great point of it I suppose.

God bless you, my own sister.

To Lady Georgiana Morpeth

DEVONSHIRE HOUSE, *November 10th, Tuesday, 1807.*

I had not any hope of hearing from you today. Never think when you have one moment's time to spare that it is not worth while spending it in writing to me, for you can seldom have an opportunity of giving so much delight.

Lady Elizabeth has just told me that my father has desired to get him a list of the stages from London to Brighton and she seems to look upon our going there as certain. If I could go there merely for health, exercise and the hope of its doing him good, and put the appearance of pleasure as much out of the question as the reality of it is, I should not—except leaving my grandmother—care much where the time till your return is spent. But if we are to pass it in dancing attendance at the Pavilion, courting the Prince and Mrs. Fitzherbert, toadying the Manners family, who are all assembled there in one heavy lump, I shall not have one moment's peace and shall prepare myself for nothing but difficulties, vexations and shame. I am more uncomfortable about it all, as I think my father is in a remarkably sociable, *animated* humour, and as the St. Albans going there certainly had great influence with him, I am sometimes afraid that we shall live " dans le sein de cette famille," and I believe it is hardly possible to find a less respectable receptacle.

Lady Heathcote is really talked of as ill as it is possible to be, and yet I should have no right to be nice about the company I go into ; or rather, no power, for I think no blame can be attached to me for that I so reluctantly live in. When once I begin on this subject, I feel as if I lost my head, and ramble on about fears and doubts, till you must, like the man in Cowper's Invalid complains to, almost wish I had. The thing that wears me most is that no sooner have I, after racking my own head and that of my friends, questioning and listening, disputing and submitting, convincing and being convinced, settled with much difficulty one line of conduct in one difficult situation, and begun putting it in practice with a great deal of trouble and tolerable success, than it makes way like a change in a Harlequin Farce, for a more perplexed and perfectly different one, where none of the old arguments will do for the new case, and no sooner do you, my kindest sister, after having directed me right and guided me safe through one difficulty, begin to think of reposing upon your Laurels, than I attack you again with all the old questions and reasonings, when you had but just done answering and combatting, and in short, make myself the greatest torment of your life, in return for your being the greatest comfort of mine.

This is " cosa da morire," and if you send me word that your patience is quite exhausted, I shall neither be surprised or angry.

God bless you, dearest dearest G.

November the 10th, Tuesday evening, 1807.

Tomorrow at 8 o'clock my grandmother and I go to Mrs. Bourchier's at Hadley, where we are to meet Caroline Lamb and her baby.

But I am glad to go on this expedition as I have, since my return, refused so many invitations to Brocket and also a plan of Caro's to come to Devonshire House for a few days, that she would have been quite affronted if I had not contrived to see her in some way or other.

I have heard no more of Brighton this evening. God bless you, my dearest G. My eyes are quite shut.

H. CAVENDISH.

I must just tell you a conversation that passed tonight at supper. Lady E. said to George she thought we should certainly go to Brighton and asked if it was full. He said, yes, but that the best thing of it was one could live very quiet there. She answered, " Oh, but I hope there are amusements for one of an evening—Rooms and a Theatre, as though the Duke never thought of those things in London he *enjoyed* them amazingly at those places," and quoted Bath. So you see what she means to accomplish at Brighton—to parade about everywhere with him and I !

y Georgiana Morpeth

JERMYN STREET [*her grandmother's*]. *Thursday morning, November 12th, 1807.*

r expedition to Hadley yesterday was very fatiguing yet one I am delighted to have made as it seemed to give real pleasure to Caroline [Lamb] and made up for the many times I had unavoidably been obliged to put off seeing her in any other way.

My grandmother, as usual, though we had not been appointed by Caro till 12, left London at 8, so that we dressed quite in the dark and passed the 3 or 4 first miles in a substantial fog, endeavouring, but in vain, to read Beattie's life outloud to one another.

When we arrived at Hadley, the Bourchiers were waiting breakfast for us and as my grandmother had provided herself with *12* muffins and as many Cracknells, we were at no loss how to employ the first part of the morning there.

We then visited Mrs. Burrows and Mrs. Munroe in an equipage I am in a fever least my grandmother should adopt in London. It is the body of a sedan chair upon the legs of a Wheelbarrow, the two handles of which are strapped onto an unfortunate man's shoulders, whose business it is to drag one from place to place, with this great inconvenience to oneself that when he has taken his first Spring, there is no possibility of stopping him if he was disposed to take one to the world's end. My grandmother is so enraptured with this safe conveyance that it is ten to one if, by the time you arrive, you do not meet John Matthews wheeling her up St. James's Street.

Caro did not come till 2 o'clock ; her baby is really beautiful, from a degree of strength, animation and vivacity that you do not often see in a child of a year old. She is grown very thin and looks heated, though in very good health ; but certainly there never was anybody whom being with child became so much, as when I left Town I thought her excessively pretty and yesterday almost as much the contrary. One hears such wonders of her both ways and every way when one is away from her, that I always feel an involuntary surprise to find her as I did, at Hadley, like another, to quote Lord B., and when she is quiet, gentle and reasonable I am glad to see her and to believe that much of what we heard must have been exaggerated. I do not mean to say that there is not too much reason to wonder at her oddity, and blame her conduct at times. Lady Elizabeth (who in general

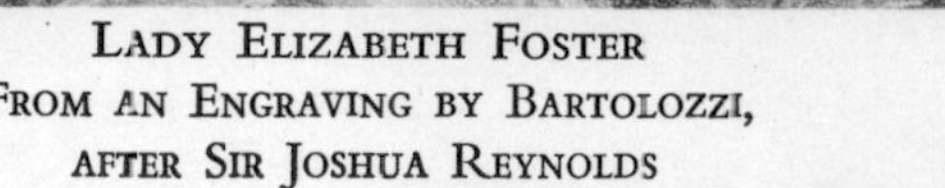

Lady Elizabeth Foster
From an Engraving by Bartolozzi,
after Sir Joshua Reynolds

Caroline St. Jules,
afterwards The Hon. Mrs. George Lamb

takes her part against any attacks upon her) says she stood in a corner one day flinging cups and saucers at William's head (a pretty pastime for him, poor man), but she says they all worked one another up and all had a share in the blame they so plentifully heaped upon her head. There is also evidently much spite in them against her. George said last night that her child was the most frightful creature he had ever beheld. I said really angrily (for if you could see it you would really think it impossible anybody should say so but from ill-nature or jealousy), that it was quite ridiculous to pretend it. He coloured, muttered and seemed very anxious Lord Melbourne and Lady E. should not hear us, but she did and told me afterwards that Lady Cowper had persuaded him to think so, for that when the boy was first born they were all in admiration of it till she began sneering about it.

I heard no news but that Spencer Cowper is going to marry a Miss Catherine Philips and that Lady Duncannon is with child again and very souffrante. How soon this is upon the Tapis and in all Lady Bessborough's letters she talks of nothing else, and it is all the old details of pains and aches all over again. It is hard upon Lady D., who is the only one disposed not to make a fuss if they would leave her to her own judgement and discretion about it.

I hope to Heaven Corise will not return with a presentiment, confided separately to every one of her acquaintances of the same event. I shall not be tame through a second 9 months' absurdity and indelicacy but give it her, with all the strong reasoning I can collect together.

The Heatons and Kendalls dined at D. House yesterday, Mr. Motteux and Mr. Moore. I exerted myself amazingly and was more Maîtresse de la maison than usual. My father was in the highest good humour and Lady E. very quiet and passive. She told me it was possible we might go Monday. I do not dare quite give up the dread of it, yet all these delays are very favorable.

God bless you dearest G.

most affec^ly^ yours, H. CAVENDISH.

To Lady Georgiana Morpeth

DEVONSHIRE HOUSE, *Friday, November 13th, 1807.*

I was with my aunt George [Cavendish] almost the whole of yesterday and she says my uncle is so much schocked at the necessity of my going out with Lady E. if I go to Brighton (which he thinks, as you do, there would be no possibility of avoiding) that he sent me word by her that I had much better remain in Town with my grandmama. My opinion however is so strongly against all this for all the old reasons, with the added one of being always pleading to him when I wish to go away, a wish for country, and, the only time he goes himself, asking to stay in Town. My grandmother agrees with me so strongly about this that I have no thoughts of not accompanying him, and must now only trust to snow, wind, rain, frost and every sort of argument that the Heavens are bringing forward upon my side of the question.

I have nothing to tell you today. Mr. Motteux supped at D. House last night to be complimented upon some fresh Suffolk supplies he had sent us. His gifts are grown so frequent that they are not now announced upon their arrival, but break upon us like the Marquis of Carabas's possessions to Whittington. " This is a very fine duck." " It comes from Mr. Motteux, my Lord." And the dear little man himself often says with an arch smile of an evening : " Were the herrings good today, Duke ? " " Pretty well." " By Jove, I sent them ! " and then a sort of triumphant laugh.

This is to show you the sort of details London, emptied of everything but this generous friend, force me to occupy myself with.

I sat all yesterday with Lady George and Anne. Anne the most solid of shepherdesses, in a stuff gown and coloured boddice [*sic*] " come to go a-shopping with dear Harriet." And go a shopping we did with a vengeance, for there is no linen or muslin that is not unfolded before their eager eyes, no box that is not unlocked, no curious little pocket book or huswife that is not spread out to them, and they courtesy and bargain and apologize and consult, till the shop keepers and I were ready to faint upon the Counters with weariness and ennui.

They have been at the Duke of Rutland's near Newmarket where the Duchess, I see, has been affronting them with all her might and main. Lady Shelley was there and they do not like her at all, the reason why they cannot tell, therefore I do not give any faith to their abuse of her. Mr. Brummel has won their hearts, I believe by sitting between them. They little think how dearly they will pay for it.

Ever yours, HARRIET CAVENDISH.

To Lady Georgiana Morpeth

JERMYN STREET, *Saturday morning, Nov. 14th, 1807.*

Miss Trimmer went out of town yesterday morning and I therefore spent almost the whole day here. My grandmother and I had a dinner after our own hearts, a little in style of Cumberland's jew, Egg shells and potatoe skins, but quite enough for people upon régimes as strict as ours. We played 5 games at Chess, read above a hundred pages of Forbes' life of Beattie, and 60 of Lord Gardenstone's[1] travelling Memorandums, not a new book but a very entertaining one. Played old songs upon the old harpsichord, and before the carriage came to fetch me, were both all but fast asleep upon our chairs.

This does not sound brilliant, yet it was the pleasantest day I have passed since my return to London, and my dear grandmother is so very kind and indulgent to me, that her ever having been otherwise, must have been owing to faults in my conduct or stubborness in my manner, that I either had not the sense to discover or the humility to allow.

The Bessboroughs and Duncannons are to be in Town between 4 and 5 today. As I hear nothing more positive about Brighton, I begin to trust we shall remain quietly here till the 10th arrives to make me half wild with joy. I long to be stunned with the dear people's noise again and wonder how I could ever send them upstairs, or rejoice when their dinner came to take them away from your room.

The fog is so thick here today that I can hardly see to write, and yet I must in a very few minutes cut a passage through it to Mrs. Kendall's, who is rather a dead weight upon my hands at present. I am to bring her here and I do not know how I shall get rid of her again when once she settles upon the Carriage.

I met Charles and Mrs. Bagot walking the other day; she has recovered all her beauty and I really never saw anything half so pretty. She was dressed magnificently, all in light blue satin and white lace. She was less grand than usual in her way of acknowledging me, and I suppose I ought to go and call upon her, which I have never yet done at her own house.

I met Lord Henry Petty yesterday and never saw any thing so smart, blooming and joyous as his appearance. Miss Beckford must be kind,

[1] Francis Garden, a Scottish judge, 1721–1793.

or something very prosperous must have happened. He has some great feather in his cap just now, but whether it is a political or sentimental one I do not pretend to determine.

It is odd how much illnature there is about Mr. Burrell's marriage; every fresh person I see begins with some story of his indifference or hers. The truth is, one half of the world is busy in resenting Mr. Beckford's wrongs, and the other half up in arms about Miss Seymour's, and Frank Primrose, Mr. Harbord, Lord Mountjoy and a swarm of rejected admirers, go about complaining of ill-usage and canvassing for the pity of all their acquaintance—making bitter complaints of Lady Perth, who by the way, having nothing else to do, is going to set up for a prize herself. Pray mention it to Mr. Howard; there is nothing like taking these things in time, and not knowing what being beforehand with the rest of the world in a few little galanteries, may not avail him in the long run.

I am afraid if my father ends by going to Brighton, I can plead no good excuse for not accompanying him and must, as you advise me, do as I can from day to day there. The weather puts it certainly out of the question while it continues what it has been for the last days of this week, but Lady E. seems to be more anxious than ever to leave Town the first fair moment and Motteux is gone to Brighton, (I am convinced by her orders) as I heard her say to him, " Now remember, if you possibly can, bring good accounts and say everything that may induce him to go there." I declare I had a great mind to have a finger in the pye too, to spite the employer, but Motteux is so odious, and my situation requires so much circumspection, and above all openness and fairness on my part, that I would not seriously do anything of the sort for the world.

I often begin a sentence arguing one way, convince myself it is wrong, chemin faisant, and end debating warmly on the other side of the question. This little criticism I think it politic to make, for fear you should.

I think my grandmother is quite established here and I never knew her so little beset by her friends and acquaintances.

Mrs. Howe heard that upon the King of France sending to have a house taken for him, Lord Hawkesbury sent to tell him he must not come within 50 miles of London. God bless you dearest sister.

ever most affec^{ly} yours, HARRIET CAVENDISH.

XIV

"THE DEVIL WAS SICK—"

NOVEMBER TO DECEMBER, 1807

ON November the 16th Lady Elizabeth was taken suddenly and very seriously ill and as usual, Sir Walter was bland, confident and nearly drained the wretched woman's life away by bleedings. No wonder that Harriet found her meek and docile. Her illness seems to have left that cold fish, the Duke, quite unmoved; indeed his spirits soared. But she recovered and started to plague them all again.

Hartington, who was now 17, had embarked on his extremely casual career at Cambridge, while Frederic Foster and Frank Lawley, Harriet's beau, were at Oxford.

There was much comparison between the three rival babies of Lady Duncannon, Corisande Ossulston and Caro Lamb; Lady Cowper taking care to be spiteful about Caro's poor little boy.

On December the 4th Harryo mentions the "Prince of the Peace." This was Don Emanuel Godoy, the favourite of both the King and Queen of Spain, who had their eldest son, the Prince of the Asturias, arrested at Godoy's instigation on a charge of conspiracy against the throne.

Lord Granville was forced to break off his negotiations in Russia, now completely under French influence, and war was declared against England on October the 31st. Granville left St. Petersburg on the 9th of November but only reached England in January 1808.

To Lady Georgiana Morpeth

November 16th. Monday. 1807.

[Russell's History of] Modern Europe at 8 o'clock is as extraordinary an exertion as my walking every morning at about the same hour to breakfast with my grandmother in defiance of fog, dirt and cold.

I am quite in spirits about Caro [St. Jules] and George [Lamb]. I like him as a companion (I cannot yet imagine a more tender regard) better every day, and their delight at seeing each other again, their conversations, " qui ne tarissent pas," and the content and satisfaction with which she now talks of her engagement to him, makes me feel my mind at ease with regard to her prospects of happiness, and I think they must increase in proportion to her knowledge of him. She is conscious of all his defects, but so enthusiastic about his merits that it does not seem to weaken her admiration of him, and she was struck with his good looks and thinness, two great proofs of love, as he looks ill and is considerably increased in size. He seems to love her more than ever if possible and I think she has it in her power to do him more good than ever one person did another.

I have at last discovered the clue to all Lady Elizabeth's manœuvres about the Prince of Wales. It is ambition, the fault of Gods and men ; ambition for Caroline, whom with a sort of second sight she sees having honours and dignities showered upon her in the succeeding reign. The night before last she said to me, making every sort of mouth and twisting the puppies in her schawl and her schawl about the puppies, that " after all one could not exactly tell what the Prince may not do for George when he is King." This is the cause of her rage if anybody says he is in a bad state of health or that lemonade and vegetables do not agree with him, and if the weather had not interfered, it might also have been the cause of a journey to Brighton, where, she told me yesterday, " it will not be necessary for us to dine at the Pavilion above 3 or 4 times."

Lady Bessborough is looking in good health and is in excellent spirits, with less of the marvellous in her conversation than I can remember her being with. The Duncannons and William [Ponsonby] come today, but the D's go on to Roehampton as the measles is in their neighbourhood in Town. By the bye I hear Lady Duncannon says of Lady Lonsdale that she is a *clever* woman, but more *satirical, dénigrante* and *caustique* than anybody ever was before her.

I have just been in to Lady Elizabeth who was taken very ill last night with spasms in her side. She is better but does not get up. Sir Walter says it will go off with fomentations entirely. She seems exceptionally low and looks ill from the great pain.

My grandmother has got a very bad cold, but I mind nothing so much as one of her winter coughs, which I am in dread of her getting this horrid weather.

God bless you, my dearest sister.

ever most affec[ly] yours, HARRIET CAVENDISH.

To Lady Georgiana Morpeth

DEVONSHIRE HOUSE, *Tuesday, Nov. 17th, 1807.*

I am very glad that you approve of what I had determined about Brighton. I begin to look upon it as quite out of the question and only regret having troubled you unnecessarily about it.

Lady Elizabeth was very unwell the whole of yesterday but is a great deal better today. Car and I dined alone with my father. Perhaps you will not believe that from the moment we sat down till we got up, the whole time of tea and again at supper, we talked of no one subject but the puppies, and Phœnix (which after consultations hours long is decided upon for the name of mine) is an incessant topic of conversation. We agreed after the evening was over, that his love and admiration of this race is quite extraordinary and I quite rejoice at having one in my possession, for it is a never failing method of calling his attention and attracting his notice.

My aunt, William [Ponsonby] and George Lamb supped with us. I really do not know what to do about William, as he certainly *dangles after me* (I think this phrase very expressive) more than ever, yet so childishly that I cannot see any way of stopping it without an appearance of affectation and Prudery. Yesterday just as I was going to dress he rushed upstairs to my room. I, without stopping to say I was glad to see him, took hold of his arm and rushed down as quick back to the drawing room, eager to get out of the region of Ladies' Maids and to avoid the impropriety of receiving Mr. William Ponsonby. My next difficulty was how to get him out of the house, as it was just dinner time, and Laughton and Jacob were pressing in every minute and banging the door to hint him away, I suppose. Soon after I got to Jermyn Street, he arrived there and when the carriage came for me, of course insisted upon being taken home. I really felt quite guilty when I got into the servants' hall here, full of our servants and my aunt's. This morning again he came to my grandmother's and when we marched down to the carriage together I saw Samuel was in a broad grin. You see all these must appear to them like appointments. But really he is so childish at times in his manner and so perfectly unconscious of there being anything extraordinary in following me (old enough to be his *grand*mother) about that I cannot say anything to him about it. [She was only two years older than he.] Caroline tells me she thinks I ought to check it, but like me, is quite perplexed how to set about it. I therefore apply for advice to your "sotto biondi capelli canuta mente"[1] and beg you will extricate me from this *delicate distress.*

My grandmother is quite delightful and her kindness to me I cannot say enough of. God bless you, my dearest G., ever yours, H. C.

To Lady Georgiana Morpeth

Wednesday morning, November 18th, 1807.

DEAREST LADY MORPETH,

I am glad to hear that Miss Seymour is reviving a little. Lady Duncannon says Mr. Burrell's marriage made her quite miserable, that she not only had as much love for him as ever, but as much hope and that there was not a look of his that she did not interpret in her favour. If he looked up as he passed the windows, she used to be in a violent agitation and come and tell Lady Jersey that he liked her as much as ever and would certainly return to her.

Colonel Leigh [who had lately married Augusta Byron] is said to be always in Town and it is another subject upon which people are tempted to be very ill-natured, but to be sure with some reason, for he certainly is "le moins marié que possible" and every body, excepting his wife, meets him at every place in England save Six Mile Bottom.

To Lady Georgiana Morpeth

JERMYN STREET, *Thursday morning, November 19th, 1807.*

The Bessboroughs and Sir Walter Farquhar dined with us today. Lady Elizabeth continues better but still has a great deal of pain in her side and does not leave her room. I think Brighton must be entirely out of the question; the ground is today covered with snow and when all the fine weather and good opportunities of the last month could not tempt my father to leave Town, it is ridiculous to suppose that he will encounter all the impediments of this. My only fear is that Sir Walter who is arrived *point blank* upon this subject will give him so much

[1] "Hoary wisdom beneath fair hair."

trouble with his advice, that he will think it less to take the journey, and when Lady Elizabeth recovers she may urge the necessity of it for her own health as an added inducement. Mr. Motteux (true to his charge) sends accounts of the climate and the astonishing effects it has had upon the Duke of St. Albans, with such stuff about open windows and sitting on the cliff etc., that if I had not made vows of Christian Charity and toleration, I could wish that some of these mild mornings he might topple headlong from the fearful height.

Mr. Sheridan got into Devonshire House yesterday nobody knows how and I had much difficulty in getting him out again. He says he never despaired of his country till now, that Ireland is in a state of frightful confusion, that rebellion is fermenting in every corner of it and only waiting for the arrival of the French there, which arrival he seems to think practicable and will be immediate, to burst forth and end only in our ruin and destruction! Never again accuse me of not talking politics; I am Mrs. Jolliffe in rather a more advanced period of life than that in which she was listening to Hume and am getting by slow stages to the very last events in the last century, which to my shame be it spoken, interest and astonish me to a degree that I hope never can be discovered to anybody but you. At two and twenty to be "bouche béante" at the great Duke of Marlborough's successes! And to read of America with the same sort of wonder and surprise that I suppose its discoverers to have felt when they first looked at it.

George Lamb was not able to come to us yesterday and it was with the greatest delight that I heard Caro declare in the morning that she did not know how she should live through the long evening without him. It would certainly have been more sentimental not. However we did just contrive to exist with the great satisfaction of finding it difficult. I have not for a long time seen her in such high spirits and at present (I always, if you observe, put in some expression of that sort; now, whilst it lasts, "pour le moment," for fear of any sudden change, which if I did not you might attribute to my inconsistency instead of hers) she has every appearance of being the happiest of persons.

She tells me there never was anything like Lady Bessborough's love and admiration of you. We [Lady B. and Harriet] are very good friends at present but for all I can do, she will fancy that every word I say is meant to convey some meaning of dislike or indifference to her.

Yet I do assure you I never before felt so anxious to show her every possible kindness and attention. If I ask what o'clock it is, she gets up and begs my pardon for not recollecting how much she must bore me and says she will not stay a moment longer. If I go out with her in the carriage, she is all the while on the defensive, and if I was always venting the most bitter reproaches upon her, she could not be more constantly hinting at my dislike and her wish to spare me the ennui she knows I feel when I am with her. In spite of this we are, as I said before, very good friends. I have seen more of her than I almost ever do in London and I am sure my manner to her is warmer and more attentive than usual. I flatter myself the style of complaint is grown almost mechanical to her, but though it may please her ear, no words can say how it fatigues my lungs to be obliged every half hour to repeat, " How can you, my dearest aunt ? Oh no ! my dearest aunt. What an idea ! " I mean to adopt groaning like Mr. Marsh, which would be very expressive and save a great deal of trouble.

London begins to look quite full. I passed [Prince] Paul in the Park the other day and he absolutely leapt with eagerness to attract my notice to the most violent bows that ever man made before. His meeting an acquaintance in the street must give him more exercise than a long walk. Frederic Byng is just come I hear, but I have no fear of seeing much of him just at present.

Corisande has just arrived in Town and has sent to beg me to go to her. I will finish my letter when I come back with a description of Miss Emma Bennet.

I am just come home from Queen Street. I think the little girl very handsome and the most engaging that ever was seen, yet I will own, only to you and pray do not tell anybody I say so, that she is a child some people would think ridiculous and others frightful. To reconcile the seeming inconsistency I will give you an exact description of her. She looks no more like a child than Mrs. Howe does. Her eyes, eyelashes and eyebrows really made me start, they are quite as big as Corisande's, excepting the eyebrows which, of course, are less black and thick. Her profile is perfectly regular and her skin a clear pale brown. She sits *bolt* upright in her nurse's arms, and fixes and bends her immense eyes in a way that " tient du miracle." She looks foreign to a degree that is ridiculous, but this Lord Ossulston does not observe, or I suppose he would knock her little brains out. I hear Lady Melbourne said when she saw her that she is not a pretty child, but would be a beautiful woman, and this perhaps is the happy medium between my admiration and what I suspect to be other people's disparagement of her.

Corise is in high health, but not in beauty ; however as she was just come off a journey and dressed " en bergère " it is not fair to judge. She is grown extremely thin and is perfectly in shape, but looks darker and older. She was rather nervous as her father was to be with her this morning. He talks of them as if they were to let him live entirely with them and his first question was whether they could lodge him for a month. This is really unfortunate, considering that they have barely room for themselves and that it is like Gulliver coming amongst the Lilliputians. However they seem ready to do everything that is right and dutiful and proud of doing as much honour to him and contributing as much to his convenience as they possibly can. I hope he is aware that Lord Ossulston has not had many cubits added to his stature since the age of 11 or 12, as such a joke as Mounsieur used to hazard to good little Mr. Delmé, would raise a storm in Queen Street, that no power, French or English, would have power to quell.

I think my grandmother will end by spending the winter in Town, and she is in such good spirits and seemed so pleased with the thoughts of seeing a good deal of you and the children, that I begin to think it decidedly the best thing she can do.

God bless you, my dearest G.

ever yours most affec^ly^, HARRIET CAVENDISH.

Hartington seems in raptures with Cambridge in several letters to his grandmother. I wrote to him once, but really " c'est perdre son latin," for he does not write in return and has hardly time to read what one sends and I know nothing annoys him so much as to receive a letter that he has not time to double docket and, I believe, make extracts from into a large copy book.

To Lady Georgiana Morpeth

November 20th, Friday, 1807.

The post is just going and I have only time to tell you that I am not more unreasonable about the delay of your return than must be expected. I have still the greatest hope that it will end by being none at all, as to send for that boy in the depth of winter seems to me madness

Lord and Lady C. I am really much happier in Town than I could have hoped to be and my grandmother's being with me is a comfort and resource not to be described.

Lady Elizabeth has been worse today, but Sir Walter says it is nothing. She was blooded this morning and I dare say will be relieved by it.

I will write a long letter tomorrow but the last bell is ringing. God bless you.

ever most affec^{ly} yours, HARRIET CAVENDISH.

To Lady Georgiana Morpeth

Saturday, November 21st, 1807.

Lady Elizabeth is better today, but she was very ill the whole of yesterday. It is a violent attack upon her chest, which is in so inflamed a state that notwithstanding her being so weak as to faint away continually, they were obliged yesterday to bleed her twice, and to put her on a blister in the night. Sir Walter says today her illness has taken exactly the turn he could wish and with quiet and proper management she will get quite well in a short time.

My aunt has just been here on her way to Brocket Hall. As William [Ponsonby] is going there with her and from thence to Roehampton, I shall have no opportunity or indeed necessity to speak to him at present, which I own is a great relief to me. He is so particularly touchy about anything he imagines to be an affront that I cannot change my manner to him in the least degree without his immediately taking it as an egregious offence. Yet if when he returns to Town there are the same reasons for doing so, I will certainly speak to him as you advise me.

Corisande has improved in looks, which I did not think when first I saw her ; at least her figure from her being grown excessively thin looks much better. I did not do justice to her little girl when I wrote last about her. She is really beautiful and I find it is the general opinion. The Ossulstons come here of an evening, which is, pour dire le vrai, heavy work. You know my regard for him and affection for her, but really to sit for hours, each other boring, by each other bored, counting the hours that seem to us years and all affectionately happy when it is time to part, is not an enlivening existence. At my grandmother's the evening seems to me only a few minutes, because one is not obliged to be company and everybody is employed some way or other. But till Corise can read or Lord O. embroider, I do not know how we shall mend the matter here.

Caroline [Lamb] is looking uncommonly well, she is, if anything, thinner, but looks in much better health than when I left Town. My aunt too looks well, but she is grown immensely large. William is very much improved, he is grown taller and larger and looks 5 years older than when I last saw him—raison de plus.

I hear nothing of Louis the 18th. If I do, you shall. My grandmother goes to Roehampton Sunday but only for a day or two. God bless you, my dearest G.

ever most affec^ly yrs, HARRIET CAVENDISH.

To Lady Georgiana Morpeth

Monday, November 23rd, 1807.

I have left myself but a moment for writing, my dearest G. I must begin by thanking you for your letter. I hope Early rising and Modern Europe will continue to make up to you for the want of more lively interests and that you will not pine for what we are so soon to enjoy, Mr. Delmé's society.

The Duc de Gramont has not yet been able to leave Gosfield, but they expect him in Town some day this week.

I went to Queen Street this morning and found Lord Henry Petty there, more animated and brightened up than I could have believed his nature admitted of. He was just going to Holland House where he was appointed by Lady H. to meet them at dinner. I hear such histories of her behaviour at the different places she has been at, that I think you were in great luck to have so little fault to find with her during her stay at Castle Howard.

To my great dismay as I was crossing from the Bath Gate on Saturday in Piccadilly, a little man jumpt from an enormous horse, and proving to be Paul, he walked with me to Devonshire House, bowing and congratulating himself upon his luck all the way. He has no idea that I ever deny myself to him and Comte Potocki when I am at home, and he says I must go out very early and never come in again, for they have called at all hours. Lord Petersham met us and looked surprised, as Paul was screaming, " Comment va le piano,

Ah, ah, ah ! ! " with his odd laugh and gestures just as he passed, and I am sure I looked as if I wished myself a hundred miles off.

Miss Catherine Philips who is to be Mrs. Spencer Cowper is very handsome, I hear.

Lady Elizabeth's amendment has been as rapid as her illness was ; she really is surprisingly better.

God bless you, my dearest sister. Forgive this hurry.

ever most affec[ly] yrs, HARRIET CAVENDISH.

To Lady Georgiana Morpeth

Tuesday, November 24th, 1807.

I still must hope you will be here before Christmas, though this fine bright morning makes me tremble. I see Lady Carlisle in my mind's eyes, basking in the kitchen garden and throwing back her three cornered handkerchief. What an odd temperature the dear woman's is, and how unlucky it is that her thinking it sultry in December should keep you all in the North, when we are freezing even in the South.

How your account of the man and women made me laugh. Georgiana will be a most terrible coquette and with her beauty, coquetry may do worlds of mischief. How all the little boys now trotting about in petticoats will suffer from the powers of her charms. I am easy about Caroline's respectable existence and I love her for being such a careful soul ; she will " vaguer " and be a pattern to her contemporaries.

The Ossulstons, George Lamb and William Ponsonby supped here last night. Corise is in very good spirits and Lord O. has a look of attendrissement and delight whenever the child is mentioned (a topic that as we have not many, we are too happy to harp upon) that is quite pretty to see.

Pray tell Lord Carlisle once for all that we know no more of the Duc de Gramont, Louis the 18th, their motives and their plans than if they were in Siberia. I think it is the hardest thing upon the Duc de Gramont. Mounsieur d'Averay, I think his name is, stays amusing himself in London, though he knows till he returns to Gosfield, the Duc de G. cannot leave the King. Corise is furious but " little o." seems somewhat relieved, and I dare say blesses Mounsieur d'Averay in his sleeve from morning till night.

My grandmother's rage for sights is terrible just now. We have been to Chelsea this morning and tomorrow we are to go with Mr. Preedy and Mr. Andrews, two reverend beaux, to see a school five miles off all through the City. It makes me so languid and fatigued that I cannot be cheerful and then she frets over my constitution, which is now proof against everything but dawdling a whole morning over Doctor Bell's system of education. Getting up early agrees with me perfectly, if I may be quiet in Jermyn Street for the first part of the day, which I enjoy of all things, but to travel ten miles, making clerical conversation, to stand over little boys reading the Testament, with my feet and nose aching with cold, and to come back here at about one, the beginning of a Devonshire House day, quite exhausted and fit only to go to bed, is what the strength and health of a horse could not endure. I fought off with the greatest difficulty this morning calling upon a crocodile in Pall Mall and I pray that no more animals may settle in the neighbourhood of Jermyn Street.

Ever yours, H. CAVENDISH.

To Lady Georgiana Morpeth

Wednesday morning, Nov. 25th, 1807.

Lady Elizabeth is still going on as well as possible. Her illness was certainly a very alarming one both from the nature and the violence of the attack to so very weak and delicate a person.

My opinion of the 3 little rivals is very decided.—Caroline's is the finest child, Corise's is the prettiest and Lady Duncannon's is the fattest, which considering its mother is rather surprising.

I went to see Lady Melbourne yesterday after I had finished my letter to you, and found her looking quite well though kept in Town much against her inclination by the remains of a terrible cold and cough she has had for some time. Corise was with me, in one of her humours, in which she constantly says everything she ought not, and amongst others she contrived entirely to forget that Caroline Lamb was in any way related to Lady Melbourne, begun abusing her for her violence and whims. Lady M., though the first person to say this herself, is the last to hear it from anybody else, and if I had not by dint of winking and kicking, recalled Corisande's scattered senses, there would have been a second edition of the Argyle Street quarrel.

The Bessboroughs, Lord Cholmondeley, Mr. Vaughan, Mr. Tierney Sir Walter and Mr. Moore dined with us. It was very dull as Lord

Cholmondeley who sat by me would tell me the story of Mr. Panton's opera during the first courses, and Doctor Fellowes' adventures at Paris during desert. Mr. Tierney seems very entertaining but the intervals in which I could listen to him were so short that I heard but little of his conversation. They played at Whist after dinner and the Hollands and Mr. Allen arrived from the play. She is in great beauty and I think rather less than she was. She raves about you and the Duchess of Bedford ; she says you are quite angelick and adored by the whole world. She represents the Duchess quite in a new light, as the most sensible woman, good wife and excellent mother that ever lived. Johnny [the Duke of Bedford] too is in high favour and, in short, Lady H. was in such great good humour that she painted everything couleur de rose. Lord Holland was very pleasant. When it was time to go she said she should come here very often whilst she remained at Holland House and I am afraid she means always to make it a resting place between home and the Theatres.

I have had Miss Berry with me all this morning. She talks rather too much of Mr. Ferguson and Madame de Starhemberg, considering she must know they are less derniers de mes soucis, but was otherwise very agreeable.

I cannot tell you how well papa and I go on together ; his spirits are so much improved with his health, that it lessens by the half one's difficulty in getting on with him and I see much more of him than I used to do which is another great object gained.

God bless you, my own dearest G. I am tired with Whitechapel but will write a longer letter tomorrow.

To Lady Georgiana Morpeth

DEVONSHIRE HOUSE, *November 26th, Thursday morng. 1807.*

I have nothing new to tell you today but that Mr. Motteux is returned and supped here last night. How much more interesting this intelligence is than none at all I leave it to you to determine. He is full of Brighton news. Mrs. Fitzherbert is very ill. The Prince was there for one night and returned to Town the day before yesterday. They say he is never in bed more than 3 hours and that the rest of the four and twenty are chiefly employed in writing to Lady Hertford. I hope for her sake she is not obliged to devote as many to reading these royal productions, especially as George Lamb assures me it is all "damned stuff." I suppose by this they have the pleasure of hearing select passages at Whitehall, where he spends as much of his time as he can spare.

I have not seen the Duc de Gramont yet, but I hear he is delighted with Corise and her child and the little picture of domestic felicity that he witnesses in Queen Street. Lord Ossulston has turned over a new leaf and is all indignation and resentment about the King of France's reception, and has thoughts of going en famille to Gosfield, meaning his empressement to be a small satire upon the country for its backwardness in this particular. What would I not give to see him there, crowing with triumph and attendrissement, pénétré with the magnanimity of his own conduct and almost crushed by the overwhelming civility of theirs—one such embrace as Lally Tollendal gave my uncle might put an end to Mounsieur mon beau fils [1] in a moment.

I see nothing but Mr. Delmé, though he has not yet been here, but he is in every street that one drives through, at every shop one stops at and is so constantly perched at Devonshire House gate whenever we drive in or out that I think we might offer him the place of Porter when anything happens to Robert. The lodge would be a nice dwelling for him, save him a great deal of expense and I should think the life would exactly suit him.

Lady Elizabeth still keeps her bed but she continues getting better every day. God bless you, dearest.

ever yours, H. CAVENDISH.

Lady Georgiana Morpeth

DEVONSHIRE HOUSE, *November 28th, 1807.*

And will you not come away? I suppose Lady Carlisle will be ready to die of laughing and think it "comical enough" when the roads are impassable and none of our letters can reach us—but it seems the oddest diversion for Lord Carlisle's mind that can be hit upon.

My father has got a little gout. Caroline and I are both confined to the house with wretched colds and Lady E. is not yet able to leave her bedroom. I attribute my cold to going to Jermyn Street last night in a thick fog.

I found Mr. Spencer and Mr. Preedy there. William Spencer [2] just come to Town in a violent hurry as he says he is going to have a share

[1] Harriet's pet-name for "Little o."

[2] A cousin of the Duke of Marlborough's.

in Drury Lane, I believe, at least he is to settle all the money concerns and bring everything in to order again—an odd person to choose for this purpose I think. He was brilliant with rouge and spirits, but must have been rather disappointed at his audience's behaviour. I did nothing but blow my nose and wink my eyes ; Mr. Preedy had one of his lethargic fits upon him and never had his open for a minute and my grandmother was nodding the whole evening in a comfortable nap. He repeated to us however (just as if we had been awake) quantities of his own poetry, of which, by the bye, he is going to publish a small volume, his bookseller having offered him two hundred pound for it, and read us a Latin epitaph he has just written upon the death of poor Mr. Sargent and contrived to introduce in the course of the conversation, all the compliments that have ever been paid him, de part et de l'autre for the last twelvemonth.

George comes every night and is as agreeable as it is possible to be, and as tranquil as can be expected. He is much better and more comme il faut in his manners than he used to be, and improved in his person from the necessity of having but 6 hours sleep and the dinners at Lincoln's inns not being the most recherché ones that ever were heard of. Caroline is charmed with all these *dawning* merits and beauties and nothing can be more satisfactory than the *apparent* state of her mind *at present.*

God bless you, my dearest best of G's.

ever most affec^ly^ yrs, HARRIET CAVENDISH.

To Lady Georgiana Morpeth

Tuesday, December 1st, 1807.

My morning has been entirely taken up by waiting for Madame Krumpholtz,[1] taking a first and delightful lesson of her.

I am quite enchanted at Jackson being about to draw the women ; send me every particular of their dress, attitude etc. and if Freddy and Harriet are to be introduced in the piece. Have your picture done, my dearest sister ; you never looked so well, and think what millions some people I know would give for a copy of it, for which seriously

[1] Madame Krumpholtz, whom Gouverneur Morris said was " the best performer upon the Harp in Europe," was the widow of Johann Baptist Krumpholtz, also an eminent harpist who drowned himself in 1790 after she eloped to England.

I would give any sum Mr. Jackson would require. If he would dr: you and copy it for me, if it was but an outline, I do not think I should ever be quite unhappy again, and in real soberness I do assure you it would add to the pleasure of my whole existence.

The report about Lord Henry [Petty] and Miss Beckford cannot have any truth in it. He laughed about it to the Ossulstons, said it was quite ridiculous, and after praising her beauty very much, said he thought her consumptive and that she certainly would not live. There is no knowing however that this may not all be an excess of prudence in keeping his secret.

The Bessboroughs, Melbournes and Duncannons dined here yesterday. Lady D. is grown fat but she does not look in beauty ; she has got the fault that Lord Lauderdale says he cannot stomach, and without any cause, as she is not with child. My aunt is grown immensely large ; I never saw so great an increase of size in so short a time and I hear from Lady Elizabeth that she frets herself about it and cannot bear to have it observed.

God bless you dearest G.

Lady John Townshend ! Oh, cousin, spare me !

To Lady Georgiana Morpeth

DEVONSHIRE HOUSE, *December 2nd, Wednesday morning, 1807.*

Lady Elizabeth's illness was certainly attended with a very great degree of alarm, but I was not aware of it at the time. There is something in illness so softening to the mind and manners of the person who suffers and to one's own feelings about them at that time, that if I was to say the only moment in my life in which I had felt anything like affection for Lady E., it would be during the last week and my conscience would be very uneasy and my heart very heavy, if joy at her danger or a wish for her death had ever for an instant come across my mind. In my behaviour to her I hope I have been right. I have been attentive to her and seen her constantly, which she has appeared much pleased with, but I have never done anything that should make my usual behaviour to her appear either cold or capricious when she recovers.

I must now explain to you some other feelings I have on this subject, as I am anxious to know if you agree with me. Her illness and, of course, absence from our society have painfully convinced me that not only I, but my father would be much happier without her. I never saw him in such good spirits, so perfectly at his ease and talking so much and so cheerfully. I should not trust solely to my own observation, but everybody has made it and even Caroline [St. Jules] has repeated it to me more than once, of course without drawing *the same conclusion.* Do not think from this that I mean to say it would be a good thing if she was *now* to leave the house. It is quite another thing. Her doing it would be attended with difficulties, reflections and probably self-reproaches to him, that make it in my mind a thing never to be imagined practicable for a moment, but I only lament to find, I think past all doubt, that if she had not rooted herself by all the ties of habit and now almost a sense of duty in his home, he would be ten thousand times a happier person. I was always certain that her character and manners could not suit him, and I am convinced that he is often silent from a wish not to embark in arguments and disputations with her.

Miss Berry is rather a thorn in my way. When I am with her, I am led to say more than I wish and repent it till I meet her again. For example, I told her the last part of what I have said to you. However she entered into it so warmly and drew the line so exactly as I meant that I do not, I hope, regret having done so. I own to you I do not wish to see a great deal of her and I beg you to tell me how you advise me to draw *this* line. She *bullies* me into more friendship and confidence in her than I ever think of giving her and yet in their proper degree I think her very deserving of both.

I begun praising Count Potocki the other morning and she grew quite red with anger, and immediately told me that Starhemberg (one must be familiar with these long dignities) said, " Esterhazy est de retour en ecstase avec tout ce qu'il a vu (which is precisely what I dislike in him) Potocki aussi content mais critiquant toujours." I suppose she has heard of Potocki's laughing at her, for she is now always abusing him, and really colours with indignation at any praise or defence of him. I am not quite sure she does not think me a little in love with him, or else she is herself, and piqued with his froideur. She complimented me a great deal upon my " plain, downright Cavendish understanding." Can you tell me why this always affronts me so much ? I immediately see myself one of my old uncles in petticoats and am ready to cry with vexation.

I had but 5 minutes' conversation with Lady Holland, but the way in which she praised you for your behaviour to Lord Carlisle proved that she thought the difficulty of doing so as great as the merit. I think I should like Mr. Brougham very much. George Lamb says he always leaves Holland House the minute she begins ordering and giving herself *airs*, and one night that George asked him why he went so early, he answered—" because I see the fetch and carry work is beginning." I think it is such a good expression.

Mr. Motteux is gone again to Brighton and our only remaining visitor is George. When Caro does not monopolize him, he is very pleasant and agreeable and certainly more so when he does not live a great deal with his family. I always know when they are in Town, if he has dined at Whitehall, before he has been 5 minutes in the room.

God bless you, my dearest sister.

ever most affec^{ly} yours, HARRIET CAVENDISH.

Caro [Lamb] and her boy have just been here. I am afraid I no longer think George Lamb and Lady Cowper so unjust, for though he is the finest, largest, healthiest creature I ever beheld, his face is as far from pretty as possible. I believe it is seeing Corise's baby that has made me think so, for her features are so very regular it is impossible to admire any others after them.

To Lady Georgiana Morpeth

DEVONSHIRE HOUSE, *December the 3rd, Thursday, 1807.*

Frederic Foster wrote a long letter to Caroline yesterday from Oxford which he ends, " Lawley is just come and I am going immediately to paint our wretched friend to him in her true colours." We are in a terrible fright, for to trust to Mr. Foster's Tact, which we must do in this instance, is but a melancholy necessity and I am sure that if he interferes at all, it must be to say exactly what one would wish him not.

I think, and I am sure you must, that I have been rather given of late to make mountains out of Molehills, but as I think in my situation I ought to think almost as much of propriety as people in a less difficult one ought of much more serious things, I must call you to a consultation upon another of my delicate distresses, the last about W.P. having ended happily in exactly the difference of our manière d'être that I wished to accomplish, without quarrelling, arguing, or going one step out of the common way to effect it. But, passons au déluge —I am afraid I shall have more difficulty about Frederic Byng, whom I do think the most forward person I ever met with and one who always contrives to make one appear more intimate with him than one has any wish to be.

I met him this morning in Hyde Park. Caroline and I were walking and he was riding. We stood still to talk to him, that he might not ride on with us, and were very civil but rather cold, as befitted our dignity. He asked me amongst other things if I was ready to go to Hungary, for that he never heard anything like Prince Paul sur mon chapitre. (Oh ! that it was not the thing that is " en extase de tout ! ") To go on with my story ; we bid him good morning, he bowed and rode into Knightsbridge. We rejoiced all the way up Constitution Hill, wisely planning to confine our walks in future to the Green Park, when, " oh ! hapless mortals ever blind to fate ! " we no sooner came in sight of the Bath Gate, than in rushed Frederic Byng with a look of triumph at his contrivance. We, however, looked so very grand that he seemed a little distressed and said he only came to look at my dog and to beg me to lend it to him in the course of the next 10 days. I said, yes, certainly, in a violent hurry and hurried off without another word. But it soon entered that careful soul Caro's head, that if Mr. Byng ever talks as if I encourage him, it will be thought rather odd after all that was said last year and my certainly having talked too much to him, if he is parading about every where with my dog in his possession. Yet how to hinder his borrowing it I do not know, or why he asks for it if he does not want it to be thought that I am on very intimate terms with him. He is in his manner to me as respectful and decorous as any thing can be, but Corise tells me that when she saw him at Thoresby, he was so black-guard and used to tell such extraordinary and coarse stories, that I am convinced his acquaintance can do one no credit.

I had no sooner despatched my letter to you yesterday than I received the following note, " Dear soul, I am come to Town for good ; the sooner we meet the better. Heaven bless you. M.B." [Mary Berry]. "Je pique mais je m'attache," would be better reading for the case in point.

Lady Elizabeth is much better. She leaves her bedroom and has seen several people.

I was pleased with Caroline Lamb yesterday. She was very reasonable and quiet. We all agree about her child ; his face is certainly not pretty, he is all retroussé like her, with tiny eyes and an odd helpless countenance and I thought I perceived a slight tint of yellow on his eyelids and eyebrows, which is very extraordinary as his hair is dark brown. I trust that when the 6th makes its appearance it will put all these first borns to shame.

Nothing ever was like the political despair this declaration of war from Russia has put us all into, and strange to tell, I am foremost in the anxiety and can think of little else.

You have heard, I suppose, that Lady Westmorland's poor little baby died on its passage home. They think it was weaned too soon, as the Portuguese nurse would not come over with it.

Lord Melbourne and George supped here last night. Lord Melbourne is very tiresome and I am afraid Caroline has taken quite an aversion to him. He harps upon the same joke, as a man who is at this moment tuning the piano forte just at my ear, does upon each note.

You can have no idea what a plague Mrs. Kendall is to me. She is the most fidgetty, teazing, unoccupied person that ever doomed me to be civil to her, and gets into the house by means of coming with old Heaton in his chaise and it is hours before she gets out of it again.

I wish I could see the dear women's pictures by a sort of second sight. Do not let Georgiana turn up her eyes in her new way ; she would look best making her " beauty face," but it would be terrible to hand her early coquetry down to after ages.

The O's are at Walton. She says Lord Tankerville's kindness is delightful. I am afraid it is rather capricious, as when first she went to Chillingham he would hardly speak to her and before she came away, to nobody else, without any possible reason for the change and he treats his own family in the same way—they are favourites by turns, during which periods the rest of the set are totally neglected, and Lord Ossulston is become quite his right hand. He will not suffer a tree to be cut down or an alteration made at Chillingham but by his directions, " So I used just to run out with some of my father's people and point out improvements." Do you see this little monarch of the groves ?

God bless you, my own dearest sister.

Ever most gratefully and affec^{ly} yrs, HARRIET CAVENDISH.

To Lady Georgiana Morpeth

Friday, December 4th, 1807.

Lady Bessborough came to supper last night from Holland House and brought the news of Lord Henry Petty's marriage with Lady Louisa Strangways [Lord Ilchester's daughter] being declared. I thought he did not look so gay and smart for nothing. They are delighted at it and Lrd. H^{d}. says if Lady H^{d}. had ever allowed him to be in love with anybody, it would have been with Lady Louisa; he thinks her so good-humoured, unaffected and pleasing. I hope it will not make Lady Maria [Fitzroy] unhappy or Miss Napier, or Miss Crewe, or Miss Beckford, for if report is to be believed one's compassion must take a very wide range upon the subject.

2 more marriages are declared, Lord Pembroke's [to Comtesse Woronzoff] and Lord Craven's. Walker went to see Miss Brunton's[1] Trousseau today,—of one her gowns the sleeves alone cost five and twenty guineas and the whole of it is magnificent beyond measure.

I am just come from Hyde Park where Caroline and I have been wading through the snow. The consequence is that my throat is sore and I am obliged to cover myself with wraps and camphorated spirits.

London is duller and more gloomy every day and the people go singing all over the streets about merry Christmas much to my annoyance.

My aunt has just been here. All this affair in Spain is supposed to have been a plot of the Prince of the Peace; Buonaparte says the Prince of the Asturias is a very great fool and he shall be able to make a great deal of use of him. My aunt is in high spirits, full of political emotion and all for dying the death of the Heroic upon the first emergency.

Frederic Foster writes very entertaining letters about his intentions in case of an invasion; to go " dans les provinces les plus éloignées chercher des Troupes" and then to come " doucement joindre les Vainqueurs."

God bless you, dearest Lady Morpeth,

ever yours, H. C.

To Lady Georgiana Morpeth

Monday morning, Dec. 7th, 1807.

I went to see Miss Berry yesterday morning and was taken up to

[1] Louisa Brunton, a celebrated actress, married to the 1st Earl Craven, 12 Dec. 1807.

her bedroom at the very top of the house. There I found Prince Paul established in a great arm chair, toujours [dans] des extases. If he has any pretensions to be a Prince or in any way a person of importance, her manner must be very mortifying to him, as she treats him quite like a child. Agnes [Berry] told me that some days ago she never saw anything so affronted as he was—that upon his saying before several people some thing that pleased Miss Berry, she said " Good little soul," and got up and kissed him.

Yesterday morning Caroline walked with Sam and met Mr. Byng at the gate. He asked where I was but said nothing more about the DOG. However whilst we were at Dinner, William Rhodes came in and with the most plaintive voice said—" Your Grace, Mr. Byng called here this morning and desired a *horse* might be ready for him in the course of 2 or 3 days. Hitton says he does not know what he must do." Papa looked astonished, as well he might, and I was obliged to come out with an explanation of the mistake. I am afraid I can do nothing about it now.

[*End of letter missing.*]

To Lady Georgiana Morpeth

JERMYN STREET, *December the 8th, Tuesday morning, 1807.*

The Ossulstons are come to Town for 2 or 3 days and supped with us last night. I made her bring her work and accompany me on the Piano Forte. The little man was *aux anges* as he is very proud of her talent and the evening passed off rapidly. Papa likes my playing on the Harp, which gives me a double wish to improve, and our concerts are, even now, very tolerable ones, when George Lamb does not sing, which he has of late been much given to.

Ten thousand thanks for your kind and entertaining letter. It came to reconcile me for not hearing from Mr. Foster, who since Frank [Lawley] has been at Oxford has not written a line to any of us and I do not dare attack him in any way as he would as likely as not tell him of it.

When I went to see Miss Berry the other morning she began upon the old attempt of becoming an evening visitor at D. House, and with such hints direct and at last, " What a much better state of things it would be, if such a person as myself might come in any time from 10 to 12," that I thought it better to tell her once for all, that it might be a much better, but was an impracticable state of things to bring about. I then described to her the really uncertain manner in which we pass our evenings, sometimes having tea in the dining room, sometimes coming here, etc. etc., and to my agreeable surprise she was convinced in a minute, gave up the point with a good grace, seemed perfectly satisfied with my expressing regret upon the subject, and therefore in this instance a little of the " downright Cavendishism " she compliments me upon, held me good and probably prevented me having a great deal of trouble.

[*A large piece of the paper is torn away here.*]

The Bessboroughs, Lambs and a few men (the little race) dine with us today. My dearest grandmother is to come in the evening. Lady E. still keeps her room and looks thin and weak to the greatest degree, but she is in everything essential, recovering fast. Mr. Delmé is going in a week to Mr. Bailey's, where he will find his last flame, Lady Elizabeth Villiers, and from thence to Bath.

[*Here the tear recurs and Harriet has written in a post-script.*]

What a disaster ! Can you submit to read it in bits ? The Deuce is in it ; a sheet of paper never so misbehaved before. Don't tell Lord Morpeth I have singed it !

To Lady Georgiana Morpeth

December 12th, Saturday, 1807.

I see in the papers today that Lord Granville is set out upon his journey and it is likely, " dans une saison si rude " as Mr. Foster said of his to C. Howard in September, to be about as unpleasant a one as can be performed. I see Lady Charlotte [Leveson Gower] will begin supping with us again, which really will be too palpably absurd.

The minute I see the man who has seen the King, in other words tiny o, I will hear all I can and send you all I hear.

I am confined to the house with my cold and as I am not Lady Carlisle, I do not see much to regret in it in such weather.

George [Lamb] and I are very good friends, but we have occasionally little fallings out. What used to be said of me when I was a child, may be applied to him now—he really has not half an hour's good behaviour in him. Caro and I are constantly scolding him for it; he is like a schoolboy, when he has been good and quiet for a long time for him he begins making a noise, teizing the dogs, spoiling the furniture and then we say, "Don't, George, pray be quiet, dear George. Oh, leave that alone," just as I do to your children when they question.

God bless you, my dearest dearest sister. My letters are grown shabby and stupid, but how should they be otherwise?

H. C.

To Lady Georgiana Morpeth

December the 14th, Monday morning, 1807.

In the innocence of my heart I was puzzling in vain to find out who these uncontroulable Lovers who can only be parted by the Ocean, could possibly be, but I now agree with Lord Morpeth and conclude I am certainly one of them.

Mr. James dined here about ten days ago and I suppose he carried some tale of wonder about it to the old Dow., though I remember I sat between William [Ponsonby] and Delmé in the same side of the table as he did, so that he can scarcely have seen me and if he had, I divided my attention very equally between my neighbours. Sometimes I think William has never himself heard a word of the matter, which I should certainly prefer. I was surprised at his so easily taking the slightest hints. I said one evening that my father had said I must not receive the foreigners of a morning; he said, very quick, why? and I answered, but very carelessly, that it was one of those things in which there was really no harm but had better be sacrificed to the opinion of others who generally reckoned it an impropriety. He did not make any remark, but he has never been here since of a morning. The day before he left Town he supped here, he is just as childish and "sans conséquence" in his manner as ever. My only dread is Lady Bessborough getting hold of any idea about it. What an interesting story she would make of it. "They adored each other ever since they were so high," forgetting how many adorations she has tacked upon my poor shoulders since that period.

C. Lamb rather alarmed me—she came up to me the day they dined there and with her most solemn face and voice, "What a delightful man my brother William is ! " But I do not believe more was meant than met the ear.

By the bye, I must tell you a thing will amuse you. George Lamb last night talked to Caroline about me in rather a mysterious manner. At last she asked him (in consequence of something he said) if he thought I had any attachment. He confessed he had, but he believed it was now over. Her curiosity was excited and she entreated him to tell her to whom. He at first positively refused but said he was certain of the fact ; at length Caro's eloquence extorted the secret and with much reluctance he named his brother Frederick ! ! ! ! what would I give to see your face ? I think after *this* one may become pretty callous as to suspicions of attachment. Pray tell me if you hear any more. I am afraid that Lady Carlisle will write to Lady Essex for an explanation which the Dowager will be too happy to undertake.

Lady Elizabeth is recovering rapidly. The Devil got well and the Devil of a Monk was he. I was in hopes all affectation and disputatious whinings would have vanished, she was so free from them during her illness and so much more agreeable for it ; but they revive and strengthen with every beat of her pulse and she really did wrangle so about all these marriages and mésalliances that last night my patience had much to do to bear it.

It is said that Mr. Skeffington is going to marry Miss Bristowe ; more steps for more Columbines. This last will be quite a satire upon the Heathcotes.

God bless you, dearest G.

ever most affec^ly^ yours, HARRIET CAVENDISH.

To Lady Georgiana Morpeth

Wednesday, December 16th, 1807.

The Hollands were with Lady Elizabeth yesterday morning. They talked a little of Lord Henry Petty's marriage [to Lady L. Strangways] and seemed pleased with it, but I am afraid he has been a gay deceiver to more than one, as Lady Holland said rather crossly, " I am heartily glad he is going to be married, for he was beginning to make himself too ridiculous with his loves."

Lady Bessborough sent to ask to dine here Saturday. I suppose Lord Granville will certainly be here by that time and Lady Holland means " to come and take a peep at us," in the evening. I see it in my mind's eye like a scene in a genteel comedy, all of them coming in at different doors and exiting again by pairs into the great Hall; Mr. Allen falling to my share, perhaps with a comparative view of society in Peru.

I suppose you have by this time heard that the Author of the Spanish letters is Southey—Lady Elizabeth is reading Semple's travels through Spain and says they are excessively interesting and entertaining. You will see a review of them in the last number of the Edinburgh Review. Let me know if I shall send them you, they are in two small volumes.

George Ponsonby is to be leader in the House of Commons which was announced yesterday as such a secret, and heard with such emotion and effect that I conclude you will hear it from many other correspondents, with comments upon it that I should be rather at a loss how to make. When Lady E told it me, with marks of admiration in every look and motion, I had not a guess whether to look in rapture or despair, to take it as a thing of course or a matter of astonishment. However, I contrived to get off like Lord Burleigh in the Critic; did not utter a word but endeavoured to look bursting with meaning.

My aunt was remarkably rational during Lady E's illness and never made an unnecessary fuss about it. Her imagination has lately been considerably less brilliant, which, of course, is an unspeakable improvement.

Did I tell you that Lord Ossulston is in transports at Lord Pembroke's marriage [to Princess Woronzoff]? I suppose he thinks it is as well to be handed down to Posterity with a parallel case.

Are you only 5 at dinner? I wish you joy of the grown-up Turkeys. I was quite happy to see them.

God bless you, my dearest G.

ever most affec^ly yours, HARRIET CAVENDISH.

To Lady Georgiana Morpeth

December the 17th, Thursday morning, 1807.

I have just been taking my 3rd lesson of Madame Krumpholtz and she played to me what Lady Mary [Lowther] played at Lowther. I never heard anything in musick to be compared to hers; the touch and expression are quite perfect. She has a hand about half the size yours and as fat as Lady Holland's, which may contribute to the very harmonious sounds she draws from the Harp, but in that respect I shall not labour to emulate her, though I think with such a captivating talent as hers one might set all personal defects at defiance.

I continue my system with tolerable perseverance as far as Diet and Early Hours are concerned, witness having dined yesterday upon 2 slices of Goose ! and breakfasted this morning with my grandmother at 9. But I find the impossibility of taking exercise make the greatest difference in my well-being. London is now, during the few hours one can see without candles, like a great cloud from the thickness of the fog and it is impossible to see across the street. I contrived however to penetrate my little eyes as far as Mr. Byng yesterday in St. James's Street ; and afterwards had Mr. Delmé for an hour at the Carriage door in Pall Mall.

George Lamb has been ill and Caroline almost as bad from agitation. One would think he was a poor emaciated being, to whom every cold must be fatal, instead of which he always shines out after any of these attacks fatter and more blooming than before. He is improved in person I think, and in manners I am sure, and I really think her affection for him is as great as one can wish it.

Dearest sister, I really do sometimes think of your coming to Town till I am almost wild with impatience and joy. Have the Children forgotten me or do they ever " play at being aunt Haryo " as they used to do when I was at C.H. ? I should have liked to see that darling Coquette receiving Henry.

What is " the Tankerville family ? " It is an alarming title considering what a very drole novel might be made of its Namesakes. The O's are settled at Walton, but he comes to Town every now and then for a day. Mr. Hill is in Town ; all I have heard of him is that he was walking up St. James's Street with another man, when Lord Ossulston met him and asked him how soon he was to set out, upon which he allongated his throat and made such an extraordinary tragi-comic face, that both his companion and Lord O, who were strangers to each other, burst into the most violent laugh, in which he very soon joined heartily. This looks Ratisbonish.

God bless you, my dearest G.

most affec[ly] yours, HARRIET CAVENDISH.

To Lady Georgiana Morpeth

Friday morning, Dec., 1807.

I have left "sub margine" with variations by Mounsieur Diji and graces by Madme. Krumpholtz to come and write to you. I could not pay you a greater compliment. I am afraid I shall grow too fond of it and never do anything else. Though I get up before 9 and am never in bed till near 2, my days pass with a most wonderful rapidity and indeed if they did not, such weather and such company would drive me distraught. Last night, for example, Caro and George sat as usual whispering in a corner and I was left on the other side of the room from 11 till ½ past 1 at the mercy of Mr. Motteux and Mr. Delmé.

The Bessboroughs come to Town tomorrow to stay till Monday. William is staying at Holland House, which I think is a very good thing for him as it will probably draw him out and force him to exertion. Lord Granville is not yet arrived but Lady E. expects he will today or tomorrow.

Lord Brooke is going to be married to Miss Shugborough Evelyn, who has an immense fortune. I have a great regard for him and am very glad of it, as I believe he is as poor as anybody can well be.

I pity you being goaded to the gravel walk by grandpapa's commands in the form of advice. I am glad he is better.

Little Delmé I find proposed to Lady E. Villiers just before he left Town, but unlike his patient adherence to Caro after her refusal, he resents this last with all his little might and will not go near her or her mother. Mr. Beckford and Miss Rigby are to be married soon. They were at the play last night, I hear, looking very happy and everybody says she is a very delightful girl.

Lady Elizabeth is better today but has still a good deal of pain in her side.

God bless you, my dear dearest sister. I am sorry to send you so shabby a letter.

To Lady Georgiana Morpeth

December the 21st, Monday, 1807.

The Bessboroughs, Sir Thomas Miller and Sir Philip Francis [1] dined here on Saturday. Lord Granville not yet arrived. My aunt is, of

[1] Now recognized as "Junius."

course, anxious to be in Town when he is, and if she would be so, with less détour and prevarication, I should not blame her for it; but there is so much contrivance, so much of representing poor yielding Lord B. as a tyrant from whose Commands there is no way of escaping, and herself as a victim to him, that it is really distressing to hear her. I do not know how she contrives to manage him as compleatly as she does; till the moment they left Town yesterday, it was undecided whether they should or no, and she told us that they return some day this week, but have not yet determined which.

Mr. Motteux and George Lamb supped here last night. Mr. Motteux is much more insupportable than ever. Miss Berry has been ill and I had one of her usual notes yesterday; "sick or well yours dear soul," etc. I had promised in my answer to go and see her this morning, but the fog is impassable and I must break my promise.

[*End of letter is missing.*]

To Lady Georgiana Morpeth

December 24th, Thursday, 1807.

I am going to confide to you a little extravagance and my *laudable motive* for it. I have taken a share in Corisande's box at the opera, for which I pay very little, as she has it only every other week and has many other subscribers. My aunt and Lady Elizabeth are to have a box, Lord Clarges', if it can be got. Lady Bessborough can think of nothing else and I see she means to go a great deal this year and is more on the "qui vive" on the subject than ever. I would have given anything to have consulted you first, but there is no putting off determining. The deed is done, the Money paid and I think it will prove of convenience and use to all parties. As I know you are kind enough to interest yourself about my economy, I must tell you that I have, after having paid this, about 80£ *in hand*, without a debt of 5 shillings in the world.

The Ossulstons, Townshends and Sir Philip Francis dined here yesterday. It was very dull and unpleasant, as the whole set were out of humour. I had felt very unwell in the morning and Sir Walter gave me, an hour before dinner, 5 drops of Laudanum, which from my being totally unused to it had such a strange effect upon me that I was all the time like a person in a dream and talked in riddles to poor little o. I was vexed after dinner at Lady John's saying to Lady E., "So I hear William Ponsonby's going to be married?" "Good God, no, after all you know he is quite a boy." "That does not signify, Lady Townshend told me she did not know the person whom he was to marry, but that it was quite certain that his marrying her had been for a long time violently opposed, but was at last agreed to and everything settled." All the rest of the evening she was lost in wonder and promising to make the most active enquiries.

God bless you, dearest. Pray do not disapprove of what I have done about the Opera.

Yrs most affec[ly], H. CAVENDISH.

We had a scene last night "qui tenoit un peu du comique," though it gave rise to most sentimental notes this morning. Caroline from 9 till 12 was most anxiously expecting George as he was to leave Town today for Brocket to remain there 10 days. Just as we were going to supper the door Bell rang, but no George appeared, and after waiting a quarter of an hour, we sent for Laughton to enquire who had been. For some time he only answered in a most mysterious manner, "It was Mr. George Lamb, but he is returned to Lincoln's Inn." We pressed him for an explanation, which he at last gave in the following words, and you know his civil emphatic manner, "Mr. George Lamb coming up stairs *rather* too hastily, made a false step and falling down, had the misfortune to—to—an unpleasant rent in his . . ." here Laughton modestly pointed to his own inexpressibles and hurried on to "I offered him *Every thing*, needle, thread, *Everything*," I conclude this impressive 'Every thing' to have been nothing less than a pair of his own best black satin, in which case I do not much wonder at his adding, "but nothing would prevail upon Mr. George Lamb to remain."

To Lady Georgiana Morpeth

Christmas Day, Friday, Dec. 25th, 1807.

Shall you like to be next door to grandmama Carlisle at the Opera? for we are just going to take the Box adjoining to hers, in preference to one quite at the top of the house. I do not mind as we may easily be quitte for a few nods and there is no other to be got. The worst is being open to the Pit, exposed to examination and completely "en proie" to F. Byng, who I remember a long time ago when we borrowed Lady Carlisle's box, was all night within an inch of it.

I am beginning a letter to you tonight as tomorrow my day will be very busy ; I receive the sacrament in the morning and dine at 5 with my grandmother. I must also call on Miss Berry in the course of the day, which I have for a long time delayed. She must be in terrible distress about Mr. Ferguson who does appear from the trial to have been about as wicked as it is possible to be. I saw a person who was present at it and says that when Lord Elgin's counsel was stating the case, his indignation was so violent that he several times said, " Mr. Ferguson, that Demon," and that nobody could blame him for it the treachery and act was so great that was proved against him. After this you shall hear Miss Berry's learned defence, as I have no doubt I shall, at some length.

Many thanks for your letter. Tell George aunt Harry will never love him any more if he makes you stay over the 6th. I envy you snap-dragon—last night we had nothing but Beer Posset, a custom that makes me sick.

God bless you, my dearest sister.

ever most affec^ly yrs, HARRIET CAVENDISH.

To Lady Georgiana Morpeth

December 27th, Sunday, 1807.

Oh, naughtiest little boy ! but I forgive him as he is such a surprising darling as to play at Cassino. I suppose Georgiana will make some request next and if you are always to be so complying I do not know when I shall see you again. What will Lord Granville say if he arrives before you and hears the reason why ?

I am in expectation of the Duc de Gramont who is gone to Lady E's room after paying me one unconscionable visit and has promised me another before he goes.

God bless you dearest G.

ever yours, H. C.

To Lady Georgiana Morpeth

Tuesday, Dec. 29th, 1807.

Lady Elizabeth told me last night that there was a report of Lord Granville being landed, but it was afterwards contradicted though they are in hourly expectation of it.[1]

[1] He reached England on January the 11th, 1808.

I hear Lord and Lady W. Russell are in the most dreadful anxiety about their second son, a beautiful boy of about 7 years old. He was bit by a dog supposed to be mad, whilst he was making snowballs with two of his schoolfellows. The part bit, was cut out within three hours and has since been burnt with caustic, so that they have great hopes, even if the dog was really mad, that taken so in time, it may not have any bad consequences; but whilst the doubt remains in their minds it is hardly possible to conceive a more terrible situation. He has behaved like a little hero. When they were going to perform the operation, he desired them not to blind his eyes, for he should like so much to see it done. He never flinched or made the least exclamation the whole time.

I must now try and recollect for you as much as I can of Lord Ossulston's account of his visit to Gosfield. He is, as I was sure he would be, enchanted with it and says Louis the 18th is the only clever Sovereign in Europe, that his manners are dignified but extremely condescending. He never, of course, says a word of his reception here, but is evidently very much out of spirits, though he struggles to conceal it; that he talks a great deal; has more information than anybody, particularly about everything that concerns England, the history and language being perfectly familiar to him. He keeps Mounsieur, the little Dukes (you will see that I here drop the style of my little authority,) and all the people about him at a great distance and in the best order possible. Gosfield is a large fine house and they seem very comfortably established there; his attention to economy even in Trifles is rigid. He received Corisande with the greatest kindness, kissed her and said to Lord Ossulston—"Pardonnez à un vieux Étranger." I think this is all that can interest you. Lord Ossulston is in a ferment and he is a dear, good, honourable little man, but his tirades against Ministers are not amusing and leave him scarcely breath to sputter out, "It's a shame, it's a stain, it's a blot upon the country," at the end of each of them.

Ever most affect[ly] yours, HARRIET CAVENDISH.

My father went to Brooks's last night for the first time. Lady Elizabeth leaves her room but does not dine with us yet.

XV

SCRAP BOOK

1808

HERE comes a sad gap in the correspondence. There are no consecutive letters belonging to 1808. No letters describing Granville's return from Russia, or how Harriet was dragged unwillingly into society, chaperoned by her aunt Bessborough, " each other boring, by each other bored " ; nothing to tell us of what she felt when Granville started to woo Miss Beckford (the rejected of Lord Henry Petty), and then gradually veered towards her. We do not know if she was aware that she was called the " Pearl " while Miss Beckford was the " Sapphire "—just the few disjointed letters that follow.

It would appear that Georgiana Morpeth came to London for her sixth confinement sometime in January, that Haryo stayed with her whilst the rest of Devonshire House migrated to Chiswick, where she shortly rejoined them. After March she came back to London and started the hated social round with Lady Bessborough.

Clifford, Caroline St. Jules' brother, is mentioned for the first time since 1802, though he and Hart had been at Harrow together and he had been brought up with the rest of them, and it would appear that George Lamb opened his fiancée's eyes to her parentage, of which she alone was ignorant. They were not married till 1809.

The one letter to Lady Spencer is the eighth of a series which Harriet evidently wrote her during her autumn visit to Castle Howard.

To Lady Georgiana Morpeth

January 1st, Friday, 1808.

I wish you, Lord M. and your dear children a very happy new year and many returns of it, and this must be pretty nearly all the burthen of my song today, for though I am going on as well as possible, I am very much weakened and fatigued, as you will not be surprised at when I tell you that I take Calomel every night and take no nourishment but a little weak Chicken Broth. Sir Walter says I must have patience, but I shall have none if I am not quite well when you come. He has just been here and says I am going on prosperously. I am afraid he will not let me get up for some days and says I must expect short returns of pain. My illness has been occasioned by excessive biliousness, which is odd considering the life I have been leading for some time; but Sir Walter says this must have been accumulating for more than 3 months. When first I came from Castle Howard I remember whenever I wrote having a pain in my side so sharp that, in the course of a letter, I have sometimes been obliged 2 or 3 times to lay down quite flat upon the couch for ease, and I often said to Caro, laughing, that if it was wrong to write to you, I should think it was a punishment for I never could write above a dozen lines without having it, but never thought seriously of it.

The reports about Hart continue to be put in every day. I think he quite hates Miss Faulkener. His new flirt is the handsome Miss Rumbold, but he says she is the most ridiculous person that ever was known. He gives very drole accounts of Lady Rumbold sitting on a front row at the play, turning round to wink at him and her daughter. Sarah Faulkener was opposite, looking very ill. He is just now wild with delight at the Miss Monsons [1] being arrived in Town. Heaven send his taste may mend before we have a sister-in-law.

God bless you, dearest. Sir Walter has allowed me a sole, to my great joy and I must leave you for it.

ever yours, H. C.

To Lady Georgiana Morpeth

DEVONSHIRE HOUSE.

I have really but a moment to write to you, Dearest Sister. Hartington came to Town last night with a cold, sore throat and a great deal of feverish malaise about him. He has been overheating and neglecting himself, but his chest does not seem in the least affected, and Sir Walter has given him a most prodigious Dose, which I hope will carry off all his complaint. Nursing him, and a very long visit from the Duc de Gramont, have taken up all my morning.

[1] These were probably Elizabeth and Charlotte, daughters of the 3rd Baron Monson.

Louis the 18th is at Wanstead. The Duc made me a great many apologies for coming to see me of a morning—said that the English customs were so severe that he was afraid to do it was to " blesser la Bienséance." Shall we be suspected of a mutual attachment?

Mr. Heaton has just told me that he hears a report at Burlington House of our having taken several Portuguese ships. I do not know if there is any truth in this.

God bless you, dearest G. Hartington has sent for me. 1000 thanks for your letter.

To Lady Georgiana Morpeth

MY DEAREST SISTER.

Hartington is quite well again, but pulled by his illness and grown very thin.

As far as I can recollect Mr. Allen's account of the reviews; Sir John Sinclair's, Wordsworth's Poems and that on the Catholic question are by Jeffery; Lancaster by Sidney Smith; the first upon the mental question and one on West Indian Affairs by Mr. Brougham and Mant's Poems by a Mr. Hallam. Mr. Lyttelton cannot be absurd enough to claim Peter Plimley if they are not really his.

Lord Henry Petty has been at Brocket where they are all charmed with him. Lady Melbourne asked him to guess the riddle about marriage; " mon premier est un Tyran, mon second est un Monstre, mon tout est le Diable." He said he would not only guess it but answer it by another—" Quand on aime son premier on ne craint pas son second et le tout est la félicité suprême." I hear Lady Louisa is quite beautiful.[1] Poor Lady Maria.

God bless you, my dearest. The Ossulstons and Townshends dine here.

ever most affec^ly yrs, H. C.

To Lady Georgiana Morpeth

Monday. [*1808?*]

DEAREST G.,

I have not seen your children, as I have only been out in the evening in a chair, but I hear they are in high health and beauty. I long for

[1] Lord Henry married Lady Louisa Strangways on March 30th, '08.

them to come and tea with us, as we dine at home. I hope the Madame will agree.

I had a thorough London morning yesterday. Mr. Ward, rather constrained in his manner and dwelling on the delights of the Duchess of Beaufort's cheerful, animated manner, which I took as a cut and appeared much depressed.

In the evening I packed myself up, toothache and all, for a party at Corisande's, which was remarkably pleasant. I found there Corise in great beauty. Caroline very fat and pretty but not in spirits, at least (though talking and exerting herself), more of her discontented, affronted manner than I have for a long time seen, but very kind to me. Lady Melbourne and Lady Cowper, looking just as usual; Lady M. with a turban and Lady C. in a dirty gown and pearls, graceful and cold. Mrs. Hope, Mrs. William Locke, Charlotte Hunlocke, a sort of resurrection.

To Lady Georgiana Morpeth CHISWICK.

MY DEAREST SISTER,

Every thing is much better than I could have expected—at least appeared to me from Papa's receiving me *for the first time in my life* with real and *demonstrative* affection; he shook hands with me, kissed me twice, looked and seemed delighted to see me, and this reconciles me to everything. His spirits are considerably improved with his health and his health by exercise and activity.

Lady E. talked as disagreeably as possible, *we* and *us* at every word,—great hopes of Brighton on her part in about 10 days, which I think puts it almost entirely out of the question. If we go, she expressed great hopes you would, and as my father would stop 2 or 3 days at Woolbeeding I wish something could be contrived for me to travel there with you.

There is not a soul here but F. Foster. Papa was excessively anxious about your face, made me give details dated from the 1st January. I said your being able to come must depend upon your face. Lady Elizabeth means to leave your boy with you about one and to call for him and see you in her way out of Town between 3 and 4.

I feel much better, my dearest sister. Papa's kindness and affection has really *elated* me. I could make any sacrifice and bear any grievances for such a reward.

I am afraid I have not been clear ; I really think Brighton out of the question and with you, Chiswick would be very bearable.

To Lady Georgiana Morpeth

CHISWICK.

MY DEAREST G.,

I am comparatively happy even here. It is very delightful to see my father as well as he is and to experience kindness in his manner that I did not think it was in his nature ever to shew, whatever he may feel.

I am perplexed about Caroline ; she is excessively reserved, but not cold or appearing the least angry with me, but today at breakfast she mentioned Clifford and appeared extremely nervous. She seems to dislike talking of George to me and her manner is very préoccupée and she has the appearance of not being unhappy but agitated. I cannot be more *clear* in my account till I see you, but I am in my own mind without a doubt that George has opened her eyes, but in what degree and to how softened a view of her situation, I cannot and do not know.

I feel quite *extraordinary* without you and long beyond measure for you to come. I am quite well and I think I may say that I have exerted myself to the utmost. I think in the midst of all my, what has been reckoned, good conduct, I have often failed to do so and have had credit given me for much more than I deserve. My wish of doing right and really acting up to my own ideas of what is so, never was so strong as it is now. I am only anxious to make fewer complaints, more sacrifices, to become worthy of her and you. I see faults now in my past conduct in my situation which is one that is much talked of but little understood, that I did not think were faults before.

God bless you, my dearest dearest sister. I send you your beautiful, enormous boy.

Caroline and I mean to be with you tomorrow morning ; she is grown very thin, but looking much better than I ever saw her in my life. Could you write me a line by Lady E. that I may hear from you how you are ? I am sure Brighton is all talk. God bless you, dearest sister.

I should like to see you alone tomorrow but if there is the least difficulty I shall not like to appear anxious about it. I dare say it will happen. Pray give my love to Lord M.

To Lady Georgiana Morpeth

Though I have but one hour to write 5 letters in, I have a superstition about missing one day writing to you, and therefore send you this scrap, for my own sake, not for yours.

Corise tells me in one of her letters that she saw Lady Boringdon and Sir Arthur [Paget] flirting very much at some assembly. I am afraid the story you told me about Lord Boringdon is too good to be true.

Caroline seems very reasonable about George and I am happy to find that Lady Elizabeth's fears of a record hasty acceptance are without foundation.

Have you seen much of the Lambs? My grandmama hears from Caroline constantly. Sarah [Spencer] and I had almost a quarrel about William Ponsonby yesterday—she begun the old story that he seemed quite a fool and I my old defence that few people are so much the contrary. Our dispute ended amicably with some little concessions on both sides. I hear from both Lady Elizabeth and Caro that he is wonderfully animated at present and seems to enjoy going out very much—anything that rouses him must do him good. I have been his champion on so many occasions that really il y va de ma gloire to have his understanding thought more highly of.

[*End of letter missing.*]

To Lady Georgiana Morpeth

CHISWICK. [*Early 1808.*]

Many thanks, my dearest sister, for your letter. I am most extremely sorry to hear both from yourself and Lady Elizabeth of a return of pain and the divided opinion of those you have consulted. You know I can give no advice. I shall be with you on Monday at 11 o'clock and with you as much of the day as I can and you please. I wonder how I bear being so much and entirely away from you. If I was given to superstition, I should fancy all manner of horrid things were to happen to me in Town; my terror of it is so great with you there and [Lady E.] here I cannot in any other way account for it.

W. Spencer is really an exertion to one's eyes and ears not to be told, himself and his tongue in perpetual motion.

Mr. Vigoureux dines and sups here every day ; I used to like him when I was so high because he eat tallow candles, made stones dance in vinegar and played all sorts of conjuring tricks. But the bore of his society to riper years is indescribable. Happy is he who sleeps or snores, whichever you think sounds best.

W. Spencer has taken to the task of conciliating my affections, an irksome one to us both. By the bye 3 days running he has said " it rained bull dogs, cats and tygers."

I had one page of notepaper from Hart. He says he has been unwell for a week which has prevented his writing. " Write, mia vita. Rumbold sends you his love." I was at first on my highest horse, but as usual tumbled off it upon reflecting that this " wild freedom " must have been the Marquis's and not the Knight's. Do you know I am by a sort of fatality adopting W. Spencer's odious, flippant, figurative style ? My nerves are put in motion. I have written a long letter to Hart, complaining of his, and laughing very much at the absurdity of his charge against me. If he wished me to be sentimental he will be disappointed, but otherwise I think he will be satisfied.

Papa is quite well and snoring *violently*, and Lady E. and I are sighing in different keys over our letters. Mr. Foster is in a terrible humour for every kind of torment that you can imagine. He makes Caro nearly cry by calling *her* an old fat Lawyer.

Will you bet me 20 guineas that we do not leave Chiswick till March ? If you were here no words can say how much I should prefer it to London. I wish you would come down here for a day or two if the weather continues to be what it has been today. It really is delightful.

The O's dined here yesterday. Lord Folkestone is his Hero at present. He quotes him every second word. Corise can talk of nothing but Mr. Eden ; his being a good *metch*. . . .

[*End of letter missing*.]

To Lady Georgiana Morpeth

Thank you, my dearest G., for your note. I am almost more obliged to you for a very short letter as it proves to me that when you have a hundred things to do you remember me.

My grandmother is full of Duncannon's little exertions. They are certainly better than total indolence, but I am glad I am not the person obliged to be delighted with them.

I told my father of the fang and the eager interest with which he made enquiries into the particulars would have amused you. I hear Walte said to Corisande the other day, "I think I have made a friend of the Duke," which entertained him extremely. I hope the drawing of it will be an easy operation.

I had a letter from Mr. Foster today. Mr. Lawley has not been at Oxford, I find, only Beilby.

God bless you, dearest G. The bell is ringing.

ever yrs, H. C.

To the Countess Dowager Spencer

CASTLE HOWARD, *November 7th, Monday, 1808. (no. 8.)*

A thousand thanks, my dearest grandmother for your letter and very interesting accounts of the French royal family. It is impossible not to feel the greatest interest for their situation, but there is certainly something in the Individuals of it I have happened to meet with that rather destroys it, and though one may rejoice at their insensibility and frivolity, for their own sake, it compleatly checks the interest and feeling any other conduct would excite in the minds of English people. The King has, I believe, great superiority both in understanding and character over Mounsieur [d'Artois] whose society I am used to, and it is so made up of noise, thoughtlessness and nonsense, that it is no wonder that compassion does not occur to me, and that when I hear of the miseries of french royalty, it conveys no distinct idea to my mind. I see that people never had so much cause for despair, but I never see the slightest symptom of it amongst them. Nothing can be a greater instance of the way in which calamity dwells upon their minds than a speech of Mounsieur de Puységur's to my sister, which I believe I wrote you word of last year, when she asked him, after some conversation about the state of their affairs, if he did not often think with regret of Paris. "Pas plus qu'à Pékin, Madame."

I am glad that I mentioned the *Castle of Indolence* [1] to you, as I am sure you will be pleased with it. There are descriptions of the

[1] By James Thompson, 1700–48.

Aeolian and British Harp, one of the Musick of Indolence and the other of Industry, and an address to Dreams, that I think beautiful poetry and 3 verses beginning, " It was not by vile loitering in ease," that I beg you to admire. Lady Stafford pointed these last out to me, and, in this instance, I admire her taste and agree with her. Honi soit qui mal y pense.

Hartington left us the day before yesterday. He has been very amiable and delightful and I miss and regret him all day long. I believe I have mentioned his picture to you ; it is impossible to see a more striking or spirited likeness. He is leaning one arm on his large Newfoundland Dog, and his watch chain and favourite seal very conspicuous. He talks of meeting me at Althorp, but I never build upon any of his plans, till I see the execution of them.

Since I last wrote G. has had a tooth pulled out ; she is better but her gums and face are still uncomfortable from very great inflammation and irritation.

We have had all the Vernon family here. Miss Ann and I renewed our acquaintance and talked a great deal of Nuneham, of Lord Harcourt and of you, my beloved grandmother.

Do you know how much you are loved, admired and honoured by every person who has the least connexion with you ? and do you know how happy and proud it makes your grandchildren to see you revered and thought of as you are, treating them as if they were your equals and your friends. I never say to you half what I feel upon this subject, but you must not think it is owing to not observing or not valuing such kindness. The Post is just going and I must have done. I have promised to write a line to my brother ; I was happy to see him as eager as ever about his journal.

most dutifully and affec^ly^ yours, HARRIET CAVENDISH.

XVI

HARYO AT CHISWICK

1809

1809 saw Corunna and the expedition to Walcheren. The younger men of the Devonshire House set were all on active service. Harriet wrote to her brother, who was now nineteen years old and supposed to be at Cambridge, but actually gadding all over the place, to give him news of them. Among these careless self-assured boys were George Cavendish (Lord George's son) and Frederick Howard, Morpeth's brother. Both were to give their lives for that England which they had always regarded as their easy heritage. George Cavendish was drowned when his transport was sunk, and though Frederick was unscathed in this campaign he fell at Waterloo.

Lord Byron refers to Frederick's death in the verses :

Yet one I would select from that proud throng
Partly because they blend me with his line,
And partly that I did his sire some wrong,
And partly that brave names will hallow song ;
And his was of the bravest, and when shower'd
The death bolts deadliest the thinn'd files along,
Even where the thickest of war's tempest lower'd,
They reached no nobler breast than thine, young gallant Howard.

Lord Carlisle's mother was a daughter of the 4th Lord Byron who was great uncle of the poet ; he was also his guardian, with the natural result that quarrels ensued and though Byron attacked Lord Carlisle in his writings with much vehemence, he made an amende honorable in the verses quoted and in a letter to Moore he wrote : " In the late battles, like all the world, I have lost a connection—poor Frederick Howard, the best of his race. I had little intercourse of late years with his family ; but I never saw or heard but good of him."

At home the great scandal of the time was that of the Duke of York and his mistress Mary Ann Clarke. He, as Commander-in-Chief, was involved by her selling commissions in the Army.

But all these events only seem to touch Harriet lightly. She is at her best when writing to Hart. She could not make him the receptacle of all her worries and perplexities, but he thought in the same way as she did and so, with a great sigh of relief, she takes up her pen and lets it run away with her. And though dear Hart was so extremely " volage " he dated and docketed all her letters, for which relief I offer him much thanks.

To the Marquis of Hartington

CHISWICK. *Tuesday, January 17th. 1809.*

I must answer your letter immediately, for every sort of reason—to thank you for it a thousand times, to tell you that nothing gives me half the delight that hearing from you does, but above all to entreat you to determine upon no plans, to settle nothing about Tutors or Tours without—I do not say consulting, if you have any objection to it, but mentioning it to my father.

All that space I give you to put yourself in a passion and get out of it again, and now listen—I do not doubt your intending to do it, but I feel sure that you will delay it till all the good effect of the communication will be lost. He will hear of Mr. Caldwell from somebody else. Lady E. will have a pretext for accusations without end against you—a satisfaction I grudge her experiencing and I shall know that all might have been avoided by your now doing what you probably mean to do a week or ten days later.

Wish a little—so will I.

I have had several conversations with my father about you and you are very much mistaken if you think his habits of indolence and carelessness have made him indifferent to his children. I am convinced that he loves us all, but he is proud of you and anxious about you and would feel, I am convinced, deeply anything like neglect in your behaviour or dislike in your feelings towards him. Of the last, I am certain he never can have had reason to suspect you.

Now stop, for I am getting into rather a passion—and shall go and look at the snow.

It would be unreasonable and foolish to attempt to judge of your affections towards him, by my own. It must be very different. I do not say that I have not often lamented his coldness and regretted the little communication between us, but I know that one expression of kindness or interest from him has more influence over me than almost anything else in the world, and I cannot imagine any situation in which his power over my heart and feelings, if he chose to exert it, would not be *almost* unlimited.

Now, dearest, dearest brother, what a very great love you are, with your extraordinary confusion of ideas and quantities of different subjects occupying you all at once. As to Sir Wm. [Rumbold]—I am not inclined to abuse him either in great or small letters but I am extremely sorry to hear that he is so unwell. You seem both of you to lead the most fatiguing lives in the world—never in the same place two days together, taking much too violent exercise and never going to bed till two or three in the morning. I cannot conceive the amusement of all this and its consequences must be bad.

The Prize Ox amuses me, the seal astonishes me, Mr. Caldwell enchants me, your stupidity does not strike me, your discretion reassures me, your hunting occupies me, your query perplexes me, for I understand Lady Essex is in a fair way to recovery and the Dow, le fut, l'est et le doit être.

Do not accuse me of not answering your letters. Write to me from Chatsworth.

Ever yours, HARRIET CAVENDISH.

I cannot get a frank—tell me I am not worth a few six pences, if you dare.

To the Marquis of Hartington

CHISWICK. *January 24th. 1809.*

I really do not know that anything gives me as much pleasure as hearing from you.

Still at Kedleston with a Lady looking over each shoulder ! I will contrive it so that you shall be the most sorry of the two, if they read what I write. I admire your temper in bearing my tormenting you about your plans and I think you perfectly in the right, as far as they concern Mr. Caldwell, but my father does not know that you have given up keeping this Term at Cambridge and questions me about it every day, whilst Lady E. keeps up a sotto voce Bass of "Delay, example, young men of fashion," which proves it will be made a grievance of but, as I said in the other case, one that does not signify, if my father hears it from you. My own opinion is that in every way you will be infinitely better at Chatsworth, that is if you remain there, but odd as it may sound, I do not reckon three months passed between K. K. Kedleston,[1] Doveridge and Sandon [2] staying at Chatsworth ! I am sorry to differ from you and probably with all the Ladies you may consult on the subject. Before I knew anything of your plan of operations for the winter, I was anxious beyond measure to see you soon in London. Perhaps I am so still, but that's my affair, and I don't mean to tell you yet. What good will either study or exercise do you, if you are to be in Jermyn Street in three weeks and to simplify the thing, how shall we convince the Duke and la Douairière that you are "staying at Chatsworth"? It is heroism, downright heroism in me, to argue upon this side of the question, but I am anxious for you not to be in Town at present, if the alternative is your staying at Chatsworth to study and "thrive like a Prize Ox."

I am glad Miss Sneyd is "elegant." I always think it more incumbent upon an Heiress to be pretty than anybody else, as it leaves a loophole for her admirers and a hope of inspiring for herself a disinterested attachment for herself.

À propos of *grandmamas*, what do you think mine was about to do the other day at Althorp ? When your letter to me arrived there, she said—"God bless me, I wonder what he can have to write about so soon again. I think I may as well look into it," and "demain Papillon" [the letter] was between her finger and thumb, when my aunt snatched it out of her hand—"Nobody shall touch the *slut's* letter (quand on est à Rome, il faut faire comme à Rome) but her own self," and sent it on to me, like a dear positive love. Pray, do not mention this, mais parlez moi de cela.

As to Lady Scarsdale's uneasiness, it is not in human indulgence not to partake of it. How do I from my heart pity all those who have to do with a woman such as Lady R[umbold]. Somebody asked me the other day which Sir William [Rumbold] preferred, you or your Chaise and four. You should have seen my dignified contempt and

[1] Lord Scarsdale's. [2] Lord Harrowby's.

'HART', AFTERWARDS 6TH DUKE OF DEVONSHIRE
FROM A WATER-COLOUR

the face of my poor antagonist, who thought it the best joke he had ever cut. I think it will be the last of the kind to me.

You will see in the papers as much as I can tell you, of the Bravery of some of our Troops, and the loss of others. Frederick Howard and Agénor de Gramont [Corise's brother] are both mentioned as having behaved most gallantly and Agénor is to be promoted on his return. It makes me quite adore them. The expression is rather strong, but never mind. A young man, unused to such scenes, distinguishing himself in them, does make me enthusiastic. Of the two Cavendishes, I have heard nothing, but you will see that Lord William Bentinck was in the principal and most responsible situation and has acquitted himself most nobly. They say, indeed, the success of the repulse was chiefly owing to him. Think of Lady William. I think it must have driven her wild, first the anxiety, then the joy. How *do* people keep their senses in such cases? Lady Charles Bentinck probably does, from having had originally so few that they could not muster into insanity. I hear nothing of her husband.

Letters have been received from Mr. Stuart. He says the lower orders are still well disposed but that the Junta is entirely made up of old women or rogues and if Buonaparte had dictated to them, they could not have acted so as to assist his plans better than they have done. You must not repeat this, but it is really too bad. God bless you.

H. CAVENDISH.

I have just seen a letter from Frederick Howard. He had a narrow escape. It was the transport he was in that ran aground. They got on board the Barfleur and came home in that. Henry Cavendish is wounded in the hand, nothing of consequence. God bless them, dear people.

To the Marquis of Hartington

CHISWICK. *Saturday, January 28th. 1809.*

DEAREST HARTINGTON,

Since I wrote we have received the melancholy intelligence of poor George Cavendish's loss. After behaving with the greatest bravery, the transport on which he was returning was sunk and himself and every man on board was lost. It is impossible to say how much I feel for his family. It is dreadful for them, having first received the news of the embarkation and supposing him safe.

God bless you.

H. C.

To the Marquis of Hartington

CHISWICK. *Sunday, January 29th. 1809.*

I am going to pour upon you all the facts that have lately occurred in the great world and all the jokes good and bad that they have given rise to. Of the festivities at Woburn, you will see something in the Papers, but not that Lord Ossory and Lady Sefton have been the victims throughout of the Duke of Bedford's " espièglerie." There is no saying in how many ways the unfortunate Dowager has been made a fool of, but as she is safe in Town again, superba di se stessa, and thinking she has made every husband faithless and every wife jealous, you need not waste much compassion upon her. She talks in raptures of the Tavistocks, calls them " the Doves," says they retire three hours every morning to read Poetry—" Broke in upon them one day and, to be sure, he reads like an angel, afraid there are no little ones coming, but happiness is never compleat." She was one of the party sent to disturb poor Lord Ossory, whom they found supping on a cold boiled chicken and a tongue. Lord Kinnaird was disguised as a French Cook, with a Bill of fare, ordering sauce piquante à la Bedford, Sefton à la superbe, which enchanted her and she immediately spread her fan before her face and said it was very distressing, everybody would take her for Lady Hinchinbroke. They carried her back to Woburn more dead than alive, as the Duchess knowing her terror in a carriage, desired the Coachman to drive up all the banks, she screaming the whole way.

Now for St. James's. The first we heard of it was from Frederick Foster. " The Palace is burnt to the ground with all the maids of honour and the Queen has singed her beard." There was a difference of opinion at Brooks's whether they should go and look at it. General Fitzpatrick said, " It is very cold and we had better stay here ; as the King is not in it, it is not worth looking at, and as to the Maids of honour, they are a parcel of dried sticks and will only make it burn a little brighter." George Lamb says the Country will be ruined by omissions. We have been within reach of the French Army without killing a man and set fire to St. James without burning a Duke.

It snows, it rains, 'tis dark, 'tis cold, 'tis dim. We do not see a soul except Corise, who when "Lor. O." is out, will brave any weather rather than an hour's solitude. She cannot recover her surprise at my not journeying up to Town every Tuesday and Saturday to go with her to the Opera. "Is it poss-sibbil? Are you quite med? Have you no wish to flirt?!!!?"

I love you, I kiss you, I curtsey to you and am

Your affectionate sister, H. CAVENDISH.

Miss Trimmer came to me the day before yesterday. A dear woman, but as Doctors give physic before some illnesses to prepare the patients, she always gives me lectures, not upon any harm I have done in the past, but in case there should be any in the future, and like another Cassandra, predicts to me many sins that I may perhaps commit. But at this moment when I feel innocent of them, this prophetic management of me only gives me a wish to laugh. For example, she comes and breakfasts with me at nine and groans all the while at the probability of my being in bed at eleven next month in Town, and when I tell her I have been at Chiswick Church—"Who can tell, my dear child, if you will go to St. George's!"

To the Marquis of Hartington

CHISWICK. *January 31st. 1809.*

"What will be thought of me, what will be said of me," I am convinced narrows more minds and destroys more happiness than anything else in the world. Walker [her maid] is rather in distress at what the world may think of *her* at this present moment. Laure and her were attacked in the gravel walk by one of the American Deer. Walker's account is—"When I perceived that the animal had butted twice at Ma'mselle, I thought—every circumstance considered—it was better to run home for help." The house is divided upon it. Some think good Generalship best displayed in a retreat, others that her friendship should have induced her to face the foe. If Laure had not had the most wonderful courage and presence of mind, she must have been dreadfully hurt, but she held the beast's ears and then its throat till her strength failed her and then ran round and round a tree till some of the servants came to her assistance. Papa is so terribly pacific in his disposition that he will give no orders about having the animal confined. We are therefore afraid of going far from the house and F. Foster walks with his sword drawn.

God bless you, dear brother—I never send a letter to you that I do not long to get it back again, half an hour after it is on its journey, but I pin my faith on your discretion, and Desks, Keys, Locks, Patent springs etc.

We are so fixed here that I do not even look forward to London as a place I am to be in again. It is a positive pleasure to me to be out of Town and with the society a little more enlarged or in one instance curtailed, I should not have a wish beyond Chiswick for a long time to come. God bless you, my dearest brother.

HARRIET CAVENDISH.

The rain poured with such violence into my old room the other night that I was obliged to remove to yours. I had much rather sleep in the British Museum at once ; I woke every minute fancying some of your nasty snakes [1] and beetles were crawling upon the pillow and to this hour I do not know what all those strange things are stuck against the wall.

To the Marquis of Hartington

CHISWICK. *Wednesday night, February 1st. 1809.*

And are you quite alone, nice brother, with nothing but Ancestors and the Queens to trifle with ? Do not be afraid of my not writing often enough. I do nothing that I like half as much, and as to the delight of receiving your letter ! oh but !—

It is perfect of you to stay at Chatsworth till the end of April and if a shade of regret mixes with my satisfaction at it, I can only say it is very imperfect of me. My father asks me every day when you are to be at Cambridge. Indeed, dearest Hartington, considering his unlimited indulgence to you, he ought not to be neglected and his entire ignorance of your plans must be in a thousand ways painful to him. I would give all I possess (which is as Walker assured me this morning in something between an hysteric and a swoon, not one farthing) that you would write to tell him that you have given up keeping this Term and your reasons for doing it.

[1] Hart was addicted to collecting strange animals. Harriet talked of his Muscovy Ducks, and now it is Snakes. After his succession he made a zoo at Chiswick.

I am extremely sorry to hear of the great affliction of those poor Cavendishes.[1] Anne is the best creature in the world and has not an idea beyond loving and pleasing her own family. It will be terrible if they are obliged to part with Henry again.

How surprized Barrow's sermons must have been upon first opening to see you and Sir William. I wonder it did not shut of itself. Do you know, it is very delightful of you both, and it is incalculable what advantage serious study, steadily persevered in, would be to you. A frivolous woman is a bad thing, but if there is one thing more contemptible than another, it is a frivolous man. And the great advantage of the contrary extreme is that with a good foundation of principle and knowledge, Archbishops may dance hornpipes for any reflections I may make upon them in consequence.

To be abused is the lot of la pauvre humanité. To have enemies because he is your friend is to be understood and regretted upon both Sir William's and your accounts, but to be above minding such attacks is, I hope, as much in both your characters as ever to do anything to justify them is far from your conduct. That your friends should be worthy of you is of course to both G. and me a most anxious wish and we are perpetually cross-questioned about Sir William Rumbold by people who wish to gratify their curiosity or to excite ours. I am as sick of being asked—" Is he a toad eater ? " as I am of answering—" You forget that question reflects as much upon my brother as upon him." I wish I dare tell them how much they betray their own littleness of mind in so eternally suspecting it and I am convinced that a person who can never believe in disinterested friendship in others, is incapable of feeling it himself. When I see the prejudices, meanness and selfishness that actuate half the people one is laughed at for not admiring and wondered at for not esteeming, I feel to detest the world and wish myself old Betty, or rather the Broom she sweeps with.

I got up to begin undressing, but saw myself in the glass making such a very cross face that I could not help laughing, which put me in good humour again and I shall write on.

Car and I have taken to gardening and except being constantly overlooked by Mr. Fletcher and a dozen Laundry Maids, we are going to create quite a Paradise. I make Frederick Foster take long walks

[1] The family of Lord George Cavendish ; Anne married Lord Charles FitzRoy in 1825.

with me in the Environs. He is really afraid of reports, will not let me take his arm if I am tired to death ; my great delight is to walk excessively fast as he is quite as infirm as people generally are at 90, he does not quite dare to stay behind but hobbles after me, too much out of breath to scold, but in a real rage. " How can anybody be such an Idiot as ever to be persuaded to walk with a woman going ten miles an hour and then stopping to faint and " Oh, Mr. Foster, I am so tired, oh, Mr. Foster, I shall die ! "—To be sure, he is a strange man, so very unlike anything else in the world.

Good night, brother mine, it is 3 o'clock and I was up this morning before 10.

Thursday.

If I read it over it will go into the fire—I beg you to put it into yours the minute you have read it. Pray, pray write to me.

God bless you.

H. CAVENDISH.

To the Marquis of Hartington

CHISWICK. *Sunday evening, February 5th. 1809.*

I was in Town the whole of yesterday. First in Park Street, where I saw Frederick Howard looking very well, grown fat and as uninteresting as if he had never been out of Grosvenor Place, talking of new musick and Vestris [the dancer]. All my enthusiasm evaporated in less than ten minutes and by the time he left the room, I could have felt as much for Lady Julia. I do not want to take from his merits either at home or abroad, however I believe few people to be as faultless, and I hardly remember hearing anything of him but praise or seeing anything but what deserves it. Yet there is a total want of something, I do not exactly know what. A possibility of living months in the same house with him on the best of terms and the most intimate footing without liking him a bit better or worse one day than another, coming from a battle as other men come from the Opera, and in short so mechanically right, that one would give the world to see him outrageously wrong. Lord Gower [Granville's half-brother] was with him and staid a good while with us. It is impossible to be more pleasing and gentlemanlike or more totally free from any sort of affectation and pretension. He has a great deal of conversation and more tact and observation than almost anybody I know. I should think the fault of his character is being too worldly minded, and the only one in his manner (but to a much less degree than poor Lady Charlotte), always looking as if he thought Lady Stafford was hid in the room, " creased like a dog's ear in some folio," ready to dart out upon him at the first offence in word or deed. It is terrible to see a mother exerting such undue influence over the minds of her children and to see Lord Gower outwardly and visibly, when she is in the room with him, you would think him a child of eight years old, afraid of being whipped.

I went from G's to Lady Maria Hamilton. She kept me ages with her and talked a great deal of you, says she has an uncommonly good opinion of you and desires me to assure you of her protection. She is more dignified and au pied de la lettre than ever. I scarcely know a person of whom I have so high opinion, a sort of veneration, and taking all things into consideration, one grain of merit in her has twice the merit that a thousand would in anybody else. Lady Abercorn came into the room whilst I was there, in a great taking, God knows about what, fanning herself with her pocket handkerchief, as red and as ruffled as a Turkey Cock. It might be jealousy, it might be anger, it might be " as who should say I am a Marchioness," it might be nothing at all. Lady Maria seemed to take it like the old woman with the Eels and I confess it gave me no one emotion, but a very considerable degree of satisfaction, when the door shut after her. She is not a favourite of mine, she is so violent and inconsistent and so prudish and severe about other women, forgetting that nobody ought to be so indulgent, that I feel disposed to take up the part of every bad character she names, not for the virtue of those I defend, but from feeling how little right she has to attack. She said one day *at* a person in every respect her superior, though perhaps not faultless, that anyone suspected of an intrigue ought to be put in the Pillory. My Aunt Spencer could hardly go beyond this, yet upon surer footing. Do you know I am shocked at this last dear love's vehement abuse of the world in general, for I really cannot draw any line or see that she does. I dined there yesterday. She was more entertaining than ever, but sparing neither friend nor foe. I found myself at dinner, to my great dismay seated between Lord Grenville and Sir Samuel Hood. It was a sort of celebrated bodkinism that quite overpowered me, but I was soon relieved by seeing them both what Lady Augusta Greville calls "set to," in a manner that took off all responsibility from their neighbours. As they eat very much like the rest of the world I was not much edified or amused. Sir Samuel has a foolish manner and does not look like a Hero ; Lord Grenville does worse for he looks like a fool, but his conversation immediately destroys that first impression and is most remarkably sensible. Lady Grenville is very pretty, at least more Tournure than anybody I ever saw and the nicest little round head and small features. She looks like his granddaughter, but I hear she is the best wife in the world and that he has the highest opinion of her understanding and judgment. Lady Hood is very handsome, much younger than Sir Samuel and by all accounts a delightful woman. Sarah [Spencer] is quite well. She looks better than I ever saw her and is the most excellent, amiable creature in the whole world.

God bless you, my dearest, dearest brother. I live upon the hopes of a letter tomorrow—I would not be Cooksey, coming without one.

H. CAVENDISH.

To the Marquis of Hartington

CHISWICK. *Wednesday, February 8th. 1809.*

I have had two notes from Anne Cavendish since I wrote last—she gives but bad accounts of Lord and Lady George and says he has been more overcome by it than any of them. I love him for feeling it so deeply. I believe my aunt's severity was only in manner and that she never has been wanting in affection and essential kindness to any of her children. Anne's youth was particularly stormy and it was not in the power of governess to subdue or manage her. Lady George was therefore obliged to exert herself and was more strict and despotic with her than with any of the others.

I wish you would not talk of red Cardinals and Dormice when the subject is a serious one—Poor Caroline Lamb has been very seriously ill but she is a great deal better and I think will go on quite well now. The disappointment was a great one [she had miscarried] and, added to her illness, has weakened her excessively.

I am delighted at your coursing and voltigeant and wish I was John Hall to see it. "Rather too high for pleasure" amuses me. It is

Delmino's mistake throughout all his proceedings and applies as much to Lady Barbara [Villiers] as to a five barred gate. I hear he is now at Lord Shaftesbury's—what a mercy it is that nothing whatever affects his spirits or seems to give him a moment's mortification. He seems at present the happiest of human beings, but I have no idea how he will do as an old man, when " the time cometh in which no man can dance."

Miss Trimmer dined and slept here the day before yesterday—I was quite happy to have her and to repose my eyes upon something so very unlike Lady E. I took her to Town yesterday, where I found my grandmother expected in Jermyn Street. She arrived whilst I was there and we were all once more assembled in that little dirty room with all the noise of a narrow London street, carriages, cries, post bells, dogs barking, children squalling etc. and John Matthews preparing " oh spare feast, a radish and an Egg," in the midst of it all. We began immediately about you—she gave me the account of her alarm about gaming and I did not mention having heard of it from you with a prudence and discretion that does me honour.

I found as usual a crowd in Park Street. Lady Maria Hamilton, Miss Butler (who enquired after you and said she was in love with you once for ten minutes because you said " no " so kindly—can you recollect the decisive moment ?) and dear little Miss Humphries, now Mrs. Dimmock, the happiest but the poorest person in the world, with a husband she adores, but hardly bread to eat. She is near her confinement, and looks quite like a football. Miss Butler is very good humoured and entertaining sometimes but with a little too much buffoonery. The Duchess of York must have given over not brooking things, for some time. Mrs. Clarke [1] is rather a clever, pretty, impudent woman ashamed of no one thing in the world, which is lucky for her. I went to Spencer House where my aunt did talk of it all in such extraordinary language that Lord Stair and I were covered with confusion. It made me think *so* much of Althorp to see his ugly face—I found there much the most beautiful creature I ever saw—Lady E. Bingham, Lord Lucan's eldest daughter. It is real, regular beauty with so much charm and intelligence of countenance and is so very striking and graceful in figure and manner, that if she is ten thousand delightful things besides, she shall be Lady Hartington with

[1] Mistress of the Duke of York.

full permission. They say she is the best and the most amiable ure in the world and not more than fifteen, which I think a great object. I thought Lady Spencer seemed rather discomposed at my excessive admiration and began immediately about Georgiana. Lady Maria, too, seemed rather in a huff when I said Lady Elizabeth would be a very good wife for you, and as she cannot have any designs herself, it must be for Lady Frances. I admire your making such a stir in all the nurseries. I hear nothing of your grown-up loves and for a wonder you are not just now supposed to be dying for anybody. Somebody told me a long story about Sir William Rumbold and Lady Burrell or Lord Egremont's second daughter, who is coming out this year, they did not know which, and somebody else, but it was all in a great puzzle in my friend's head and I could not make it out clearly, but the pith of it seemed that he was in love with these three Ladies all at once.

[*A large piece is cut out here, presumably by F. L. G.*]

Were you at Church this morning? And do you know that I went here, though they are in hourly expectation of the steeple falling in and crushing the congregation. I took Mrs. Brown [the Housekeeper at Chiswick], who talked the whole way of " Dear Lord Hartington, God bless his kind soul." She never can resist the drive but had rather be hung than go to Church in its present precarious state.

Goodnight and God bless you, my own best and dearest brother. All the clocks in the neighbourhood are striking two, my eyes are quite shut and what little sense I have has been asleep for the last 3 hours.

Ever yours, H. CAVENDISH.

To the Marquis of Hartington

CHISWICK. *Saturday night, February 11th. 1809.*

I am half delighted and half unhappy. Your letter to my father has had the greatest success. He seems pleased and has mentioned having heard from you several times today. Lady E. is silenced, has turned herself into another key, " love of Derbyshire and improved health "—

But you have had a fall from your horse, you have hurt your head and Carrington thought it necessary to bleed you. Heaton [the Devonshires' lawyer] assures us that it is nothing, but my anxiety for

Monday's Post is not to be told and if it brings me no tidings of you I shall go to G. and if she has none to La Douairière and if that fails, to Chatsworth.

And now, my adventurous brother, will you have done riding, fishing, horses, voltigeant over bars to edify John Hall and leaping over everything that comes your way to please Sir William [Rumbold]. I do trust, as you say nothing of it, that this fall has not been a bad one, but promise me that you will not ride carelessly in future. Somebody laughed at somebody for driving slowly and cautiously and asked why he did and somebody else answered (it would not have been pretty in him) " because his friends are not yet tired of him "—A l'applicazione, signor.

I have been in Town again all this morning—I took Mrs. Brown with me. She has not yet recovered Chance's [Hart's dog] death and lamented over it for near an hour. We then dwelt upon all your perfections and the trouble is she cannot say too much of your kindness and generosity to her, but there is in the dear woman's head such a confusion of times and topics that it is difficult to follow her thread of ideas. The dear dog and the sweet child, with every now and then a touch of the Monkey and John Brown.

G. had been at a supper at Lady Castlereagh's, where she had been, to quote her note to me about it—" sickened of London for the rest of the season, nothing but dull and ugly old men and all the women whom she had been trying to avoid and neglecting to call upon ever since her arrival in Town." I made her give me a detailed account of it, with a view to my letter. Lady Hinchinbroke, all covered with steel, full of vivacity and enquiries about you and jokes about the members' close attendance at the house. I see her—if you don't—bending down in a high voice—" Ought not we to be jealous of Mrs. Clarke ? " Lady Cowper in the velvet, protecting Kitty Monck through the crowd. Dow Essex in Crimson d°, taking pretty good care of herself. Lady Charlotte Leveson in grey cloth, looking as if she was doing penance and wishing, I am sure, to sink into the earth. Lady Bath, a little heap of good humour, esprit and affectation, with nothing like shape but an immense Turban upon the top of it all—and Puységur at Lady Harrowby's feet, one of the most agreeable women in the world and perfectly good and respectable, but always provoking me by—

Good night, my dearest brother—I am so tired I do not know what I say—the dear woman never provoked me in the course of her life, yet God only knows what I might not have been going to accuse her of in my first sleep.

Sunday. Feb. 12th. 1809.

I was on the point of forgetting Lady Warwick, Lady Augusta and Lady Caroline Greville ! Lady Augusta looking very handsome and blooming but just as she did last year and just as she probably will do the end of this, so you need not hurry or trifle up to see. She told G. a quantity of very long stories and Lady Caroline was all smiles, nods and protections. I am always afraid of telling you that this family bore me till I wish to scream because I am not sure that you do not suspect me of talking *at* you, which I hate to be done to myself so much, that I dread being supposed to do it to others. I have no prejudice against Lady Augusta ; I think her uncommonly handsome, good humoured and unaffected, but I think her unworthy of you and I cannot believe that you are not of my opinion. Nothing shall make me think that such a woman would have it in her power either to captivate or fix you. I know that I am *romantic* as to my idea and wishes about the woman you are to marry, but it is for reasons so *very* flattering to you, that you must not blame it. Yet I shall not (whatever I may say in speculation), break my heart when the deed is once done, if it is to nothing worse than Lady Augusta—Oh ! yes I shall—you must not, shall not, cannot like, Warwick's daughter, Clonmell's sister and oh, Lord Brooke, whose very look is bore, indefatigable bore and whose " tongue keeps good the promise of his face." If you do marry into this kingdom of detail, I shall adopt Mr. Hill's plan, who used to say that when Lord Brooke began a story he went on working it up till there was nothing for it but to pretend to go into a fit, for nothing short of that would satisfy him as to the degree of astonishment and interest he wished to excite in his hearers.

Corise dined here today ; she is a nice love and very entertaining. She thinks all this affair of the Duke of York " very good for the moral." Her politics are impayable. She says Lor' O has quite a line of his own. Poverino !

God bless you, best dearest kindest brother. Pray burn this letter the instant you have read it.

As a Young Man

In Later Life: from an Engraving

William, 5th Duke of Devonshire

To the Marquis of Hartington

CHISWICK. *Tuesday, February 21st. 1809.*

Tell me, do you believe that I have been all this time calm, good tempered, " like a tame fowl expecting a shower ? " Oh ! to describe my rage and indignation after my unexampled goodness. Three letters without waiting for one from you, eight pages each and you send me " good bye love, dinner's ready," and not a word from you since.

If I had not communications of the utmost importance to make to you, nothing should induce me to write to you again, oh nothing, oh but nothing !

You will today or tomorrow or next day, receive a letter from my father, by which you will see that he has taken alarm as to your intentions and certainly is in some respects dissatisfied with your plans. Do not let him know that I have told you of his letter to you having passed through my hands, but I wish you so much to know of the conversation that passed between us this morning with regard to you. He brought me the letter you wrote to him and his answer and, with a kindness and confidence that I can never feel grateful enough for, he desired me to tell him if there was any objection to his sending it, if it would vex you and said smiling, " I am afraid he will think me a little cross." Is not this indulgence and kindness and was I wrong in telling him that I felt convinced you only wished to know *from himself* what his wishes were about you and would never misunderstand the interest and anxiety that might make him ever blame or differ from you ?

Perhaps my father may have had reason to think you a little inconsistent and we must forgive him for not understanding perpetual motion.

God bless you dear, dearest, dearissimo brother. I have not time or I would write to you about Primroses, Crocuses and Cowslips, the only things I see.

William Ponsonby was here yesterday morning. He looks very ill, is grown thin and pale but is in good spirits and very pleasant and amiable.

Pray, are coursing and writing incompatible ? Are you aware that though rather addicted to neglecting my friends, I never was neglected before and have no guess how I shall brook it much longer ? Is Mr.

Hunlocke's appetite for his dinner a good reason for writing me only half a page? Or in other words, is there no time in the day but one in which you can employ yourself about your sisters, for Lady Morpeth is equally affronted with you? But I am astonished, thunderstruck, at being slighted. Oh heavens, mercy me!!!

Most affec^ly^ yours, H. CAVENDISH.

To the Marquis of Hartington

CHISWICK. *Wednesday, February 22. 1809.*

I am triste à mourir tonight. Lady Elizabeth has been in one of her most odious humours. Caroline [St. Jules] honouring the shadow of her shoe tye. William Spencer and Frederick Foster both a little drunk and very riotous and my father snoring in happy forgetfulness of us all.

London I hear is very dull, nobody thinking of anybody but Mrs. Clarke and the House sitting every night and all night. We have just got a print of her, which Papa says is like me, but it is so great a compliment to me inasmuch as it is a thousand times better looking than I am, that it confuses and distresses me etc.

God bless you dearest—not one word more, to save your life or mine, till I hear from you.

H. CAVENDISH.

To the Marquis of Hartington

CHISWICK. [*received*] *February 27th. 1809.*

Did you ever hear of the monkey who made use of the cat's paw to pull the hot chestnuts out of the fire? A l'applicazione. I have been all over the place after my father. He bids me tell you he thinks you had better not accept the offer of the hounds, that he has several reasons for your not doing it, which he will tell you when he has time.

To adopt your phraseology, "ce qui m'accable, m'épouvante" is that you do not seem to be aware of how very angry I am at your not having written to me. I do not believe I shall ever write you another long letter. La Douairière says she has had a long letter from you, so your being ill did not prevent your writing to her. I think it is a story. I like your daring to send me such short and impertinent notes. I condescended to walk all down the lane to meet the blue cart. You should have seen me walk back again, at least a head taller.

If you are really ill, you are a poor, nice sick love and I am not angry.

God bless you, own dearest brother.

To the Marquis of Hartington

CHISWICK. *Tuesday, Feb. 28th. 1809.*

I dined at Spencer House yesterday and found the whole Camden family assembled. Lady Camden never opens her mouth and Lady Fanny never shuts hers—a happy variety in one family. Lady Georgiana, the new one is, alas for her, Lord Camden in a pink satin drapery. It was a very pleasant dinner. Lord Euston, Lord Ipswich, Lord Gower, Sir William Scot and General Grenville. Lord Euston looks very little older than his son and infinitely better looking. Lord Gower is grown thin and shy and if he was thick enough to have a shadow, I am sure he would be afraid of it. He is very pleasing but Trentham and Castle Howard are not good schools for ease of manner and conversation. All that race seems to think it wrong to talk of any interesting subject and keep (as if it was upon principle) to fires and Operas etc.

I was with Lady Maria Hamilton for a long time the other morning. Lady Selina Stewart was with her and I think her the most beautiful little woman I ever saw. I hear she is not at all foolish, which her manner appears to be, and very good and amiable.

The Miss Rumbolds were walking in Hyde Park yesterday morning—they met the Miss Faulkners and all talked of you—I assure you I do not. I trust to Sir Wm's acting as ballast to the heads of all his family.

God bless you, my dearest brother. Write to me, write to me, write to me—and believe me

Most affec[ly] yours, HARRIET CAVENDISH.

XVII

EPITHALAMIUM

MARCH TO JUNE, 1809

THE happy state of things at Chiswick could not last for ever. Lady Bessborough could not allow Harriet to fritter her time away while storms gathered on the horizon. For some time they had all feared, and Lady Bessborough had been aware, that the inevitable solution of the Devonshire House problem was a marriage between the Duke and Lady Elizabeth, and therefore she steeled herself to further the *mariage de convenance* between Granville and Harriet that had been in the air for some time.

But while it still remained so Harriet continued to write long fluent letters to Hart; detailed accounts of her sister's illness and of Lord Paget's elopement with Lady Charlotte Wellesley. This was the famous "double divorce" of the time, the protagonists being Lord Paget (created Marquis of Anglesey in 1815), who after divorcing his first wife, Lady Caroline Villiers, a daughter of the Jerseys, married Lady Charlotte Wellesley (*née* Cadogan). In Harriet's letters we only have an account of the elopement and much commiseration for Lady Paget and do not learn that she, in turn, married the 6th Duke of Argyll.

Harriet returned from nursing her sister in Park Street to Chiswick and was half horrified and half fascinated by a new, dangerous conveyance, the tandem; Caro St. Jules married George Lamb, and over all hung the thunder-cloud of the Duke's approaching marriage to Lady Liz.

To the Marquis of Hartington

PARK STREET. *Tuesday, March 7th. 1809.*

I should have written to you before if I had not been entirely occupied about my sister, for the last 5 days she has been very unwell and is still tormented with the eternal pain in her face. She had another tooth out and for 2 days after was really in tortures, not only in her mouth but all over her head. She has kept her bed and I have been with her the whole time, scarcely out of her room day or night. This *is* a good excuse for not writing.

My Father came to Devonshire House today, where I shall dine but I mean to sleep here till G. is quite well as she likes me to be in her room. I have only been to Church and to walk in Hyde Park at the most unfashionable hours. You must not, therefore, expect London to have made me more brilliant. I have entirely lost all taste for a Town life and only wish to keep as much out of it as possible.

Are you quite alone ? " Is there indeed no Rumbold in the room ? " I do think entire solitude " oltra il dovere " [" beyond the claims of duty "] and I am afraid of its giving you a disgust of Chatsworth and bringing you before the appointed time to this destruction of all good resolutions and good deeds. I see nothing but Doctors and Dentists. How should I know who misses you, who spins ? I do nothing but heat bread and milk and drop laudanum.

By the bye, I heard of one Ball. Lord Palmerston and Lady Cowper, Kitty Monck (screaming to the fiddlers), Mrs. Bagot, Frank Primrose and Puységur. Corise by herself, I believe, for she mentioned no Partner in the pleasing toil. I saw Lady Rancliffe at Church and I think her very pretty with the most beautiful figure I ever beheld. She had with her what I suppose was a Miss Parkins, very short and very smart with a pot of rouge on each cheek.

Pray write to me dearest, dearest Hart—I will write to you again when I have time or de quoi, but such a letter as this I am ashamed of. I will let you know how Lady Morpeth goes on. God bless you.

To the Marquis of Hartington

PARK STREET, *Wednesday, March 8th. 1809.*

DEAREST BROTHER,

G. is a little better today—the pain continues but with less violence and in other respects she is well.

I dined at Devonshire House yesterday and found it cold and dismal ; London is full of impenetrable fog and horror at Lord Paget's elopement—he went off the day before yesterday with Lady Charlotte Wellesley. It is in every way shocking and unaccountable. He has left his beautiful wife and 8 or 9 children and she a husband whom she married about 5 years ago, for love, and who is quite a Héro de Romance in person and manner, with 4 poor little children. He left a letter for Lord Uxbridge saying that he had a great esteem and affection for Lady Paget but could not resist taking the step he had done. I have heard nothing of her or indeed any particulars but those I have told you. Pray, dearest Hartington, marry somebody you will like to stay with. I believe Lady Paget is a very great fool though do not imagine that I mean that or anything as an excuse for him—I think him inexcusable and detestable.

How the White Hart will ring with my aunt Spencer's comments upon this event and how dearest Douaire Zara and Sarah will mourn over the world and its enormities. They can none of them say or feel too much, yet the miserable destiny Lady C. Wellesley has prepared for herself will bring its own punishment and it is impossible not to feel the greatest compassion for her.

There is not a [print of] Mrs. Clarke to be had for love or money—Coleman's broad grins will set out this morning. I have got a terrible cold, which makes me cross and a headache which makes me stupid. I had a very bad night and never shut my eyes till just 4 this morning—I am not used to a street house and the watchman takes entire possession of my mind and I listen for him and to him with the sort of anxiety I should feel if I knew he was attacking instead of guarding, his quarters. G. too talks in her sleep, which has an effect upon my nerves not to be described. Last night just as I was dropping asleep, she jumped up in bed and cried out in the most theatrical manner—"Suspend!" Every night we have long conversations, for if I answer her she goes on for an hour.

God bless you dear, dearest Hartington—write your duties and never mind me. It delights me to hear from you but I am never angry when you do not—H. CAVENDISH.

My Mornings are engrossed but not enlivened with conversations. Lord Carlisle writes to know if he may wait on yr. Ladyship—Lady Carlisle coming up etc. are sounds that meet my resigned ear as regularly as the clocks strike 2 and 3. Miss Berry who is grown but much—oh but, oh but, but, but—much more emphatic than ever, comes every now and then.

Major Ponsonby and Mr. William are always sending for me and in short I am nurse, porter and invalide all in one. I get little notes from Corise at all hours to propose to me opera, assembly, etc. She does not understand the possibility of anything keeping one from them.

God bless you—my attempts at kindness are poor—are you alone, and poorly and shall you have courage to continue so till April?

Most affec^{ly} yrs, H. CAVENDISH.

F. Foster is grown very cross and plagues our lives out. His jokes and attacks are unimportant and have often no merit but being tiresome. He calls Caro " a fat old lawyer " and " a hideous attorney," which cuts at her better half she can but ill endure.

George is called to the Bar and sets out in a day or two upon the circuit, after which I think something must be determined.

To the Marquis of Hartington

PARK STREET, *Thursday, March, 9, 1809.*

G. is much the same today—the pain continues but the gum is in such a state of inflammation that I think it may account for it. Just after I sent my letter yesterday Farquhar arrived from Uxbridge House. He had seen the letter Lord Paget had left with his father. It was to say that he was as well aware as any body could be of the villainy of his conduct and the ruin and infamy it would bring upon himself—that he had the greatest esteem and affection for his wife and adored his children, but that he had long been irresistibly attached to Lady Charlotte. He had begged for foreign service, exposed himself in every way (which, by the bye, every body says was really the case—that no commanding officer ever put himself so forward in danger), hoping from day to day to die in the bed of honour—that when he returned from Spain he was unfortunately thrown again into her society and though his eyes were open to all the dreadful consequences, he could not resist doing what he had done—and having ruined her, thought himself in honour bound to ruin himself also—that he should now go with her to some Island in the Archipelago where he might never be heard of more, only begging that any spark of regard that his family and friends might have felt for him should be all turned to the consolation and welfare of his wife and children.

Sir Walter also saw Lady Charlotte's letter to her friends, which was to say that no human being ever would hear of her again as she should in future live only to the man who was willing to sacrifice everything for her sake. Sir Walter knew her and talked of her with abhorrence —she has left her husband in a very dangerous state of health and 4 poor little deserted children. Henry Wellesley made some discovery the day before she went off—very high words passed between them and he told her that either she or him must leave the house. The next morning, before any body was up, she walked out into the Green Park—where she met Mr. Arbuthnot[1]—he spoke to her and she only begged him not to delay her, that she was going to take a step she should probably repent to the latest hour of her life. Her manner was so hurried and extraordinary that he was convinced she said this to get rid of him and that she was going to drown herself and watched her till she had passed the water. She got into a Hackney coach and drove to Ld Paget's home, from whence they eloped. There are many reports this morn^{g}—some people say they are still in Town, that his family have got at him and are trying to persuade him not to leave England, others that Henry Wellesley and him fought yesterday and that Lord Paget was killed—I shall probably know the truth before I send my letter. It is a dreadful tragedy all together and the horror and consternation at it is what it ought to be—deeply and generally felt. She has very little beauty but I believe her powers of pleasing to have been uncommonly great and her Coquetry unfortunately in proportion. It is an awful lesson and a warning to women; what must her feelings be if she has any. There can be nothing so terrible as to bring misery upon a man really attached to one—it would be better a thousand times to die oneself and think only of what she occasions to Lord Paget, and probably the last act of this eventful history is yet to come.

Mr. Wardle moved last night in the house of commons that the Duke of York must have been guilty of the charges made against him and consequently unfit to be Commander-in-chief. Mr. Perceval made so fine and judicious a speech, proving so much inconsistence and falsehood in the evidence of Mrs. Clarke etc., that it is supposed it will turn the scale in the Duke of York's favour.

Lord Morpeth means to vote against Mr. Wardle's motion and supposes most people will—it will not be ended for 2 or 3 days.

[1] Diplomatist and intimate friend of the Duke of Wellington.

Farquhar has just been here ; he thinks G. much better. There has been no Duel. God bless you, dearest brother.

Most affecly yrs, HARRIET CAVENDISH.

To the Marquis of Hartington

DEVONSHIRE HOUSE. *Thursday, March 16th. 1809.*

A thousand thanks, my dearest, dearest brother for two of the most delightful and entertaining letters that ever were written—indeed they are not ill-bestowed—I read them till I know them almost by heart and think them what I think you—better, dearer and droller than anything else in the wide world. Lord Paget is alive—the report of the Duel was false, but many of his friends say that he is in so distracted a state that they should not at any time be surprised to hear of his having destroyed himself. He said to his Aide de camp the morning he was leaving his home to join Lady Charlotte, " The best thing you could do for me would be to run your sword through my body." He seems to have acted as much upon a false idea of honour as from the force of passion. He believed himself to share the ruin he had brought upon her and forgets in this desperate and fallacious reasoning the sacred claims that a wife and children have upon him and how absurd it is to talk of honour at the moment of abandoning them.

Lady Paget is in great distress but I fancy his conduct to her has for a long time been inexcusable. He has written to Lord Uxbridge to say that hers has always been irreproachable and that her encouragement of Sir Arthur and Lady Boringdon, for which she has been so much blamed, was in obedience to his express command. You should hear Miss Berry upon the subject—" oh it is a pretty story, a very pretty story. Lady Charlotte leaves 4 children, the youngest four months old and just weaned, oh, but it is a pretty story. Lord Paget devotes himself to ruin and disgrace and for what a strapping lass I would hardly hire for my kitchen maid—oh, but it is the very prettiest story." And so she goes on crescendo with anger—*the*'s and *but*'s till entire loss of breath forces her to stop.

I am very glad you have written to Papa. I hear the next Term begins on the 12th of April and I wish to know if you mean to be in Town at all before that time.

I have very little to tell you, I have been out no where and mean my first gaiety to be next Saturday's opera. There was a very small supper here on Saturday.

Delmino just returned from Lord Shaftesbury's, still smiling because he has not lost his teeth but in other respects dejected and meek. Wm. Montague who talked to me from 12 till 2 without once stopping —I was very glad of it, for being quite stupified with a bad cold, it saved me all trouble and there was nobody else I wished to listen to. He gave me an account of every place he had been at, every person he had seen, every book he had read, every cold he had had, every joke he had cut, every Lady he had admired, every acquaintance he had made, since last July. I eat oranges, blew my nose, looked at Wm. Ponsonby's immoveable gravity and every 10 minutes said "Indeed! Really! Dear me! No!"

I called on Lady George yesterday and found Anne very low and looking extremely ill. Charles [Cavendish] came into the room, grown very tall and stout and desiring me to write immediately to you to inform you that Miss Gayton is married to the revd. Mr. Murray, a brother of Sir James Ponsonby's—a man of about 50. It is said that her parents insisted upon it but that she is miserable and not in the least dazzled by her reverend prospects.

F. Foster spends his life with Miss Beffin and Miss Riddesdale—one the Lady who has neither arms nor legs and the other a dwarf who is to be seen in Clarges Street whom he says is remarkably agreeable and much better looking than any of us.

Lord Monson is very dangerously ill and going immediately to Bristol. They say she appears fond of him, at least is very attentive to him and that their little child is beautiful.

Sarah Faulkener is growing as large as Lady Castlereagh. Lady Emily Cecil is become a beauty. Lady Rancliffe is all the fashion. Lady Cowper confined to her couch with a chill. Mr. Goldburne [*sic*], who squints, in love with Lady Selina Stewart but nobody can make out if he has proposed or if she has refused. He rather thinks he has but his brother assures him he has not. This may come of squinting— nobody who did not could doubt. Lady Primrose is at every assembly, improved beyond measure and by some people reckoned the prettiest woman in London. Lord Primrose has not grown an inch. Frank [Lawley] has jilted Kitty Monck! This is all "they say," for heaven be praised I have not seen one of their faces.

God bless you Dearest—G. is much better, that is, she has still a great deal of pain but she has less irritation in her nerves and very great inflammation still in the gums may account for it. God bless you once more.

To the Marquis of Hartington

CHISWICK. *Sunday, March 26th. 1809.*

Really if I did not look upon a letter from me just now in the light of a punishment I would not send you one, *but* in about ten days my Father talks of being in Town, I shall probably see many sights, hear many things, meet your loves by dozens, and *then* not one word shall you receive till you have retrieved your character and sent me some more of those delightful letters. To value them as I did was fully to deserve them.

My love, the Lilacks are all coming out. It has been much colder these two last days, which the gardener says is a good thing as it will prevent the flowers being too forward. Drury Lane is burnt to the ground. The Duke of York has written to the House of Commons to make a request, which request the House of Commons has declared to be a breach of privilege in His Royal Highness to make. I hope half this news will be uninteresting, the other stale.

I cannot understand why I hate the thoughts of going to Town so very much. Chiswick is not in its present state very attractive. William Spencer is staying here and c'est presque tout dire on the disagreeable side of the question. He looks like a starved cat, tries one's spirits by his perpetual rattle, his manners are full of familiarity and conceit and his conversation of bad jokes and bad taste. People say he is brilliant, but I think they must mean noisy, which sometimes does as well. All I know is, if he is—— I am ashamed of giving so much abuse to one person and shall have none left for dear square little Monsieur Vigoureux, who dines here almost every day, gets drunk and comes into the drawing room singing "Maudit amour, raison sévère" and spouting from all the old French operas and romances. Frederick Foster, complaining from morning to night that "Mr. Tooth aches," and every now and then a coach full of Bessboroughs, is all our society. What I enjoy is independent of all these good people; walking before breakfast and most part of the day in all this delightful weather, my own dear little room, once upon a time receiving a letter from you and every day one from G. In London I am never either so good or so happy. "Le matin je fais des projets et le long du jour des sottises." But in April when you come, if you will walk with me, talk to me, dance in moderation, flirt with discretion, give me my Lapis lazuli and be a perfect love as you were at Althorp, I shall be the happiest of Ladies.

God bless you, dearest brother.

Ever yours, H. C.

To the Marquis of Hartington

PARK STREET. *Monday, April 3rd. 1809.*

G. is very unwell and I am again entirely taken up with nursing her. It is now a decided nervous complaint. Bailey and Farquhar met here last night and have ordered her strong nervous medicines, taken in great quantity and if the pain does not yield I expect them to order her to the sea, which I am convinced will be at last the only thing really and thoroughly to reestablish her health. I feel scruples about writing to you, for I go no where, see nobody and think of nothing but nerves and Valerian. Your last letter delighted me, but for words to describe the admiration and gratitude for the beautiful Lapis etc. with the additional satisfaction of not paying the Tax of Mr. F. Stanhope's acquaintance for it. Its success is brilliant and the only reason I mean ever to go out again is to display it.

I do not think Caro's marriage will take place till the middle of May—shall I not see my nice tall brother till then? La Douairière is settled in Jermyn Street again—a great love but literally living upon Turnip Tops. I get up every morning at 8 o'clock, breakfast with her and walk all over London. She amuses me more than I can describe. I find what I dislike most in Town is going out of an evening—the bustle of the streets before any of my acquaintances are out of their first sleep entertains me to the greatest degree.

God bless you—I am glad you like hunting, but I expect to hear of your breaking your neck every day.

Your obedient humble servant, HARRIET CAVENDISH.

To the Marquis of Hartington

DEVONSHIRE HOUSE. *April 23. 1809.*

It is now twelve o'clock and I am but just enough recovered to write. No, there never was ever anything so terrible, so provoking, so unhappy. Listen! I always lock my door whilst I am undressing. In future I swear it shall be wide open to the whole house. It never happened to me to forget it before, but precisely last night it did because (I suppose) it was the only time in my life that it would be a real grievance to me not to remember it. I opened the window shutters that I might find it impossible not to wake by break of day. In consequence of this precaution I woke every half hour, wondering why you did not come. At last the day looked so far advanced that I determined to get up and wait for you below stairs.

Now for the "dénouement." I found the outward room door locked, a collection of Coals, chips and a candle erected before it having long made fruitless efforts to come and make themselves into a fire. Walker and old Mary in the deepest consternation. Half past nine and the Marquis gone!

Now tell me, was there ever anything so very provoking! I really had rather sat all night in the porter's lodge. Pray, dearest Hartington, write to me all you would have talked about and condole with me. Mary was touched by my extreme distress and stood by me an hour endeavouring to comfort me.

Write me word if you thought me quite mad when you found me locked up. The thing that vexes me most is that I hardly saw you or spoke to you last night, putting it all off till the morning. I wish you joy of this fine day for an open carriage. To be in a *Tandem* (in that night) and a fog does not seem to me the height of felicity, tho' if you had staid another day, I should have strongly recommended your passing it with Doctor Willis.[1]

God bless you, dearest. Had Lady Augusta continued being there and did you behave well to all "les dames d'amour"?

To the Marquis of Hartington

PARK STREET, LONDON. *Monday, April 24th. 1809.*

I was really quite delighted to hear from you today, for till I did, I felt as if I was still locked up in my room and you still at the door. How very much you make me laugh, cry, rejoice and grieve. You deserve your cold most thoroughly and I try not to pity you for it. I have been singing your parody all the morning and it goes better to the musick than the original.

[1] *The Alienist.*

I went to the Opera Saturday and made a great many enquiries about the ball to hear something about you, but everybody made me the same speech—" I saw Lord Hartington's head." This was very unsatisfactory and comes of towering above your sex. Mr. Montague, by the bye, is enchanted with your admiring his sister, but he seems doubtful if she will survive another ball. Lord Gower says when you begin to dance with her, you lift her very high from the ground and that she is never near it again till the end of it. Do you know I mean, I believe, to go to Mrs. Montague's ball on purpose to look at you as I suppose I shall not have that gratification anywhere else for the one night you stop in Town.

George Lamb arrived yesterday and Caroline is perfectly happy. He is grown thinner, looks very well, and is really a very excellent, delightful creature. I believe the marriage is to be on the 17th. People put me quite out of patience with wondering and speculating upon what Lady Elizabeth's conduct will be in consequence of it. What should she do, but what she always has done, " sit absolute on her unshaken throne " and really feeling as independent as I do of her, both in mind and conduct, it is of much less importance to my happiness than I once considered it to be.

God bless you, dearest.

Most affec[ly] yours, HARRIET CAVENDISH.

To the Marquis of Hartington

PARK STREET, *Wednesday, April 26th. 1809.*

Thank you a thousand times, dearest, I am glad your cold is gone and to hear of your good intentions, as I suppose the Vollero in chorus is not your only occupation, though it is the only one you mention.

I mean certainly to go to Mrs. Montague's ball; to see your feats of agility, and quite long for it. I have not heard much of you, excepting from Mr. Montague who thinks you all perfection and employed above an hour in telling me so—you know he is not given to abridge. Oh, if your Cambridge friends could have seen me, impressing the Vollero upon you, playing it again and again, note by note, passage by passage! I thought my father seemed very much pleased with Sir William—I never can make out why every now and then àpropos de bottes, you fancy that I object to your friendship for him. I think you both of you want rousing at times, to exertion in many ways and there is danger of your suffering yourselves to lead a life very unworthy I believe of him. I am sure of you but your wise sister thinks you both so young that you may sometimes be allowed to be foolish and both sometimes so foolish that it is well for you you have the excuse of being so young. I have not decided yet what to give Caro myself. The vision of you and the arm chair thrilled me—" allow me to present you with a chest of drawers."

I walked in the Park yesterday morning and met your loves by dozens—the two Miss Faulkners, Miss Bouverie and perhaps Miss Montague, a pretty little dark thing with a tribe of brothers and sisters. Mr. William Montague fastened himself upon me in the opera room in spite of a quarrel having taken place between Corise and the whole family—" and he the cause "—for she resolutely refused having him at her party, which was resented by the remaining 15 branches. I believe " Lor' O " thought him too short—I know Corise did.

The opera was very thin but pleasant; Mr. Eden was in the box for a long time and he is very agreeable, though there is something I do not like in his manner—a forced manner as if he thought all his words were being written down and that it was therefore necessary always to be saying good things. Mr. Lawley was also in the box for a good while—I wish you could be acquainted with him, I am certain it is impossible that you should not like him and yet I think you are now prejudiced against him. He is really the most excellent and amiable of human beings and whatever you may think of it, I can assure you that mine is an impartial opinion.

The Lady Grevilles have lost their uncle, old Charles Greville. Ld. Carlisle says Delmino is smitten with Lady Caroline in consequence of Lady Barbara's cruelty. I think it will be hard if he cannot succeed—the novelty of a lover may do something and I should imagine him to be the first and perhaps the last so she had better *snap!* (to quote F. Foster).

G. is much better and I hope by the time you come she will be almost well. I hear Lady Jersey incessant and I do not expect G. to bear it much longer without calling for nervous supplies—shall I rush in with the Physick chest?

God bless you again.

Most affec^ly yrs, H. C.

To the Marquis of Hartington

Monday, May the 1st. 1809.

DEAREST HARTINGTON,

I was at the Opera on Saturday and we had a great many people at supper here after it—this has been my only dissipation and as (Heaven be praised) it is one in which I do not set my eyes upon any of your loves, I am afraid accounts of it will not be interesting to you. I long for Wednesday but I am afraid that in spite of your threats and at the risk of becoming "no sister of mine" in consequence that I shall not be able to go to Mrs. Montague, at least if the violent cold that seems to be coming into my head does not leave me before it. I want to see you and to talk to you beyond measure and if you require it, I will sit up all Wednesday night, with the lock of the door in my hand. I have just been sending an excuse to poor dear Mrs. Bocher [Bouchier ?] whose head is turning, I hear, with the Prince's attention. She thinks Lady Hertford a blind and pink roses and pink shoes abound more than ever. At eleven I come home and find Corise who is not well, "and is bore" because she cannot stand the fatigues of Assemblies; Caro and George, Frederick Foster and some stray Ponsonbies. This account of my day is my excuse for my letter. Do you mean to come from Cambridge in Sir Wm's Tandem ?—I met one the other day—the first horse seeming to have a very independant spirit and a wretched man in it, having no more command over him than you have over your understanding when you get into one. I heard very great praise of Sir Wm. the other day (not because he drives a Tandem) and a lot of what he used to be. People say (I never give up my authorities) that he is more improved than anybody ever was, that he used to keep the worst company of any man in London and was really the greatest puppy (ne vous Déplaise) that ever was seen and that now he is quite the reverse. He seems to me to be remarkably popular and I hear everybody speak well of him.

Write me one line by return of post, dearest brother, to say what time you shall be in Town and if I may announce you for dinner to his Grace. God bless you.

Most affec^{ly} yrs, H. C.

To the Marquis of Hartington

CHISWICK. *Thursday, May 11. 1809.*

I cannot describe to you the delight I feel at being here with nothing but G. and the 6, in the most delicious weather and out of London and all its perplexities. It is a proof of a very weak mind, I am afraid, never to feel good or act wisely but when I am surrounded by green trees, what Mrs. Brown used to call Daffydowndillies, sheep and muscovy ducks, but so it is. Yesterday when I left London I was to quote you " afraid of having no reward in the next world " and today a sort of Mrs. Trimmer. I shall not sleep here after tonight but I mean to come every day and all day whilst the weather continues what it is now. I long to hear from you what day you mean to be in Town. Will you drive me to Epsom? I am assured by my friends that it would not be too much for your ponies, but I do not care, if you have no wish to go.

The only drawback to our enjoyment here is that at about two, innumerable drab coloured coaches drive down with every Howard that ever was devised, Cawdors, Sloanes etc. It is a sad thing to marry a large family. God bless you my dearest, dearest, dearest brother—some people think one as expressive—I do not.

Ever most affec[ly] yrs, HARRIET CAVENDISH.

To the Marquis of Hartington

Saturday, May 13th. 1809.

DEAREST HARTINGTON,

I went to Lady Stafford's last night and oh, the dullness, crowd and heat! Not one single anybody I ever wish to set my eyes upon again yet one or two things rather gratified my curiosity and I have just seen as much of the world as I wished to do. I am in the greatest admiration of Miss Montague—I think her uncommonly pretty and more cleverness and interest in her countenance than all the rest of the young ladies put together. Lady Augusta Greville I cannot admire in any way—she bores me almost as much as Lord Brooke, who never ceased giving me details of his puppy—Stewart's relation—till I nearly screamed, put it upon the heat and somebody treading on my toes and in the hurry escaped. Lady Rancliffe plunged down upon a couch by me and told me that she had never before found an opportunity of forming a friendship with me!!! I was on the point of saying "pray don't let us find it now." Nothing could be more flat than our attempt at imitating it and I left her very much disappointed, I am afraid, in me upon further acquaintance.

God bless you dearest—what day do you come?

To the Marquis of Hartington

LONDON. *Tuesday, May 23rd. 1809.*

I have been at Chiswick today—it was delightful and fresher and sweeter than anything you can conceive. Early in the morning I drove with Corisande, who was in a bad way and wanted air. She thinks of nothing but her party which is to be on Thursday week, to begin with a dinner, then the christening of her frightful child and to end with musick. We called on Lady Conyngham [the Prince's favourite] who was drest out to have her picture painted and more en représentation than usual. We are to dine there some day next week, to meet Lord Scarborough who wants to hear me play on the piano forte. He is the man who used to be called Doleful Dick and wear knots of blue ribbon on his cravat to testify his constancy to Lady Scarborough, who was not at the time allowed by her family to speak to him. He looks like Don Quixote and thinks every woman he sees is in love with him. I mean to sham it.

The whole house is keeping your birthday and some female is singing so extremely loud that it entirely distracts my attention. Tell me if you have left any of the eighteen pence and if your eyes are like each other again.

[*The rest of this letter has been cut off.*]

To the Marquis of Hartington

LONDON. *June 24th. 1809.*

MY DEAREST HARTINGTON,

I am reconciled to your departure by the good I trust Brighton will do you. I have just been with my aunt Spencer who says she has seen Farquhar and that he thinks it is absolutely necessary for you to attend most *minutely* to your health just now and early hours, the sea air—of a morning especially—and perfect quiet will very soon brace you and recover you entirely. I long for all those things for myself, as my spirits are in a perfect fever and bathing is as necessary to me as to dogs during Hydrophobia. How delightful it would be! I really hardly wish ever to be with anybody I love in London, the place of all others I most dislike and detest. We would get up at six, walk before breakfast on the finest sands in the world, improve our minds, drive, dip, eat (you I mean, for my system is to be but a spare one) and I mean to return to Town as narrow as Miss de Vismes.

God bless my brother—H. CAVENDISH.

To the Marquis of Hartington

LONDON. *June 29th. 1809.*

DEAREST HARTINGTON,

Your account of your good health quite delights me. I am one foot on sea, one foot on shore, that is, waiting to be called for to go by water to Richmond, to dine there and return to Cork and Orrery.

The supper last night went off admirably, excepting that your loves were all absent, I mean, in mind. The dejected ones lamenting you and regretting their fate and the sanguine ones busy in examining their prospects of worldly good.

Lady Morpeth sat at supper between Lord Granville and Baron Tripp, Lady Harriet Cavendish between Lord Hinchinbroke and Mr. Pierrepoint, odd but respectable.

God bless you, my dear love. G. and Thomas are knocking at the door. Write, I entreat you and believe me—

Most affectionately yours, H. C.

XVIII

"TO DOUBT IS TO DECIDE"

JULY TO DECEMBER, 1809

GEORGIANA MORPETH and Harriet cast care aside and went to the seaside. Harriet continued to write to Hart about "*la pluie et le beau temps*," but did not once mention the problem that never left her. Granville was courting her. What was her answer to be? It says much for her integrity that she did not allow her father's dreaded marriage to Lady Elizabeth, which took place on October the 19th, to influence her decision.

Never had she needed advice so sorely and to whom could she turn? It would appear strange that it was to Selina Trimmer, but on consideration, Selina was not such a bad choice; Harriet's heart and head were at war and she was frightened of the counsels of her heart. Selina was the arch-advocate of reason and so she turned to her. Haryo's distraught letters are almost painful to read. She has all the intolerance of youth; she is implacable towards her aunt. She, who had laughed at Granville, mocked at her aunt, found them in league against her. Her aunt, her namesake, had been her lover's mistress and was still his confidante and he and she were in league against her—Harriet. She judged them both without pity. But she was undecided. Why?

Granville she had known and disliked all her life, but *this* Granville—what was there to be said in his favour? Why could she not say "No" and have done with it?

Her father's marriage to Lady Liz had not proved such a trial as she had expected. Each time she inclined towards Granville she was repulsed by the feeling that her aunt was directing their destinies. Why did she not refuse him? She knew of their liaison. She was to become an ideal wife to him. She was to bring up *their* children with her own. She did not love him but—ah! she was in love with him.

"Adored Granville who would make a barren desert smile," she wrote as a bride.

Outwardly she was wise in her choice. She certainly never gave a sign that she regretted it. But the last letter to Hart? And the very last letter to Selina? Those short notes are pregnant with reserve. Had Georgiana Duchess been alive, her beloved Emma, I do not believe she would have written as she did on those winter evenings from Chiswick.

To the Marquis of Hartington

BURE. CHRISTCHURCH. *Sunday, July 1809.*

We have been in daily expectation of you, my dearest brother—where are you and why have you not honoured us with any communication of your intentions? Have you been at Brighton or in Town or giving away Sir William?[1] Pray let us know immediately and if it is practicable, pray come and see us. Muddiford is delightful to us and perhaps would be to you for a short time but I really believe it is the most retired place in England. We have the prettiest and most comfortable little cottage that ever was seen about a quarter of a mile from the sea. The sands are excellent and the bathing better than any place I have been at. I must not forget to mention a piano forte, which with Ladies Morpeth and H. Cavendish are attractions enough for any reasonable Individual, as Lord Boringdon would say. G. and George send their best love and unite in my entreaties.

We were very much pleased to hear of Sir William being so well married. If by any chance you are with him, pray give him our best remembrances and congratulations. God bless you dearest—

To the Marquis of Hartington

BURE. *Tuesday, July 25th. 1809.*

It was neither swooning nor suicide, but a violent passion into which I put myself, upon receiving your letter, and out of which I shall not be till I have put it upon every side of this paper, a punishment severe enough for any crime and which I congratulate myself upon having it in my power to inflict.

There would be some reason in any body else pleading eighty miles

[1] Sir William Rumbold, 3rd Bart., married on July 13th, 1809, Harriet Boothby, daughter and co-heiress of Lord Rancliffe.

out of their way as an excuse for not keeping an engagement, but as with you it is in general an inducement and there is not a race, ball or vulgar woman in England that has not made you do twice as much, your sisters have a right to reject that plea entirely.

And now dearest, dearest adored brother of mine, tell me when I shall see you, where and how, for I suppose it would be now unreasonable to expect you here. When we leave the Isle of Wight we shall go to Paultons where Mr. Sloane and Lady Gertrude [1] have bothered me ever since I have been in their neighbourhood to ask me to go.

Pensari, o caro and believe me.

Ever yours most affec^{ly}, H. CAVENDISH.

If you do not write to me immediately, Hampshire will not hold me. The disappointment was unspeakable—to your sisters, [little] George, the bathing man and the Christchurch company of strolling players from whom a petition to the Most Noble Marquis etc. to order a play has been upon my table for the last week.

To the Marquis of Hartington

BURE. *Thursday evening, August 10th. 1809.*

I am this moment returned from Mr. Rose's, where we have been what George calls tea-ing with a vengeance. The Ladies Greville are really very nice girls and made the evening much more tolerable than it would have been without them. We walked in spite of a violent thunder storm as the air was delicious and the effect of the lightning on the sea and the Needles quite beautiful. Lord Warwick quite tormented me, made me play on the piano forte, compared me to thunder, lightning, and his old aunt, told me my talent for musick was a gift of God given me to support me through all trials and console me under all misfortunes, talked to me of Miss Beckford, assured me that she is the link between man and angel sent here to prepare us for Heaven and teach us how to behave there.

There was a Mrs. Brown, the doctor's wife in a corner of the room, with her hands spread before her face ; she had once seen five villages on fire from a flash of lightning and whether she thought herself still on the spot or expected Bure to be on flame if she set her eyes upon it, no power could persuade her to uncover them. I sat close to her with a sort of modest triumph, known only to a Coward. Thunder

[1] Mr. Sloane Stanley had married Lady G. Howard.

and lightning are nearly the only things I am not afraid of and therefore I make the most of the rare virtue and console, fan and allow for the amiable weakness of my friends with an ostentation not to be described.

We go to Paultons the day after tomorrow. My letters from thence will probably be as dull as Mr. Sloane's stories, but I promise you they shall not be as long.

On Wednesday we have determined to embark for the Isle of Wight. The Lambs, I hear, leave Cowes on the 12th, so that we shall just miss them. I am to write to Sarah to take rooms for us at the Inn at Ryde. Write to me, my dearest brother, never mind your letters being short and do not use all the Devil's apparatus but at the first table, on the first sheet of paper, of the first things that occur to you, make a letter to your humble servant and most affectionate sister,

HARRIET CAVENDISH.

To Miss Trimmer

BURE, *Friday, August 11, 1809.*[1]

MY DEAREST SELINA

Hart left us the day before yesterday—I do not think it necessary to feel any alarm about him as to his loves. He cares for none of them and is too babyish in his manner about and to them, to give any reason to them to hope or complain. He wishes them all married most cordially and feels real relief as they go off his hands. He is a most amiable creature and only wants a little steadiness and right sort of ambition, to make him all one can wish ; but his danger is resting satisfied with comparative superiority and by constantly associating with people inferior to him in understanding and acquiring habits of indolence, mental indolence, I mean, of all things the most hurtful and difficult to conquer.

God bless you, my dearest Selina ; I hope to improve as a correspondant when I begin my tour and as we leave Bure tomorrow you may hope for my next letter being a brighter one.

Ever most affec^{ly} yrs, HARRIET CAVENDISH.

To the Marquis of Hartington

PAULTONS. *Monday, August 14th. 1809.*

The Post yesterday brought me 6 letters, a piece of good luck (as

[1] The dates of this and the previous letter are irreconcilable, although each is clearly dated.

Mary Gladwin with a low curtesy observed to Mr. Dupper when he proposed to her) that does not happen to everybody, every day. Yours was quite delightful. You should have seen G. pamer de rire over it and you have the particular art of making everything you describe as present to one as if one saw it.

Were you surprised at Lord Boringdon's marriage? Miss Talbot is a most delightful person, extremely pretty and agreeable. How they all do surprise me by accepting him. His success, just as to that, is wonderful. I do not envy his wife and happy in my mind was she who ran [that is the first Lady Boringdon who eloped with Sir Arthur Paget].

Mr. Grenville is here in a Pepper and salt Coat and black inexpressibles, looking like some rare bird. Mrs. Leigh,[1] but not the Colonel, a Doctor Halifax, Mr. and Mrs. Hammersley expected.

I heard the greatest praise of Lady Rumbold the other day from Miss Campbell. Who have you, are you going to have, at Chatsworth? I am writing like a newspaper when London is out of Town and it has nothing to say.

Mr. Sloane, the old one, tells long stories from morning to night which, however, he is very kind in not seeming to wish one to attend to much. He is a very respectable, good sort of man. His son, Lady Gertrude's better half, or rather her worse quarter, for in size and intellect it is impossible to be more insignificant, keeps up a continual joke, that is joke in his own acceptation of the term and is really a torment to one's patience and understanding. Lady Gertrude is amazingly improved, not as you may suppose by being with her husband but by being away from her Father. God bless you.

To the Marquis of Hartington

AT LORD CAWDOR'S, GOLDEN GROVE, LLANDILO.
SOUTH WALES. *September 12th. 1809.*

DEAREST,

How various her employments whom you probably have been calling idle. I confess, however, that I ought to have answered your last delightful letter sooner. I received it at Ryde in the midst of expeditions par terre et par mer and was too much hurried to answer it at the time. My aunt confined her spirit of enterprize within very narrow limits and Lady Anne would think few things worth the peril

[1] Formerly Augusta Byron.

of going in a coach and four. Lord Spencer, Sarah, the Morpeths and I went over every part of the Island. We found the Lambs at Cowes. Caro much more extraordinary and entertaining than ever, leading the sort of life people do in a Harlequin farce, perpetual shifting of scene, dress and company, lodging at an apothecary's, dining at the Duke of Gloucester's, enfant de famille at Mrs. Knox's, an Irish lady who gives assemblies in London, one minute on a Pillion, the next in a boat, but the wand to effect these changes always in Columbine's hand—Lady Spencer exclaiming—" William Lamb is an angel, nothing like the school of adversity ! "

From Ryde we returned to Paultons and found much the same sort of people that I described to you when I left it. Mr. Jekyl, who talked of you,—" and a most forward, impudent woman of about forty, making such love to him at a dinner at Lady Cork's that it was really disgusting to see it. I really never witnessed such a shameful attack —a Lady Water, Water I think it was "—Park ? ? ? I screamed with feelings not to be described ! Poor dear branch of the family, doing her little possible to make herself agreeable to the head !

Badminton was the next stage of our Tour and much the pleasantest. The Duchess [of Beaufort] and Lady Harrowby are in very different ways delightful persons.[1] Lord Granville was there and they love him as we do you, which is not saying peu de chose. So many people tell me that I am going to be married to him that perhaps it may be as well for me to begin acquainting my friends that I am not. I do not wonder at the reports or blame people for giving credit to them and it is only from thinking myself pretty good authority upon the subject that I take the liberty of contradicting them.

The Boringdons came to Badminton three days before we left it. She seems to suit him exactly and to like him extremely. She is not striking au fait de beauté, but what some people may admire very much ; a pretty figure, a remarkably animated countenance, good hair, good eyes, good teeth, not a fine but not a bad complexion, a great want of manner, a loud voice. More perfectly at her ease than any one I ever saw before, but not the ease of a person used to the best company. She is wonderfully well informed and accomplished, paints and draws admirably, dances quadrilles and Waltzes to perfection, very sensible in conversation, good humoured and enjoying

[1] Granville's sisters. He had asked the Duchess to invite Harriet.

herself to the greatest degree. In short, she is a very estimable, but not a very interesting, person ; she has no great charm or attraction about her, but nothing against attaching one to her. One is glad to see her once, without feeling very anxious to see her again, excepting Borino who has given her the most satisfactory proof to the contrary.

Lord Worcester is a very nice goodhumoured obliging boy, dying to be acquainted with you and as fond of musick, dancing and me as your Lordship. God bless you, dearest, dearest brother.

Ever yours, H. CAVENDISH.

To Miss Trimmer

October 8th. 1809.

I was hurried yesterday, my dearest Selina, and had not time to say half I wished to do—our anxiety is very great upon the change that may have taken place at D. House.[1]

Lady B. acts in every way a most extraordinary part. We have every reason to believe (from confidences betrayed de part et autre) that she obtained a promise from Lord [Granville] before he joined us at B. [Badminton].

Ought I, my dearest Selina, ever to think of a man, over whom she has such claims or such influence as this ! I found also that she had tried to alarm him by telling him that I meant to quarrel with my father, if any change in Lady E's situation took place. 2 days before he left B. he talked to me in the most serious manner of my extraordinary situation with regard to her and the difficulties it placed me in, begged me not to think him impertinent, but he could not resist saying that he thought *the way in which I meant to act*, was calculated to inflame everything and said a great deal of respect to Parents etc. I was astonished and begged him to explain himself. He said he had been told that I had determined to quit my father entirely and go and live at Lord Spencer's, that such a breach between parents and child etc., etc.—I had hardly patience to hear it out. I answered that not only I had never said anything of the sort but that I had never felt it, that my respects and affection for my father would alone prevent my taking such steps, that my conduct would be just what it always had been, whatever might and certainly would be, my suffering. He seemed as much astonished as delighted—again begged my pardon and so it dropt.

[1] The marriage of her father to Lady Elizabeth Foster.

What is it that awaits me at my return, my dearest Selina? Is it possible Lady B. should have fabricated an alarm to answer any purpose in frightening him from any idea of connecting himself with me or are our worst fears indeed to be verified? You must let me see you as soon as I return, my dearest Selina. I cannot tell you what an incalculable blessing your friendship is to me and the consolation it is to be able to place the most entire confidence in you—I will not rely upon myself—I will pray for the assistance I feel so much in need of and hope from it that peace, which I am sure the world cannot give.

Lady B. is an awful example of what self-indulgence and yielding principles will end in. If upon the subject of the last part of my letter, you should find it necessary (which I do hope and trust it will not be) to speak to my sister, I wish it might be so contrived that she may not think I know anything of it—I dread any vexation for her, any fancy she might take of my having been close with her or any subject of gêne between us.

God bless you, my best and dearest friend. Whatever my fate may be, if I can but keep myself steady in principle, act as you would approve and make religion the great rule of my conduct, I cannot be very miserable. There is here so much to suffer and so little to enjoy that I am more than ever convinced of the folly and madness of those who live for this life alone. Help me to become worthy of a better and believe me—ever yrs, HARRIET CAVENDISH.

Will you write me a few lines immediately, which will still find me here—the day of our departure is not settled.

To the Marquis of Hartington

STACPOOLE. *October 14th. 1809.*

MY DEAREST OF BROTHERS,

I cannot resist writing you one line, but you must excuse its not being more for I have a bad headache and a great many letters I must answer.

I am surprised and glad that I bear so well what I always expected to bear so ill.[1] A great deal must be painful, but there are considerations for which tutti si puo soffrir and nothing can diminish my respect and affection for my Father. I mean my conduct to be what it always has been. My mind was early opened to Lady Elizabeth's

[1] The Duke's marriage to Lady Elizabeth.

character, unparalleled I do believe for want of principle and delicacy, and more perverted than deceitful, for I really believe she hardly herself knows the difference between right and wrong now. Circumstances have altered her conduct and situation at different times but she has invariably been what even when a child I understood and despised.

God bless you—I am certain you will feel and act as you ought. I look with confidence and happiness to those whose affection and kindness will make up to me for every other suffering, and am with more attachment to you than to almost anything else.

Ever yours, H. C.

You may give the enclosed to Caro [St. Jules]—I trust she knows nothing yet or if she does—as she always has done. I hope I never need mention the subject to her even when she does.

To Miss Trimmer

After Oct. 19th, 1809.

MY DEAREST SELINA,

I cannot thank you enough for your letter. My sister is quite well and supports herself under this trial exactly as we could wish her to do. May my dearest grandmother find herself equal to it. At present no very painful, no ostensible change is to take place, and I believe we shall at our return find everything apparently exactly in the same state. I rejoice, as it would be too much for G's spirits probably if it was to be otherwise. I shall be impatient to see you, my dearest Selina ; I have much that I wish to say that I am not at liberty to write. My mind is strongly occupied and my situation a most extraordinary one. I never felt so much in need of the friendship and advice of those I love and esteem.

I do not know what my fate will be, but I earnestly pray that it may not be embittered by a consciousness of acting either in a wrong or a weak manner. I cannot think that I ought to alter either my manner or conduct in any respect at my return. I may suffer more, but nothing should influence my respect and affection to my father ; —it was not in the power of circumstances to encrease my bad opinion of Lady E.

I pity Lady Bessborough from the bottom of my heart. I attribute most of her faults to vanity indulged and weakness encouraged. I forgive her most sincerely for any artifice or duplicity in her conduct to me. I have no merit in doing so for she has been the sufferer.

[*End of letter missing.*]

To Miss Trimmer

October 1809.

MY DEAREST SELINA,

It is very kind of you to use the word " indulge " when you ought to reproach me for not having acknowledged your last letter sooner.

I believe you are now with my grandmother, from whom I received an answer yesterday to one of mine, upon the subject of Lord G. and our meeting at Badminton. I do hope I may trust to her discretion in not mentioning what I say to Lady Bessborough as I know everything goes to him through that channel. I dare not say to her what I otherways should do, for that reason, and yet when I can venture to place confidence in her it is a real happiness to me.

After my sister's last letter to you, Lord G's manner varied perpetually but was never that of a man free to act in an open, sincere manner. He certainly at times, especially the last evening, betrayed great interest in me, and seemed to feel more than he was at liberty to show, but if there are obstacles to his seriously thinking of me, it is both weak and selfish to act so as to place me in a very difficult situation as he does everything to occupy me and to attract the attention of others, without committing himself, or making any sacrifice of the slightest gratification to himself. This conduct does not belong to a character to which I could wish to trust the happiness of my life. He professes great impatience for my return to Chiswick—my conduct there will not be difficult if Lady B. does not make it so by jealousies and tracasseries—I wish she would give no more importance to his manner and attentions than I do, and experience might I think teach her the same lesson. I used, when I was a girl, to think turning my back was dignity and flirting violently with any one person when I was told I had flirted too much with some others, prudence and propriety. My ideas upon this subject are altered and I think I may, without much vanity, say improved. I do not understand Lord Granville's inconsistence but I neither resent nor lament it and only wish to prove by the quiet and steadiness of my own manner that both my feelings and conduct are independent of the changes in his.

I trust you will come to Chiswick to see me act up to my sense of what is right and to approve of my practice, as I know you will of my theory. Pray (I need not say it, though) keep this for yourself and the fire—my envelope is equally for the best and kindest of grandmothers, with whom concealment in this case is only another word for necessity. [*The " envelope " is missing.*]

To Miss Trimmer

Oct. 1809.

MY DEAREST SELINA,

I am very sorry to hear of you at Holywell, for selfish reasons, —for my devout grandmother I rejoice. It is all I can do to keep up my spirits for the various difficulties I have to encounter at my return, but I have many comforts, many blessings—your kindness and friendship first in the list, my dearest, best of friends.

Ever yrs, H. C.

P.S.—Read to yourself.

Lady B. means to be at Chiswick—you can have no idea of the manœuvering of her conduct—she has acted fairly by no one person —a directly different part to each and then obliged to have recourse to artifice and duplicity to try and reconcile the whole—" What shipwreck has she made of honour, dignity and fair renown ! "

To the Marquis of Hartington

CHISWICK. *October 29th. 1809.*

MY DEAREST BROTHER,

As I do not know anything of your arrangements, engagements, terms etc. I cannot beg you to come at any particular time, but I do long to see you. I cannot tell you how much I look forward to seeing you, particularly just now, when there are so many subjects I wish to talk to you about and do not like to write.

The state of things here is better than I could have expected. Every circumstance of the change is compleat and, painful as it is at times, much better to be borne than I had dared to expect. Her manner is less offensive from no longer being a perpetual struggle to put forward claims and require attention to which henceforward nobody can dispute her right. F. Foster for the first time in his life, I believe, has shown good taste and what is better and natural to him, good feeling. He is neither elated nor significant, more attentive in his manner to us and exactly the same to her. Caroline [" Caro-George "] comme au commencement jusqu'à la fin, the best and most amiable of human beings but impenetrable as to what she thinks or feels on the subject. My Aunt Spencer talks like herself and recommends moderate conduct in terms of coarseness and violence that would astonish Billingsgate. Sir Walter is Scotch and Mr. Vigoureux poor. This may not sound liberal but never was problem so well proved.

Of the World and its opinions I know nothing and care less. I pity those who look to them for happiness and despise those who form their opinion from them.

God bless you now, my dearest of brothers, and I do long to see you and am ever most affec^ly

HARRIET CAVENDISH.

To the Marquis of Hartington

CHISWICK. *Saturday, November 4th. 1809.*

I regret any delay in your coming but perhaps it is better as G. and I go to Holywell on Monday and do not return here till the end of the week. You will have power to bear " the woman," partly because your patience will not be so severely tried as you expect. I am already reconciled to some things, accustomed almost to all ; I do long to see you, my dearest, dearest brother—my fingers are grown stiff and my ideas all embrouillés—a pretty picture of a correspondant. Mrs. George is charming my ears with something about Shepherds and Flora—F. Foster is absolutely bursting with rage at the weather. It is raining as it never rained before. He says he wishes he could affront, vex or pique it—that he has a great mind to go out into it sans parapluie sans redingote, to look, to stare at it, to lay down under a tree with a book. This is all very well said but it proves what a melancholy dearth of subjects the person who writes it must have.

Lord M. is gone to Castle Howard for a fortnight upon business, G. to Town for one hour's conversation with, or rather attention to, Lady Jersey.

Bless you, my very best and dearest brother—I do long most impatiently to see you.

Ever yrs, most affec^ly.

To the Marquis of Hartington

CHISWICK. *November 15th. 1809.*

I left Holywell yesterday, having expected your arrival that evening every moment in spite of all the reasons that made it improbable. I hope you mean to write to me before I come but still more that you will be here very soon.

The Duchess mourns comme de saison and is not embellished by it. She goes on much the same as she always has done.

The Bessboroughs, Duncannon, Lord Granville and Mr. Ellis dined here yesterday and the two last are here still.

Frederick Foster is full of his jokes but has behaved perfectly with regard to all that has passed here. His judgment in general is so very much what it ought not to be and his love of rank and consequence so great that I was afraid he would have been particularly disagreeable, but fortunately he has been as quiet and considerate as possible and I really feel grateful to him for it. He has good principles and good feelings, which I think Heaven in mercy to mankind gave to everything belonging to her. I am quite ignorant of Caroline's [" Caro-George "] opinions and feelings and I had rather continue to be so. The other Caroline [" Caro-William "] is like a Volcano on the subject.

There is a very disagreeable paragraph in the Papers today, a mock account of a ball and rowing match here. It has no merit but ill-nature and I think such things are not worth a moment's pain. I trust to your judgment to act exactly as you ought when you come, which is saying a great deal and paying you the highest possible compliment. There is a very distinct line to be drawn in our conduct to her and you have the sense to see it and strength of mind to follow it.

God bless you now, my dearest, kindest, best of brothers—I long to see you and do not exactly understand why your present reasons for delay should be much prolonged.

I hope you bring your curricle, for in spite of wind and weather, perils and hair breadth's scapes, I must go in it.

I have been practising on the harp till my fingers are so sore and tired that I can hardly make my pen go.

Delmino dined here yesterday. He is grown thin and deplorable. He is so used to disappointments in love that I never attribute his gloom to that and loss of appetite he certainly cannot complain of. What are the sorrows of such an empty head?

The dear Douairière and Miss Trimmer never seemed well pleased with you till now, but the cry of No Popery prevails and I see the latter is in dread of a Catholic question. God bless you again and again.

Ever most affec[ly] yours, HARRIET CAVENDISH.

To the Marquis of Hartington

CHISWICK. *Thursday, November 16th. 1809.*

MY BEST AND DEAREST HARTINGTON,

I feel such confidence in your affection that I am certain the knowledge of my happiness will add to yours and if anything can increase mine, it is that conviction. Lord Granville's character and attachment give me a security in looking forward to uniting my fate with his that I could not have believed I should ever feel at such a moment as this.

He proposed to me the night before last, but from some communication he thought it necessary to make first to part of his own family, I have been bound to secrecy till today.

Are you coming, my own adored brother, and do you approve and are you happy?

Ever most affec[ly] yours, H. CAVENDISH.

To Miss Trimmer

MY DEAREST SELINA,

I send you the enclosed bracelet as a little remembrance from me. On Sunday (Dec. 24th, 1809) I shall have a right to the Initials I have had engraved upon it.

I do assure you, my dearest Selina, that at this most important and interesting moment I often think of all your past conduct to me, with affection and gratitude not to be expressed.

God bless you, my dearest friend.

Ever yrs. most affec[ly], HARRIET CAVENDISH.

INDEX